The Normans in their Histories:
Propaganda,
Myth and Subversion

The Normans in their Histories: Propaganda, Myth and Subversion

Emily Albu

THE BOYDELL PRESS

First published 2001
The Boydell Press, Woodbridge

ISBN 0 85115 656 8

The Boydell Press is an imprint of Boydell & Brewer Ltd
PO Box 9, Woodbridge, Suffolk IP12 3DF, UK
and of Boydell & Brewer Inc.
PO Box 41026, Rochester, NY 14604–4126, USA
website: http://www.boydell.co.uk

A catalogue record for this book is available
from the British Library

Library of Congress Cataloging-in-Publication Data
Albu, Emily, 1945–
    The Normans in their histories: propaganda, myth, & subversion /
Emily Albu.
        p. cm.
    Includes bibliographical references and index.
    ISBN 0–85115–656–8 (alk. paper)
    1. Normans – France.   2. Normandy (France) – History – To 1515.
3. Normans – England – History – To 1500.   4. Civilization, Medieval.
I. Title.
D148 .A59 2001
944'.2 – dc21   00–051948

This publication is printed on acid-free paper

Printed in Great Britain by
St Edmundsbury Press Ltd, Bury St Edmunds, Suffolk

Contents

To my mother, Doris Albu,
and to the memory of my father, Emil Albu

Maps

Abbreviations

ANS   *Anglo-Norman Studies*, see under *Battle*

Battle   *Proceedings of the Battle Conference on Anglo-Norman Studies 1–4* (1979–82), ed. R. Allen Brown (Woodbridge, 1980–3); from 5 (1983) published as *Anglo-Norman Studies*

CW   *The Classical World*

EH   *The Ecclesiastical History of Orderic Vitalis*, ed. and trans. Marjorie Chibnall

EHR   *English Historical Review*

GF   *Gesta Francorum*

GG   William of Poitiers, *Gesta Guillelmi*

GND   William of Jumièges, *Gesta Normannorum Ducum*

MGH AA *Monumenta Germaniae Historica, Auctores Antiquissimi*

MGH SS *Monumenta Germaniae Historica, Scriptores*

RS   Rolls Series

TRHS   *Transactions of the Royal Historical Society*

Preface

The late Paul Alexander introduced me to Norman histories when he encouraged me to write a comparative study of the Byzantine and Norman historical traditions. I began this project with a two-year fellowship at Radcliffe/ Harvard's Bunting Institute, where the Normans drew more and more of my attention until they eventually edged their rivals to the periphery. In four years I completed a draft of the revised work surveying the Norman tradition.

Then I had to put the manuscript aside for many years until an NEH summer stipend and an ACLS fellowship allowed me to resume this study. During all that time Lucia Gates was a constant friend, whether sharing childcare or sharing ideas. Lucia also read an early draft of the manuscript and offered generous advice. At a critical moment, Gregory Nagy welcomed me as a visiting scholar in Harvard's Classics department, while Michael Maas introduced me to the literature on ethnography and prodded me to write.

I am grateful to friends and colleagues at the University of California at Davis, who provide a nurturing environment for teaching, research, and writing. I cannot imagine a better place to work and live. From the vantage of sunny Davis, I came to suspect the darkness that I had seen in the Norman histories when I read and reread them in Boston. So I read them again in the sunshine, just as a test. When I was ready to write the final draft, the UC Davis Humanities Institute gave me a fellowship along with a quiet office, for which I owe thanks to Georges van den Abbeele and Ron Saufley.

Peter Brown, Cassandra Potts, Leah Shopkow, Hugh Thomas, and David Traill read the manuscript and offered invaluable suggestions and corrections. For Chapter Three I benefitted from Joanna Drell's advice, while Jean Blacker and Noah Guynn were especially helpful in their corrections of Chapter Six on histories in Old French. I am grateful for information supplied by Piotr Gorecki, Ralph Hexter, John D. Niles, David Spear, Peter Wallace, and others whose ideas I acknowledge in the notes. At UC Davis I have received research assistance from Jeffrey Brien, Christopher Case, Heidi Lypps, and Rachel Ward, while Nate Greenberg made the maps and Andrew Lazo proofread sections of the final manuscript and checked references, with help from Gail Nichols, Mike Winters, and the interlibrary loan staff of Shields Library. Caroline Palmer at Boydell & Brewer gave much-valued encouragement.

I dedicate this book to my parents, who nurtured my scholarly curiosities in a loving home. My daughter Emily overcame her early childhood disgust at the realization that her mother studied dead people, and she matured into the biggest booster of this work even when it consumed her mother's attention. Finally, I could not have written this book without the constant love of Alan Taylor, who has given me a tranquil life, a haven from the contentious world of the Normans.

Emily Albu
June 2000

Outline Genealogy: The Family of Rollo*

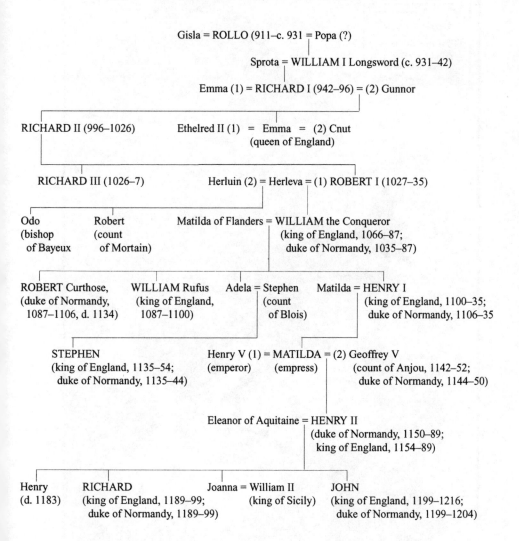

Gisla = ROLLO (911–c. 931 = Popa (?)

Sprota = WILLIAM I Longsword (c. 931–42)

Emma (1) = RICHARD I (942–96) = (2) Gunnor

RICHARD II (996–1026)   Ethelred II (1) = Emma = (2) Cnut
(queen of England)

RICHARD III (1026–7)   Herluin (2) = Herleva = (1) ROBERT I (1027–35)

Odo   Robert   Matilda of Flanders = WILLIAM the Conqueror
(bishop   (count   (king of England, 1066–87;
 of Bayeux   of Mortain)   duke of Normandy, 1035–87)

ROBERT Curthose,   WILLIAM Rufus   Adela = Stephen   Matilda = HENRY I
(duke of Normandy, (king of England, (count   (king of England, 1100–35;
 1087–1106, d. 1134) 1087–1100)   of Blois)   duke of Normandy, 1106–35

STEPHEN   Henry V (1) = MATILDA = (2) Geoffrey V
(king of England, 1135–54; (emperor)   (empress)   (count of Anjou, 1142–52;
 duke of Normandy, 1135–44)   duke of Normandy, 1144–50)

Eleanor of Aquitaine = HENRY II
(duke of Normandy, 1150–89;
 king of England, 1154–89)

Henry   RICHARD   Joanna = William II   JOHN
(d. 1183) (king of England, 1189–99;   (king of Sicily) (king of England, 1199–1216;
            duke of Normandy, 1189–99)   duke of Normandy, 1199–1204)

* with the dates of comital, ducal, and royal power.

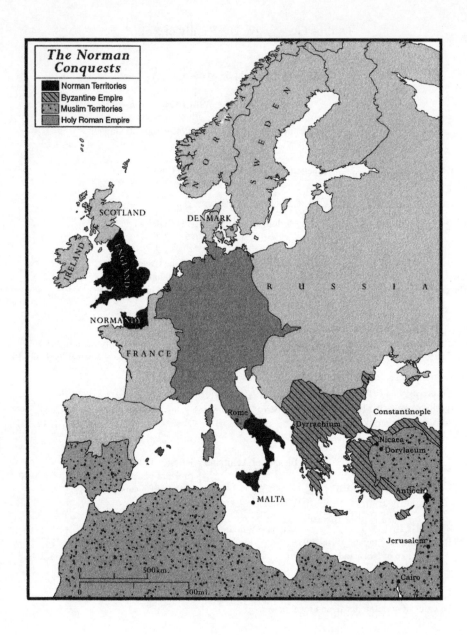

The Norman Conquests

- ■ Norman Territories
- ▨ Byzantine Empire
- ⋰ Muslim Territories
- ▓ Holy Roman Empire

NORWAY

SWEDEN

SCOTLAND

DENMARK

IRELAND

ENGLAND

RUSSIA

NORMANDY

FRANCE

Rome

Dyrrachium

Constantinople

Nicaea

Dorylaeum

MALTA

Antioch

Jerusalem

Cairo

0   500km

0   500mi.

Introduction

No good song is ever sung about a traitor. All peoples curse the
apostate and the betrayer as a wolf, and judge him worthy of
hanging, and they tie him on the gallows if they can and brand him
with every sort of abuse and insult.[1]

(Orderic Vitalis, *Ecclesiastical History* 2.314)

THROUGHOUT the ninth century, vikings assailed the Frankish coast,
burning and looting centers of Carolingian civilization and learning. In
911 King Charles the Simple, great-great-grandson of Charlemagne, ceded
Rouen at the mouth of the Seine to Rollo, the leader of one marauding band.
Charles hoped that these vikings, blessed with land and the salvation of
Christianity, would keep their pagan brethren away from the Seine and away
from Paris. The Rouen vikings, however, sometimes did just the opposite,
calling in their Scandinavian kin to threaten Paris when the French king
menaced them. Less predictably, the counts of Rouen became the dukes of
Northmannia/Normandy and forged a powerful domain, with far-flung interests and connections. Rollo's great-great-great-grandson conquered England;
Norman nobles wrested southern Italy from Lombards and Byzantines, and
eventually defeated the Arabs to create the Kingdom of Sicily; and on the
First Crusade, Normans under Bohemond took Antioch and made a Norman
principality in Syria.

Under Rollo's descendants Normandy survived at the center of this expan-
sion for nearly three centuries until 1204, when the French King Philip
Augustus snatched the ducal title and authority from the English King John.[2]
Those remarkable three hundred years begged for historians not only to cele-

---

1 For Orderic's *Ecclesiastical History*, references are to volume and page number in the
   edition of Marjorie Chibnall (Oxford, 1969–80), 6 vols. (hereafter cited as *EH*).
   Except where indicated, all translations are my own.
2 Henry I (duke from 1106 to 1135) died without a legitimate surviving son, but direct
   descent from Rollo continued through Henry's sister, Adela, whose son Stephen
   claimed his grandfather's dominion over both England and Normandy. Count Geoffrey
   V of Anjou challenged Stephen, claiming sovereignty on behalf of his wife, Henry's
   daughter Matilda. By 1144 Geoffrey had overrun Normandy and entered Rouen, where
   the archbishop declared him duke. But in 1150 Geoffrey gave Normandy to Matilda's
   seventeen-year-old son Henry. Upon Stephen's death in 1154, the young man ascended
   the English throne as Henry II. The years of Geoffrey's regency (1144–50) thus interrupted the lordship of Rollo's heirs, who nonetheless regained control with Henry II,
   great-grandson of William the Conqueror by the female line.

1

brate Norman achievements but also to verify the legitimacy of Norman princes and to authenticate the rights of Normans to inhabit and dominate their lands. Many writers took up the challenge, beginning in the late tenth century with Dudo of Saint-Quentin, a cleric and ambassador from Vermandois who claimed a commission from Duke Richard I and his son Richard II. This series concluded with the twelfth-century vernacular histories of Wace and Benoît, supported by King Henry II of England. In between came a wide variety of works, including William of Jumièges' epitome and continuation of Dudo, William of Poitiers' panegyric of William the Conqueror, William of Apulia's verses on the conquests in southern Italy, the anonymous *Gesta Francorum* ("The Story of the Franks") by a crusader who set out for Jerusalem with Bohemond's army, and the masterwork of the monk Orderic Vitalis, the *Historia Æcclesiastica* ("Ecclesiastical History").[3]

These histories employ various styles, poetry or prose or a mixture of the two, in Latin that may be classicizing or inspired by Christian devotional texts, or in the French verse of emerging romance. Despite such diversity, these histories form a distinct literary tradition marked not only by their common focus on the Normans but also by their tendency to mine one another for data and inspiration. For nearly two hundred years Norman historians wrote their own revisions and continuations of the *Gesta Normannorum Ducum* ("Story of the Norman Dukes") begun by Dudo.[4] Although neither the author of the *Gesta Francorum* nor the chroniclers of Normans in Italy and Sicily knew that tradition, their works nonetheless became an integral part of it when twelfth-century historians like Orderic and Wace wove their tales into pan-Norman narratives.

Because Normans left a voluminous historical record in a virtually continuous sequence, it should be easy to answer the question, "Who were the Normans?" But this problem continues to vex Norman scholarship, provoking heated debate.[5] Today historians still puzzle over these questions:

---

3 The word *Gesta* meant "deeds" or "exploits" in Classical Latin, and came to acquire the sense of "héroic story" or simply "story" [J. F. Niermeyer, *Mediae Latinitatis Lexicon Minus* (Leiden, 1976), 467].

4 Elisabeth M. C. van Houts, "The *Gesta Normannorum Ducum*: A History without an End," *Battle* 3 (1981), 106–18. Leah Shopkow, *History and Community: Norman Historical Writing in the Eleventh and Twelfth Centuries* (Washington, D.C., 1997), explores a broad range of works written in Latin on the history of Normandy.

5 The seminal work is R. H. C. Davis, *The Normans and their Myth* (London, 1976). See also G. A. Loud, "The '*Gens Normannorum*' – Myth or Reality?" *Battle* 4, ed. R. Allen Brown (Woodbridge, 1982), 104–16, 204–209; David Bates, *Normandy before 1066* (London and New York, 1982); Eleanor Searle, *Predatory Kinship and the Creation of Norman Power, 840–1066* (Berkeley, 1988); Cassandra Potts, "*Atque unum ex diversis gentibus populum effecit*: Historical Tradition and the Norman Identity," *Anglo-Norman Studies* 18, ed. Christopher Harper-Bill (Woodbridge, 1996), 139–52; Ian Short, "*Tam Angli quam Franci*: Self-Definition in Anglo-Norman England," *Anglo-Norman Studies* 18, 153–75; Emily Albu, "The Normans and their Myths,"

What criteria marked a person as a Norman, and what were the indisputable qualities of Normanness? How Scandinavian did Normans remain? How Frankish did they become? How different were they from their neighbors? And finally, since Normans were so successful at conquest, why did they then disappear as a distinctive ethnicity by the early thirteenth century?[6]

A few Norman historians, especially beholden to their patrons or awestruck by conquest, defined Normans through the broad strokes of panegyric. So William of Poitiers celebrated the hero who conquered England, while Amatus, Malaterra, and Ralph of Caen, respectively, commemorated victors over southern Italy, Sicily, and Syria. Their histories transformed Normans into the champions of Christendom. But most historians of the Normans subverted the text of achievement and legitimization with subtexts of treacherous leaders and a lawless society. From Dudo to Wace, monks and courtiers alike expressed similar disillusionment with the Normans and their princes.

Although they had read neither Dudo nor his successors, observers like William of Apulia and the anonymous author of the *Gesta Francorum* nevertheless reached the same conclusions. Their Normans can be fearsome warriors, like *Hugo Insanus* ("Mad Hugh"), the crusader who defended a fortress tower single-handedly against a Turkish attack, or like another Norman named Hugh, who greeted a Byzantine envoy at Melfi, in southern

Haskins Society Journal 10 (forthcoming). Two volumes by David C. Douglas offer an overview of Norman history that builds on the classic studies of Ferdinand Chalandon, Charles Homer Haskins, and Carl Erdmann: *The Norman Achievement, 1050–1100* (Berkeley and Los Angeles, 1969) and *The Norman Fate 1100–1154* (Berkeley and Los Angeles, 1976).

6 Charles Homer Haskins opened the debate with this positive assessment of Norman assimilation [*The Normans in European History* (New York, 1966; reprint, Boston and New York, 1915), 247 (page citations are to the reprint edition)]: "Wherever they went, they showed a marvellous power of initiative and of assimilation; if the initiative is more evident in England, the assimilation is more manifest in Sicily. The penalty for such activity is rapid loss of identity; the reward is a large share in the general development of civilization. If the Normans paid the penalty, they also reaped the reward, and they were never more Norman than in adopting the statesmanlike policy of toleration and assimilation which led to their ultimate extinction." On the submersion of Norman identity in post-Conquest England, see Hugh M. Thomas's forthcoming work on assimilation and ethnic identity in England after the Norman Conquest. In southern Italy, as Joanna Drell has shown in her study of charters from the Principality of Salerno ["Cultural Syncretism and Ethnic Identity: The Norman 'Conquest' of Southern Italy and Sicily," *Journal of Medieval History* 25 (1999), 187–202], aristocrats sometimes identified themselves as Normans, but they did so in dwindling numbers through the twelfth century. Noting that "the chief effect" of the Norman invasion of southern Italy "was to add further elements to an already disunited land," G. A. Loud ["How 'Norman' was the Norman Conquest of Southern Italy?" *Medieval Studies* 25, ed. Antonia Gransden (Nottingham, 1981), 30] even asked ". . . how far was it really a conquest?"

Italy, by knocking his horse out from under him with one bare-fisted punch.[7] But Normans could also play a subtler game, surprising their enemies with a more artful ruse. The histories recount many victories achieved by treachery. A favorite Norman stratagem was the feigning of illness or death in order to escape danger or to penetrate a stronghold. Duke Richard I, Robert Guiscard, Roger I of Sicily, and Bohemond all claim some version of this legend.[8] The Norman hero appears as trickster as often as warrior.

Norman historians perpetuate the image that deceit as much as ferocity contributed to their successes. In hostile territory, when their enemies outnumbered them, trickery could bring about the victory that arms could not. But once the battles end, what kind of citizens do the tricksters become, and what kind of societies will they build? According to their own historians, the Norman people were unruly, their communities volatile. Indeed, the very traits that had ensured their conquests worked against the creation of stable and satisfying societies, exacting an emotional toll from people who could neither trust nor be trusted. If we take Norman histories as the benchmark, the evidence suggests that the interior life of Normans was as unsettled and unsettling as the societies they created. In their histories, Normans come to exhibit varying degrees of malaise, pessimism, and anxiety over the inability of warriors and tricksters to become stable rulers or liegemen.

Are these histories or the men and women they describe any different from others in the medieval west? Until more of those histories are studied as literary works, I cannot answer that question. This book treats only the Norman tradition. It may help to remember, however, that all medieval historians wrote with ethical intent, in this resembling their Roman predecessors. Sallust (86–35 B.C.E) shaped his *Jugurtha* and *Catiline* to expose the moral decline of Roman society. His ethical stance influenced later Roman historians including Tacitus, who himself attacked the criminality of the Julio-Claudian emperors.

Medieval writers rarely knew those Roman histories but found their own ethical models in the Old and New Testaments, which present patterns of a fortunate human condition devolving into betrayal through sin, followed by "punishment, exile, and the hope of restoration."[9] Augustine pioneered the way for the new Christian historians who considered it their duty to unmask

---

7 Anonymous, *Gesta Francorum et aliorum Hierosolimitanorum*, ed. and trans. Rosalind Hill (London, 1962), 8.20 (hereafter cited as *Gesta Francorum*); Geoffrey Malaterra, *De rebus gestis Rogerii Calabriae et Siciliae Comitis et Roberti Guiscardi ducis fratris eius*, ed. Ernesto Pontieri, 2nd ed., vol. 5, pt. 1 (Bologna, 1925–28), 1.9 (hereafter cited as *Historia Sicula*).

8 Marguerite Mathieu has reviewed instances of this myth in her edition of William of Apulia, *La geste de Robert Guiscard* (Palermo, 1961), 46–52.

9 Susan M. Shwartz, "The Founding and Self-betrayal of Britain: An Augustinian Approach to Geoffrey of Monmouth's *Historia Regum Britanniae*," *Medievalia et Humanistica* n.s. 10, ed. Paul Maurice Clogan (Totowa, N.J., 1981), 33–53, at p. 35.

evil and highlight redemptive virtue. So Gregory of Tours denounced the cruelty of the rulers in chaotic Merovingian Gaul while a generation earlier, Jordanes played a more subtle game in criticizing the Goths. In an exemplary study of history as literature, Walter Goffart has shown how Jordanes' habit of evasion undercuts the formal praise of his narrative.[10] Jordanes' *Getica* ("Gothic History") relegates the greatest Gothic lords, even Theodoric, to minor roles and thus depreciates their accomplishments. Countless medieval historians besides the Normans honed their craft by reading Jordanes.

If Normans were not alone among medieval peoples in displaying violence or treachery, Northmen and the first Normans were ahead of the curve, precipitating the collapse of law and order in late tenth-century France, which Thomas Bisson aptly calls "a crisis of fidelity in the millennial genera-tion."[11] By the example of their success, first Northmen and then Normans schooled their neighbors in the fine art of violence as a strategy as well as a way of life. Although treason and deception are important themes in much of medieval literature and thus not the exclusive possession of Normans, these themes held particular resonance for Norman historians, who sought the social origins of this pathology among their own people and identified stages of its development.[12]

When I began to study the Norman histories, I simply planned to survey their own tradition from its beginnings in the epic history of Dudo to its final flowering in the vernacular romance histories of Wace and Benoît. My aim was to present a literary interpretation of Latin and Old French texts which have not always been read with attention to language and tone. I wanted to

---

[10] *The Narrators of Barbarian History (A.D. 550–800): Jordanes, Gregory of Tours, Bede, and Paul the Deacon* (Princeton, 1988), especially 62–68.

[11] Thomas N. Bisson, "The 'Feudal Revolution,' " *Past and Present* 142 (1994), 27. This brilliant article probes the revolutionary changes in patterns of violence and power in western Europe, from the tenth century to the twelfth, showing how "wilful, exploita-tive lordship, including that addicted to violence, became an institution even as it was discredited in the eleventh century," until such bad lordship became normative and expected in the twelfth. Concerning the violence attributed to vikings, Niels Lund has argued that vikings distinguished themselves *not* for their plundering of Christian Europe, a practice established before they entered the scene, but rather for their success at a game played with gusto by their southern neighbors ["Allies of God or Man? The Viking Expansion in a European Perspective," *Viator* 20 (1989), 45–59]. J. M. Wallace-Hadrill, on the other hand, assessed the viking incursions by the panic they inspired in their Christian victims and the devastation they wrought on towns, country-side, and people of Francia ["The Vikings in Francia," in *Early Medieval History* (Oxford, 1975), 217–36]. From the evidence in Frankish sources, Wallace-Hadrill concluded that contemporaries were not exaggerating when they claimed unprece-dented savagery in viking attacks. As we shall see, the vikings' Norman heirs refined viking models to terrorize their own foes and each other as well.

[12] On the theme of treason in medieval literature, see Emanuel J. Mickel, *Ganelon, Treason and the* Chanson de Roland (University Park, P.A. and London, 1989). Mickel places Ganelon's treason trial within its historical, literary, and legal context.

show how, for each of these works, the style *was* the history, not simply an annoying rhetorical stratum to dig through and discard in search of pay dirt. And I thought it useful to view the individual histories in their literary and historical context. No study has followed the entire literary tradition from the Latin and Old French histories of Normandy and the Anglo-Norman realm through the chronicles of the crusades and the Norman principalities in Antioch, Italy, and Sicily.

This book pursues these original intentions. But it also reveals within the histories patterns of convulsion and deceit that offer clues to the Norman identity. Beneath the splendor of the Norman achievement, the histories expose a culture of mayhem and predation that threatened societies and individuals. From his vantage point in twelfth-century Normandy, for instance, Orderic Vitalis frequently bewailed the destruction wrought by Norman arrogance.[13] William the Conqueror's deathbed lament, as reported by Orderic, details the treachery of friends and kin that shaped William's experience and forged his character.[14] Orderic's own memories of abandonment by his family recall that same language of betrayal (*EH* 6.552–54). As it does in other Norman histories by writers as disparate as William of Apulia and Wace, the mood of the *Ecclesiastical History* turns dark. But if "no good song is ever sung about a traitor," Normans in their histories nonetheless inspired many a fine requiem to their treachery.

---

[13] See, for instance, the indictment presented by the venerable monk Guitmund (*EH* 6.8–12). Chapter Five discusses this example and many others.

[14] *EH* 4.80–94.

1

Dudo of Saint-Quentin

WHEN they commissioned the first history of Normandy in the late tenth century, the dukes faced a delicate problem.[1] How should they present their past? How should they explain where they had come from and who they had become? How should they defend the legitimacy of their hereditary claim to Normandy? These were knotty questions for Normans whose viking ancestors had ravaged Christendom, converting to Christianity themselves only gradually after the land grant of 911. By the end of that century, the Norman dukes wanted an official history that would show how far they had traveled from their pagan past. They may have wanted the history to send the contrary message at the same time: just as Norman dukes could call in their viking cousins to harry the Franks, so they could also summon the wolves within themselves to devour any foe.

For the Norman duke Richard II (996–1026), the issue was by no means academic. The viking founder, Rollo, was his great-grandfather, and the ducal history was the history of his own family. So the problems of Normandy's origins and the evolving Norman identity had far-reaching consequences. A twenty-first-century solution might be to hire a public-relations firm to create photo opportunities or plant stories in the popular press. The duke found the tenth-century equivalent; that is, he engaged a Frankish literary artist, a scholar and cleric who, in exchange for benefices, would write a history that was both elegant and credible.

Dudo of Saint-Quentin got the job. He was a canon of Saint-Quentin when the count of Vermandois dispatched him on an embassy to Duke Richard I (942–96), probably late in 987 or early in 988.[2] After that mission, Dudo

---

[1] This chapter draws on my articles, especially "Dudo of Saint-Quentin: The Heroic Past Imagined," *The Haskins Society Journal* 6 (1994), 111–18; and "Normans and their Myths." Though Richard II (996–1026) was the first to style himself duke, I follow convention and use the terms "duke" and "duchy" to describe the Norman princes and their lands from 911 onward.

[2] *De moribus et actis primorum Normanniae ducum, auctore Dudone Sancti Quintini decano*, ed. Jules Lair (Caen, 1865), 4.128 (hereafter cited as Dudo). For a translation

visited Rouen again and again, until at last he began his history of Richard's realm.

In a long panegyrical letter to Adalberon, the bishop of Laon, to whom he sent his manuscript, Dudo explained the genesis of this work. Here he assured the bishop that he did not compose this history voluntarily or at his own initiative.[3] On the contrary, as Dudo tells the story, in the last two years of Richard's life and reign, the old duke one day astonished the cleric by flinging his arms around him and importuning him to write about the customs and deeds of the Norman land and especially of his grandfather Rollo.[4] At first Dudo refused. Only after some days of ducal pleading did he relent and accept the burden. While he was in the early stages of his work, *heu proh dolor!* ("alas and alack!") Richard died. Dudo insists that he would have quit the task if Richard II, the son and heir of Richard I, along with Count Raoul, the old duke's half-brother, had not begged him to keep his promise.[5] Medieval historians often posed as reluctant writers, but Dudo embraced this affectation with panache.

Surely this Frankish cleric was an excellent choice for recording the heroic tale of the first Norman dukes. Dudo was well-educated in the tradition of the fast-fading Carolingian renaissance, which emphasized classical learning.[6] He also turned out to be one of the most talented spin doctors of the Middle Ages. He created an entertaining narrative that idealized the Norman dukes and yet was so convincing that virtually everyone believed him for over 800 years. Indeed, Dudo's version of early Norman history dominated the genre of Norman historical writing that he inaugurated, providing the mythic, thematic, and narrative structure for subsequent Norman histories, from the mid-eleventh-century epitome and continuation of Dudo by William of Jumièges to the vernacular verse histories of Wace and Benoît.[7] Though

and notes, see *Dudo of St Quentin, History of the Normans*, trans. Eric Christiansen (Woodbridge, 1998). Leah Shopkow fixes the dating of this embassy, in *History and Community*, 35–36. Before this book appeared, I benefitted from reading it in typescript, as well as the doctoral dissertation on which it is based ["Norman Historical Writing in the Eleventh and Twelfth Centuries" (University of Toronto, 1984)].

3   Dudo, pp. 115–20.

4   Dudo, pp. 119–20. Eric Christiansen (*Dudo of St Quentin*, xxiii–xxiv) notes that Dudo was imitating Heiric of Auxerre's account of the commission from his abbot, Lothair, to write a verse *Life of St. Germanus*. See also his note 31, on p. 178.

5   A charter of Richard II, dated 1015, confirms Dudo's continuing ties to the ducal court by allowing him to bequeath to the congregation of St. Quentin the benefices he had received from Richard I. [*Recueil des actes des ducs de Normandie, 911–1066*, Mémoires de la société des antiquaires de Normandie 36, ed. Marie Fauroux (Caen, 1961), 100–102].

6   See Leah Shopkow, "The Carolingian World of Dudo of Saint-Quentin," *Journal of Medieval History* 15, no. 1 (1989), 19–37.

7   Chapter Two discusses Dudo's impact on William of Jumièges and later writers in this tradition, including Orderic Vitalis and Robert of Torigni.

many later writers accessed Dudo via William's *Gesta Normannorum Ducum*, others continued to read Dudo's sometimes difficult Latin, as the thirteen surviving manuscripts attest. Both directly and indirectly, therefore, Dudo of Saint-Quentin played a fundamental role in defining and evaluating Normans and Normanness.

Despite his initial reluctance, Dudo produced a long and complex manuscript (187 pages in Jules Lair's printed edition). To read this work from beginning to end is to enter and traverse a strange borderland where late Carolingian erudition meets a rough-and-tumble frontier territory. Despite the singular influence that this pioneering document exerted on the tradition of Norman historical writing, few modern scholars seem to have made their way through the complete Latin text, poems and all. Yet it is worth examining in some detail.

First, what should we title the work? The seventeenth-century editor, André Duchesne, rephrased Dudo's description from his dedicatory letter to call it *De moribus et actis primorum Normanniae ducum* ["On the Customs (or Character) and Deeds of the First Dukes of Normandy"]. This unwieldy name has stuck, despite the suggestion that the manuscript tradition supports the simpler *Gesta Normannorum* or *Historia Normannorum*.[8] Although other Normans play strong supporting roles, as we shall see, the clear ducal emphasis argues for Duchesne's choice.

The *De moribus* aims to cover more than a century, from viking raids and the creation of the duchy to the death of Richard I in 996. In Lair's edition the structure appears logical and straightforward, with its four books dedicated successively to an unrepentant viking named Hasting and to the first Norman dukes: Rollo, William, and Richard I. Leah Shopkow has demonstrated the elements of hagiography in these lives and has shown the link to serial biographies of saints.[9] In the *De moribus* this pattern serves particularly to emphasize the direct succession of dukes through the male line. Surely one motive behind Dudo's commission was the dukes' eagerness to validate first William's claim to Rollo's title and then the challenged claims of Richard I.

Proof of legitimacy posed a problem because the dukes, Rollo and William, had no sons from Christian marriages. Conjugal relations *more danico* ("in the Danish fashion") allowed a father to postpone his choice of heir and, at the opportune moment, designate the child he preferred. But such a system entailed risks, including suspicions of spurious paternity and refusal to accept a concubine's son. Other Christian peoples, most dangerously the neighboring Franks, could challenge such a child's legitimacy, as could kin within the ducal family. Dudo's history aims to answer and repel such threats.

---

8 Gerda C. Huisman, "Notes on the Manuscript Tradition of Dudo of St Quentin's *Gesta Normannorum*," *Anglo-Norman Studies* 6 (1984), 122.

9 *History and Community*, Appendix 1, 277–80.

By its structure as much as by explicit affirmation, the *De moribus* proclaims Rollo's line the worthy, lawful rulers, just as it makes Hasting the undeserving assailant on the land.[10]

By emphasizing the legitimate transfer of authority, Dudo's schema creates the appearance of progressive civilizing. Beneath this tidy surface, however, lurks a world in disarray. Throughout the tenth century, the duchy and its rulers experienced dramatic changes. Dudo's mythic history may have failed to give us the documents, names, and dates that would let us trace the milestones that mark Normandy's progress in this turbulent time. But Dudo has left evidence just as precious in the myths and stories interpreting the origins of a society riddled with perfidy and injustice.

Now and then a critic surfaced to question Dudo's accuracy. A nineteenth-century scholar, for instance, added a marginal note to a twelfth-century manuscript, expressing annoyance at the rhetorical thicket he had to penetrate in order to retrieve useful information. In his panegyric to Adalberon, Dudo had written this fawning apology: "Nearly half of this work seems to have no regard at all for the business of utility unless, by you as reaper, it is weeded of superfluous thistles." At the midpoint of this sentence (after "Nearly half of this work seems to have no regard at all for the business of utility") the reader has added "*certe*" ("that's for sure").[11]

Today Dudo's readers understand that his characters are literary creations, their stories shaped to create a meaningful narrative. But for eight hundred years historians valued the *De moribus* simply as a document of fact – indeed as the sole witness except spare chronicles for the early Norman period. In 1865 the editor, Jules Lair, defended Dudo's reliability, claiming that he drew upon authentic recollections from the ducal family derived from the half-brother of Richard I, Raoul d'Ivry (whom Dudo addressed in an introductory poem as *relator hujus operis*, "the narrator of this work").[12]

Despite Lair's defense, historians developed growing apprehensions about Dudo's suspicious data. In 1880 Sir Henry Howorth pronounced Dudo's

---

10 On the Normans' strategy of limiting acknowledged heirs in order to legitimize the succession, see Searle, *Predatory Kinship*, 93–97.

11 Dudo, p. 119, note (a). Lair suggested that the marginal note in ms. N was that of l'abbé de la Rue.

12 Dudo, 27–30. Lair believed that the count of Ivry, Raoul, "had taken care to collect all the traditions of the ducal family, and he found himself in a good position to do so because he was the brother of Richard I, and since only a single generation separated him from the conquerors." Lair went so far as to suggest that only the occasional verses should count as Dudo's original contribution, amplifying the prose account he heard from the Norman prince. On the other hand, D. W. T. C. Vessey, ["William of Tyre and the Art of Historiography," *Medieval Studies* 35 (1973), 438] argued that, despite Lair's enthusiastic protestations, no information can be traced to the supposed informant, Raoul, or to the ducal court. Shopkow offered the reminder (*History and Community*, 153) that *relator* "can also mean appellant, in which case [Dudo] meant only that Raoul urged him to write."

stories about Rollo "a huge waste of rhetorical commentary. . . . I have now examined Dudo's account of Rollo from beginning to end, and have shown reason for believing it to be a mere farrago of distorted and altered fragments from the old annalists; that we have nothing in it of any value or reliability; and that the whole history of his reign must be re-written from other materials."[13] In a study published in 1916, Henri Prentout scrutinized Dudo's narrative one paragraph at a time and found "very few definite and fresh facts about the history of the first Norman dukes."[14] Dudo's once splendid reputation lay in shambles.

Still historians continued to mine his work because they could not find sources to replace him.[15] Giving up Dudo meant facing a void, a critical hundred years without a history. As late as 1945, the Earl of Onslow was poking through the wreckage, trying to salvage a detail here or there, struggling (to use his own metaphor) "to winnow the truth from the falsehood in his writings."[16]

Because Dudo does not readily yield facts to such harvesters, this enterprise produced only frustration. But when historians began to read Dudo on his own terms, they uncovered a valuable cache. Marc Bloch regarded Dudo's narrative as "an infinitely precious piece of evidence" because it revealed "the mentality belonging to a particular environment and age."[17] R. W. Southern agreed: "What [Dudo] set out to do, and – according to the standards and opinions of the best judges of his own and the following century – succeeded in doing, was to tell in the noblest style the story of a noble destiny."[18]

Although Dudo cared little for authenticating details from Normandy's first hundred years, he did create a plausible heroic version of Norman origins from the potent combination of Roman and Christian, Frankish and Scandinavian elements.[19] And he endowed his story with an essential truth about the persistence of Scandinavian traits among the Normans. However

---

13 Henry H. Howorth, "A Criticism of the Life of Rollo, as told by Dudo de St. Quentin," *Archaeologia* 45, no. 2 (1880), 248, 250. For a review of the criticism, see David C. Douglas, "Rollo of Normandy," *EHR* 57, no. 228 (October 1942), 417–18; reprinted in his *Time and the Hour: Some Collected Papers of David C. Douglas* (London, 1977), 121.

14 Henri Prentout, *Étude critique sur Dudon de Saint-Quentin et son histoire des premiers ducs Normands* (Paris, 1916), 431.

15 David C. Douglas recalled the admonitions of Francis Palgrave, published in 1851 (*Collected Works*, 2. 500): "You may abandon the history of Normandy if you choose, but if you accept the task, you must accept Dudo or let the work alone." "Rollo of Normandy," 418 n. 12; reprinted in *Time and the Hour*, 135 n. 12.

16 Richard William Alan Onslow, *The Dukes of Normandy and their Origin*, ed. A. L. Haydon (London, 1947), 31.

17 *Feudal Society*, trans. L. A. Manyon (Chicago, 1961; reprint, London, 1989), 1.28.

18 "Aspects of the European Tradition of Historical Writing: I. The Classical Tradition from Einhard to Geoffrey of Monmouth," *TRHS* 5th ser., 20 (1970), 192.

19 See Trevor Rowley, *The Norman Heritage, 1055–1200* (London, 1983), 10.

quickly the Northmen assimilated, Dudo understood that it was critical for them to harry neighbors and foes with threats of Scandinavian affinities.[20]

Reading the *De moribus* in its entirety corrects misunderstandings that have arisen from the process of quarrying chunks without understanding their place in the whole. For instance, historians liked to cite Dudo as evidence that Rollo and his heirs all styled themselves "duke." When the study of early documents revealed that, until Richard II, the rulers were "counts," historians blamed Dudo for "gross – and quite deliberate – inaccuracies. . . . In Dudo's opinion, the very first Norman leader, the Norwegian viking Rollo, was the first duke of Normandy. This was just not true."[21] A closer look at the complete text, however, cuts short the long-lived debate. In fact, Dudo bestows the title *dux* not only on Rollo and his progeny in Normandy, but also on characters like Rollo's father in Scandinavia (2.2). Rollo himself is *dux paganorum* (2.25) before becoming *dux Northmannorum* (2.26). Eleanor Searle has deduced that "to Dudo, *dux* meant 'warleader.' "[22] Virtually everyone now understands that no historical account offers a neutral, unbiased reckoning of events. That was the elusive ideal of those nineteenth- and early twentieth-century historians who found Dudo wanting.

Although Dudo apparently had access to archival materials and to the duke's own memories and family records, he preferred to shape the Norman story by drawing on literary models of proven antiquity. Dudo's Carolingian school training prepared him to take Vergil's *Aeneid* as the template for an epic history featuring heroes who came by sea to a new homeland, where they would fight and eventually intermarry with the old inhabitants, whose religion and language they would adopt.[23] The fusion of these two cultures would produce a people of unique energy and promise, destined for greatness.

---

20 Norman dukes "became increasingly gallicized. Nevertheless it was to the interest of the Rouen leaders well into the eleventh century to emphasize their Scandinavian character. Richard I owed everything to it." Searle, *Predatory Kinship*, 124.

21 Bates, *Normandy before 1066*, xiv.

22 Searle, *Predatory Kinship*, 296, n. 15. She notes that this was true for the chronicler Richer as well. The Romans had most commonly used *dux* in this military sense.

23 Lair's footnotes to the edited text point out Vergilian echoes. Christiansen has added others in the notes to his translation. Many readers have commented on the influence of the *Aeneid* on Dudo's history. See, for example, Southern, "Aspects of the European Tradition, I," 192. More recently, Eleanor Searle rightly asserted that "the *Aeneid* is the organizing principle of Rollo's saga." Searle, "Fact and Pattern in Heroic History: Dudo of Saint-Quentin," *Viator* 15 (1984), 126. Searle argued that Dudo organized his history with Rollo as Aeneas and Richard I as Aeneas's son, Ascanius. See also Searle, *Predatory Kinship*), 64; and Pierre Bouet, "Dudon de Saint-Quentin et Virgile: *L'Énéide* au service de la cause normande," *Cahiers des Annales de Normandie* 23 (1990), 215–36. Bouet concludes with appendices that list allusions to Vergil in the *De moribus*, Books One and Two. For additional commentary, see Eric Christiansen, *Dudo of St Quentin*, xxi–xxiii, and his notes, 177–229.

It was not unusual for a scholar of Dudo's day to turn to Vergil. While the Augustan poet remained popular throughout the Middle Ages, he met an especially enthusiastic reception with Carolingian readers, whose interests Dudo inherited. Dudo and his contemporaries read the *Aeneid* as a kind of grand history. Tacitus was virtually unknown. Livy, Suetonius, and Sallust reached a somewhat larger audience. But when Western medieval historians looked for classical models, they usually chose the epics by Statius and Lucan, and, above all, by Vergil.

Dudo did insert allusions to other classical authors, often culled second-hand from Carolingian texts. Introductory verses recall Horace and Persius. The narrative begins with a geography lesson that mimics and globalizes Julius Caesar by dividing all the world into three parts: Europe, Asia, and Africa.[24] Dudo invokes Scipio, Pompey, Cato, and the *gloria Romae*, and he imitates Lucan's epic on the Roman civil wars. He knew Statius and Ovid. But Dudo mined the *Aeneid* most of all, and he did so with particular skill and intelligence.

First he hinted at a parallel between his epic history and Vergil's epic by maintaining a Trojan origin for his vikings. This was not an original idea. As early as the first century B.C.E. Roman writers were noting claims of the Aedui and Arverni, peoples in Gaul, that they were Trojan descendants, too, and therefore kin to the Romans.[25] In the seventh century C.E. the Franks discovered their own putative Trojan origins, which later the Bretons would sometimes emulate.[26] Newcomers into the Roman world in late antiquity and the Middle Ages might dignify their ancestry by tracing their genealogy back to the Trojans, preferably to Aeneas. Such a mythic history could validate their claims to be the new Romans, sharing an imagined kinship with the old Romans. But it could also implicate them in a web of ancestral deceit.[27]

---

24 Although the idea comes from Jordanes' *Getica* 4, the language echoes Caesar's *Gallic War* 1.1.

25 For references in Julius Caesar, Lucan, Tacitus, and Sidonius Apollinaris, see Pierre Bouet, "De l'origine troyenne des Normands," in *Mélanges René Lepelley: Recueil d'études en hommage au Professeur René Lepelley*, ed. Catherine Bougy, Pierre Boissel, and Bernard Garnier (Caen, 1995), 403. In two of his letters (*Ad Atticum* 1.19.2 and *Ad Familiares* 7.10.4), Cicero also mentioned the Aedui's claims of Trojan descent. [Susan H. Braund, trans., *Lucan, Civil War* (Oxford, 1992), 231, note to line 1.427.]

26 Pierre Bouet, "De l'origine troyenne des Normands," 403–406. R. W. Southern outlined this pattern in "Aspects of the European Tradition, I." See also Colette Beaune, "The Political Uses of the Trojan Myth," in *The Birth of an Ideology: Myths and Symbols of Nation in Late-Medieval France*, trans. Susan Ross Huston, ed. Fredric L. Cheyette (Berkeley, 1991), 226–44.

27 The ancients recognized Troy's endemic treachery, which surfaced when King Laomedon perjured himself by refusing to pay the gods their due for building the massive walls of Troy. Horace's third Roman Ode features Juno rehearsing this story and proclaiming the eternal condemnation of the city "along with her treacherous ruler

Dudo devised a clever route along this genealogical path, co-opting the Gothic claim that he found in Jordanes' sixth-century *Getica*.[28] Dudo asserted that the vikings who came to Normandy were descended from Aeneas's compatriot, Antenor, who escaped Troy to found a new home in the west, and that the *Danai* became the *Dani*.[29] This presented a neat etymological proof of his thesis, and few readers seem to have complained that Antenor was Trojan and the *Danai* were the Greeks.[30]

Still, Antenor must have seemed an odd choice for the Normans' progenitor. Surely some members of Dudo's late tenth-century audience knew Antenor's ancient reputation as a traitor who escaped the holocaust at Troy precisely because he was the man who betrayed his own people to the Greeks.[31] The survival of both Aeneas and Antenor provoked suspicions about them in antiquity.[32] The strongest, most consistent indictment focused

and people" (*cum populo et duce fraudulento*; *Ode* 3.3.24). Throughout late antiquity and the Middle Ages, Troy developed into a hotbed of intrigue and betrayal, perhaps best exemplified in Chaucer's *Troilus and Criseyde*. See Lee Patterson, *Chaucer and the Subject of History* (Madison, 1991), 84–164.

[28] *De origine actibusque Getarum*, ed. Theodore Mommsen, in *MGH AA* 5, pt. 1 (Berlin, 1882), 60–66.

[29] Dudo, 130. Bouet, "Dudon de Saint-Quentin et Virgile," 228, gives Dudo's probable sources for the tradition that Antenor had traveled to the Illyrian territories: the *Chronicle* of Pseudo-Fredegar, *Liber Historiae Francorum*, and the *De gestis Francorum* of Aimoin de Fleury.

[30] Eventually someone noticed. By the twelfth century, the master historian of the Norman tradition, Orderic Vitalis, gave Antenor a son called Danus, who left his name to this new people, the *Dani* or Danes. Pierre Bouet has plausibly suggested that Dudo was confusing *Danai* (Greeks) with *Dardani* (a term for the Trojans), derived from the Dardanus, ancestor of the kings of Troy ("De l'origine troyenne des Normands," 407).

[31] A half century later, writing an abridgment and continuation of Dudo's history, William of Jumièges explicitly acknowledged Antenor's betrayal of Troy [*GND* 1.3.(4)], as we shall see in Chapter Two. Antenor's reputation for treachery reached a wide medieval audience through the first-century C.E. works of Dares and Dictys, translated from Greek into Latin in late antiquity. Medieval readers believed the claims of Dares and Dictys to be participants in the Trojan War, fighting on the Trojan and Greek side, respectively, and therefore reliable witnesses. Both featured Antenor as the Trojan who entered into secret negotiations with the Greeks and betrayed the city to them in exchange for his own survival and enrichment. This charge against Antenor survived throughout medieval literature, surfacing most notoriously in Dante's *Inferno* (Canto 32). Deep in the bowels of Hell, the second ring of the ninth circle, home of traitors to their native land or party, is called Antenora. On the betrayal of Troy and its medieval variations, see Colette Beaune, "The Political Use of the Trojan Myth," especially pp. 228–29.

[32] Meyer Reinhold, "The Unhero Aeneas," *Classica et Mediaevalia* 27 (1966), 195–207; esp. 198. It seems likely to me that Dudo's persistent linking of Norman dukes to Vergil's Aeneas also has an ironic intent. As Meyer Reinhold has shown, the unheroic Aeneas was suppressed under Julius Caesar, Augustus, and their imperial heirs, who claimed descent from the hero Aeneas, though cowardly qualities surfaced in Ovid's provocative version of the Trojan prince seen through the eyes of Dido betrayed. Early

on Antenor, whom Dionysios of Halicarnassus even named as the person who freed the Greeks from the horse and signaled the Greek ships to emerge from hiding. Vergil's Antenor was a whitewashed figure, mentioned only twice: as the father of three sons killed in the great war and lamented by Aeneas in the underworld (*Aeneid* 6.483–84) and, more prominently, as the fortunate fugitive who has already found solace and a new home in Italy, while Aeneas still wanders through dangers, as Venus complains to Jupiter (*Aeneid* 1.242–49).

The learned Dudo must have known the accusations that impugned Antenor's character. Consequently, his introduction of Antenor as the ancestor of the vikings (and thus of the Normans) gives a sinister cast to the upstart Normans he was pretending to honor, even as it subtly reminds the Normans' enemies that they were dealing with the descendants of a dangerous traitor. On another level, of course, this invented Trojan thread fashions just a small and curious line in an intricate web of allusions to the *Aeneid*. For instance, passages describing the horror of night raids by viking bands echo Vergil's description of the fall of Troy.[33] Throughout his history, Dudo lifted words and phrases, imitated Vergil's dactylic hexameters, borrowed its primary theme, and finally even stole its hero.[34] Vergil's Aeneas is a complex character. Dudo broke him down into simpler elements in order to illustrate the progressive civilizing of the Norman dukes.

The first of Dudo's four books focuses on Hasting, the archetypal viking, actually a composite figure that Dudo drew as an anti-Aeneas.[35] Hasting has the passion that Aeneas rarely shows, and he directs his considerable energies toward evil. He lusts after murder, mayhem, rapine. Hasting hungers for civilization, but only to devour it. Here is just one especially obvious example of Hasting as the anti-Aeneas: his goal is to go to Italy, to find Rome, and to demolish it.[36] The language that describes his eager departure on that adventure echoes *Aeneid* 3.529–32, where Aeneas first arrives in Italy. Hasting

---

Christian writers such as Tertullian, Lactantius, and Orosius assailed Aeneas's image, as did Dictys and Dares. Ovid, Christian polemicists, the Latin poets of the Trojan war, all these influenced medieval writers up to and including Chaucer and John Gower. Thus the ancient tradition of the unhero Aeneas reached the medieval west as a potent foil to the Vergilian Aeneas.

33 Dudo, 1.4; *Aeneid* 2.265.

34 This history is prosimetric, that is, it is written in alternating poetry and prose. The predominant meter is dactylic hexameter. See the appendix on Dudo's meters in Eric Christiansen, *Dudo of St Quentin*, 236–37, and his notes to the translation.

35 Felice Lifshitz has argued that Hasting's tale is only prefatory material, and she excludes it from her discussion of narrative structure. "Dudo's Historical Narrative and the Norman Succession of 996," *Journal of Medieval History* 20 (1994), 101–20. But Hasting's character offers an important foil to Rollo's relative civility. The clusters of poems also support the division of this work into four books.

36 For this episode, see Dudo, 1.5–7.

sails to Italy, finds the biggest city he has ever seen, enters it by a ruse, wrecks the place and slaughters nearly everyone in it. But just as Hasting is glorying in the achievement of his lifetime ambition, he learns that the place is not Rome. To him it seems a big city, but to the Italians it is merely the obscure village called Luna.[37] Dudo has a healthy sense of humor – and by Book Two Hasting has also learned how to laugh – but here the viking is not amused. He rages around the nearby territories, wreaking havoc until he feels a little better, and stomps back to France. He soon returns to Dudo's pages apparently transformed into a pawn serving Frankish interests against Rollo's viking band (2.13).

But Rollo, the focus of Dudo's second book, is the viking who will adopt some of Aeneas's traits and settle in the new homeland. Like the Trojan hero, Rollo has to flee treachery and chaos in his old home and face wandering and tiresome diversions. Dudo even provides him with a storm scene, almost obligatory in epic, whose Vergilian components include the hero's prayer and a shipwreck.[38] While Juno stirred up the winds against Aeneas, postponing his fated arrival in Italy, evil spirits provoke the storm against Rollo, hoping to thwart his predicted baptism. Rollo also has to encounter his own consciousness (and here I think he is most like Aeneas) as he gradually comes to understand the destiny predicted through visions that others must interpret for him. This is Dudo's equivalent of *Aeneid* 6, where the hero descends to the underworld and meets his father, Anchises, who shows him the glory toward which he is working.

Although none of Dudo's Norman dukes braves the land of the dead, Dudo teases us with that idea when he puts Hasting at Luna and has him penetrate the town by feigning death, from which he awakens to slaughter the monks who are giving him his last rites.[39] Hasting gains no insight from his *faux* encounter with the other world. This anti-Aeneas still longs to destroy human life and undermine Christendom. Dudo means to contrast him with Rollo, whose interior life – his dreams – and growing self-knowledge lead him to found a civilizing dynasty.

Driven out of his Scandinavian homeland by an evil king, who has killed

---

[37] The myth also seems to play with an imagined link between presumptuous ambition and lunacy. On the travails of this once rich Roman town, see Silvia Orvietani Busch, "Luni in the Middle Ages: The Agony and the Disappearance of a City," *Journal of Medieval History* 17 (1991), 283–96.

[38] Dudo, 2.8–9; cf. *Aeneid* 1.81–156. Leah Shopkow ("Norman Historical Writing in the Eleventh and Twelfth Centuries," 603–604) has shown that this scene follows the *Vita sancti Germani* of Heiric of Auxerre, though Dudo understood that his model was imitating Vergil.

[39] Norman sources attached this folktale motif of feigned death to Bohemond and other Norman heroes. Marguerite Mathieu (*La Geste de Robert Guiscard*, 46–52) cites frequent examples along with the likely prototype: in Icelandic sagas, most notably *Heimskringla*, Harald Hardrade takes a Sicilian town by this stratagem.

Rollo's brother Gurim, Rollo tarries on the island called Scanza. Physically and emotionally exhausted, he falls into an anxious sleep, when he hears a divine voice (*vox divina*) saying, "Rollo, quickly get up! Hurry! Sail across the sea! Go *ad Anglos*, where you will hear how you will return, saved, to your country and enjoy perpetual peace there without any harm" (2.5).[40] At first Rollo persists in believing that the dream is urging him to conquer the *Angli* (Angles), and so he sails to England, against the advice of a spiritual guide, a Christian Anchises, who correctly interprets the dream to mean that Rollo must accept baptism and join the *Angeli* (angels). This is, of course, a famous literary trope, best known from Bede's tale of Gregory's decision to preach to the Angles/angels, but Dudo gives it a broader comic effect.[41] Just as Aeneas made a false start, misinterpreting Apollo's command (*vox; Aeneid* 3.93), so Rollo misunderstands the voice in his dream and heads for England.

In England another vision corrects his error. Rollo's second dream (2.6), arguably the formative myth of Norman identity, deserves close examination. The pagan Rollo dreams that he stands on a mountain in France. Out of the mountain top flows a spring that purifies him of leprosy and lust. Around this mountain flock thousands of birds of different colors, but all with red left wings. All seek the spring, refreshing themselves peaceably and nesting together at Rollo's bidding. When Rollo awakens, a Christian captive explains the symbolism. The mountain is the church of France, and the healing spring holy baptism that washes away the leprosy of wickedness and sin. The multitudes of birds are the men from various lands, who will carry Rollo's shields and rebuild the walls of ruined cities in service to him. "*You* the birds of various kinds will attend; *you* the men of various realms will obey as they lie down in service to you" (*Tibi aves diversarum specierum obtemperabunt; tibi homines diversorum regnorum serviendo accubitati obedient*).

This seems to be an inclusive vision of Normanness that transcends constraints of racial purity or bloodline. The mixed heritage of the Normans will continue to be a distinctive feature of the Norman self-concept, "a point of tension," as Cassandra Potts has observed, "and a point of pride for Normans in the tenth and early eleventh centuries as they struggled through the creative processes of state-building and regional identification."[42] But the

---

[40] Dudo's *velociter surge* recalls the *surge velociter* of Acts 12:7, when an angel awakens Peter in prison, freeing him from his chains and leading him to safety. But the coded language that obscures the hero's destination alludes to Apollo's prophecy to Aeneas, as he begins his wanderings after Troy's destruction: "*Antiquam exquirite matrem*" (search for your mother from ancient times; *Aeneid* 3.96). Christiansen, *Dudo of St Quentin*, 188, n. 128.

[41] *Bede's Ecclesiastical History of the English People*, ed. B. Colgrave and R. A. B. Mynors (Oxford, 1969), 132–34. Christiansen, *Dudo of St Quentin*, 188, n. 128.

[42] "*Atque unum ex diversis gentibus populum effecit*," 139. The Latin quotation comes from a history of the monastery of Saint-Wandrille, written in the 1050s: *Inventio et miracula Sancti Vulfranni*, ed. J. Laport (Rouen, 1938), 21. See Elisabeth M. C. van

interpretative voice in Dudo's account promises that conversion to Christianity will bring Rollo supreme power over these peoples, atop an autocratic social structure.

The concept intrigues Rollo as he sails to France and fights the natives there for the right to settle in his adopted homeland. But Dudo soon presents episodes that suggest the hostility of the war band to Rollo's dreams of domination. In the first of these scenes, a "confrontation . . . in the best saga style," Hasting makes a cameo appearance, brought in by the Franks as a consultant for viking affairs (2.13).[43] "You come from that same people," says the Frankish prince to Hasting, whom the narrator here identifies as "inciter of all wickedness." "Give us advice on dealing with them." Hasting answers testily, "Just send envoys to them to see what they have to say." "Please," comes the rejoinder, "you go right away." Clearly no fool, Hasting responds, "I won't go alone." So the Franks dispatch two soldiers who know Danish. With his armed escort, Hasting stands on the riverbank, from a safe distance interrogating Rollo's vikings:

> "Officers of his royal majesty order you to say who you are and where you come from and what you want."
> "We are Danes from Denmark, come to conquer France."
> "What is your lord's name?"
> "Nobody, since we are equals in power."[44]

This assertion of an egalitarian warrior society fits the stereotype of social equality among Scandinavians. But the vikings' insistence upon this ideal also defies Rollo's dream of his rule and strikes against the dynastic ambitions of his successors.

After speaking with these viking warriors, Hasting reports back to the Franks, apparently goading them into combat by provoking the war party to challenge the ferocity of Rollo's vikings.[45] Dudo inserts a hint that Hasting has perhaps collaborated with Rollo. As the tide of battle turns against the Franks, Hasting and a companion turn tail and run away *hilares* (merry). Had Hasting lured Charles into a fight he knew his fellow vikings would win? Were Hasting and Rollo co-conspirators? This episode is one of many

---

Houts, "Historiography and Hagiography at Saint-Wandrille: The '*Inventio et Miracula Sancti Vulfranni*,' " in *Anglo-Norman Studies* 12 (1989), 233–51.

[43] Frederic Amory, "The Viking Hasting in Franco-Scandinavian Legend," in *Saints, Scholars and Heroes: Studies in Medieval Culture in Honour of Charles W. Jones*, ed. M. H. King and W. M. Stevens (Collegeville, Minn., 1979), 272. On the questions of Dudo's relationship with Old Norse poetry, see the summary of scholarship in Eric Christiansen, *Dudo of St Quentin*, xvi–xviii.

[44] "*Quo nomine vester senior fungitur?*" *Nomen* can mean either "name" or "title," so this question may read: "What title does your lord use?" The answer, then, is "None."

[45] 2.13. Dudo identifies the head of this war party as a belligerent standard-bearer suggestively named Roland.

reminders that, no matter how far he has come, Rollo has more in common with Hasting than with Charles.

The next scene emphasizes the differences, in both custom and disposition, between viking and Frank. With Hasting gone for good, Rollo makes his famous treaty with the vanquished Charles, the treaty that grants him Rouen and the beginnings of the Norman state. Once again Dudo uses humor to convey a darker subtext. When the Franks order Rollo to kiss the king's foot as an act of fealty to his new lord, he designates another viking to perform the duty for him (2.29). Refusing to stoop, this viking grabs Charles' foot and raises it to his lips, toppling the king. It is an aptly symbolic gesture for the union of Scandinavian and Frank, and it sends a message not only to Charles and the Franks but also to Rollo, whose command has provoked a menacing response from a defiant viking who will bow to no king. The air is charged with threats all around, and the vikings' laughter taunts Rollo as much as Charles.

Small wonder, then, that a royal bride and oaths of loyalty do not prevent conflicts in the promised land of Normandy. Imitating the structure of the *Aeneid*, the second half of Dudo's history records these struggles between the new settlers and the old. According to Dudo, Rollo's son William Longsword inherits his father's passion for law and order and far surpasses Rollo in Christian sensibilities. This version of William Longsword adopts the part of Aeneas that is reverent, filled with religious awe, obedient to the will of the gods. But because William is so trusting, enemies can lure him into an ambush and assassinate him (3.63). Angels take the martyr's soul to heaven, and when his grieving men prepare the body for burial, they discover a key on a chain around his neck. It unlocks a chest containing William's most valued treasure, a monk's habit (3.64). He had never wanted to be a powerful lord, Dudo suggests, but aspired only to the spiritual life.

William left a young son, Richard I, who must fight the continuing wars in the new homeland, insurrections within and attacks from Frankish counts, the German King Otto, and the Franks' King Louis IV. But one danger especially, at William's death, threatens the survival of the duchy: hoping to reabsorb Normandy into their direct control, the Franks dispute the boy's legitimacy and, therefore, his right to inherit William's lands and powers. If William left no heir, the Franks might reclaim the duchy.

To refute these charges, Dudo must first argue that William fathered the boy, a claim made more difficult by Dudo's depiction of William as a man with ascetic longings. Then he must show that William designated a concubine's son as his successor. Dudo never mentions William's Christian wife, Leutgarde, and so implies that Richard is the duke's only child.[46] This simpli-

---

[46] Searle, *Predatory Kinship* (93–97) shows how Dudo and the Norman rulers followed the early medieval patterns of constructing kinship to foster their own political interests.

fies the matter, but questions still remain. If William had acknowledged the boy, why was the child living in Bayeux instead of at the ducal court in Rouen? Dudo answers that William Longsword had wanted the boy's mother, an unnamed *matrona venerabilis*, to elude the clutches of a Scandinavian rebel named Riulf. So when the woman was pregnant with Richard, William sent her to the safety of Fécamp (3.66). As the child matured, William entrusted him to a tutor in Bayeux, where he might learn the Scandinavian tongue no longer spoken in Rouen (3.68). So eager was the pious William to equip his son for preaching to the pagan Danes that he endured the boy's absence. But, Dudo insists, the father missed his son very much and visited him at Easter, persuading the nobles there to swear fealty to Robert should William face a fatal turn of fortune's wheel.[47]

Growing up in Bayeux, the boy learned to operate in both the old pagan world and the new Christian realm. Richard did become bilingual, speaking a Scandinavian dialect as well as French. He eventually married a pagan-born Danish lady, and so fostered the old Scandinavian ties of kinship. He knew how to handle both Frankish bishops and viking mercenaries. In Dudo's pages Richard matures into a powerful synthesis of viking and Frank – cool and rational, ruthless and calculating against his enemies, but passionate in his defense of Christianity, pious in his own way. It is this synthesis that Dudo finds uniquely Norman. And it was Vergil's Aeneas who led Dudo to the creation of such a hero for his epic history.

Of course, Dudo did not simply imitate the *Aeneid*. Dudo's history is a composite of many genres: satire, lyric, panegyric, biblical prophecy, hagiography, as well as ancient epic and perhaps even saga.[48] But its organizational structure as epic history or Vergil parody best discloses the two extremes of Dudo's attitude toward the Normans, whom the text extols and the subtext treats with delicious wit.

The fourth and final book, on the reign of Richard I, dominates this narrative, being longer than the first three combined. At first this imbalance seems

---

[47] Many historians of early Normandy invoke this tale as evidence that Scandinavian dialects were no longer spoken in Rouen, and they see this as proof of the rapid assimilation of Normans into Christian and Frankish culture. But Dudo is using (and perhaps inventing) the language issue to answer critics who challenged Richard's legitimacy. For a more complete discussion of this passage, see my article "Scandinavians in Byzantium and Normandy," in *Peace and War in Byzantium: Essays in Honor of George T. Dennis, S. J.*, ed. Timothy S. Miller and John Nesbitt (Washington, D.C., 1995), 114–22. After considering the history of Scandinavians in Byzantium, I suggest that in Normandy assimilation might have come more slowly than we have imagined.

[48] For elements of hagiography, see Victoria B. Jordan, "The Role of Kingship in Tenth-Century Normandy: Hagiography of Dudo of Saint Quentin," *The Haskins Society Journal* 3 (1991), 53–62. On Biblical influences, see Felice Lifshitz, "Dudo's Historical Narrative," 109–14. On the broad range of Dudo's sources and models, especially those from the Carolingian curriculum, see Shopkow, *History and Community*, 146–53.

only natural. After all, this duke was Dudo's initial patron and contemporary. The historian frequented Richard's court and knew witnesses to Richard's life and reign. The book lingers, however, on tales of Richard's minority and youth, neglecting altogether many of the mature years, the quarter century (c. 965 – c. 990) when Dudo's supposed informants were in their prime. Critics have suggested that Dudo skipped over these years because he favored the *Annales* of Flodoard of Rheims, a reliable source until 966, over oral accounts and so virtually ended his history when Flodoard stopped, with the wars between Normandy and Chartres.[49] Only with the building of a magnificent church at Fécamp (dedicated in 990) did Dudo take up the narrative again for an abbreviated finale.

But a myth-maker of Dudo's caliber would hardly disregard a quarter of his century simply because he lacked a written source. After all, Dudo imaginatively constructed Hasting, for whom he had little evidence. Then did Dudo simply run out of time or energy, or did he lose interest? Nothing in the narrative suggests haste or impatience with a task he shows every sign of relishing. On the contrary, Dudo chose to focus on the drama of Richard's childhood, which features the turmoil surrounding a weak Carolingian king, with the consequent hazards for Normandy.

It is a compelling story. At William's assassination King Louis abducts the boy and holds him hostage on the pretext of protecting and educating him at the royal court. Richard's tutor rescues him from the king's vice, and two loyalists in the Norman side, Bernard the Dane and Bernard of Senlis, conspire to keep the child safe within Normandy, even as Louis and Duke Hugh the Great scheme to divide Normandy among themselves. But the Bernards outwit these foes, buying time until Richard is old enough to take the offensive himself. By the late 950s Richard is attacking Theobald, count of Chartres and drawing the ire of neighboring counts, Geoffrey II of Anjou and Arnulf I of Flanders, along with the Carolingian king Lothar (954–86).[50] This formidable alliance counters Richard's attack and nearly brings disaster to Normandy, until the young duke enlists pagan Scandinavians to terrify his enemies into making peace in 965. This treaty is a watershed for Richard, assuring his survival even as it halts his aggression. For Dudo the peace of 965 marks the end of Richard's heroic period and so makes a fitting denoue-

---

[49] Flodoard of Reims, *Les Annales de Flodoard*, ed. Philippe Lauer (Paris, 1906). In a forthcoming article ("The Man from Vermandois: Dudo of Saint-Quentin and his Patrons") Leah Shopkow argues that by virtually ending the narration in 965, Dudo could avoid detailing the struggle between Capetians and Carolingians. This was a volatile issue that pitted Normandy and Vermandois against one another and so strained Dudo's conflicting allegiances.

[50] Bates, *Normandy before 1066*, 14–15. On the precarious condition of early Normandy, see also Potts, "*Atque unum ex diversis gentibus populum effecit,*" 139–52.

ment for the narrative, to which Dudo need only add the postscript of Richard's last years.

What sort of people are these Normans, who have survived such obstacles? And what is the character of Richard, the boy rescued to secure his people's domain? The very structure of Dudo's work provides an answer, because the pagan vikings frame this struggle. The *De moribus* begins in Scandinavia itself, where injustice predominates: the narrative opens with human sacrifices (1.2), a people descended from a traitorous ancestor (1.3), and youths driven out of their homeland to fend for themselves in foreign lands (2.1). The deceit of Hasting at Luna illustrates the consummate infidelity of these pirates, who attack trusting innocents, like wolves in sheepfolds (1.7).

At the end of Dudo's history, Scandinavians appear again with Richard's importation of these pagans to join his battle against a faithless king and count. But when the Franks finally capitulate and sue for peace, Richard finds his Danes difficult to mollify (4.119). To Richard's polite request that they return home, the Danes threaten, "Never will we grant a lasting peace!" They angrily remind the duke that many Northmen have answered his call, and others are even then outfitting ships to join them. "For you we will conquer France, which we have invaded. But if you're not happy with that, we'll take it for ourselves. Choose which you prefer, either for you or for ourselves." These Danes know how to turn the screws even on Richard. Their menacing language argues only for might, never for peace and justice. This close contest between Richard and the Danes exposes the Normans' kinship with their wild cousins.

Only the duke's sophistication will eventually trump the pagans' rough threats. Indeed, this must be the moment for which his father had prepared him, when William dispatched the boy to Bayeux to learn Danish so that he could preach to the pagans (3.68). And preach he does, for sixteen days, on fidelity and infidelity, on the fallen angels and God's creation of mankind as a faithful and just replacement for the lost and damned (4.121). When people, too, fall from grace, explains Richard, God sends Christ to redeem them from sin and duplicity and to promise resurrection for souls of the faithful and the just. But when Richard's sermon on Christian ethics and on the mysteries of heaven and hell fails to win the vikings to the duke's will, he reverts to his back-up plan: under cover of darkness Richard bribes the Danish leaders to betray their compatriots, tricking them to leave France (4.122–23).

See how far Richard has progressed from his grandfather's pagan origins, and how much he has retained of the viking's wiles. By guile and by violence, Rollo and his progeny fight to establish and maintain control. Dudo's surface narrative presents this struggle as a quest for peace and justice. Dudo preserves or invents a single major act of Rollo's reign in Normandy, for instance, an act that pretends to symbolize the new duke's enforcement of law.[51] This is the now famous judgment of the missing plow. In a rare glimpse of tenth-century peasants, Dudo looks to the countryside, where a farmer obeys Rollo's new edict to leave all plows and livestock in the fields, trusting the duke's surety for protection of property (2.31–32). But when the peasant comes home for lunch, his wife upbraids him for being so credulous, and while he eats, she steals into the field and removes the plow. When the peasant reports the plow missing, his wife attacks him again and dispatches him to the duke, who gives him five gold coins in recompense, but also sends agents to interrogate villagers. Under torture by fire, none admits to the crime. An exasperated Rollo asks the bishop, Franco, why God did not reveal the thief. Answers Franco, "Fire has still not touched the culprit." So Rollo summons the peasant to identify exactly who knew about the plowing equipment left in the field. "My wife," he replies. The woman denies any guilt until a thorough flogging elicits her confession at last. "Did you know that your wife was the thief?" Rollo asks the husband. "Yes, I knew." So Rollo had both hanged, writes Dudo, and their execution put an end to thievery in the land. It is a cautionary tale for any who would test the duke's justice.

A cautionary tale of another sort dominates the next book. Rollo's heir, William Longsword, proves too trusting and too eager for peace and so succumbs to the deceit of the Flemish Count Arnulf I, "infested with guile" (3.62–63). Arnulf and his "four treacherous men" lure William to a meeting on an island in the Somme, offering fealty if William will protect the count from King Louis, Herbert of Vermandois, and Hugh the Great. Believing Arnulf's sincerity, William kisses him to seal the concord, then boards his boat. But Arnulf's "four wicked men" summon William back to the island, pretending that they have neglected some detail. When the credulous duke returns alone, the henchmen reach for concealed weapons and assassinate "alas! the innocent William" in plain view of his companions, who watch helplessly from the riverbank. Adopting the tone of a (still extant) Latin lament for the death of William Longsword, Dudo describes the wailing of Normans and Bretons as a chorus of angels carries the martyr's soul to heaven.[52]

---

51 Dudo may have drawn on events from the reign of Duke Richard II to illustrate his argument that Rollo nurtured peace and law in his land. See Mathieu Arnoux, "Classe agricole, pouvoir seigneurial et autorité ducale. L'évolution de la Normandie féodale d'après le témoignage des chroniqueurs (Xe–XIIe siècles), *Le moyen âge*, 5th ser., 6 (1992), 35–60.

52 The anonymous *Planctus*, probably written soon after the murder, ends nearly every stanza with a plaintive call for lamentation: *Cuncti flete pro Willelmo innocente interfecto* ("All weep for William the innocent, murdered"). This poem makes Longsword "a lamb mangled by a wolf" (*ovem lupo laniatam*). Jules Lair, ed., *Étude sur la vie et la mort de Guillaume Longue-Épée, duc de Normandie* (Paris, 1893), 66–68; "Complainte sur la mort de Guillaume Longue-épée," in Philippe Lauer, *Le règne de Louis IV*, Bibliothèque de l'École des hautes études 127 (Paris, 1900), 319–23; "Der

This mistake of trusting too much is one that no other Norman duke is likely to make. Rollo's descendants, wary of Normans and neighbors alike, became adept at surveillance, as Rollo himself learned to do when his Frankish wife harbored two knights sent by her father, King Charles (2.33). In this instance, Rollo relieved his anger by executing the Frankish knights in the market place of Rouen.[53] But Dudo's narrative more often works to remove Franks from the lists of Normandy's principal enemies, invoking the Vergilian model: the foreign and native peoples must overcome their hostilities to unite and create a uniquely vigorous civilization, joining Scandinavian cunning and ferocity with Frankish Christianity and culture. An outsider to Norman society, Frankish by birth and education and outlook, Dudo elevates the Frankish connection. So he has the Frankish nobles pronounce their approval of Rollo and urge their king to ally with him (2.25). The longer their contact with the Franks, the more civilized these Normans become. The second duke, William Longsword, is himself half Frank. In describing Frankish–Norman hostilities, furthermore, Dudo takes care to divert blame away from the king and onto a villain like Arnulf of Flanders. Often the verse interludes carry this editorial commentary. In a series of four poems that freeze the action before the battle of Chartres (4.107), for instance, Dudo addresses each of the chief adversaries. How, asks Dudo in the delicately worded poem to King Louis, can Louis be deceived by the *odibilis* ("loathsome") Arnulf?

Verses in the *De moribus* even argue passionately, if not persuasively, that the Norman–Frankish link will ultimately exalt France.[54] As early as I.7, when Hasting turns his booty-laden ships from Italy to France, Dudo breaks

---

Planctus auf den Normannenherzog Wilhelm Langschwert (942)," ed. Phillipp August Becker, *Zeitschrift für französische Sprache und Literatur* 63 (1939), 190–97. Robert Helmerichs has collected the manuscript evidence, commentaries, and translations at this website: www.ukans.edu/carrie/Planctus/

53 Commentators disagree on the reasons for Rollo's anger here. Rollo's *comites* (the same companions who have consistently challenged his princely prerogatives?) have come to inform him that Gisla has hidden these envoys, having failed to report their arrival to Rollo. The *comites* ridicule Rollo by calling him uxorious and by further charging that he has never even had sex with his wife, who has taken in these Franks to attend her. Dudo implies that Gisla has indeed lavished "all the goods" on her Frankish compatriots, "and she made them stay much too long" (*cunctaque bona illis largiens, nimis diu morari fecit*). Enraged by these insinuations, Rollo saves face through a public execution. For alternative interpretations of this passage, see Christiansen, *Dudo of St Quentin*, 197, n. 220.

54 This is a familiar impulse for optimists living in a cultivated society confronted by barbarians. Cf. the *Getica* of Jordanes, which Dudo knew. Walter Goffart has shown how the *Getica*'s happy ending, with the birth of a son to a Gothic princess and an east Roman prince, promises a happy union of Goths and Romans (*Narrators of Barbarian History*, 68–75).

into poetry to address France, once victorious in battle, lord of many peoples, strong, and law-bringing:

> Now you lie prostrate, sitting on your weapons, ashamed,
> stunned and dazed, weak, worried, and gloomy,
> downtrodden, reprimanded and scorned, rebuked,
> . . .
> Now quickly get up, get back to your weapons, press on!
> . . .
> Another progeny is sent forth from Denmark over there.
> . . .
> At last you will make a treaty, finally in tranquil peace
> your realm and your name will measure up to Olympus.

The power of this union, joining the civilized with the virile, will restore France's lost might. At least that is the literal meaning of this poem, which recollects Vergil's fourth eclogue, often called Messianic because it foretells the birth of a child who will usher in a new golden age. Christians widely interpreted this poem as Vergil's prophecy of the Nativity. Here is Dudo's allusion to this famous poem:

> Altera progenies Dacia dimittitur illa.

> (Another progeny is sent forth from Denmark over there.)

Compare it with *Eclogue* 4.7:

> Iam nova progenies caelo dimittur alto.

> (Now a new progeny is sent forth from heaven on high.)

Dudo infused irony into this line, replacing "heaven" with "Dacia" and Vergil's *alto* ("lofty") with *illa* ("that"), which can suggest distance (from the civilized world) or renown or even notoriety: "that infamous Denmark." Perhaps Dudo jests when he aligns a viking assault with the heavenly dispatch of a child who brings redemption.[55]

Two more Vergilian allusions in these verses war with one another to offer conflicting messages. On the one hand, that final line echoes the injunction of *Aeneid* 6.782, where the spirit of Anchises promises his son, Aeneas, that the fighting between Trojan exiles and native Italians will lead ultimately to their union and the creation of a mighty empire. On the other hand, the first line above recalls *Aeneid* 1.295, as Zeus makes the same promise to Venus:

---

[55] It is possible that Dudo is only following Carolingian wisdom, which portrayed the invasions as a divinely inspired corrective unleashed against sinners. See Simon Coupland, "The Rod of God's Wrath or the People of God's Wrath? The Carolingian Theology of the Viking Invasions," *Journal of Ecclesiastical History* 42, no. 4 (1991), 535–54.

25

wars will end at last, and Romans will govern a mighty realm in peace. This reference holds a more ambiguous assurance for France, since Zeus at once sends Hermes to earth, "so that the lands and citadels of new Carthage may open up/ to welcome the Trojans, and Dido, ignorant of fate, might not keep them out of her lands" (1.297–300). Do these Vergilian allusions identify France with Italy, or with Carthage? The latter possibility holds sinister overtones for the Franks.[56]

Apostrophes to Rouen overshadow those to Paris in Dudo's pages, but France is never far from the writer's mind. The Norman dukes themselves sometimes share Dudo's Francophile inclinations. When it suits them, they seek Frankish approval and authorization for their power just as they adopt the Frankish language, religion, and culture. In all eras of their history, whenever they encounter other societies, Normans gravitate toward the more prestigious identity. But in Dudo's pages, the Norman dukes also revel in their link to a dangerous viking past. Dudo's own patrons, the Richards I and II, are particularly adroit in using the threat of Scandinavian ferocity to intimidate foes. And they locate this ferocity not only in their pagan kin but also, pointedly, in themselves. However swiftly or completely the Normans may have assimilated into Frankish and Christian culture, in their histories they keep this sense of themselves as essentially untamed.

Dudo proves adept at managing this tension. As he makes each Norman prince more civilized than his predecessor, he also emphasizes the persistence of their feral instincts. So each of Dudo's four protagonists who commands a book of his own boasts a personality distinct from the others. Hasting is the deliciously wicked viking, while Rollo emerges as a redeemable marauder, capable of salvation. Rollo's son, William Longsword, matures into a statesman and a devout Christian, who is still capable of a good viking rage. As a child, Richard remains out of focus, the pawn in maneuverings by stronger personalities. But the adult comes alive though language and gesture – a smile for the bishop who asks him to call off his wolves, obscure court-speak for French negotiators, heroic exhortations to battle for Norman and Scandinavian warriors, straight talk for Scandinavian warlords, and erudition in a sermon for awestruck pagans, a tour de force that caps Richard's career as Christian statesman and fulfills his pious father's wish. Among the four principal characters, Richard stands out as the most

---

[56] Did Dudo also amuse himself by mixing a pun into the Vergilian allusion of the first line above? He has replaced Vergil's *saeva sedens super arma* ("sitting on savage arms"; *Aeneid* 1.295) with *super arma sedens verecunda* ("sitting on arms, ashamed"). Perhaps the change is appropriate enough since Vergil's subject, *Furor*, has become *Francia* in Dudo's version. But by late antiquity we find some authors using the neuter plural *verecunda* to mean "genitalia." So we can read *verecunda* as the first in a string of adjectives modifying abject France or as a substantive noun in apposition to *arma*.

nuanced and most intelligent, the consummate high-stakes player in games of danger and intrigue.[57]

Dudo draws such characters with shadings of heroism and cunning. He can also sketch Frankish kings as hapless victims of their own bad judgment, tricked by villains whose evil deflects guilt away from France. These foes of the Normans, among the liveliest of Dudo's creations, include Riulf, the head of the Danish party at the ducal court, who protests William Longsword's alleged pro-French stance by organizing a rebellion (3.43–44); Count Arnulf of Flanders, "filled with a viper's venom," the contriver of William's assassination; and Count Theobald of Chartres, "infected with the venomous spite of treachery" (*venenifico perfidiae infectus livore*), beguiler of King Lothar and mortal enemy of Richard I (4.110).[58]

Some of the slyest conspirators match wits in the power struggle of Richard's minority. Dudo signals the importance of this episode with prefatory verses rivaling the poems at the beginning of his history. As he approaches Richard's book, he writes invocations to each of the nine Muses. Finally, after Greek-studded poems addressed to Robert, archbishop of Rouen, and fresh prayers, Dudo launches into his famous story of William's extracting promises of protection for his young son, whom he then packs off to Bayeux to grow up fluent in Scandinavian (4.67–68). Following William's assassination, Richard's Breton and Norman supporters produce the boy, bring him to Rouen, and crown him duke while his father's body still awaits burial. As Count Berenger of Brittany proclaims, "We should put this boy in place of his father so that he is our duke and patrician," the nobles swear allegiance to Richard over sacred relics (4.69). While the young duke (no more than nine or ten years old by Eleanor Searle's reckoning) sets up residency in Rouen, Dudo celebrates the event with a paean to "Rouen, spreading far and wide on the banks of the Seine,/ rich in all goods including fierce fighters," now blessed with the new duke Richard, "whose goodness and piety and reverence will cause you to ascend to the Elysian fields at last" (4.69). This poem artfully fashions a moment of calm before Richard's captivity and the machinations that will free him.

At first no one seems to harbor suspicions when the Carolingian King Louis IV, rides into Rouen with his retinue (4.70). The people receive him joyfully, assuming that he will move against the Flemings to avenge William's murder. But instead, he lingers in Rouen, detaining Richard and refusing the boy's guardian when he asks permission to take the child to

---

[57] For a ready example of such a character whom Dudo would have known well, consider the dedicatee of the *De moribus*, Adalberon; cf. Felice Lifshitz, "Dudo's Historical Narrative," 107–108.

[58] Felice Lifshitz has described why Dudo, writing when Normandy found itself surrounded by enemies, might want to define "the Thibaudian and Flemish houses as vicious and diabolical." "Dudo's Historical Narrative," 108.

another home. When the townspeople realize that their duke is a prisoner, mobs gather in the streets, threatening the officials they deem responsible: "By your negligence we've lost Duke William, our special advocate. But this boy won't be driven into exile by your treacherous plotting. We will kill all you perjurers and the king – you deserve it! – and we will free Richard, the sovereign child, so he isn't forced into exile." In the heat of the moment, the ducal retainers first attack the crowd, then turn on the king and his men. The terrified king sends for Bernard of Senlis, described here as "prince of the Norman army," to help him "quickly, for the love of God." Now this Bernard, Richard's kinsman, emerges as the first of the shrewd politicos at the Norman court. Bernard refuses to come to the king's aid, sending only a terse message that he expects to die in this sedition. But when pressed, he advises the king to take the boy in his arms and go as a suppliant, begging the people and soldiers for mercy. Louis, it seems, dares not face the rabble, but he surrenders the boy to a Norman garrison.

The Normans have Louis cornered in a palace in Rouen. There the king pleads with Norman princes (4.71):

> I came here out of compelling obligation, at the horror of your lord's death, and to comfort you on account of what happened. But I met more sadly with the sorrow of an even more painful woe, because your people, from the town and countryside, and fighting men along with a mob of peasants wanted to rub me out and my men, too, and tear us to pieces in sudden death. But by your advice, you rescued me, Bernard, from the pestilential foe in such a great insurrection. Tell me what I should do now.

Bernard tries to calm the king and manipulate him into leaving the Normans in peace, so that they can control their own destiny. He says

> You are very upset about what the peasants and townspeople did to you. So it is important for you to be rendered innocent of deceit and public evil. In short, because our lord, Duke William, was in all respects blessedly loyal to you, it is fitting for you to authorize and solemnly decree that Richard, the boy of great promise, possess the land by legal right of inheritance. You should swear it with a sacred oath of holy faith and laying your hands on sanctified relics, and swear that you will never harm him, and in turn, that you will be his helpmeet and defender against all earth's people.

Bernard continues his lesson on the obligations between king and lord: "Thus you will be able to rejoice in our service and military support, as we will in your guardianship and governance. And if anyone should quarrel with you, we'll rub him out." Here Bernard pointedly uses the same verb – *conteremus* – that Louis had used to describe the Normans' recent threats against his own person. It serves as a reminder, if the king needs one, that these people are useful as allies just as they are dangerous as foes. "And," concludes Bernard, "if anyone should rise up against us, cast him down to the ground by the power of your might."

Louis pretends to acquiesce, straightway confirming the boy's hereditary right to possess the land. Laying his hands on holy relics, in God's name the king swears to aid Richard against all his enemies, and compels his men to swear likewise. But amid the ritual oaths of fealty, Dudo interjects the language of deceit and guile. The king speaks *in dolo* (4.71) and *fraudulenter* (4.72), tricking the Norman princes to return Richard to his custody with reminders of the oaths he had sworn and promises to educate the boy in his palace, like a proper prince. Louis's arguments become increasingly melodramatic: "Since his father died in my service, I'll be considered crueler than a beast if I don't come to his aid" (4.72). Dudo invests the custom of foster parenting with ominous weight. "Tricked by the dissembling appeals of the deceitful king, the Norman princes handed over Richard." Dudo adds, for any readers who have not yet gotten the message, "The king pretended in word and deed to be a helpmeet of good will, but in his heart he bore a purpose of ill intent."

The scene ends with lugubrious verses to Rouen: "Weep for your captive boy, alas!" This takes Dudo as far as he is willing to go in condemning a Frankish king, so he hastens now to divert attention away from Louis's guilt and toward a panoply of characters, the deceitful and the loyal. Back at his court, Louis first receives legates from count Arnulf, whom the narrative identifies as "fouled by the unspeakable crime." His spokesman paints a different picture, of a falsely maligned invalid, too sick to come in person and defend himself against lying defamers. To prove his innocence, Arnulf is willing to undergo judgment by fire and to kill the assassins, if that will appease the king. But perhaps such extreme measures will not be necessary. Before deciding, let the king see the rich gifts the envoys bring – ten pounds of the purest gold – and hear the promises of annual tribute and military service. (Not right away, presumably, since Arnulf's gout keeps him home-bound.) The king should not desert his servant, accused of such a crime *sine re* ("without cause"). And here the envoy turns skillfully from bribery and excuses to threats. "Do not destroy what has been entrusted to you. You can destroy all the Flemings more easily than you can pulverize [the verb again is *conterere*] glass vessels with a hammer."

Blinded by the gifts, the king's advisors find the Flemings' counsel eminently reasonable. "You shouldn't prejudge the case," they argue. "He is willing to prove his men innocent or exile them." And responding to the threat, they agree, "You ought not destroy what you hold," adding besides, "It isn't your obligation to avenge all who are killed, but to pacify the survivors who are squabbling on account of the death." But after appealing to his royal role as peacemaker, they conclude, "Remember the woes and disgrace which the Normans inflicted on you in Rouen and beware lest, dealing worse things upon you, they take Normandy away from you." Seeing that they have won their case, Arnulf's men freely expose their full wishes: "Hold the son Richard forever, and the usufruct of his realm evermore. Oppress the inhabitants of that land with the harsh yoke of rule and servitude, and compel them to serve you obediently." And so Louis, "tricked and blinded by the persuasion of their wicked counsel and the gifts," exonerates Arnulf and keeps Richard under close surveillance.

Dudo's audience has received an entertaining presentation featuring characters skilled in sophistry and bribery. The narrator's voice offers a running commentary, peppered with words for treachery, injustice, and evil. How can the Normans survive amid intricate intrigues? How can their duke, a mere child, remain alive in this viper's nest? The answer is, of course, quite nicely, using the Normans' own innate qualities, nurtured through long experience of trickery.

One incident serves as a wake-up call for the Normans, betraying to the boy's tutor, Osmund, that Richard is in fact the king's prisoner. Osmund had taken his charge riding in order to teach him the noble sport of falconing (4.73). But when the queen Gerberga informs Louis of the child's absence, the enraged king threatens Osmund with blinding if he should ever take Richard away again. And Louis assigns three retainers to guard against the duke's escape. Alarmed, Osmund sends a message to the people of Rouen, revealing the king's deceit. At special masses in all the churches of Normandy and Brittany, the people pray for God's aid and lament for their duke. They fast and walk barefoot in sackcloth. Priests and monks pray, sing hymns, and give alms on Richard's behalf. Meanwhile, writes Dudo, the boy was at least getting a royal education in the palace, learning to speak properly in "varieties of discourse, . . . in the mellifluous sweetness of the ways palace folk speak" (*mellifluo palatinae sermocinationis dulcamine*; 4.74) These are skills that will serve Richard well.

Eventually Norman prayers and fasting move God to free the boy, using Osmund as agent for this miracle (4.75). By pretending that the child is ailing and needs special care, Osmund manages to remove Richard from the king's compound. This feigned illness echoes Hasting's trickery at Luna, and this ruse becomes a favorite motif in Norman histories.[59] While loyal castellans protect the boy in a secret fortress, Osmund rides out to consult with Bernard of Senlis. After a celebration and thanksgiving in verse, Dudo recalls the conversation as Bernard breaks the silence of a dark night (4.76). "What's going on with you, Osmund? Have you no good news about my nephew?" "My lord," he answers cautiously, "if I rescue him from the hand of the wicked king, what will you do about that?" "I will elevate you and enrich you with many fees. I will exalt you and make you wealthy with benefices. I will

---

[59] On this feigning of illness, see G. A. Loud, "*Gens Normannorum*," 112.

restore my nephew in the hereditary realm of his father, and I will compel the Norman and Breton princes to serve him."

Encouraged by these assurances, Osmund reveals the truth to an exuberant Bernard, who hastens to Hugh the Great, duke of the Franks and father of the future king, Hugh Capet. Hugh the Great is himself a rival for the throne long held by Carolingians and thus a potential ally for the Normans. Dudo creates another vignette through the tentative dialogue of Hugh and Bernard, who has taken his cue from Osmund's initial approach to him. When Hugh asks, "Why have you raced to me so unexpectedly and so early in the day?" Bernard answers, "I come to you for advice, since King Louis holds my nephew in closer custody and with tighter oversight. If by chance someone rescues him from the king's hands, what sort of help will Your Mercy bestow on him?" Exclaims Hugh, "Everyone is amazed at what King Louis is doing! That boy's father was deceived and killed because of his faithfulness to the king, and now the king holds the son captive. If only someone would free the boy from the king's chains, and bring him to me!" "Lord," asks Bernard, "what will you do if what you have asked for should be fulfilled?" "Subjug-ating Normans and Bretons to him," promises Hugh, "I shall have him possess whatever his father held. I will aid him against the king, and I'll vigorously help him against Arnulf and all the conspirators." Then Bernard, "heaping prayers on prayers," falls at Hugh's feet as a suppliant, begging him to reward his trust in the duke's sentiments and promises, and confessing that he has the boy. Delighted at Richard's rescue, Hugh swears on relics that he will do what Richard and Bernard ask. Here Dudo highlights Hugh's promise by inserting verses to the Great Duke – "powerful and strong, flourishing,/ Great and renowned and worthy" – urging him to remember his promises of aid and help the deserving boy hold his father's lands.

Armed with Hugh's oaths of protection, Bernard returns to Richard, kisses him, and whisks him off to Senlis with a great army (4.77). But King Louis now labors under a double sadness: first, that he had taken the boy prisoner, and second, that the boy has escaped. The latter seems to trouble him far more, if we judge by his actions. For he sends a legate to Hugh, asking him to force Bernard to return the boy. Hugh replies that such a request supposes a massive military effort: "Unless I take from Bernard the castles Senlis and Coucy, Thourotte and Creil, I cannot press him by any efforts to return Richard, his beloved nephew." While Hugh fends off Louis's diplomatic foray, the Normans and Bretons rejoice, and Richard's protectors scheme. The two Bernards dominate the plotting. Bernard of Senlis consults in secret with Bernard the Dane of Rouen, agreeing to use go-betweens in future so that they can trick the king by adding the element of surprise to their inge-nuity, foiling his intention, says Bernard of Senlis, "to destroy us all."

Meanwhile the king, further distressed by Hugh's rebuff, summons Arnulf to advise him (4.78). Arnulf, whose mind Dudo always describes as turning to the destruction of Normans, also has reason for trepidation. He tells Louis

I'm terrified with a trembling of massive fear (*ingentis formidinis pavore exterreor*) and I'm shaken to the inmost marrow over what will come, fearing that the Normans and Bretons will unite with Duke Hugh, who is quarreling violently with you, to the destruction of our union. I am terrified that they'll take up military force and rise up against us as one. But I'll give you a plan to counteract this so we don't fall into the hazard of a ruination to come. Blind Hugh's eyes with gifts and benefices so that he can't rightly thwart what you do. Yield to him Normandy from the Seine to the sea, so that you can hold in peace everything on this side of it. Thus divided, the Normans will be devastated, and they won't be stirred up to struggle against us any more. So you will diminish and disarm the power of those men, when they aren't fighting for their one and only lord.

It is a shrewd plan, contrived by one of the most dangerous villains in Dudo's pages. To intensify the melodrama of this scene, Dudo launches into verses here, scolding "Arnulf, inventor of wickedness, plotting, and woe." This poem warns Arnulf that he will not prevail. But it will take all the Normans' wiles to sabotage this scheme.

The king dispatches a delegation of bishops to compel Hugh to go before him (4.79). To Hugh's question – "For what business did you force me to race here, with special legates claiming your due?" – Louis replies, "So that you return to me Richard, whom Osmund stole and led off to count Bernard." Hugh repeats his old protest, that he would have to muster force to storm Bernard's fortress. And here Louis makes the offer that Arnulf has suggested:

So that you are a helpmeet to my interests, and not an antagonist, I'll yield to you the counties of Évreux and Bayeux, for you to possess even from the Seine all the way to the sea. But I shall hold the lands on this side of the Seine, and I shall satisfy my will from these. Let us be in harmony and in agreement in every matter, as king and duke should be, in perpetuity. Going out on this side of the Seine, I'll besiege Rouen, and you ride out with full military might to attack Bayeux. So we'll wear away those haughty upstart [*advenas et superbos*] Normans and subject them to our power. They'll either become meek and subdued or they'll be driven out and quickly flee back to Denmark.

Here is an optimistic wish from a weak Frankish king. As Arnulf predicted, Hugh finds this an offer he cannot refuse. Forgetful of his pact with Bernard to aid Richard, and seduced by benefices and cities, he swears fealty to Louis, as *miles* to his *senior*, and then returns home, presumably to muster his forces against the Normans.

But Bernard of Senlis accosts him before he can act (4.80). In a speech loaded with the language of trust honored and faith broken, he gets right to the point:

Duke great and very faithful, outstanding up to now in all merits and loyalty – but I'm amazed that you lied to an innocent boy, whom you promised with Christian oath to defend. You should have kept your oath unbroken, not befouled it with a gift of presents and land. The Normans and Bretons know what you pledged to the boy, and Frankish princes rejoiced at the plan. What infamy is fouler than this? What is more loathsome than such blasphemy? The news of such perfidy and the wickedness of such an evil-doing duke is spreading throughout France. Everyone is whispering how such a duke and advocate was deceived and how he lied for gifts and a land grant.

Overwhelmed with shame, Hugh sighs: "By the true and pure works that you have related, you have reminded me that I forgot the sacred oath to defend, aid, and avenge the boy, and so I received as a gift from the king the land from the Seine to the sea to possess by hereditary right from him – all this against the oath which I swore to you and that boy." Hugh regrets his perjuring counter-oath to Louis, by which he promised his loyalty and support "unless he should ever countermand what he has given me." Hugh pleads with Bernard to find him a loophole.

You are a count of remarkable ingenuity and tremendous energy and cleverness, and shrewd in all sorts of dealings. I beg you to rescue me by some ruse from the blasphemy of this rumor. In sixteen days, the king and I will hasten to Normandy – he to besiege Rouen and I to Bayeux, as we swore. So we will crush the Normans and Bretons and reduce them to humble service. If any should be obstinate and rebellious, we'll send him packing, and anyone who should take up arms will be killed. If you have any shrewdness and ingenuity, I beg you to release me from the guilt of this perfidy.

Seeing that Hugh is being honest with him now, Bernard changes his tone, but reserves a touch of sarcasm: "Because you are a very gracious lord – and because the boy is my dearly beloved nephew – I'll calculate better than even I usually can, to see if by chance I can find a way to confound your plan." Soon enough, confident in his counter-plot, Bernard of Senlis tells the other Bernard his news and his scheme: instead of defending the city against the king, he will gather monks and priests to welcome Louis. Trusting that Bernard can prevail in any contest of trickery, all the Normans agree to cooperate in this strange request, even as Louis begins his assault and Hugh moves to Bayeux with a great army (4.81).

The Norman leaders initiate their secretly contrived maneuvers. So Bernard the Dane sends a message to the king, promising the surrender of his city if only Louis will stop despoiling the land and hasten to Rouen with his bishops and princes. A joyous king arrives to find Bernard at the gate to meet him in apparent friendship. The next morning at dawn, Bernard disarms the kings with a devilishly clever speech:

Utterly invincible lord king, for a long time now you have been pure and steadfast in your faithfulness and praiseworthy in your every work. We lost our duke and advocate by Arnulf's perfidy, but by the grace of God we've recovered you as our king and advocate. We don't care about the son whom Osmund stole from you and carried off. We who are beholden to him won't ever do military service to him, because it's a better plan for us to be royal retainers and palatines rather than bodyguards and servants of such a count. But still we're amazed at the incredible news we've heard, and we are really stunned at this report that you ceded to Duke Hugh, who has always been intractably quarrelsome with you, the ample land that stretches from the Seine to the sea's edge, and even now he is assailing the land around Bayeux and occupying it with a great army. It's a small prize, sweetest king, and a small contingent for military and civil service, that you kept for yourself. You increased your enemy by twenty thousand armed men. Who has seen stronger men in war, more prudent in counsel than the men of Coutances and Bayeux? If you had held a military force like William's, you could have been lord over the counsel and arms of all these people. Didn't William, relying on half of this army, with Hugh and Herbert in his retinue, conduct you in safe custody to King Henry? Who will protect and defend, benefit and do good to this city which you have retained?

Here Bernard reminds the king of the wealth of Rouen and its value as a trading port between Franks and English. All this Louis is surrendering to his enemy, Hugh. "Well then," Bernard concludes, "take the city, since we don't have the wherewithal to be able to live in it. And give it to Hugh so that he can rebel against you with less trouble."

We'll speed back to Denmark by ship, with all our people, and we'll collect a bigger army, and we'll lay waste this land just as Rollo once did.

(Nos Daciam, cum omni genere nostro, praepete navigationis cursu repedabimus, et hanc, majore collecta multitudine militari, ut Rollo quondam, devastabimus.)

"It won't be yours or Hugh's in the end."

Dudo has packed Bernard's language with reminders that Normans are Northmen, virtually indistinguishable from their Danish kin. What separates the Normans now from the old country and their old ways? *Nos Daciam* puts the subject and object together ("We ... Denmark"). At most they are a swift bird's flight (*praepete*) apart. In their viking past, Bernard's people got rich pillaging the land they now hold in service to the king, and it would suit them just as well to return to marauding.

This argument befuddles the king. Why should he lose Normandy to Hugh, his venerable enemy, when the Normans are offering the duchy without a struggle? Why should he provoke fresh assaults from Scandinavia? Now *he* needs advice from Bernard, who has a ready plan: "Send a legate to Duke Hugh the Great, refusing him the Bayeux countryside and insisting that he cannot occupy it for more than three nights and stay in it any longer, because he is acting out of evil counsel." Louis agrees. He retracts his promises to Hugh and thus releases that duke from his own commitments to the king and against the Normans. Hugh marvels privately at the craftiness of the Norman princes (4.82). Back in Paris, he cannot resist asking the king how this happened: "Why did you take away what you voluntarily gave me?" And the dim-witted king argues the Norman point of view, lecturing Hugh on the indivisibility of Normandy.[60] "Indeed," he concludes, "after Rollo was driven out of Denmark, he held legal claim to it as a whole [*integre*] for himself, and it has not been divided by anyone since then. The Danish-born people can serve only one lord" (*Gens Dacigena nescit famulari nisi uni soli seniori*). The Normans will soon disabuse Louis of any delusions that he can be that lord. For the Frankish king, this reckless game can only lead to further bamboozlement: a fresh invasion of pagans under the Danish king (4.86) and capture by the Normans (4.87) will persuade Louis that the lordship of Normandy exacts too high a price.

Louis's defense of a united Normandy controlled by Duke Richard marks an important moment in the *De moribus*. Here at last, in Dudo's account, the Normans possess all the dimensions of a distinctive ethnic community. Almost from their origins, according to Dudo, Normans have jointly held most of the properties that make them a people: a collective name, a common myth of descent, an association with their own land, a shared history, and a distinctive culture formed by the union of Scandinavian and Frank.[61] The king now confirms the legal right of this *gens Dacigena* to their land. The crisis of Richard's captivity, furthermore, has elicited a response that confirms the Norman identity. When Flemish count and Frankish king ally with Duke Hugh the Great against them, the Norman people resist (4.70), and the magnates, too, put aside their feuds to join against a common foe. In this defiance the Normans display a sense of solidarity that marks their final progression to a unique *gens*.

The tale of Richard's minority (4.70–82), by far the longest episode in the *De moribus*, draws attention to this culmination of Norman identity formation. It also shows Dudo at his best as a storyteller who creates ingenious characters, whose minds we fathom largely through their own language, in the manner of Scandinavian saga. The dialogue alternately obscures and unmasks the motivations of Norman and Frank, Fleming and Dane. Dudo's style engages the audience by pressing us to fill in the blanks, to analyze the speaker's intent and motivation, to anticipate the twists of plot.

---

60 *Tellus Northmanniae non nisi unius senioris unquam tuebitur advocatione, nec debet esse divisum quod decet esse continuum.*

61 These six characteristics of an ethnic community come from Anthony D. Smith, *The Ethnic Origins of Nations* (Oxford, 1986), 22–31.

*

Dudo's abundant dialogue pulls the reader into his Norman world. But another element of his literary style has had the opposite effect. Readers from the eleventh century to our own age have sometimes skipped over the difficult, even intimidating poems that introduce the work and punctuate the narrative at critical points. Typically these verses freeze the action to present some eulogy or exclamation, jolting the reader away from the actors to a pose of the author. Even as they pretend to intensify the narrative, therefore, they more often undermine it by edging the writer into the foreground and emphasizing that it is his voice we hear. The cumulative effect may have annoyed even some of the earliest readers. In any case, only a minority of extant manuscripts include the nearly eighty poems.[62] With these verses restored in the printed edition, the *De moribus* has proved intimidating to all but the most intrepid readers.

Prefaced by a long letter to Adalberon – its prose studded with assonance, alliteration, puns and Biblical references – the text then presents eight pretentious poems loaded with proof of classical learning, even slipping in some liturgical Greek. Like Horace in his volume of odes (books 1–3), Dudo will begin his *opus* with a display of technical competence in a variety of meters. First come fifty-one hexameters to his book, then a short poem to Richard II. There follow fifty lines on the poet's anxiety over his inadequacy before such a daunting task. But he will trust in the Lord, who created heaven and earth, raised Lazarus from the dead, and redeemed all humanity with His own death. Bolstered by faith that a God of such powers can succor him through his own labors, Dudo forges ahead through three poems to Robert, archbishop of Rouen, and one to count Raoul before closing this series with a metrical prayer. Dudo has begun with a display of his erudition and piety and homage to his benefactors. He could not have known that this display would so dishearten readers that many would proceed no further.

Some scribes decided to tackle the narrative by eliminating the poems altogether. But removing the verses from Dudo's prosimetrical work does not strip away mere ornamentation. The verses signal Dudo's literary ties to an era that was swiftly passing. Steeped in the poetic conventions of

---

62 See the chart of the extant manuscripts, noting those with and without the poems, in Huisman, "Manuscript Tradition," 123. Huisman counts fourteen manuscripts, but Christiansen (*Dudo of St Quentin*, xxxiv–xxxv, n. 80) points out that "the one in the Bodleian Library (Coll. R. James 28) is a seventeenth-century compilation which merely includes two fragments. Three of the thirteenth-century MSS (Douai Bibliothèque Municipale 880, Antwerp Plantin-Moretius 17.2, and Paris, Bibliothèque Nationale n.a.l. 1031) lack book 4, and seven MSS lack the poems." We cannot know how many scribes chose to leave out the poems and how many simply copied an earlier manuscript with verses already missing.

Merovingian and Carolingian writers, Dudo found inspiration in Carolingian saints' lives, whose style and content he appropriated.[63] Prosimetry lent dignity and a sense of antique substance to his work on parvenu dukes and people. Some poems accomplish still more. Consider the earliest verses to appear in the narrative itself (I.3). Here they are, along with the prose passages that precede and follow them:

Now the Dacians call themselves *Danai* or *Dani* [Danes] and boast that they are descendants of Antenor, who slipped from the midst of the Argives when the lands of Troy were destroyed and who entered the Illyrian lands with his men. Indeed those very Dacians were then driven out by their own people in the manner just described, and under the leadership of Hasting they were fiercely driven away to the borders of the vast territories of Francia.

> He is accursed and fierce, too cruel and savage.
> Plague-bearing, dangerous, grim, ferocious, profligate.
> Plague-bearing and fickle, insolent, vain and lawless.
> Deadly, pitiless, wily, everywhere insurgent.
> Traitor and inciter of evil, double-dealing dissimulator.
> Unscrupulous, haughty, corrupting, deceitful, and reckless,
> Gallows-bait, defiled, unbridled, contentious.
> Scion of plague-bearing evil, increment of guile.
> Not to be censured with ink but with charcoal.
> And towering above all others in crime by so much
> As the distance up to starry Olympus.

Hither and yon he contaminated the fugitive heathens, mixing them together and usurping their resources for himself and his own. He assailed the domain of Gallic power, appropriated for himself the Frankish realm. He violated the priesthood, trampled the sanctuary. By words and deeds he harried the Frankish king, sojourning in his cities, much to their sorrow. He growls around the garrisons' walls, like a wolf around sheep-folds. He cares not a lock of wool for the Franks, who have withdrawn to their garrisons out of fear. He pursues them all as the lion after deer.

Readers who have worked their way through Dudo's prologues may take this excerpt in stride, but those who come to it without such preparation will note its extravagance and range of styles. True, Dudo's fondness for rhyme, rhythm, and metaphor throughout the history eases the transitions between poetry and prose. The concluding prose here, for instance, boasts epic similes comparing Hasting to both wolf and lion. Still, the blunt listing of Hasting's

---

63 Leah Shopkow, "Carolingian World," 19–37. Shopkow identifies the *Vita sancti Lamberti* of Stephen of Liège and the *Vita sancti Germani* of Heiric of Auxerre as two primary models, and she nicely educes evidence to suggest that Dudo received his remarkable education "at a traditional Carolingian centre, probably Liège."

qualities, abruptly inserted as the viking bursts onto the scene, means to shock. Here Dudo has used his favorite meter, the dactylic hexameters of ancient epic, appropriating it for the non-classical parade of attributes. Medieval poets love such lists, and Dudo has compiled a catalogue of dastardly adjectives. But the collection is far from arbitrary. The repetition of *pestifer* ("plague-bearing"), three times in the emphatic opening position in a line, hurls out the threat of a pox that will infect lawful societies. A rare word, the vivid *exlex* ("outlaw"), concludes the second of two consecutive lines begun by *pestifer* and introduces an important theme, the struggle between the forces of law and lawlessness. Hasting is *impius*, in implied contrast to the pious and dutiful Norman dukes who will follow him. *Pius* is, of course, Vergil's epithet for Aeneas, and the last two hexameter lines show how skillfully Dudo can draw from his Vergilian well. *Aeneid* I.347 describes Dido's brother-in-law:

Pygmalion more monstrous than all others in evil. . . .[64]

With this allusion to an archetypal villain, Dudo appeals to cognoscenti who remember Vergil's use of the Olympian metaphor to measure the abyss:

. . . Then Tartarus itself
yawns straight downward and reaches into the darkness
twice as far as the upward look to heavenly Olympus.[65]

These lines, then, link Hasting to hell and to the traitor Pygmalion, underscoring the explicit accusation of treachery a few lines before. On the surface, this seems an odd charge to level at the viking who directs his crimes, however vicious they may be, against foreigners, and not against his own kin. But the term *proditor* ("traitor") may insinuate that Hasting, like all vikings and so all Normans, is Antenor's true heir.

Many of Dudo's poems, like this one on Hasting, let the writer interject coded messages into the narrative. Although some poems become tangled in bombast, Dudo can also write the sweetest panegyric (2.67, 68), gentle threnody (4.127), or a loving hymn to Rouen (4.69). Some of his best verses tie together distant threads in a complex narrative with recollections from the past or a glance into the future. So at the betrothal of Richard I to Emma, daughter of Hugh the Great (4.102), a poem foretells that this union will produce no child, but instead, by divine will, "a heavenly maid . . . / of Danish stock, a noble girl, kind,/ lovely, far-famed, and revered,/ worthy, well-chosen, and celebrated,/ cautious in counsel, circumspect, and wise" will bear for the Norman warrior "a worthy/ heir of a dear lineage."

---

[64] *Pygmalion scelere ante alios immanior omnis.*
[65] *. . . Tum Tartarus ipse/ Bis patet in praeceps tantum tenditque sub umbras/ Quantus ad aetherium caeli suspectus Olympum* (*Aeneid* 6.577–79).

The most memorable poems manipulate suspense, or heighten or change the mood by interrupting the prose narrative at dramatic moments, as in Book Four (95–98). Incited by Arnulf (claims Dudo, here as elsewhere eager to absolve the Frankish King Lothar and his Queen Gerberga, the apparent culprit this time), the German monarch Otto has joined his brother-in-law Lothar to attack Normandy. While the allied army moves against the duchy, Dudo freezes the action to address Arnulf in verse (4.95). When Otto stands before Rouen, Dudo reproaches him, too:

> Otto, great and venerable king,
> Why are you trying to mangle with your hostile company,
> and to infect with your wicked effort,
> and to take away the princely office from
> Richard the celebrated and sacred,
> noble and just, upright and modest,
> marquis and holy patrician,
> a duke now, too, magnanimous and brave . . .?[66] (4.96)

In the ensuing battle, the victorious Normans devastate the allied army "as lions against cattle . . . as wolves against sheep" (*ut leones super pecudes . . . ut bidentes lupi*; 4.97). Arnulf slinks back to Flanders by night, while the broken King Otto laments the death of a beloved nephew (4.98). In jubilation Dudo addresses verses to each of the four major players in this drama. He dismisses Otto with a series of brisk commands:

> Go now, flee, at once, at once!
>
> (Nunc i, nunc fuge, nunc, nunc.)

With more majestic periods he reminds Lothar of his nobility and his family's glory. He asks why such a king should harass Richard and risk a second capture by the Normans, then reassures Richard that fear of the Lord makes his enemies flee and that God will protect him while he reigns as just judge. Finally, Dudo spits out a sibilant warning to Arnulf, whom he brands with a damning list of pejoratives. From these verses Dudo expertly moves to rhymed prose and a scene of terror by night as Germans and Franks flee before Richard and his Normans (4.99). This long section shows how artfully Dudo can exploit the prosimetric form to build suspense and reinforce the

---

66 Otho, rex magnus recolendus atque,
   Cur Ricardum, percelebrem sacrumque,
   Nobilem, justumque, probum, modestum,
   Marchionem, patriciumque sanctum
   Et ducem nunc magnanimumque fortem,
   Ambis infesto laniare coetu
   Et maligno contaminare nisu,
   Et honorem tollere principatus?

heroic mood. Echoing Vergil and perhaps also the developing *chanson de geste*, Dudo invests grand confrontations with epic style.[67]

Although some readers have found the poems expendable, excluding them obscures Dudo's virtuoso performance and weakens the cohesion of his art. Only the complete prosimetrical text gives us the full range of mood and tone, Dudo's broad assault on our senses. Dudo's prose, too, extends from the baroque and flowery to the simplest dialogue, which animates his panorama of characters.

But is this prosimetrical work history or epic, lyric or melodrama? It contains elements of these, as well as hagiography, threnody, panegyric, and satire laced with irony. Eleanor Searle called it "heroic history," while I have elsewhere emphasized its comic elements as parody of Vergil.[68] The *De moribus* resonates on many levels and, in its own day, too, must have appealed to more than one audience. Since Duke Richard II could not actually read the elaborate Latin history he commissioned, nor grasp its subtle allusions to classical works, he must have appreciated, in a more general way, the history's paean to his ancestors and the legitimization of their rule and therefore of his own. Dudo thus satisfied the dukes' charge for an imposing work that dignified the origins of Normandy and the ducal family and, at the same time, warned neighbors that Normans came from dangerous stock. But Dudo was also writing to amuse himself and a select, genteel audience of Frankish prelates like bishop Adalberon, whose training in Latin language and literature allowed them to appreciate classical allusions, which often linked Normans with bestial cruelty. Some of the tension in the narrative comes from this delicate balance in a work written for these varied audiences. Sparks fly from the clash of cultures, values, and literary genres.

Irony may have suited Dudo's own personality, but the particular circumstances of his history almost require it. It let him speak to several groups at once, each clever in its own way, one reading at the surface level, and others catching an underlying message.[69] It would be wrong to assume, however, that Dudo always plays to the cultivated Frankish audience when he uses his ironic tone. Consider a brief encounter at King Louis's bedchamber just after the Bernards have persuaded Louis to call off his assault, dismiss Hugh, and receive Normandy in peace (4.86). Now the Danish king Harold has arrived with pagan fighters to support the claims of young Richard. Men from the Bessin and the Cotentin, Norman loyalists all, have pitched their tents in

---

67 Cf. 2.24, Rollo's flight from the battle of Chartres. In these short lines that answer one another, Prentout (191–95) sees evidence of the *chanson de geste*.

68 Eleanor Searle, "Fact and Pattern," 119–37. Albu, "Dudo." Shopkow called it comedy in the broadest sense (*History and Community*, 66–95).

69 For a helpful discussion of irony in another medieval author, see Don A. Monson, "Andreas Capellanus and the Problem of Irony," *Speculum* 63 (July 1988), 539–72, especially p. 541.

King Harold's camp beside the river Dives. This puts Louis in a fine mess, and Bernard of Rouen wants the pleasure of bringing the bad news to the king. So Bernard rises very early, races to the king's lodging, and shouts into the apartment where Louis sleeps with his bodyguards: "Lord king, wake up! and in private counsel search out with your men what should be done." In calculated understatement, he adds, "These people [the Danes] don't behave like the Franks, ever so full of contriving cleverness." Essentially, of course, Bernard is cheerfully delivering the news that the Normans have outsmarted Louis. It is a delicious moment for Bernard and for Dudo's Norman audience. But they cannot savor it for long. The king allows one of his men to shoot back an insulting rejoinder to the count, left standing outside: "Go right back to bed! We don't care about that sort of thing." Chagrined by the Franks' nonchalance, Bernard heads home again. Every potential audience, Norman or Frank, finds a moment to laugh, and a moment to wince, in this scene.

The Normans get the last laugh in Dudo's work. Heirs to the "contriving cleverness" of their Scandinavian ancestors (4.88), they outwit the Franks at every turn. Finally King Louis and Hugh the Great must lay their hands on holy relics and swear to grant the boy Richard all "that his grandfather Rollo had acquired for himself by force and strength, by arms and battles" (4.90). Other foes rise up against him, but Richard "came to be considered preeminent in all the land of the Normans, Bretons, Franks, and Burgundians" (4.99). His enemy, Count Theobald I of Chartres, complains that virtually all the western peoples, from the Scots and Irish to the Saxons and Aquitanians, obey his rule (4.103). Here Theobald exaggerates to rouse the Frankish king against Richard, but this hyperbole exposes legitimate anxieties about the extent of Norman ambitions.

Dudo gives almost the final word to Richard when he interprets his own acts as the Christian fulfillment of his grandfather's visions (4.126). Dedicating the monastery of Fécamp at its refoundation in 990, Richard delights in standing on a holy mountain. "For this is the mount on which my grandfather saw himself standing and washed in the salvific font, according to the salvific mystery of the divine vision, and in a dream saw himself being purified of the leprosy of vices that afflicted him." It is a noble view, linking Richard to Rollo in salvation and destiny.

But the *De moribus* suggests other bonds between Christian Norman and pagan viking, embedded in the quite different language of a persistent wolf imagery. Dudo's favorite metaphor for the northern peoples, when they go marauding, is that of the ravening wolf.[70] Biblical metaphors of wolves and sheep provide one obvious influence and context for this image. In Jesus'

---

[70] Stephen O. Glosecki packs valuable information and insight into "Wolf," an entry in *The Encyclopedia of Medieval Folklore*, ed. Carl Lindahl and John Lindow (forthcoming). Glosecki highlights the ironic ambiguity of wolf imagery in Norse myth, with its extremes of "wolf beneficent and wolf malevolent." This is a powerful ambiguity

coded language, sheep signify the faithful, whom wolves ever threaten. So Jesus charges the apostles: "Go your ways: behold, I send you forth as lambs among wolves."[71] Classical models, too, and the Aesopic tradition inform the wolf/sheep symbolism. Here as well, wolves are sly predators who ensnare the innocent.[72]

Beast epics and fables entered school curricula, offering moral instruction and wisdom shared by educated persons throughout the medieval West. But the wolf's northern provenance and the wolf pack's rapacity make these beasts especially apt symbols for vikings and their Norman heirs. In Dudo's audience among the Normans, some people would have known that the Old Norse *vargr* meant both "wolf" and "outlaw." Perhaps some at the Norman court even remembered the cataclysmic bond between the wolf Fenrir, offspring of the trickster Loki, and Odin, the father of the gods: at the "wolf-age," Fenrir would break his chains and destroy Odin, issuing in the apocalypse. As for the Frankish Dudo himself, it is impossible to know how much, if any, of this Scandinavian vocabulary or folklore he absorbed during his visits to Rouen. But the frequency and power of the wolf imagery in his work may betray some consciousness of ancient knowledge that invests these metaphors with a heightened sense of doom.

Dudo associates this wolf metaphor with the Scandinavians' long internship to pagan savagery in the feral north country, where the civilizing light of Christ was slow to shine. For instance, when Dudo's archetypal viking, Hasting, and his viking pirates invade a monastery by artful ruse, they hunt down the trusting innocents like wolves in sheepfolds (1.7).[73] When Hasting tricks the Frankish army into attacking Rollo's forces, he speaks "under-

---

that Norman historians exploited by both celebrating and demonizing their Northmen/Norman wolves.

71 Luke 10:3. The Vulgate has: *Ite: ecce ego mitto vos sicut agnos inter lupos.* Cf. Matt. 7:15; 10:16; Luke 14:4–7; and John 10:11–16; 21:15–17. For medieval parallels, see Susan E. Deskis, "The Wolf doesn't Care: The Proverbial and Traditional Context of Laȝamon's *Brut* Lines 10624–36," *Review of English Studies* n.s. 46 (1995), 41–48. In a paper delivered to the Medieval Association of the Pacific ("A Wolf among Hermits: The Irish Saints and their Lupine Relations," 1991), Kevin Roddy analyzes five lupine encounters from the lives of Irish hermits. These wolves sometimes offer the saints unusual opportunities for Christian charity.

72 See, for instance, the various versions of *Ysengrimus*, featuring the legendary contests between the wolf and the fox. *Ysengrimus: Text with Translation, Commentary and Introduction*, ed. and trans. Jill Mann (Leiden, 1987). The wolf in the *Ecbasis Captivi*, an eleventh-century beast-poem of 1229 hexameters, may represent the slyest of predators, the devil himself. For references to readers who have allegorically interpreted this wolf as the devil, see Jan M. Ziolkowski, *Talking Animals: Medieval Latin Beast Poetry, 750–1150* (Philadelphia, 1993), 158–59.

73 Earlier (1.3) Dudo has described Hasting's rampage throughout France: *Fremit circa muros praesidiorum, ceu lupus circa caulas ovium* (He growls around the walls of strongholds, as the wolf around the folds of sheep). The language here recalls *Aeneid* 9.59–60 as Turnus prowls around the walls of the Trojan camp.

girded with a poisonous and wolfish artifice" (*venenifera vulpinaque arte suffultus*; 2.13). Having attached this metaphor to pagan brutality and craftiness, Dudo then transfers it to the first Norman and his subjects, as a verse apostrophe to Rollo foretells that Rouen will one day flourish under his rule: "The wolf and the lamb will pasture together in this field" (2.2).

Despite this benign Biblical imagery, Dudo's wolves never entirely relinquish their pagan essence. Rollo's son, William Longsword, may desire peace and a monk's repose, but when Bernard the Dane taunts him as "effeminate" and so incapable of leading his Danish-born war band against the rebel Riulf, Longsword reverts to the warrior stance of his Scandinavian allies: "My sword will devour the perjurers' flesh," he vows. "Let us fall upon them as wolves upon sheep" (3.45). Longsword's son, Richard, may play the cultivated gentleman, but his Normans can assault their enemies (in this instance, Saxon warriors dispatched by the German king Otto to support the Frankish king) "as lions against the flocks, and they began to mow them down and kill them with spears and arrows and pluck them from their secure places as wolves do sheep" (4.97). Against his archenemy, Theobald I, "count of malevolent intent," Richard leads a raiding party at dawn (4.112):

In the first encounter at combat they fought with shortened javelins and lances, but in the second with flashing swords. Then the hardy band of Normans, joining shields and overlapping one shield with another, advanced with a line of swords flashing and attacked the armed Franks who opposed them. Hacking at those in front and on the left and right, the Normans knocked them all down and completely broke apart the enemy's battle line, trampling the dead bodies, a thick mass of opponents, and turning to fight against the survivors scattered in little bands here and there. Here! here! the Franks are slaughtered, the motley army is chastened and destroyed. For the warlike and savage Norman people dash to and fro, penetrating the battle lines, like wolves through sheepfolds, fiercely killing and laying low the enemy troops.

Here the mask of civilization falls, and Richard and his men hunt down their prey, who run in panic and seek out hiding places in vain. Eager for a truce, the wary bishop of Chartres dispatches a monk to Richard, requesting surety of safe conduct and a guide to lead the bishop into the Norman camp, "so that your devils and wolves don't devour him and chew him up" (4.115). Richard, "most serene duke," smiles as he grants this request from the bishop, whose fright will facilitate the negotiations.

Just beneath Dudo's surface narrative of heroic grandeur and progressive civilizing, in fact, lurk continuing reminders of bestial cunning. The recurring wolf image transmits a warning: Beware the Normans. Although they look like their civilized neighbors, you will find predatory wolves just beneath the Christian veneer. The threats give Normans a potent psychological weapon, and Normans cultivate their treacherous reputation.

Do we hear one last echo of the pagan wolf at Richard's wake, as the mourners howl out their grief (4.129)? Four times in one chapter Dudo uses a form of *ululatus* or *ululo*, the noun and verb for "howling": "The clamor of their howling reached the summit of Olympus" (*plangorque ululatuum culmen Olympi tangebat*); "there was unbearable howling throughout all the houses" (*ululatusque intolerabilis erat per cunctas aedes*); "no one could distinguish what the clergy or what the people were hollering over the sounds of howling" (*nemoque poterat discernere quid clerus, quidve vulgus concrepabat pro vocibus ululatuum*); "as country people and peasants bit the ground with their teeth, a crowd of the poor, bereft of solace, howled [*ululabat*] in pain."

Ululatus is a common term for the sound of mourning. Dudo's language here recalls Vergil's lament at the death of Dido, where houses shake with women's howls (*Aeneid* 4.667–68): *femineo ululatu/ tecta fremunt*, and especially echoes the keening as Troy falls (2.487–88):

> ... penitusque cavae plangoribus aedes
> femineis ululant; ferit aurea sidera clamor.
>
> (... and deep within the house the vaulted halls
> howl with women's wails. The outcry strikes the golden stars.)

Vergil uses the noun or verb nine more times, twice in laments for the dead.[74] He associates it always with beasts or with females who are savage or crazed or tormented by anguish. So Vergil's Amazons celebrate victory in battle *magnoque ululante tumultu* (*Aeneid* 662: "with a great resounding uproar"), and women "fill the heavens with rattling screams" (*tremulis ululatibus*; *Aeneid* 7.395) when the Fury Allecto whips them into a frenzy and drives them "into the woods, in the desolate reaches of wild animals" (*Aeneid* 7.404). With its otherworldly connotations, the word portends woe, as when Nymphs shriek out the nuptial song at the pseudo-marriage of Dido and Aeneas (*ulularunt*; *Aeneid* 4.167–69) or when Dido, dying by her own hand, invokes infernal goddesses including Hecate, whose name is "screamed at cross-roads by night" (*ululata*; *Aeneid* 4.609). In Vergil's underworld (*Aeneid* 6.257) "dogs seemed to howl [*ululare*] through the shadows" as Hecate approaches.

Twice the howling of wolves haunts Vergil's pages. Just before landing on the Italian shore, Aeneas sails past the home of Circe and hears the din of lions, bears, and pigs, changed by the goddess from men into beasts. As Neptune speeds Aeneas and the Trojans past Circe's lair, the last sound we hear is the howling (*ululare*; *Aeneid* 7.18) of Circe's wolves. Finally, in Vergil's *Georgics*, among the portents that shadow the year of Julius Caesar's assassination, "lofty cities did not cease to resound all night long with the

[74] *Aeneid* 9.477; 11.189–90.

howling of wolves" (*lupis ululantibus*; *Georgics* 1.485–86). In eddic poetry, as well, this sound forebodes death, and its repetition at Richard's demise makes a striking valediction for Dudo's old warrior, who had grown up speaking Danish, fought alongside pagan Danes, and acknowledged as heir his son by a Danish consort (4.125).[75] The women's ululations recall more than ancient memories of grieving for the dead; they also evoke the frights of pagan demons and the netherworld, the baying of wolves by night, and the incursion of the wild and the terrifying into the civilized realm.[76]

According to the historians who followed Dudo, the Normans' feral qualities by no means died with Richard. Virtually all the Norman historians describe self-perpetuating cycles of brutality and treachery, repeated in every generation within Normandy and in the Norman diaspora. Following Dudo's lead, these historians use symbolic language to suggest critical moments that reinforce an explosive and predatory identity. Dudo's history has introduced most of these crises, beginning with abandonment by Scandinavian neighbors and kin, who forced vikings to leave their homelands and survive by plunder and trickery (1.1; 2.1–4); then the clash between their idealized ancestral social structure, featuring egalitarian war bands, and the new hierarchical society of feudal Christendom (2.3); hostility between princes and the proud nobles they would rule; and the stress between Christian Europe and the Normans who kept their ties with pagan kin, summoning them to terrorize and slaughter Christian enemies, as Richard I does when he calls in his "devils and wolves."[77] Later works in the Norman historiographical tradition repeat these themes, adding new stages: feuds between families and the

---

75 Dudo has his advisors counsel marriage with the Danish Gunnor after Emma, daughter of Hugh the Great, dies childless. The Normans press this union "so that from a Danish father and a Danish mother may be born the heir of this land, who will be its defender and advocate" (4.125). On the wolf's howl as omen of death, see Stephen O. Glosecki, "Wolf."

76 The word *ululare* often has eery connotations. At Trimalchio's dinner party, for instance, a guest named Niceros describes his encounter with a werewolf on a moonlit night (Petronius, *Satyricon* 62). Niceros swears that he witnessed his companion, a soldier, leave their path and head for a graveyard, where he undressed, urinated all around his clothes, "and suddenly he turned into a wolf . . . as soon as he turned into a wolf, he started howling and ran off into the woods" (*postquam lupus factus est, ululare coepit et in silvas fugit*).

77 4.115; cf. the similar episode of Richard's minority (4.84). We see the seeds of hostility between princes and nobles in the notorious scene when a defiant viking kisses the king's foot at Rollo's command (2.27). Rollo's son and grandson must each face would-be usurpers: Riulf's rebellion threatens William Longsword's tenure so much that the duke contemplates abandoning Normandy altogether (3.43–46), while the more bellicose Richard I drives Raoul Torta and his household into exile in Paris (4.92). On the possible twinning of Raoul from Rioul/Riulf, see Leah Shopkow, *History and Community*, 75. Frequent insurrections will come to dominate Norman histories after Dudo.

45

divided loyalty of children, whose father was often a Norman conqueror but whose mother might be one of the conquered peoples.[78]

As a Frankish outsider, Dudo is a representative figure among the historians of the Normans. His dual viewpoint produces ambivalence, an ironic tension, and sometimes even a hostility that will characterize Norman historical writing to the end. In this respect, as in so many others, Dudo was almost the perfect choice for court historian. But it must be obvious that the *De moribus* does have a major flaw: Dudo's classicizing Latin was not an easy read. While its relatively wide circulation testifies to the history's prestige, nonetheless many potential readers found its Latin impenetrable. For this audience, William of Jumièges wrote a simplified and condensed version nearly a half century after Dudo put down his pen.[79] Whether encountered directly or through a mediator like William's *Gesta Normannorum Ducum*, the *De moribus* became the foundation document for much of Norman historical writing, even as the historians moved toward shedding the classicizing voice of epic and finding their own voices for the narratives of predatory Normans.

---

[78] See Chapter Five, below, for an articulate example of the conflicted son, the pan-Norman historian Orderic Vitalis. On Orderic's English boyhood, see Marjorie Chibnall, *The World of Orderic Vitalis: Norman Monks and Norman Knights* (1984; reprint, Woodbridge, 1996), 3–16. Feuding families are a common phenomenon. In the *Gesta Roberti Wiscardi*, for instance, the sons and grandsons of Tancred of Hauteville often turn against one another, as when Humphrey treacherously seizes his brother Robert Guiscard while they dine together (2.314–19); see Chapter Three, 137. So, too, in Orderic's *Ecclesiastical History*, such feuds are legion, perhaps especially in Books Nine to Eleven, as the sons of William the Conqueror fight one another for their inheritance. On his deathbed, William had foreseen this fraternal strife as he reviewed his own lifelong attacks from kin who ought to have protected him (7.15; vol. 4, pp. 826); see Chapter Five, 204–205.

[79] Gerda C. Huisman, "Manuscript Tradition," 135, argues, "The fact that so many manuscripts survive from the eleventh and twelfth centuries (ten in all), of Norman as well as of English origin, indicates that Dudo's *Gesta Normannorum* was still being read after William of Jumièges wrote his *Gesta Normannorum Ducum*. The assumption that Dudo's work was fairly soon superseded by William's must therefore be rejected." Yet Dudo's history survived primarily for an elite audience.

2

The *Gesta Normannorum Ducum* and the Conquest of England

To Rouen

Ah city, how much richer you are than most others
In the good works you promote, in your soldiers of Christ!
See how your wise duke, pious, holy, and good,
Snatched from the treachery of powerful enemies,
Accomplishes God's tasks that suit you, too,
Ever adhering to the path of righteous judgment.
But because I was not then your resident,
I cannot adequately relate what he worked hard to do.
If only you possessed eloquent poets
Who might have elegantly recorded the good he pursued!
But as to your failings in bards – you have no teachers.
Train your unnumbered children in the arts now
So that they know how to record in many-metered song
Whatever the great father's heirs will accomplish.[1]

(Dudo, *De moribus* 4.109)

FIFTY years after Dudo wrote, native-born Norman historians were fulfilling his hopes. By the time that William, great-grandson of Duke Richard I, conquered England, the Normans had produced a cadre of artists prepared to sing their duke's praise. William's victory at Hastings in 1066, his crowning as king of England, and the establishment of Norman dominance over the island kingdom provided ample inspiration. The Norman audience

---

[1] O civitas fecundior quam pluribus/ Fertilitate boni, militibusque sacris!/ Tuus ecce dux prudens, pius, sanctus, bonus,/ Tantorum procerum erutus insidiis,/ Peragit Dei quae sunt, tibique congrua,/ Recti per cuncta tramite judicii,/ Sed, quod colonus non fui quondam tuus,/ Nescio digerere quae studuit facere./ Utinam poetas possideres garrulos,/ Quis bona quae studuit elucubrata forent!/ Quod vatibus culpa est, cares rhetoribus. Instrue nunc pueros artibus innumeros,/ Successio quidquid peraget magni patris,/ Carmine multicano elucubrare ut sciant. (Dudo 4.109) Dudo works a nice pun into line 12, with the Normans' *pueros . . . innumeros*: their "countless children" cannot count, that is, they do not understand meter.

47

for their own history had grown, too. At the ducal court in Rouen were men who could both write and read histories of Norman achievements. In a dedicatory letter to William the Conqueror, the monastic chronicler William of Jumièges prefaced his own *Gesta Normannorum Ducum* ("Story of the Norman Dukes," completed c. 1070) with words acknowledging the cultural revolution: "At your majesty's side are noblemen well-trained in the liberal arts – men who go about the city with swords drawn, ousting the miscreants' treachery and striving by ever watchful defense to guard Solomon's bench of divine law."[2] And while the monk was commenting on these literate courtiers, a cleric among them – the Conqueror's chaplain, William of Poitiers – was preparing his own *Gesta Guillelmi* ("Story of William," c. 1073–74), a panegyric in Dudo's classicizing mold.[3]

Even in Dudo's time, Rouen was attracting something of a literary coterie. Warner (Garnier) of Rouen, its best-known writer after Dudo himself, has left satiric verses ridiculing yet another poet, the Irish Moriuht, who wandered upon the scene.[4] If we can believe Warner's outlandish invective, Moriuht had lived a life straight out of a Byzantine romance. Vikings kidnapped him and his wife, taking them off as slaves to separate markets. While sailing to Northumbria, Moriuht's captors amused themselves by urinating on his bald head, stripping him naked, and raping him:

> Subditur obprobriis et tunc pro conjuge Danis
> Conjugis officium cogitur esse suum.

> (He is subjected to insults and then forced
> to perform conjugal duties like a wife to the Danes.)

The poet lingers on these episodes of Moriuht's humiliation. But Moriuht's fortune changed once he reached shore. There he found himself purchased by a nunnery, whose inhabitants he charmed with his poetry. The seduction of several nuns, however, finally led to his ouster, at which point he remembered his wife and began searching for her at slave markets across northern Europe.

---

2 Elisabeth M. C. van Houts, ed., *The* Gesta Normannorum Ducum *of William of Jumièges, Orderic Vitalis, and Robert of Torigni*, 2 vols. (Oxford, 1992, 1995), vol. 1, p. 4 (hereafter cited as *GND*).

3 *The* Gesta Guillelmi *of William of Poitiers*, ed. R. H. C. Davis and Marjorie Chibnall (Oxford, 1998). See also Guillaume de Poitiers, *Histoire de Guillaume le Conquérant*, Les classiques de l'histoire de France au moyen âge, ed. Raymonde Foreville (Paris, 1952).

4 "Satire de Garnier de Rouen contre le poète Moriuth (X–XIe siècles)," ed. H. Omont, *Annuaire-Bulletin de la Société de l'Histoire de France* 31 (1891), 193–210; Lucien Musset, "Le satiriste Garnier de Rouen et son milieu (début du XIe siècle)," *Revue du Moyen Age latin* 10 (1954), 237–66; van Houts, "Scandinavian Influence in Norman Literature of the Eleventh Century," *Anglo-Norman Studies* 6 (1983), 107–109. Eric Christiansen wonders if Warner might even have been Dudo's pupil (*Dudo of St Quentin*, xii).

Three times during his quest he sought advice from pagan gods, once even sacrificing a girl to win the gods' favor. Twice more he escaped from marauding vikings, until at last he discovered his wife toiling in a spinning-mill near Rouen. He succeeded in persuading the duchess Gunnor to buy her freedom, and the Irish couple moved to Rouen, where Moriuht could ply his trade – and attract Warner's ridicule for doing it so poorly.

However much *Contra Moriuht* be fact or fancy, its picaresque story illustrates the rough-and-tumble vitality of an early Norman world whose crudity competed with Christian sensibilities. In Warner's satiric view of early eleventh-century life, even viking incursions fertilized Rouen's cultural soil. To the courts of Gunnor's husband and son, the Richards I and II, vagabond poets and scholarly envoys alike were bringing tales from the literary and folk traditions of peoples who lived throughout northern Europe and beyond. Characters and themes from Ireland and Scandinavia mingled with Carolingian learning, whose own origins reached back to classical antiquity. All these elements entered Norman culture as it was developing in the tenth and early eleventh centuries.

We know few details about literary society in Rouen during the half century following Dudo, Warner, and Moriuht. But the general progress is clear. As Duke Richard I worked to consolidate his hold over Normandy, his patronage and Gunnor's elevated Norman cultural life. The Norman ecclesiastical revival occurred under Richard's control, as he placed his relatives in positions of episcopal power. In the Seine valley, restored monasteries resumed their old functions of collecting, copying, and preserving manuscripts. Though not always peaceful even after Richard's troubled minority, as Dudo reports, the long reign of Richard I offered crucial stability.[5]

Dudo celebrated a milestone, the transmission of the duchy from Richard I to his son, Richard II, who ruled for three decades (996–1026). But Richard II faced a potential catastrophe avoided by previous dukes. For while his father, his grandfather William Longsword, and great-grandfather Rollo managed the succession through "Danish marriages," Richard II produced two sons of equally recognized legitimacy. When Richard III (1026–27) succeeded his father, the second son Robert (called "the Devil" and, more generously, "the Magnificent") challenged his authority. Only the early demise of Richard III, under suspicious circumstances, saved Normandy from protracted civil war. Robert (1027–35) held the duchy until he left on pilgrimage, bequeathing Normandy to his own son, William, the future Conqueror (1035–87).

Dynastic stability and lengthy stretches of single power, along with ducal policies, fostered monastic and episcopal learning and nurtured a vigorous literary culture. At last, during the Conqueror's reign, the restored monastery of Jumièges produced a native-born Norman history, the successor of Dudo's

---

5 Bates, *Normandy before 1066*, 24–38.

work. This *Gesta Normannorum Ducum* by William of Jumièges was to become the centerpiece of Norman historical writing, and so requires detailed attention here.

The Conquest itself inspired an outpouring of celebratory works in the late 1060s and early 1070s, and William's *Gesta Normannorum Ducum* was long assumed to be part of that corpus. But the monk of Jumièges was probably already at work in the 1050s, abbreviating and continuing Dudo's *De moribus*.[6] By the end of that decade he had completed his task, having added a chapter for Richard II, another for the brothers Richard III and Robert I, and a final chapter for Robert's son, William. After the Conquest he returned to his text, perhaps at the request of King William himself, who attended a ceremony at Jumièges dedicating the new abbey church on July 1, 1067.[7] William, king and duke, had ample reason for desiring an expanded *Gesta Normannorum Ducum* that legitimized his elevation to king of England just as Dudo's history had legitimized the earliest succession of Norman dukes, to whom King William traced his lineage in the direct male line.[8] For his part, William the monk might have hoped that his additions would draw the king's favor upon his monastery. So the chronicler made a few revisions to his earlier work, added events up to early 1070, and wrote an epilogue and a fresh dedicatory letter to the new king.

This monk has left few clues about himself other than his name and monastic affiliation. He never defines his own ethnic identity, though he was probably born and raised in Normandy. Among Norman writers, only Orderic Vitalis repeats his name, in all three instances where he does, calling him "Calculus." This presumably indicates William's monastic duties, which would have encompassed the computing and recording of dates significant for the monastery as well as producing other monastic records and annals.[9] In performing these tasks, William Calculus created the most popular of all Norman histories. Forty-seven manuscripts of his *Gesta Normannorum Ducum* in its various redactions survive today, attesting to its wide circulation. While Dudo's *De moribus* had its own audience, as its thirteen surviving manuscripts suggest, William's *Gesta* far surpassed it in readership, really replacing it as the central piece in the Norman historiographical tradition.[10] Along with Orderic, William of Poitiers also knew the *Gesta*, which later

---

6   For notes on the chronology of William's writing, see van Houts, *GND* 1, xx–xxv. For more on William and his *Gesta*, see Shopkow, *History and Community*, especially pages 39–41, 83–90, 153–55.

7   This enticing suggestion comes from Elisabeth M. C. van Houts, "History without an End," 111.

8   On the generally pro-ducal and pro-Norman view of the *Gesta*, see van Houts, *GND* 1, lii.

9   E. van Houts, *GND* 1, xxxi.

10 For a discussion of the various versions of the *GND*, see van Houts, "History without an End," 106; and van Houts, *GND* 1, xx–xxi; xcv–cxxviii.

became a principal source for the vernacular histories of Wace and Benoît de Sainte-Maure.

But Norman historians were not content merely to use the *Gesta Normannorum Ducum* as a source. By the early twelfth century, at least four copyists had revised this text, making stylistic changes or inserting episodes, and in at least two cases adding material on the succession of Robert Curthose to the deeds of his father, William the Conqueror. One of these writers appended a brief conclusion, "On William's Death" (*De Obitu Willelmi*), while the scribe known as the "A redactor" began his manuscript with Dudo's text and took up William's history only with Book Five, where the *De moribus* ended. But two well-known Norman historians made more extensive additions to their copies of the *Gesta Normannorum Ducum* – practice, it turned out, for their own histories. From about 1109 to 1113 Orderic Vitalis entered material into his manuscript at Saint-Évroul. And finally in the late 1130s, using Orderic's version, Robert of Torigni, then prior of Bec, altered many chapters and added eighteen others to the seventh book. Before he became abbot of Mont-Saint-Michel in 1154, Robert composed an eighth book on the reign of King Henry I until 1135, with some references as late as 1137. In these different versions the *Gesta* circulated throughout Normandy and Norman territories.

With its various incarnations, therefore, the *Gesta* illustrates the interdependence of texts in the Norman historiographical tradition. This tradition, of course, is not completely self-contained. As he acknowledged in his prefatory letter, William of Jumièges researched his subject *de diversis . . . codicibus* ("from various books").[11] To Dudo's material he added ideas borrowed from late antique writers like Augustine, Jordanes, Martianus Capella, and Isidore of Seville, as well as excerpts from saints' lives and annals like Adrevald of Fleury's *Miracula Sancti Benedicti* (a tenth-century "Miracles of St. Benedict") and the *Historia Francorum Senonensis* ("Seine History of the Franks;" c. 1035–40). He had access to records from his own monastery library and even, it seems, to oral epic, for instance to a heroic tale on the rescue of the young Duke Richard I from palace arrest.[12] As Norman power broadened, Norman historians drew upon a variety of western medieval sources and in turn influenced a wide circle of French, Italian, and English works. Yet the influence of Norman histories upon one another remains a dominant feature of this tradition, as the fate of William of Jumièges' *Gesta* demonstrates.

Why was William's *Gesta* so popular with his fellow Norman historians and with a wider audience?[13] Norman monasteries may have included this text in their libraries as a matter of course, considering it an essential holding

---

11 For William's sources, see van Houts, *GND*, 1, xxv–xlv; and Jean Marx, ed., *Gesta Normannorum Ducum* (Rouen and Paris, 1914), xvi–xvii.
12 *GND* 4.3–4; van Houts, *GND* 1, xxxviii.
13 On its audience, see Shopkow, *History and Community*, 223-26.

for the study of Norman history in a Christian and monastic context. Its style and format made it easy to read, its brevity made it easy to copy, and its apparent artlessness made it easy to trust. Where William copied Dudo, he condensed the master's account to one-third the length of his original, converting Dudo's sometimes difficult verse and prose to a Latin whose simplicity made the text both accessible and credible. For some readers, finally, the *Gesta* was also appealing as a living document that beckoned them to interact with it. In his epilogue William wrote, "I leave it to wise and eloquent men to add on noble deeds." But even without William's invitation, the episodic nature of this history welcomes interpolation as Dudo's complex and unified narrative does not. A scribe could insert a timely detail or even entire chapters, putting his own stamp on the work as a whole. And as the *Gesta Normannorum Ducum* accumulated tales of particular interest to the new generation or chapters that carried the *Gesta* beyond the conquest of England, it remained relevant.

Perhaps William's simplicity disarmed medieval readers as it has modern historians, who have often elevated William at Dudo's expense. In exposing Dudo's errors and bombast, for instance, Henri Prentout suggested that William used intelligence in rejecting Dudo's fables and rhetoric. An admiring Prentout acclaimed the monk *toujours plus sincère et plus exact*.[14] Likewise, in the nineteenth century, Thomas Forester wrote about William:

> This historian is vastly superior to Dudo of Saint-Quentin, but still he has committed the error of copying and adopting the, more or less, monstrous fables of his predecessor, and his work has had the misfortune of being disfigured by a continuation, the author of which has so interpolated it, and made so many injudicious additions, as to have essentially altered its character.[15]

We now know that this "disfiguring" continuation is the work of several minds and hands, including Robert of Torigni and the master of Norman history, Orderic Vitalis. Orderic's reworking of William's *Gesta* served as practice for his own monumental *Ecclesiastical History*, just as Robert's apprenticeship to the *Gesta* prepared him to expand the *World Chronicle* written by Sigebert of Gembloux. Orderic and Robert raised the *Gesta* material to new artistic levels. Indeed, the best stories in the *Gesta*, tales that emphasize character and dialogue, are their additions or the interpolations of others. Yet modern historians have often preferred the spare data of William's original, from which they could fashion their own interpretive stories. They

---

14 Prentout, 237. See also p. 189, where Prentout prefers William's account of a peasant rebellion to Dudo's.
15 *The Ecclesiastical History of England and Normandy*, trans. (London, 1853–56), 1.376, note 1.

approved of a chronicler who offered up the facts with minimal commentary, apparently undistorted by the passage through an analytic mind.

For his part, William of Jumièges did not believe that he was bowdlerizing a monument of medieval historical writing. On the contrary, he thought that he was improving on Dudo. In the dedicatory letter, he did acknowledge his debt to the master.[16] He repeated that testimony when he reached the end of Dudo's *De moribus* with the death of Richard II, again affirming his belief that Dudo's information came directly from Count Raoul (4.20). But while he could not ignore Raoul's testimony, William disdained Dudo's fancy Latin.[17] The monk's foray into more elaborate syntax, in his introductory letter, suggests that William could not keep his language under control when he felt required to roll out a prolegomenon for his royal master.

Even if he were capable of sustaining a narrative like Dudo's, William would have eschewed the ornate style. He had little use for classicizing pretensions, and he could not resist sniping at Dudo's unseemly erudition. So William's letter explains that he writes "not in the elegant and weighty style used by rhetoricians, nor with the venal wit and glitter of polished utterance, but in an unadorned style and plain language that is simple and clear for every reader." As he began and ended his task, William tagged this work as "to be assigned to the library of chronicles" (*cronicorum bibliothece delegandum*; "Dedicatory Letter") and written "in the chronicle style" (*cronico . . . stilo*; "Epilogue").[18] In keeping with this genre, he arranged events in chronological order, typically featuring a single episode in each chapter. This simplifies and disrupts Dudo's story lines, changing psychologically complex vignettes to primitive accounts with little visible artistry and limited description, dialogue, character development, interpretation, and wit.

The effect seems to be just as William desired. He was not simply epitomizing Dudo. Through his new interpretation, he aimed to correct, and perhaps even suppress, both the rhetorical flamboyance and the seductive stories of his source, finding these to be two sides of the same coin and equally distasteful in their elitism and worldliness. William was as hostile to Dudo's courtly sensibilities as he was to his Latin style. He shows no tolerance for Dudo's irony or the wit that Dudo aims, for instance, at coalitions of vikings with Normans or at the business of taming the dukes' passions. Such episodes William abbreviates almost beyond recognition even as he emphasizes tales with a higher moral purpose. All this harmonizes with William's monastic education and temperament.[19] His learning and interests are

---

16 *Principium namque narrationis usque ad Ricardum secundum a Dudonis, periti uiri, hystoria collegi . . . .*

17 Shopkow, *History and Community*, 129–32, and van Houts, *GND* I, lv.

18 On the meaning of "chronicle" for William, see Shopkow, *History and Community*, 153–54.

19 On the monastery of Jumièges, see van Houts, *GND* I, xxii–xxx.

predominantly Christian, steeped in the consciousness that the monastic life
teaches. He presents himself as "a monk of Jumièges," and he always places
"Christian" and "monk" above "Norman" when revealing his own interests.
So the monastic library at Jumièges held the texts that helped shape
William's world view: the Bible and its commentaries, saints' lives, liturgical
works, and writings of the church fathers. Compare the more expansive
reading of Dudo, who absorbed the cathedral school learning of Lotharingia
and northern France, including much secular ancient literature along with the
Christian. It is not surprising, therefore, that William's tastes and viewpoints
are so radically different from Dudo's.

William's dedicatory letter to William the Conqueror, presenting to the
king the second redaction of the *Gesta Normannorum Ducum*, opens and
closes by linking the prince's conquest to his piety and orthodoxy. From its
first word, *pio*, the letter sets the tone:

> Pio, uictorioso atque orthodoxo summi Regis nutu Anglorum regi
> Willelmo, Gemmethicensis cenobita, omnium cenobitarum indignissimus
> Willelmus, ad conterendos hostes Sansonis fortitudinem et ad discer-
> nendum iuditium Salomonis abyssum.

> (To the pious, victorious, and orthodox William, king of the English by the
> grace of the highest King, the monk of Jumièges, William, of all monks the
> unworthiest, [wishes] the strength of Samson for crushing enemies and the
> profound depth of Solomon for rendering judgment.)

These Biblical commonplaces introduce a letter acknowledging the need for
Samson's brawn, but emphasizing a higher moral purpose. As the Bible and
liturgy influence his vocabulary and syntax, likewise Christian piety
pervades William's work. So William praises the dukes whenever they
perform pious acts, both as an honor to their memory and perhaps, too, as a
nudge to the current duke toward peaceable sensibilities and away from his
pagan legacy. Like the *Gesta* proper, this letter suppresses the crimes and
other failings of the dukes while applauding their piety. The letter especially
praises the Conqueror's father, Robert, whose death on his return from Jerusalem has won him the ring and cloak of eternal glory. Like the letter, the text
will downplay Robert's sins to stress his redemption through pilgrimage.
This pattern the *Gesta* follows throughout.

The introductory letter further reveals the monastic center of the writer's
consciousness by protesting the impropriety of worldly concerns for a clois-
tered religious. William of Jumièges fears that the attractions of pagan adventures would lead monks away from their pursuit of the heavenly Jerusalem.
"It is unseemly [for such monks] to be seduced by a vulgar puff of air with its
slight but ruinous, flattering allure and to be ensnared in the world by that
enticement." This is a telling admission and one that explains a great deal
about William's flattening of Dudo's thrilling tale. William is dull on
purpose.

The monk of Jumièges found Dudo's stories superfluous as well as dangerous, because they did not support his purpose of preserving "the virtues of excellent men [*virtutes optimorum uirorum*], whether they distinguish themselves in secular or divine affairs, so that those who live blessedly in the eyes of God should also live usefully in the attention of men." Medieval historians commonly profess that they are recording the past as a moral lesson or as a memorial to the good and likewise as a punishment for the evil. These assertions are more than mere convention, especially for a monk who expected that his *Gesta* would remain before the eyes of the dukes, even influencing their conduct. William does not always excise deeds of violence or betrayal, since the act of reporting them might bring shame to the perpetrators or a blemish to their memory, and so might discourage others from committing like crimes. Indeed, violent acts are also an unavoidable element of the Normans' story. But William restricts their impact and censors epic description that might glorify them. He prefers to offer examples to emulate rather than those to avoid.

With this mission in mind, William downplays the endemic treachery of Normans, not only dissociating the Norman dukes from their viking past but also emphasizing the treacherous world in which the Normans lived, an environment that justified the Normans' own behavior. Dudo's tales had led him in that direction. But William does not follow Dudo's argument to its end by identifying treachery as an inevitably Norman trait. He presents, instead, a cautious optimism about the future under Christian dukes. Writing while young William the Bastard offers the promise of greatness, and revising in the exhilarating wake of the Conquest, William of Jumièges is working at the apogee of Norman achievement. He strikes a mood that will not last long among Norman historians.

In the process, William subverts Dudo's structure. Though it may appear that William is simply abridging his source, nonetheless he is making choices as he shapes his chronicle. So he begins not with Scandinavia and the dispersion of raiders, Hasting and then Rollo, but with Carolingian Christendom, whose monasteries promulgate the faith. This is how the narrative opens:

> From the time when the Frankish people restored their strength and shook from their neck the yoke of Roman brutality, the church of Christ grew mightily, bearing scented fruit far and wide, and flourished all the way to the western frontier. Finally in those days their kings, relentless in war and nourished by the power of the Christian faith, always won stunning victories over the enemies who surrounded them. Under their guidance Christ's vineyard was growing and producing countless branches of the faithful. From it, naturally, burst out many flocks of monks, which, like bees from their hives, produced many sorts of honeycombs from the world's various violets in their heavenly homes. For from them the construction of the eternal Jerusalem was raised up before the eyes of the everlasting king, to gleam like shining stars forever into eternity. So you see the church flour-

ished with extraordinary power under different kings of the Franks for many years until the four sons of the emperor Louis broke the peace.[20]

The first villain is the Roman oppressor, from whose ancient empire the Franks finally carved out their own Christian realm where monasteries flourished. But the wars waged among the sons of Louis the Pious devastate Frankish Christendom, leaving it vulnerable to attack by heathens, including Björn Ironside and his mentor Hasting, "most wicked of all pagans." The *Gesta* focuses initially on the Catholic Franks as they struggle against these Northmen, who do not become the heroes until after their conversion and transmutation into Normans. Until then, the vikings are evil forces that harry the coast and sail up rivers, "destroying towns and burning abbeys." When William describes viking raids in some detail, he features the burning of Saint-Quentin and especially of his own establishment at Jumièges [1.5(6)–7(8)], borrowing material from Adrevald of Fleury's *Miracula sancti Benedicti*.[21] Monasteries, as centers for civilizing and Christianizing and sometimes as targets of viking assaults, reside at the heart of William's consciousness.

Just when we think that he has reconstructed Norman history within a Francocentric and Christian framework, we begin to see how intimately William cares for the Scandinavians in and around his Norman world. He soon repeats Dudo's explanation for the expulsion of Danes from their homeland: lust and multiple sex partners led to overpopulation [1.3(4)–4(5)]. The people had no choice but to reject most of their sons, driving them out to find their own fortunes through violence against others. So King Lothbroc exiled his own son, Björn Ironside, accompanied by his evil tutor Hasting, both ready to fight against Christians. Björn and Hasting invaded almost all Neustria *Normannica feritate*, "with the fury that characterizes the vikings."[22] In the next sentence William distinguishes these Northmen from his own Normans, when he writes that they eventually learned to ride horses *more nostratum* ("like the people of our land"). But the use of *Normannus* and the adjective *Normannicus* to mean either "Scandinavian/viking" or "Norman" renders both Normans and their northern ancestors sometimes indistinguishable, as they are in French today, when *les Normands* are Norsemen or Normans.

From William's viewpoint, Normans and Northmen do operate in the same sphere. Steeped in his own Norman culture in a way that Dudo, the Frankish outsider, could not have been, William reports this vision in a piece-

---

20 I.1. On June 25, 841, three sons of Louis the Pious fought at Fontenoy. One of their brothers, King Pippin I of Aquitaine, had already died in 838.

21 Most of 1.5(6)–6(7) comes from the *Miracula sancti Benedicti*, ed. Eugene de Certain (Paris, 1858), 71–73.

22 The translation is van Houts's.

meal fashion, without the clarity of a foreigner's perspective or the discipline of a classical education. But the pieces, like Dudo's portrait, point to a Norman identity grown from Scandinavian roots and reinforced by continuing Scandinavian contacts. Even as William reaffirms these ties, he works to distance the Norman dukes from their pagan ancestors. So he makes Rollo a less dominant figure and even omits Rollo's dreams, though these dreams are central to Dudo's message.

William's letter explains his most self-conscious deletion, that of Rollo's adventures before his baptism:

> Of course, I have excluded from my historical survey the genealogy of the pagan-born Rollo and many of his deeds in his pagan youth, before he was finally reborn to holy infancy at the font that brings salvation, and also his dream and many things of this sort, since I consider them completely fawning and presenting no pretext of anything honorable or edifying.

Here William does not claim to have omitted these tales because he judged them untrue, as Prentout and others have assumed. Instead, William pruned Dudo's tales of Rollo's adventures expressly because he wanted to de-romanticize the swashbuckling pagan.

So William of Jumièges condenses Dudo 2.1–8 into a single chapter. In the early pages of the *Gesta*'s second book, Rollo is nearly invisible, emerging only at the end of chapter three, as the viking war band chooses him leader by lot when Archbishop Franco offers a truce. This addition of the random choice undercuts the tension within the war band, critical to Dudo's construction of Norman identity, though William does include a sentence that assigns to Rollo the central traits of Northmen and Normans, nicely abbreviating Dudo 2.12–13:

> And so Rollo, appointed as leader, plotted with his men to demolish Paris, scheming in his sly heart and thirsting with a pagan instinct for the blood of Christians the way a wolf does. [*GND* 2.4(10)]

> (Rollo igitur prelatione potitus de Parisiaca euersione corde uersuto cum suis tractans, Christianorum sanguinem paganico instinctu lupino more sitiebat.)

This single sentence hints at Dudo's pattern and shows how clearly William understands the wolf imagery, which he links explicitly with pagan predation and scheming.

Excising tales of Rollo's pagan youth, William cuts out much fine material from Dudo. Robert of Torigni found this so unsatisfying that he retrieved many of the excluded adventures from Dudo and restored them to his copy of the *Gesta*.[23] But William allows only truncated versions of Rollo's rampages

---

23 E.g. in 2.7(13) and 8(14).

through France, as in *Gesta* 2.8(14), for instance, where Rollo ends a three-month truce by ravaging the countryside yet again *solita rabie* ("with his usual madness") and in 2.11(17). This final incursion prompts the French to demand that their king act in their defense.[24] The king does so in his own passive way by offering Rollo land and his daughter in exchange for the vikings' conversion to Christianity. Here the *Gesta* engineers for Rollo an abrupt metamorphosis from pirate to lawful prince. The Rollo of William's account accepts the king's deal *consulto suorum* ("on his men's advice"), without any of the tension that electrifies Dudo's scene with Charles and the viking compelled to kiss the king's foot. This most famous of Dudo's stories William omits altogether. As we have seen, this tale not only provides amusement but it also offers insight into Norman hostility toward their lords. Removing it weakens the history's thematic unity and any explanation of the Norman identity. So, too, in the *Gesta* all Rollo's men embrace Christianity [2.13(19)]:

> And when the pagans see that their leader is a Christian, they set aside their idols and with one mind adopt the name of Christ, flocking to baptism.

Only here, with the vikings' harmonious conversion, does William's *Gesta* shift its sympathies from Franks to proto-Normans.

But this early divergence away from Rollo does not mean that William erases pagan characters and paganism. William merely replaces the pre-conversion Rollo with another viking, the Anglo-Scandinavian Björn Ironside, a supposed protégé of Hasting.[25] Even as William de-emphasizes the pagan ancestors of William the Conqueror, he glamorizes Björn by conceding to him magic protection against foes, a common characteristic of heroes in Scandinavian sagas:[26]

> He was called Ironside [*Costa Ferrea*] because if he stood unarmed in battle and a shield did not protect him, he would scorn any available force of arms and yet remain uninjured, imbued by his mother with very strong magic potions.

The mood of saga lingers in the air. Indeed, William's most recent editor has shown how deeply Scandinavian legend influenced his writing.[27] So much a part of William's world are Scandinavian characters, stories, and customs that

---

[24] This passage truncates Dudo 2.25–29.

[25] Elisabeth M. C. van Houts, "Scandinavian Influence," 107–21, especially pp. 112–17; and by the same author, "The Political Relations between Normandy and England before 1066 according to the *Gesta Normannorum Ducum*," *Actes du Colloque international du Centre national de la recherche scientifique, nr. 611: Études Anselmiennes*, ed. Raymonde Foreville (Paris, 1984), 85–97.

[26] 1.4(5). See van Houts, ed., *GND* I, p. 17, note 6.

[27] E. van Houts, "Scandinavian Influence."

they surface at surprising moments, even if haphazardly, showing continuing ties between Normans and Northmen.

The reader has to work hard, however, to construct a pattern out of William's chaotic material. It is difficult, for instance, to understand why William dropped Dudo's enigmatic tale of two soldiers sent by the French king and harbored by Gisla, Rollo's Frankish bride. Did he find it improbable or simply expendable as he abbreviated a long work? Or did he remove it with more conscious thought, because he wanted to delete Dudo's hints at continuing Franco-Norman hostilities? In any case, Robert of Torigni put the episode back in his copy [2.(21)]. The *Gesta*'s abridgment of Dudo 2.17–20 into one brief chapter [2.7(13)] abandons other connections that William might have been eager to press. Here Dudo describes Rollo's departure from a siege of Paris in order to return to England and protect his harried ally, king "Athelstane." In the *De moribus* this episode establishes Rollo's increasing Christian sympathies and concern for human obligations. Dudo even has Athelstane belittle the rebellious English, who are unworthy to rule their own land, and offer Rollo half his kingdom. Rollo's supposed claim to England would have given the *Gesta* a thematic unity and would have pleased King William, if only the monk could have anticipated the Conquest as he wrote his earlier redaction, or cared to retrieve this adventure for his final version.

But William does keep some of Dudo's essential elements, not only the *gesta* form, for instance, but also a faint memory of an egalitarian heritage, a recollection that makes Normans especially volatile. Here is William's version of Hasting's meeting with Rollo's war band, which provokes the vikings' assertion of their equality [2.4(10)]:

> So when Hasting came to the riverbank, he spoke to [Rollo's men] with words like these: "Hey! mighty soldiers, from what shores did you sail here? What are you looking for in this territory? What is your lord's name? Tell us. For we are messengers, sent to you by the king of the Franks."
>
> Rollo answered him like this: "We are Danes. We share equal lordship [*equali dominio fungimur*]. We have come to uproot the people from this land, since we want to subdue the country to our own rule. But who are you, who speak our language so fluently?"
>
> He answered, "Have you ever heard of a certain Hasting, who arrived here as an exile from your lands with a vast number of ships and who more or less devastated this realm of the Franks and reduced it to a desert?"
>
> Rollo answered, "Yes, we have. Hasting began with good luck but came to a very bad end."
>
> Hasting said to him, "Are you willing to submit to King Charles."
>
> "Never," answered Rollo, "will we submit to anyone, but whatever we get by force we will claim under our own rule. Report that, if you please, to your king, whose messenger you boast you are." Hasting promptly reports all this to his leader.[28]

28 "Veniens itaque Hastingus iuxta aque decursum, talibus illos adorsus est uerbis:

This is a fine interchange, retaining some remnants of Dudo's repartee. But here is Dudo's original, more powerful in its artful simplicity (2.13):

Hasting and the two [Frankish] soldiers stood on the riverbank and said, "The counts of a powerful realm order you to say who you are and where you come from and what you are looking for."

"We are Danes from Denmark, come to attack France."

"What is your lord's name?"

"Nobody, since we are equals in power."

Then, because he wanted to know what they were saying about him, Hasting asked, "Whose story did you hear, so that his sailing here made you come? Did you ever hear about a man born in your own country, Hasting, who sailed here with many a warrior?"

They answered, "Yes, we have. He came here under good auspices, made a good beginning, but he came to a bad end and met disaster."

Then Hasting said, "Are you willing to bend your neck to King Charles of France, and bow down to serve him, and get a great many land grants in return?"

They answered, "We'll never be subject to anyone, and we will never devote ourselves to anyone's service whatsoever. The land grant that pleases us best is what we claim for ourselves with weapons and the toil of battle."

Then the Franks asked, "What are you going to do?"

To which the Danes replied, "Get out of here as fast as you can and don't hang around any longer, because we don't much like your wrangling, and we're not going to tell you what we're going to do."

Dudo's exchange creates distinct personalities. His Danes are laconic and aggressive. Hasting's final question, with its language of groveling submission, seems designed to provoke the vikings whose mettle he has already ascertained. In the next scene he goads the Franks to war by proclaiming them no match for Rollo's band. William has no interest in such suggestive interpretation. By having Rollo answer Hasting's questions, he also dilutes the force of the vikings' assertion of equality even as he excises the defiance

---

'Heus,' inquit, 'robustissimi milites, quibus ab horis huc aduecti estis? Vel quid in hac regione queritis, aut quo uester senior censetur nomine, edicite nobis. Francorum sane regis sumus legati uobis directi.' Cui interroganti sic Rollo: 'Dani,' ait 'sumus, equali dominio fungimur, terre huius colonos extirpare uenimus nostre ditioni patriam subdere cupientes. Tu uero quis es, qui tam facete nobis loqueritis?' Ad hec ille: 'Audistis,' infit, 'aliquando de quodam Hastingo, qui a uestris partibus exul cum multitudine nauium has adueniens, hoc Francorum regnum magna ex parte pessumdedit et in solitudinem redegit?' Cui Rollo: 'Audiuimus;' inquit, 'Hastingus enim bono omine cepit et cuncta malo fine compleuit.' Hastingus ad hec: 'Vultis,' ait, 'Karolo regi subdi' 'Nequaquam,' Rollo intulit, "alicui subiciemur, sed quecumque armis adquiremus nostro iuri uindicabimus. Regi, cuius te legatum gloriaris, audita si uis renuntia.' Hec Hastingus cuncta expedite suo refert duci."

of men who mock a domesticated viking's service to a Frankish king. So, too, he omits the wit from these exchanges, just as he has eliminated the trenchant interview between Rainald, "prince of all France," and Hasting, the meeting that sends Hasting before Rollo.[29]

A rare and provocative addition, however, underscores Dudo's point in claiming a Trojan ancestry and Greco-Roman ties for his proto-Normans.[30] For here William turns directly to Dudo's source, Jordanes' *Getica*, for a genealogy that traces Gothic origins back to Noah [1.2(3)].[31] Jordanes lets his Goths be warlike, of course. But he also feminizes them through a story of Amazons as Gothic women.[32] William retrieves this curious tale of Amazon queens Lampeto and Marpessa, who assail Asia and subdue it for over a century after renouncing their Gothic husbands because these men were gone so long on a campaign of their own [1.2(3)]. These gleanings from Jordanes deepen the *Gesta*'s Germanic and pagan elements in mysterious ways.

But William tears himself away from this digression, with some reluctance, to pursue other Goths, putative ancestors of his Normans [1.3(4)]. Leaving the island of Scanza, they sail to a mainland home that they also call Scanza, in homage to *Scanza insula*.[33] From there they penetrate deep into German territories, settling at last in Dacia, a region that William also identifies with Denmark. The migrations and peoples seem a mishmash, apparently conflating sources and traditions with little attempt at integration. Among the Gothic kings in Dacia, for instance, were Zeutas, Dicineus, and the famous Zalmoxis, whose wisdom elevates this Gothic tribe over "almost all the other barbarians," making them "nearly equal to the Greeks." The god Mars they claim was born in their midst, and "they used to appease him with effusions of human blood."

If this is merely a random listing from Jordanes, the juxtapositions nonetheless create neat coincidences, linking Dacia, Zalmoxis, and Mars within three adjacent sentences. All have connections with wolves and exiles.[34] And immediately following Zalmoxis, Mars, and blood sacrifice, comes the *Gesta*'s nod to Antenor:

---

29 Dudo II.13; this is the same prince who gleefully flees the battle along with Hasting.

30 Van Houts, *GND* I, xxxvi–xxxvii.

31 *Getica* 9, 25–41, 47–55.

32 Goffart, *Narrators of Barbarian History*, 80–81.

33 Jordanes expected his audience to notice this imitation of a "Greco-Roman conceptual framework," as Goffart remarked (*Narrators of Barbarian History*, 89 n. 331). Goffart quotes Livy (*Ab urbe condita* 1.1.3–4), where Aeneas and Evander name their landing places in Italy "Troy." Vergil, too, makes Aeneas plan to call his new city "Pergamum," after Troy's citadel (*Aeneid* 3.132–34).

34 Mircea Eliade, *Zalmoxis, The Vanishing God*, Comparative Studies in the Religions and Folklore of Dacia and Eastern Europe, trans. Willard R. Trask (Chicago and London, 1972), especially chapters 1 ("Dacians and Wolves") and 2 ("Zalmoxis"). Eliade (p. 73) briefly treats the passage in William of Jumièges [1.3(4)].

They even boast that Trojans came from their stock and that Antenor, with two thousand soldiers and five hundred men, escaped the city's destruction because of its betrayal which he had perpetrated. After many distractions he arrived in Germany by sea, and soon was ruling in Dacia, called Denmark from one Danaus, a king of their stock.[35]

The causal phrase in William's awkward Latin confirms Antenor's medieval reputation as a traitor who engineered the fall of Troy and saved his own life through deceit. This shows that the Antenor story had penetrated to William's level and was not simply the possession of a few intellectuals among the ecclesiastical elite, suggesting that a wide audience may have understood Dudo's implications that Normans carried a blood line predisposing them to treachery. The conflation of mythic layers, linking Zalmoxis and Mars and Antenor, furthermore, reinforces Dudo's symbolism of treason and exile.

William also retains more overt traces of Dudo's wolfish pattern, as we have seen with Rollo's assault on Paris [2.4(10)]. As in that instance, whenever he copies Dudo's wolf metaphor, William connects it explicitly with Scandinavian paganism. Consider, for instance, this passage describing the preparations of vikings under Hasting and Björn for their attack on Christian lands [1.4(5)]:

> Ships are built, shields repaired, breast-plates mended, helmets and armor polished, swords and lances sharpened; the army is carefully supplied with weapons. Then on the appointed day the ships are dragged down to the sea. Sailors board eagerly, banners are raised, sails flutter in the winds, and the pernicious wolves sail off to mangle the Lord's sheep, offering their god Thor a taste of human blood.

> (Fabricantur naves, innovantur scuta, resarciuntur thoraces, poliuntur loricae et galeae, acuuntur enses et lanceae, omnique telorum apparatu accurate munitur exercitus. Inde vero statuto die pelago impelluntur naves, ad eas propere festinant milites, elevantur vexilla, librant ventis carbasa, vehuntur lupi pernices ad lacerandas dominicas oves, deo suo Thur humanum sanguinem libantes.)

In their lust for destruction, these vikings deliver the whole countryside to Vulcan, burning Saint-Quentin with beastly rage (*ferali rabie*), slaughtering the bishop, deacons, and Christian people [1.5(6)]. The pagans even burn to the ground William's own monastery of Jumièges, leaving it a lair for beasts for thirty years.

Eventually Hasting submits to baptism, but he emerges from the font "a ravening wolf" [*et exit rapacissimus lupus;* 1.9(10)], that is, still a pagan at heart. Thus he can perform the favorite ruse of vikings and Normans,

---

[35] On the identification of Denmark with Dacia on medieval maps, see Eliade, *Zalmoxis*, 72–73, and note 146.

feigning death to gain re-entry into the monastery at Luna. Once Hasting has pierced the defenses under pretense of seeking a Christian burial, he and his men prowl the town in a wolfish frenzy [. . . *lupina rabie . . . grassatur* I.9(10)]. Before his conversion, Rollo, too, attracts lupine allusions as he plans an assault on Paris [2.4(10)]. Like wolves at twilight, Rollo's pagan pack steals into the sheepfolds of Christ, burning down churches, leading women captive, slaughtering the people, making all the land a place of mourning [*ut lupi uespertini uehuntur pagani ad caulas Christi . . .* 2.11(17)]. Here William alludes to the "twilight wolves" (*lupi vespere*) of Zephaniah 3:3, the corrupt judges who pollute Jerusalem.[36] Men like these and the treacherous prophets (*viri infideles*), continues the Hebrew prophet, induce God to turn cities into a wasteland, empty of all people (Zeph. 3:6). The *Gesta*'s reference to this passage deepens the sense of lamentation for Rollo's assault on the devout. But when the *Gesta* introduces Rollo's Christian son, William Longsword, it uses the heroic simile of a fearsome lion [*quasi leo . . . terribilis* (3.1)]. The images offer a neat contrast between father and son, the pagan wolf and Christian lion, the destroyer of civilization and the nurturer of righteousness. The contrast also signals that, for William of Jumièges, the Norman dukes have already reached their apogee in William Longsword.

In Dudo's book on Longsword, William of Jumièges found one ducal character he could hold up as a model for Norman princes. This is not surprising, since Dudo drew Longsword's portrait from the *Lament on the Death of William Longsword*, appropriating both its pious tone and its reverence for Jumièges, whose re-foundation myth it tells. The *Lament* may even be a product of the chronicler's own monastery at Jumièges, which it celebrates as the place to which the duke wished to retire.[37] In any case, Dudo's borrowings from the *Lament* made Longsword an attractive figure for William of Jumièges, who highlights this duke's spiritual development and his role as peacemaker. The *Gesta* takes care to affirm the succession and legitimacy of nearly all the Norman dukes, but none more than Longsword. Whereas Dudo had the barons press Rollo to acclaim his son as heir, William of Jumièges has an old and weary Rollo, of his own accord, summon nobles and order them to acknowledge William.[38] "Meum est," inquit, "mihi illum subrogare, uestrum est illi fidem seruare" ("My duty," he said, "is to step aside for him; yours is to swear fealty to him"). Rollo's eloquence secures a smooth succession.

His heir is a hero that William of Jumièges can admire. Legends from Jumièges supply the monk with a motivation for Longsword's monastic ambitions (3.7–8). So the *Gesta* has Duke William, riding to the hunt, happen

---

[36] I am grateful to Peter Brown for pointing me to Zephaniah here.

[37] E. van Houts, *GND* I, xxviii–xxix.

[38] Shopkow, *History and Community*, 83–84. See also John Le Patourel, "The Norman Succession, 996–1135," *EHR* 86 (1971), 225–50."

upon two monks clearing the land at Jumièges. He scorns the monks' offer of bread and water and hurries on to the chase. But after a boar charges him and sends him hurtling from his horse, the duke, on coming to his senses, seeks out the monks again to accept their charity and to promise them help.

The people of Rouen have already recognized Longsword's piety by offering him a benediction as he entered their city (3.6). From the walls they shouted, "Benedictus qui venit in nomine Domini" ("blessed is he who comes in the name of the Lord"). Among Norman *laudes regiae* this blessing occurs only twice, both times attested in William's *Gesta*.[39] Perhaps William inserted it here to foreshadow Longsword's impending martyrdom. For this is the Jews' proclamation to Jesus as he entered Jerusalem on Palm Sunday, only days before his crucifixion (Matt. 21:9). William has the Normans repeat this benediction with an ironic edge when King Louis IV rides into Rouen to steal Longsword's son and claim the duchy for himself (4.6). Here the blessing is a ruse contrived by Bernard of Senlis and Bernard the Dane to lull the king into complacency. The Bernards have surmised that the king will feel no compulsion to endanger the child if he imagines that the Normans venerate him as their true lord.

The blessing does trick the king and provides a temporary respite from dangerous circumstances. The Normans and their boy-duke find themselves in these straits through the jealousy of Franks and Bretons, but also through native treachery, the work of the devil (3.2):

> After [the Bretons] were defeated, because the devil stirred up very many evil men, fresh insurrections break out against the duke [*iterum intestina aduersus eum insurgunt molimina*]. For Riulf, inflamed by the furies of treason [*perfidie succensus furiis*] and having infected many people with the venom of discord, snatched up arms, attempting to cast him out of the realm.

Although these rebellions fail, another Riulf will eventually join Arnulf, count of Flanders, to assassinate Longsword (3.12).

From Dudo's account of this murder, the *Gesta* omits two superb speeches [3.11–12; cf. Dudo 3.63–64]: Arnulf's vow of supplication, dripping with false humility, and the assassins' plea that the duke return to the island for one final message. Yet the simplicity of the *Gesta*'s description has a power of its own as it highlights Arnulf of Flanders, here the embodiment of evil. Motivated by arrogance and lust for domination (3.10), this villain had conspired against his neighbor, Count Herluin, "whose fortress called Montreuil he snatched by deceit" (*fraude*). Herluin then sought justice from Duke William,

---

[39] E. van Houts, *GND* I, 84–85; H. E. J. Cowdrey, "The Anglo-Norman *laudes regiae*," *Viator* 12 (1981), 37–78.

who successfully besieged Montreuil and returned it to its rightful owner. For this compassionate act, claims the *Gesta*, Longsword earned Arnulf's rage (3.11):

> Meanwhile Arnulf of Flanders, breathing out the frightful poison lurking in his treacherous breast and grieving in his savage mind for the fortress he had lost, deep in his heart took to plotting the duke's death, implicating many Frankish magnates, who were infected by the guileful sophistry of this inhuman man and unspeakable murderer. With one mind they all conspire in the death of the excellent prince, committing themselves by oath to the crime. Eager to complete the deed that his deceitful mind had contrived, Arnulf sent messengers to Duke William, reporting that he wished to have a bond of friendship with him and an indelible peace.

So Arnulf lures William to the island, where the princes embrace, "swear many oaths of sacred friendship, and share many kisses of peace," while Arnulf "spins a spider web of trifles and distractions" just like "the traitor Judas" (3.12). This sets the stage for the murder, committed there by "four sons of the devil." Allusions to demonic forces, throughout this episode, both diminish Dudo's emphasis on the Normans' endemic treachery and justify Norman guile as an essential defense.

The minority of Richard I, son of William Longsword, provides more ammunition for this argument, as enemies plot to wrest the duchy from the Normans and their young master. As in Dudo, Arnulf of Flanders is the villain who engineers Longsword's assassination, then escapes punishment by seducing Louis (4.3):

> Blinded by gifts and by the traitor's wily deceits, the king absolved him of the crime, though he deserved to be hanged, and turned his wrath on the innocent boy, imitating the example of Pilate, who dismissed a murderer and condemned Christ to death on the cross.

Dudo (4.72) detailed the bribes that bedazzle the king's advisors and win over the king, too, persuading him to detain Richard. At this point, Dudo interposed a long address to Louis, fifty-eight lines of verse, urging him to release the child, son of the innocent holy martyr of Christ. This confluence of innocence, martyrdom, and Christ in Dudo's poem may have brought Pilate to William's mind. If this seems plausible, it suggests that William was at least reading Dudo's verses, even if the poems influenced his writing only infrequently and obliquely.

So misguided is this Pilate (King Louis) that he continues to protect Longsword's murderers, even as his greed makes him keep Richard under virtual house arrest in the royal palace. Louis perjures himself by promising the Normans of Rouen, *licet subdole* ("albeit treacherously"), that he was taking Richard away for but a brief time, to raise him like a prince's son at a king's court (4.2). Only by assessing the weaknesses of the Normans' opponents, namely, their avarice and envy, can Bernard the Dane outwit them and save Richard (4.6).

In fact, the theme of nearly universal deceit permeates the *Gesta*, but perhaps nowhere more than in Book Four. The fear of treachery motivates Hugh the Great to entrust his son Hugh to Richard I "so that safe under his protection he would not be injured by the tricks (*fraudibus*) of his enemies" (4.12). Richard himself remains in danger, hunted by coalitions of powerful foes. Theobald, count of Chartres and Blois, for example, incites Queen Gerberga, mother of the French King Lothar, to rouse her brother Bruno, archbishop of Cologne and duke of Lotharingia, "to use any means possible to capture Richard" (4.13). "Guilefully deceived" (*subdole deceptus*), Richard sets out to speak with Bruno, who has lured him under the pretext of arranging a peace. Only occasionally does William of Jumièges imitate Dudo's dialogue, but he does so here with flair, as Richard narrowly avoids his father's fate thanks to the warning unexpectedly tendered when he meets two of Theobald's soldiers on his way to the parley (4.13):

> One of them asked him, "Where are you heading, most illustrious of men? Do you want to be duke of the Normans or a keeper of sheep outside your homeland?" After these words, he fell silent. The duke answered, "Whose soldiers are you?" The other replied, "What does it matter to you whose we are? Aren't we yours?"

Clever enough to heed this cryptic warning, Richard rewards the soldiers (who have betrayed one master for gain from another) and rides home, leaving Bruno "cheated by the discovery of his wicked tricks" (*delusus . . . detectis nequitie sue fraudibus*).

Yet again Richard's enemies scheme to trap him. In a chapter loaded with a vocabulary of duplicity (4.14), the *Gesta* reports Theobald's plan to have King Lothar entice Richard into French territories, allegedly so that Richard can perform the service he owes his royal lord, fighting against their common foes. Just in time, as he waits with his army on the banks of the River Eaulne, Richard learns that his enemies stand on the opposite bank. There lurk the counts Baldwin of Flanders, Geoffrey of Anjou, and Theobald of Chartres, poised to attack and kill the duke, "when he should be seized by royal treachery" (*dum regia preoccuparetur proditione*). Again Richard barely escapes back to Rouen. Now "having publicly unmasked the king's deceit, he recognized his animosity toward him." Soon King Lothar goes on military offensive against Richard, invading Normandy and even capturing Évreux through the treason of Gilbert Machel (4.15). But Duke Richard crushes in battle the instigator of this assault, Theobald of Chartres. Dudo (4.114) had delighted in Theobald's fourfold punishment: he saw his liegemen fallen in battle, he himself fled wounded, his son died that same day, and Chartres burned to the ground. The monk adds that these were Christ's retribution for his crimes.

These multiple treacheries compel the Normans, at last, to use the weapon they have always held in reserve: Richard calls in the Danes [4.16(16)–17(17)]. Here again William insists that the deceit of the Normans' enemies justifies the Normans' counter-trickery. The *Gesta* adds a few details to Dudo's account (4.114–24), including the substitution of a specific character, King Harold of Denmark, for Dudo's generic *gens robustissima Dacorum* ("very hardy Danish people"). The Scandinavians burn strongholds to the ground and carry off the survivors into slavery. The sounds of lamentation subside into silence, with not even a dog left to bark (*nullo cane latrante*). "While Normandy remains free of pagan raids, France is carried off captive, with no one resisting."

In this resumé of Dudo, the *Gesta* omits any hint of Richard's difficulty in diverting the Danes from their pillage once the French agree to a treaty. And though Richard's sermon and conversion of the pagans contribute to the thematic progress in the *De moribus*, William condenses this to a simple summary: "Having successfully concluded these affairs, the duke converted many pagans to the Christian faith with his holy preaching. The rest who decided to persist in their paganism he sent to Spain, where they fought many battles and destroyed eighteen cities." William seems eager to pass quickly over the entire episode, even its salvific conclusion.

Despite William's care to dissociate his Norman dukes from their Scandinavian affinities, the *Gesta*'s fourth book continues to hold contrary memories. In the early chapters, for instance, Richard's arch-enemy and the architect of his father's murder, Arnulf, stresses the Normans' Scandinavian connections when he presses King Louis to chase the Normans back to Denmark, their homeland (4.3). In Arnulf's view, Louis should even concede much of the duchy to Hugh the Great, just "to force this treacherous people (*haec gens perfida*) to get out of the country" (4.5). William has omitted Dudo's verbal signs linking Richard with wolves; tears and laments mark his death, but no howling (4.20). Still, the *Gesta* keeps one slight allusion, when the Kings Otto and Louis leave the siege of Rouen, following the fleeing Arnulf, and the Normans search them out and cut them down *quasi bidentes*, ["like sheep;" 4.11(11)].

This slender wolfish reference may well be inadvertent. When he is being careful, William of Jumièges prefers to sever the dukes from their pagan ways. His moralist leanings even bring William to delete Richard's illegitimate offspring from Dudo's list of his children. Robert of Torigni will reinstate them and add the names of their own children, since this line of succession allows Robert to discuss the family's good deeds toward his monastery of Bec. But generosity toward monasteries does not present a strong enough pretext for William of Jumièges to acknowledge Richard's illegitimate children. More single-mindedly than Dudo, William wants to read Richard's life as an *exemplum*. While Dudo does summarize Richard's brilliance as "like a star in the sky" (4.65), William praises his pious acts, his foundation of churches and monasteries, and his commitment to peace (4.19). For William, Duke Richard excels because of his protection of monks and clerics and his care for the poor, orphans, widows, and captives. This is the behavior that closes William's account, these the deeds that he wishes to commemorate in Richard and encourage in Richard's successors.

Still, among William's additions to Dudo's account of Richard's reign is a story too hot for Dudo to relate when writing under this Richard's son. The incident occurs while the king holds the young duke at his palace:[40]

> So while he was detaining the boy at Laon, the king stunned him with very bitter insults when he returned from fowling, calling him the son of a whore who had seduced another woman's husband, and he threatened the boy that if he did not desist from such senseless acts, he would brand his knees and deprive him of every honor.
>
> (Vnde cum apud Laudunum Clauatum moraretur, puerum ab aucupio regredientem acerbissimis confutans conuiciis, meretricis filium ultro uirum alienum rapientis eum uocauit et, nisi a talibus resipisceret, cauteriatis genibus, omni illum honore priuari minatus.)

These threats startle the young duke and his guardian, in part because they reveal that Louis is holding the child prisoner. But the insults also shock because they raise a delicate issue, impugning the very legitimacy of Richard's claim to the duchy. Longsword had taken a wife, Leutgarde (Leyarde), *Christiano more*, but Richard's mother, Sprota, was the duke's wife *more Danico*. While unchristian liaisons served the dukes' dynastic ambition, they also left their heirs vulnerable to charges of illegitimacy, which would not only humiliate a child like Richard but could even serve as pretext for challenging his right to land and office.

This is the sort of scurrilous detail that a contemporary of Richard I and his son would have to suppress, however much it might have amused Dudo. It is even surprising to find this in the *Gesta*. Though William was writing nearly a century after the incident, he remained sensitive to the importance, for Rollo's dynasty, that each duke be the legitimate successor. Why, then, did William supply this anecdote? Perhaps he found it so incendiary that he included it to illustrate the king's audacity, which demanded a Norman response. But perhaps, too, this story offers a glimpse into William's own sensibilities. The good monk cannot have approved of Danish marriages, with their affinities for polygamy and concubinage. At two other places, as

---

[40] 4.3. For the Norman versions of this episode, and the various threats ascribed to Louis, see Eric Christiansen, *Dudo of St Quentin*, 212, n. 341. Dudo has Louis lash out at Osmund, threatening him with blinding and his lord with a knee-roasting (probably meaning a sound whipping); but William of Jumièges makes Richard the direct recipient of Louis's rage and adds the accusation of bastardy.

we shall see, William hinted at troubling irregularities in the ducal inheritance.[41]

Since Dudo stops with the death of Richard I and the succession of Richard II, William must proceed without him for the reigns of Richard II, Richard III, Robert I, and William the Conqueror. The new chapters, drawn more independently than the first four, show even more clearly William's monastic interests and values, and likewise stress the edifying aspects of ducal deeds. William continues to imply that the treachery of their neighbors compels the Normans to respond in kind, that necessity reinforces the Norman tendency toward rebellion. Left to his own devices, William of Jumièges also directs his attention often to the Danes and to England.

In his first chapter of the new section, William at once spotlights his monastic concerns (5.1). This panegyric to Richard II praises him not only for his military successes but especially for his cultivation of monks, concluding:

> Though he was dedicated to action in the world, still he was wholly Catholic in faith, and toward God's servants benevolent and devoted. Under his governance flourished many flocks of monks, who rushed out like bees from many hives of sacred activity, bringing golden honey to the heavenly treasures.

But the narrative turns at once to rebellions, first a peasants' revolt (5.2), then an insurgency of magnates led by the duke's half-brother, William (5.3). Of course, any period of transition is potentially dangerous, but William's narrative stresses the subversive nature of William's subjects and kin. So chapter two begins:

> Well then, as Richard entered young manhood, though he had such an abundance of fine qualities, still it happened that a hotbed of noxious discord burst out within the duchy of Normandy.

First, the peasants seized this moment to demand the right-of-way through forests and passage along rivers. William writes that they met together and sent representatives to Richard II, who cut off the envoys' hands and feet, returning them useless to their families (*inutiles suis remisit*) as a deterrent to their peers. Meanwhile, Richard had dispatched his uncle, Count Raoul, to disperse the remaining rabble, who promptly quit their assemblies and went back to their plows. Like most medieval historians, William does not probe social causes of unrest. Though ducal abuse of the hunt had probably roused the embattled peasantry, the *Gesta* suggests no pretext for the complaints.[42]

---

[41] See below at 6.2 on suspicions concerning Robert's role in his brother's death, and at 7.8(18) on the mockery of Duke William's maternal ancestry.

[42] Marx, ed., *GND*, 73, n. 2 suggests this provocation, following Christian Pfister, *Etudes*

Instead, William insists that the peasants were fomenting rebellion because they wanted to make their own laws governing the profit from forests and waters and so live according to their own pleasures. Without any apparent sympathy for the people's cause, the chronicler approves of the duke's sense of privilege as well as his tactics in restoring order, which William describes with some relish.

The episode parallels Dudo's tale of Rollo dispensing rough justice against peasants who falsely claimed restitution for a missing plow (Dudo 2.31–32). Both stories, prominently displayed at the beginnings of reigns, feature suppressions of the peasantry. Although competing nobles and neighboring rulers posed the greatest threats to ducal control, class warfare also played a potentially dangerous role. Did ethnic struggles, operative when Rollo's Scandinavians subdued a Frankish peasantry, still function at the end of the tenth century? It does seem likely that the Normans' social structure, featuring magnates with distinct ethnic ties, continued to exacerbate class frictions. Although the Norman chronicler wants to emphasize the civilizing impulse of the new duke, this hostile encounter between Richard II and his people does not bode well for peace. Dudo's thematic progression of increasing civilization dissolves in William's *Gesta*, replaced by continuing sedition, as social reality overwhelms the narrative.

Even as the new duke was crushing the peasants' revolt, at the same time he faced a challenge from his brother William, made "haughty and rebellious" by "the arrogance of some wicked men" (3.3). "Enticed by the cunning of these evil men," the brother "spurned Richard's lordship and withheld the obligation of his fealty." The *Gesta* turns this incident into an epic tale, recounting the slaughter in battle of some insurgents and the exile of others, Richard's imprisonment of his brother in a tower in Rouen, William's escape down a rope hung from a high window, and the fugitive's plea for Richard's forgiveness when he came upon him hunting in a glade in Vernon. So moved was Richard by his brother's remorse that he came to love him dearly, granting him the county of Eu and a beautiful bride from a noble family. "With these incidents quelled at last, the land of Normandy lay silent before Duke Richard."

But all was not quiet, as the next sentence reveals. The English king Æthelred II (976–1016), husband of Richard's sister Emma, "longing to inflict damage and disgrace upon the duke," dispatches a fleet against Normandy, confident that his soldiers can bully his brother-in-law. But common people join knights in the Cotentin, mustering to repel the English invasion. An English survivor reports to Æthelred (5.4):

---

sur le règne de Robert le Pieux (996–1031) (Paris, 1885), 101–102. See also Mathieu Arnoux, "Classe agricole," 45–51.

> Your serene highness, we never even saw the duke, but to our destruction we skirmished with the particularly fierce people of one county. Not only are the men extremely brave warriors, but the women are fighters, too. They attacked our strongest soldiers with the carrying-poles for jugs and smashed the men's brains out. Be assured that these women killed all your soldiers.

Here is a reminder that Norman subjects, women and men, are people to be reckoned with. The *Gesta* reports that the king realized his folly and flushed.

This debacle so humiliated Æthelred that it propelled him further toward brutality, this time against Danes living peacefully in his kingdom. On Æthelred's orders, according to the *Gesta*, the English tie babies to doorposts and knock their brains out and bury women waist-deep before tearing the nipples from their breasts and setting ferocious dogs against them (5.6). Reports of such atrocities grieve the Danish king Svein, who seeks vengeance and enters into a pact of mutual aid with Richard II (5.7). All this section (5.4–9) shows the chronicler's compassion for pagan Danes and interest in Scandinavians. These chapters reveal Norman ties to England, too, reinforced through Emma and her children, who further bind Normans to Danes.[43]

The madness (*uecordia*; 5.11) and cunning (*nimiis uersutiis*; 5.10) of another of Normandy's neighbors will force Richard to import Scandinavian ruffians as his father had done. This time Richard II "calls for the aid of two kings from lands across the sea, namely Olaf of the Norsemen and Lacman of the Swedes, with a great number of pagans," to counter the predation of Odo, count of Chartres (5.11).[44] While the Bretons aim to surprise the foreign army as the men gather booty, the pagans discover their tricks (*dolos*) and devise snares to foil them, digging trenches to trip the Bretons' horses. Trickery begets trickery, and the Normans of the *Gesta* find themselves playing the game taught them by necessity.

Again William of Jumièges attributes wiles to others, as one of Odo's allies, Count Hugh III of Maine, eludes capture through deceit. Losing his horse in battle against the Normans, Hugh must escape on foot through Norman territories. He hides his breastplate in a plowed furrow and dons a shepherd's cloak, hoisting a sheep-pen onto his shoulders. Thus disguised, he keeps encouraging the Normans to pursue the enemy, whom he reports to be fleeing only a short distance ahead of them. Once the Normans race out of sight, Hugh cuts through the forests to Maine, arriving home bloody from the

---

43 Emma's sons by Æthelred were the æthelings, Alfred, murdered in 1036, and Edward, called the Confessor, king of England (1042–66); as the *Gesta* reports (5.9), by her second husband, the Danish king Cnut, she had another son, "Harthacnut, later king of the Danes, and a daughter, Gunnhild, who married Henry, emperor of the Romans."
44 On Olaf and Lacman, see van Houts, *GND*, vol. 2, p. 20, n. 1.

briars but safe. It is a story told at the Normans' expense, since an enemy saves himself through a ruse, in the Norman fashion.[45]

Ultimately, the French king Robert, fearing for the safety of France, must broker a peace treaty between Richard and Odo (5.12). Richard "returns in delight to his kings" (*ad suos reges*), converting Olaf to Christianity before sending them back to Scandinavia. All this passage echoes the last campaign of Richard I, even to the conversion of one pagan king and some of his men, with both kings promising to return if ever Richard should need them again. This book ends, as it began, with praise of Richard II, a duke famous for his "extraordinary exploits" as well as a supporter of monks and clerics and the poor (5.17). But the episodic account of his reign has done little to illustrate this. Not only has William of Jumièges obscured Dudo's sense of progressive civilizing, but with his indifference toward personalities, he also allows the dukes to flow together in the reader's memory. The Norman people, too, are virtually indistinguishable from their neighbors. The *Gesta* does note the bravery of the Normans under Richard II (5.15): "In his time the Normans always used to rout their enemies, to turn their backs to no one." They are also disloyal and prone to rebellion, but in the *Gesta*'s pages no more so than other peoples, as treachery everywhere threatens the fragility of order. So at the end of this book (5.16) Reginald, count of Bourgogne-outre-Saône and son-in-law to Richard II, falls captive to his enemy Hugh, count of Chalon, by a trick (*captus dolo*). Only the Normans' reliance on pagan kin and their ties to Scandinavia and England distinguish them from other Christians in a duplicitous realm.

With the accession of Richard III (1026–27), son of Richard II, William of Jumièges becomes a contemporary and sometimes even an eyewitness of the events he chronicles (6.1). For the most part, he does not like what he sees. While he finds young Richard a worthy heir to his father, "the perfidious Enemy" (*perfidus hostis*) soon breaks the peace by enlisting "the cunning of some malevolent men to incite his own brother Robert to rebel against him" (6.2). William offers glimpses of Robert's character, the volatility and weakness for evil counsel that drive him against Richard (6.3). When Richard besieges his brother within Falaise, he forces Robert to surrender. Swearing peace, the brothers go their separate ways, Richard back to Rouen, where "he died, as many people said, by poison, leaving his brother Robert as heir to his duchy" (6.2). Though no writer until William of Malmesbury expressly charges Robert with the poisoning, the *Gesta*'s phrasing here plants the suspicion by placing the death, rumors of murder, and plausible motive within the

---

[45] Compare the gusto with which Normans tell similar stories of their own deceit: Emily Albu, "Bohemond and the Rooster: Byzantines, Normans, and the Artful Ruse," in *Anna Komnene and her Times*, ed. Thalia Gouma-Peterson (New York and London, 2000), 157–68.

same sentence.[46] Given his rebellion, described earlier in this chapter, Robert has not only a motive for murder but also a recent history of hostility. When he seeks redemption through pilgrimage early in 1035, "preferring to become a poor man for Christ rather than burn in the fires of Gehenna" [6.11(12)], does he set out with this crime on his conscience?

Even without fratricide, Robert needed forgiveness, according to the *Gesta*'s account of a troubled reign. First, wicked men lead Robert to suspicions against the Archbishop Robert, whom he besieges in the town of Évreux, then drives into exile (6.3). But when Robert begins to listen to good advice and to behave well, according to the *Gesta*, evil men test their theory that Robert has become a coward. From this point on, rebellions form the leitmotif of Book Six, as William of Bellême (6.4), Robert's cousin Hugh d'Ivri (6.5), and Alan of Brittany (6.8) plot sedition in the duchy. Normandy suffers repeated pillage when one faction or another seeks retribution.

Normans also find themselves drawn into the conflicts of their feuding neighbors. Baldwin V of Flanders rises up against his father Baldwin IV (6.6), and Constance, widow of the French King Robert, conspires to dethrone her son, Henry, and replace him with another son (6.7). In both those familial intrigues, Duke Robert proves the hero, restoring justice among unjust neighbors. But when the duke attempts an invasion of England on behalf of his cousins, the æthelings Edward and Alfred, versus King Cnut, a storm drives Norman ships to Jersey [6.9(10)].[47] Taking a broader Christian view rather than a narrowly Norman one, William makes a rare first-person assertion, venturing the opinion that God foiled Robert's plan so that the pious King Edward could later ascend the throne without bloodshed. If the *Gesta* has a primary theme, it is not the acclamation of Norman grandeur and conquest, but rather an affirmation of the gentle righteousness in Christian living.

In a fractured world, where son attacks father, and mother schemes against son, the *Gesta* makes Robert the peacemaker. But this duke also needs both respite from and redemption for his turbulent life. So in the midst of the chaos, he announces a pilgrimage to Jerusalem, against the advice of counselors who fear worse turmoil if he abandons Normandy to his child.[48] Despite their pleading, Robert proclaims William as his heir and leaves with a shower of almsgiving [6.11(12)]. At this point in the *Gesta* Robert of Torigni inserts fantastic tales of Robert's legendary ostentation on his supposed stop in Constantinople, but William of Jumièges takes the duke

---

[46] See van Houts' n. 3, p. 47 of *GND* 2.

[47] "The story [of this aborted invasion], which is unconfirmed, should be treated with caution, but it cannot be summarily dismissed." David C. Douglas, *William the Conqueror: The Norman Impact upon England* (Berkeley, 1964), 163.

[48] William may have been as old as eight, though Robert of Torigni gives his age as five; van Houts, *GND* 2, p. 81.

directly to the Holy Sepulcher, where he sheds countless tears and offers countless gifts of gold. On the return voyage Robert falls ill and dies, finding a foreign tomb at Nicaea, where his men bury him in the church of St. Mary [6.12(13)]. William of Jumièges imagines that God willed Robert's death on return from pilgrimage, "so that his blessed soul, just now made dazzlingly white by the splendor of his excellent works, might not later be entangled in worldly affairs and thus accumulate stains." This requiem suits no one as well as the fractious Robert.

As feared, the years of his son's minority are turbulent ones. The opening chapter to the *Gesta*'s Book Seven, in language as rhetorical as any William writes, introduces civil discord as a theme of this book [7.1(1–4)]. Evoking Scripture as his teacher in these matters, William recalls how "the son's house is destroyed by the wickedness of an evil father, but on the other hand is strengthened by the merit of a good one." So Christ rewards the boy-duke for his father's redemptive pilgrimage, snatching Robert's son from the snares his people set.

> From his childhood many Normans veered away from fealty to him, throwing up ramparts in many places and constructing very strong fortifications for themselves. As soon as they gain confidence in their defenses, at once hostile plots and insurrections break out in their midst, and fierce conflagrations are set everywhere in the land.

The chronicler writes that he cannot hazard naming all the perpetrators, since he wishes to avoid "their inexorable hatred."

> Still, I whisper in your ear, when you stand next to me, that they were no other than these who profess to be his liegemen, on whom now the duke has heaped great honors.

In this confession, the monk reveals the volatile nature of the duke's Norman kinsmen and intimates, sometime rebels now at the center of power. Writing decades later, Orderic Vitalis adds details into his redaction of the *Gesta*, supplying names and deeds to support William's charge. From his vantage point Orderic can proclaim that the Normans are dangerously troublesome when given free rein to indulge their penchant for rebellion, and in this book in particular Orderic restores and intensifies Dudo's theme of the treacherous Normans. For his part, William of Jumièges does not exactly define treachery as an essential feature of Normanness. Yet here in the final book of his *Gesta* he comes close when he describes an instigator of this rebellion [7.7(17)]. This man, Guy, was the young duke's cousin, a grandson of Richard I and thus a rival claimant to William's title. The *Gesta* features the depth of Guy's betrayal when "like Absalom, he began to turn many magnates from their fealty to the duke and to ensnare them in the chasm of his own perfidy" (*in sue perfidie voragine*).

75

So dire is the duke's situation that he must take the precarious step of seeking aid from the French King Henry. Together Henry and Duke William fight the Norman magnates at Val-ès-Dunes, crushing the rebels. At last William can show his strength by destroying hostile fortresses, "so many castles of thugs and homes of criminals" [7.7(17)]. He still has to battle with the Angevins [7.8(18)] and their count, Geoffrey Martel, "a man crafty in every way" (*vir per omnia versutus*), who attacked his neighbors, captured Count Theobald, and as ransom "violently extorted from him the city of Tours with several strongholds" before he turned his assault against Normandy and Duke William.

Even here, after Val-ès-Dunes, Normans ally with neighbors against their duke, as a Norman garrison surrenders the stronghold of Domfront, which William must now besiege. But the duke interrupts this assault to ride all night to Alençon, another rebel fortress that he has learned is vulnerable to attack. At a fortification across the river from Alençon, the defenders' mockery so angers him that he rouses his forces to attack the citadel and burn it to the ground. Capturing those who had taunted him, he has his men drag them before all the townspeople and then cut off their hands and feet. William of Jumièges tantalizes his readers with the incident, but Orderic Vitalis inserts the critical details into the *Gesta* [7.8(18)]:

> So without delay, as he had commanded, thirty-two men were maimed. For they had beaten pelts and fur garments to mock the duke and had called him a *pelliciarium* [a dealer in pelts], as a contemptuous insult because his mother's parents had been *pollinctores* [burial assistants who washed and prepared corpses].

Orderic's repetition of the pun, linking animal skins with the human bodies that William's grandparents had prepared for burial, is a humiliation too fresh for the duke's contemporary to handle. Although the monk of Jumièges does not mention the charge of bastardy here, it must have been on his mind. Maybe it is surprising that he dared even allude to it, especially since Jumièges depended upon Duke William's good will, and the chronicler is careful elsewhere not to offend. This is one of three slight allusions – the others being the French king's derision of young Richard I and the rumors of poisoning in the death of Richard II – that suggest irregularities in the ducal succession. But the presence of this incident, even tenuously noted, hints at the monk's antipathy to the habit of keeping concubines or marrying "in the Danish fashion" and then legitimizing the children of these unions. This incident marks one of the parallels between the lives of Richard I and William II, since both suffer humiliation for their alleged bastardy and their mothers' humble status.[49] In the very next chapter [7.9(21)] the *Gesta* notes the pres-

---

[49] Shopkow (*History and Community*, 83–84) sees the parallels in the *Gesta*'s lives of these two dukes, particularly concerning the succession.

sure from Norman leaders, who urge the duke to provide a legitimate heir of his own. And so duke William marries Matilda, daughter of Count Baldwin of Flanders.[50]

The duke must face yet another assault [7.10(24)].

> To be sure, from the moment when the Normans first tilled the fields of Neustria, the French were always wont to envy them, rousing up their kings against them and asserting that the Normans had violently stolen from their ancestors the lands which Normans now hold.

Certainly this is the obvious indictment to level against Normans: Since they had captured French lands by force, so the French king had every right to take back his ancestral territories by the same means. The *Gesta*'s repetition of this charge may be another sign that its author harbors hostility toward Norman predation. But the *Gesta*'s language softens the blow, making the Normans harmless inhabitants who work the land (*Normanni arua Neustrie ceperunt incolere*). So, too, when the French instigators succeed in rousing King Henry to invade Normandy, his army's preoccupation with arson and rape makes French troops the true predators and leaves them vulnerable to a dawn attack by Norman defenders. The Norman forces slay many of the invaders and send the rest back to France, where they reconnoiter to launch another onslaught [7.12(28)], which the Normans repulse yet again.

Rebellions and invasions – treachery from within and without – have formed one continuing storyline of William's *Gesta*. But the conquest of England and perhaps the Conqueror's own influence propel William into a narrative on another plane. As he has often stressed the lawful ducal succession, so here he emphasizes the legitimacy of the duke's claim to England [7.13(31)]. In the version of William of Jumièges, King Edward has promised England to William and has sent Harold to seal the pledge with oaths. Harold's subsequent renunciation of the oaths makes him a perjurer from whom the duke must seek justice in battle. For while William's power in Normandy soars, in England Harold wrongly takes the throne at Edward's death.[51] The new king's infidelity and madness turn all the English away from him, claims the chronicler, and a strange star (Halley's comet) portends another change in kingship, which belongs to Duke William by right [7.14(34)].

The duke stands poised to attack. But if this is a triumphal history, the *Gesta* devotes little attention to the triumph. At this climactic moment,

---

50 The marriage occurred sometime between October 1049 and 1051, but did not receive papal sanction until 1059. William of Jumièges does not mention the objections to this marriage.

51 For a summary of "the singular authority that William exercised over his duchy on the eve of the Norman Conquest," see C. Warren Hollister, "Normandy, France and the Anglo-Norman *Regnum*," *Speculum* 51 (April 1976), 204–205.

William of Jumièges keeps his spare style, granting to the battle of Hastings only a few lines [7.15(36)]:

Then the duke, taking precautions against a night attack, ordered his army to be ready at arms from nightfall till the welcome dawn. But at daybreak he arranged his armies of troops into three divisions and set out calmly to meet the dread enemy. He entered into battle at the third hour. The carnage lasted till night. Harold himself fell, mortally wounded, at the first encounter of the troops. When the English learned that their king had met his death, fearing for their own safety now that night was coming on, they turned around and sought refuge in flight.

The narrative of battle is plain, almost matter-of-fact, but the chronicler takes care to locate the responsibility for the deaths of so many Englishmen, who perished as God's retribution for earl Godwin's betrayal of Alfred Ætheling [7.16(37)]. This recalls the *Gesta*'s Biblical simile in 7.6(9), condemning as "a traitor like Judas" the English earl who dined with Alfred and offered him the kiss of peace before surrendering him to King Harold in London and certain death. When Duke William slaughtered Englishmen at Hastings, he was thus acting as a righteous avenger for the murder "unjustly perpetrated by them."

This fits the ducal view of the Conquest as promulgated by all the historians who sought the new king's favor. This view turns the Norman myths inside out by proclaiming the English, in one way or another, as traitors whom the righteous duke must overcome. So the *Carmen de Hastingae Proelio* lets Duke William condemn Harold before the king's envoy, who has ordered the Normans to sail away before the battle (lines 233–34):

"The bond of our alliance he has wickedly dissolved
    by holding unjustly what should by right be mine."

("Fedus amicicie nostre dissoluit inique,
    Dum tenet iniuste que mea iure forent.")

Here William rehearses to the legate Harold's "perjured hand" (*periura manus*; line 241) and secret oaths, falsely sworn (*furtiua . . . periuria*; line 239), and then addresses his troops with similar reminders (lines 260–65):

"You Normans poised for outstanding accomplishments:
The lying and infamous perjuring king and adulterer
    is scheming and laying snares for us.
For he is accustomed to conquer not by force but by deceit,
    and pledging fealty with his lips, he offers death.
So we should beware not to be deceived by him. . . ."

("Normanni faciles actibus egregiis:
Falsus et infamis periurus rex et adulter
    Molitur nobis tendit et insidias.

Eius enim mos est non ui set uincere fraude,
Spondendoque fidem porrigit ore necem.
Ergo cauere decet ne decipiamur ab illo. . . .")

It seems no coincidence that the *Carmen* puts these words in the duke's mouth, distancing itself from accusations that seem incongruous when they come from a Norman. Later generations of writers, shielded both from the euphoria of the Conquest and the wrath of the Conqueror, will challenge this interpretation more overtly. But writing at about the same time as the *Carmen*'s author, William of Jumièges also attaches Norman labels to the enemy, though in much abbreviated form.

Following the battle of Hastings, the Conqueror quells resistance in London, and the English submit to his election, anointing, and coronation [*Gesta* 7.16(37)]. The new king returns to Normandy [7.17(38)]. The chronicler lingers over his royal presence at the dedication of the church of St. Mary at Jumièges, devoting more space to this event and the succession of the new archbishop of Rouen than he had to Hastings. But another rebellion interrupts the peace, as Count Eustace of Boulogne, "corrupted by the wiles (*uersutiis deprauatus*) of some Englishmen from Kent," attacks Dover [7.18(39)]. Orderic will lay the blame on Norman oppression, but William of Jumièges stresses the duke's innocence. So Eustace and the wily English scheme, "while the victorious king was staying in Normandy, with his zeal for good works, in his usual upright way increasing his reputation for devotion and gracing his beloved homeland with his beloved presence" (*patriam sibi gratissimam gratissima illustrans presentia*). These words of praise offer the king a pious alibi for any trouble brewing in England. Perhaps William of Jumièges is also encouraging his duke to remember Normandy and not let England drain his time and affection.

For the chronicler, the conquered English are traitors because they plot to overthrow their new master [7.19(40)]. The Conqueror leaves Normandy to his son Robert (Curthose) and returns to England, where "again he found many of these people whose fickle hearts a treasonous plotting [*preuaricatrix conspiratio*] had turned away from loyalty to him." The *Gesta*'s language keeps stressing English treachery as the conquered conspire to reclaim their own country. William of Jumièges even insinuates that these bandits (*latrunculi*) are unchristian when they intrigue to surprise knights who are hurrying barefoot to church at the beginning of Lent. The English rebels panic "after the detection of their schemes, treacherously hostile to God" (*detectis Deo contrariis eorum perfidie machinis*), and they hide out to wait for Svein, king of the Danes, whom they have summoned to their aid. The *Gesta* does not hint that this is an old Norman trick, but rather continues to attach the language of treachery to "perfidious" English who try all means possible to resist the Conqueror. So, too, the rebels send envoys to York "to expose their luckless contrivance of folly." Their acts are "brash," as the results show, when the Normans retaliate by slaughtering everyone, even non-combatants, children, and old people in the city to which the rebels flee. English resistance brings all manner of pestilence upon the land, as when two sons of Harold return from Ireland with reinforcements, "like the most savage pirates, wiping out the country's population by fire and rapine" [7.20(41)].

The *Gesta* contrives a powerful contrast [7.21(42)]. On the one hand, there are the English rebels, whose "madness" has plunged them into "ruinous conspiracies" and whose "ill-conceived rashness" has ultimately led them to piracy along remote coasts. On the other, there is King William, whose wisdom moved him to build "very safe strongholds at strategic sites, which he fortified with elite military garrisons and with an abundant force of mercenaries." The book ends here with the very next sentence, in a burst of alliterative applause:

> Finally *for a little while* the storm of wars and rebellions are quiet. Now he masterfully controls the reins over the whole English monarchy, and prosperously appropriates its glory.

> (Tandem bellorum ac seditionum tempestate *parumper* conquiescente, iam totius Anglice monarchie et habenas potentius temperat, et gloria prosperius potitur.)

The proviso, "for a little while," is Orderic's addition, inserted not only because he wrote decades later, when he could see how short-lived was the peace, but also because his vision of Norman history argued against a tranquil conclusion. But William of Jumièges gamely tries to end his story on a grand note.

William's hope rests on a foundation of quicksand. In his epilogue the chronicler bids farewell to King William, repeating the popular pun on *angeli* and *Angli*: "So I wish that the devout and orthodox king himself under the protection of the angels control the English happily, subdue them bravely, and govern them justly." Then he turns to William's son Robert, heir to the duchy, to continue the history of Norman dukes, hoping that Robert, then in the bloom of youth, will prove a proper successor to his ancestors in his virtue as in his name. For the story of the Norman dukes has come full circle from the first Robert, the Christian name taken by Rollo at his baptism, to this Robert, the Conqueror's son.

William of Jumièges never continued the history to encompass Robert's reign. Perhaps the monk died before he could fulfill this promise. But if he did live longer, he may have lost his appetite for further writing, as Robert's rebellion against his father subverted the desired cycle, leaving no closure to William's tale.[52] Later Norman historians, Orderic and Robert of Torigni and Wace among them, will see the irony in the bonds that unite Robert/Rollo

---

[52] Shopkow, *History and Community*, 90.

with Robert I, Northman with Norman. Although William of Jumièges quit his *Gesta* before he had to acknowledge these ties, he probably perceived them well enough. And though he wishes to encourage the dukes with reports of their piety, explaining lapses into barbarism as responses to the strife that envelops them, the lapses eventually overwhelm his narrative. Presumably, the Normans of William's day justified their behavior by blaming perfidious neighbors. Time and again William tries to believe that argument himself. But even as William writes his history beyond Dudo's chronological scope, Dudo's damning patterns surface more and more. William is not a profound analyst. Yet in the end, could he have witnessed the last years of the Conqueror or the beginning of Robert's reign and still kept some semblance of optimism?

Only in the immediate afterglow of conquest do Normans produce truly optimistic histories. And even then it is a rare enthusiast who can write a persuasively upbeat account, like Geoffrey Malaterra's on the subjugation of Sicily. The Conquest of England naturally creates the largest share of such panegyric, of which the *Carmen de Hastingae Proelio* ("Song of the Battle of Hastings") and *Gesta Guillelmi* ("Story of William") by William of Poitiers are good examples.[53] Their surface narratives justify Norman aggression and rejoice at Norman victory. Some observers of the Bayeux Tapestry would include it, too, in this group. But in their own ways, all three of these works document the Normans' ties to paganism and treachery.

If the editors of the Oxford texts are correct, the *Carmen* is our earliest literary record of the Conquest, written perhaps within two years following the battle of Hastings.[54] The heavily rhetorical "Song," with its elegiac couplets following a proem in hexameters, shows the influence of Carolingian verse and so reveals its grounding in the same literary tradition that produced

---

[53] *The Carmen de Hastingae Proelio of Guy Bishop of Amiens*, ed. and trans. Frank Barlow (Oxford, 1999), which replaces the edition by Catherine Morton and Hope Muntz (Oxford, 1972); *The Gesta Guillelmi of William of Poitiers*, ed. R. H. C. Davis and Marjorie Chibnall (Oxford, 1998).

[54] Though R. H. C. Davis ["The *Carmen de Hastingae Proelio*," *English Historical Review* 93 (1978), 241–61; reprinted in R. H. C. Davis, *From Alfred the Great to Stephen* (London and Rio Grande, Ohio, 1991), 79–100] argued that the *Carmen* was a twelfth-century literary exercise, produced c. 1125–c. 1135, the *Carmen*'s editors, Morton and Muntz concluded that it was written "at least before 1072 and very probably before the autumn of 1067" (xix). The question has provoked lively debate, as evidenced by the discussion led by R. H. C. Davis and L. J. Engels, in *Battle* 2 (1980), 1–20. Elisabeth M. C. van Houts ["Latin Poetry and the Anglo-Norman Court 1066–1135: The *Carmen de Hastingae Proelio*," *Journal of Medieval History* 15 (March 1989), 39–62, at p. 55, n. 45] concurred with Morton and Muntz, finding that "the *Carmen* must have been written at the latest in September or October 1067." For the history of this controversy, see pp. xxiv–xl in the edition of Frank Barlow, who also concluded that Bishop Guy wrote the *Carmen* soon after Eustace attacked Dover in the autumn of 1067.

Dudo. Its author, "neither a Norman nor a lover of Normans," was almost certainly Guy of Amiens, born in Ponthieu, a county traditionally hostile to Normandy.[55] So it may be a significant detail, when the *Carmen* describes the Norman battle-line at Hastings, that Guy reverses the left and right sides, as if he were watching from the English vantage point. Still, he writes to win the favor of the new king, whose wife he came to serve as chaplain.[56]

This complex mix of background and motives leads Guy to reveal an array of feelings about his nominal hero, who is Caesar to Harold's Pompey, with all the ambiguity that Lucan's epic had provided these Roman combatants. At some moments he takes pains to conceal a tactical blunder, like the duke's folly in allowing the late-arriving English to cut off his exit from the peninsula where he had stationed his troops.[57] Occasionally he even shows delight in cunning, as when the Normans trick the English into surrendering London after the battle of Hastings.[58] But at other points he offers up provocative details about a character whose flaws he seems eager to expose.[59]

William of Poitiers, formerly a knight and then chaplain to Duke William, wrote his *Gesta Guillelmi* between 1071 and 1078, shortly after William of Jumièges completed the *Gesta Normannorum Ducum*.[60] Readers from both his own day and the present have judged William of Poitiers "essentially a

---

55 Morton and Muntz, *Carmen*, xlii.
56 Orderic Vitalis (*Ecclesiastical History* IV.9) identifies Guy as "most eminent among the clergy who served her spiritual needs," when she traveled from Normandy to England for her coronation in 1068. By then, writes Orderic, Guy "had already put in verse the battle between Harold and William." Perhaps this chaplaincy was Guy's reward for producing the *Carmen*. For an explanation of the Caesar/Pompey motif at lines 365 ff., see Morton and Muntz, ed., *Carmen*, xxxvii. Chapter Three, below, discusses more fully its use in the *Gesta Roberti Wiscardi* by William of Apulia, who likewise identifies his Norman hero with Lucan's despotic Caesar. Concerning motives that may have driven Guy to write the *Carmen*, see Morton and Muntz (*Carmen*, xxv), who suggest that Guy wished to bring peace between the feuding King William and Count Eustace of Boulogne; and Elisabeth van Houts ("Latin Poetry," 55–56), who has proposed that Guy dedicated the poem to Lanfranc, King William's trusted advisor, in the hope that Lanfranc would mediate the strained relations between Bishop Guy and Pope Alexander II.
57 Morton and Muntz (*Carmen*, xxxvii) cite this passage as an example of Guy's "literary evasion," as he resorts to weighty rhetoric whenever he wants to muddy the waters over problematic episodes.
58 G. A. Loud, "*Gens Normannorum*," 112 cites this episode as the one that marks the *Carmen* "in this if in nothing else part of the mainstream of the Norman tradition."
59 Morton and Muntz, ed., *Carmen*, xli–xlii. Guy sometimes makes tactless references to William and even makes William's enemy, Eustace II of Boulogne, its "second hero" [xxii and xxxvii, following Frank Barlow, "The *Carmen de Hastingae Proelio*," in *The Norman Conquest and Beyond* (London, 1983), 200]. If recent editors are correct in their early dating of the *Carmen*, King William and Count Eustace had not yet reconciled when Guy was writing.
60 On William of Poitiers and his *Gesta*, see the introduction to the *Gesta Guillelmi*, ed. Davis and Chibnall, xv–xlvii.

propagandist rather than a historian, who carefully altered earlier material less favourable to the duke."[61] Perhaps he considered himself more an epic poet like Lucan or Vergil, with a license to shape heroic material. Even though he protests that he writes only the truth, his carefully embedded assurance of his master's perfection contradicts any claim to objectivity (1.20):

> Poets were allowed to conceive, from their own inmost being, the wars to which their pens gave birth, and to expand on the facts however they liked by ranging over the fields of creative imagination. But we will purely praise the duke or king, to whom nothing impure was ever beautiful, never deviating a single step from the path of truth.

> (Parturire suo pectore bella quae calamo ederentur poetis licebat, atque amplificare utcumque cognita per campos figmentorum diuagando. Nos ducem, siue regem, cui nunquam impure quid fuit pulchrum, pure laudabimus, nusquam a ueritatis limite passu uno delirantes.)

William of Poitiers is a partisan whose unswerving aim is homage to his king. "We desire that he be praised by the constant favor of the people," affirms the poet about the man he describes as *prudens, justus, pius ac fortis* ("valiant, just, devout, and brave"), a hero with the eloquence of Cicero (2.12).[62] Elsewhere throughout his *Gesta Guillelmi*, the writer emphasizes issues of trust, fidelity, and legitimacy. In doing so, he reverses the Norman myths, changing both events and interpretations to favor Duke William, making him a principled man beset by treacherous foes.

Duke William makes his first appearance in the *Gesta Guillelmi*, at least as the text has come down to us, as an armed knight riding to the rescue (1.6). By beginning with the hero's adolescence and passing quickly over the years before his adulthood, William of Poitiers neatly avoids the question of the boy's legitimacy, though the problem haunts the book, as we see in the preoccupation with the justice of William's rule in Normandy and the legality of his claim to England. Lawlessness marked William's minority, when the boy confronted villains unrestrained by the order and piety that a strong Christian ruler should enforce (1.7):

> They were all neglecting the right, eager to avoid no wrong.

> (Fas quidem negligebant omnes, nefas nullum devitare curabant.)

Such men naturally resist the temperate laws that the duke imposes when he reaches maturity, laws that will end the slaughter, burning, and rapine (1.6). Norman historians like Dudo, Orderic, and Wace would argue that this is Norman territory in its usual state of affairs. But William of Poitiers turns the

---

61 Morton and Muntz, *Carmen*, xviii n. 2, agreeing with the conclusions of Raymonde Foreville, *GG*, xlii–xliv.

62 Compare, for instance, this central passage on the duke's piety and justice: 1.47–48.

story around by claiming that the duke restores order at Val-ès-Dunes and thus brings the Normans back to their civilized condition under his authority.

Hereafter, for the rest of Part One, this *Gesta*'s hero continues his struggle against wrong. The emphasis is quite different from that of the *Gesta Normannorum Ducum*. Although both writers focus on moral issues, William of Jumièges presses the duke to behave well while William of Poitiers insists that he does, in fact, always act on the side of justice.[63] The vocabulary of the *Gesta Guillelmi* relentlessly continues this theme. The forces of good clash with the forces of evil. Men faithful to justice and the feudal bond struggle against the unfaithful, while the duke's probity ever confronts his enemies' turpitude. Terms like *amicitia, fides*, and *justitia* recur, as the good duke and king forges peaceful order out of turmoil. When King Henry withdraws from his union with William, for instance, one chapter contains eight forms of *amicus* or *amicitia/inimicitia*, along with other assorted terms for law and its opposite (1.13). This passage concludes with the assertion that the king "unjustly alienated himself by his injustice." This is far from an isolated example. Consider Geoffrey of Mayenne's perfidy (1.33; 40), Count William of Arques' false oaths of fealty (1.23), and the defense of the duke's attack on Brittany (1.42). These episodes explicitly contrast the villains' disruptive evil with the duke's love of justice. Part One concludes by stressing these qualities. Admired by the Roman emperor and champion of Byzantium, Duke William earns kingly stature within the larger European community even before the Conquest.

The use of ethical and legal terms increases as William of Poitiers presses the duke's legal claim to England. The *Gesta Guillelmi* lays the groundwork, first establishing the legality of Edward the Confessor's title to the throne (1.14), then emphasizing Edward's choice of Duke William as his heir, a decision witnessed and solemnly confirmed by Harold (1.41–42).[64] But Part Two opens with the crowning of Harold, in a work heavy with villains, the most vile.[65] Like a melodrama, this *Gesta* has aligned the forces of good and evil against one another. So when Duke William meets Harold's envoy before the battle of Hastings, the *Gesta* reviews the treaties, the broken promises, and the illegality of Harold's claim (2.11). Against such a usurper, the duke

---

[63] See van Houts, *GND* 1, liv–lv, on the writing of William of Jumièges, whose chapters often have a formulaic ending that reinforces the moral lesson he wishes to convey.

[64] William of Poitiers is drawing on claims that Duke William and his agents had already articulated. See G. Garnett, "Coronation and Propaganda: Some Implications of the Norman Claim to the Throne of England in 1066," *TRHS*, 5th ser., 36 (1986), 91–116; and E. M. C. van Houts, "Historiography and Hagiography," 233–51.

[65] 1.3–4; 2.8. Cf. the similar treatment of Harold in the *Carmen*, which attacks him as *rex . . . sceleratus*, "a wicked king [who] readies treacherous weapons (*perfida tela*) for a brother's destruction" (lines 129–30). "A jealous Cain," he kills his brother, Tostig (line 137), having waged a "worse than civil war" (*plus quam ciuile . . . / Bellum*) against him, like Lucan's combatants (cf. Pharsalia 1.1).

can only win a just victory. The *Gesta* reinforces this theme by using a legal metaphor to describe the beginning of the decisive battle. The Normans strike first just as the prosecution attacks first in a court of law (2.17). And when Harold falls, the *Gesta* caps its indictment with a counter-eulogy that exults, "You will never wear the crown you stole *perfide*" ("treacherously;" 2.25). This direct address condemning the villain's corpse acts much like Dudo's verse apostrophes, interjecting ethical commentary of high drama. It is a technique that William of Poitiers has used before, in reproaching the perjuring Harold (1.46), for instance, or in urging England to accept her Norman lord (1.32).

William's coronation "in the sacrosanct solemnity of the Lord's day, 25 December 1066," assures that his heirs will inherit England, which the Conqueror rules by hereditary right and by the law of war (2.30). The crowning of the lawful king also brings England the corollary of justice, peace (2.33, 35), which William's rule has already conferred on Normandy (1.10, 30, 59; cf. 2.45), and redoubles the honor that the duke has conveyed upon his people. At the same time it confirms God's approval of the Norman aggression against England, which William of Poitiers has gone to great pains to justify by stressing divine inspiration (2.1), papal support (2.3), Norman valor at Hastings, and especially the justice of the Conqueror's claim.

The Conqueror himself is a Christian epic hero for whom William of Poitiers repeatedly interjects praise into the narrative. Near the end of the first part, for example, he describes the duke's lifelong piety, orthodoxy, and zeal against heresy, all passions that qualify him to be God's chosen king (1.47–51). Inspired by his father's example, Duke William understands that only the heavenly realm endures. Like his forefathers he therefore builds and supports monasteries until Normandy rivals late antique Egypt in the number and sanctity of her holy establishments. Duke William spares and comforts the poor and weak (1.32, 48); he shows clemency to his foes (1.25, 28, 38; 2.25). He works tirelessly, not out of personal ambition, but for love of his *patria*, her people, and Christ their savior (2.28, 48).

The duke's worldly talents complement his spiritual inclinations. He is eloquent (2.12), tireless in the performance of his duty (1.16–17), and fearless in the face of danger (1.30; 2.10–12, 22). He earns the admiration of his own nobles (1.21) as well as kings and counts, emperor and pope (1.11, 13, 59; 2.3). Occasionally William of Poitiers reaches beyond stock panegyric, hinting at the Conqueror's unique vigor. The rash courage of his youth (1.11–12) mellows into the meticulous planning and decisive action of a man who knows that his cause is just (1.25, 33, 34; 2.24).

The duke's self-confidence surfaces again and again during the English campaign: in his jaunty warning to a captured spy (2.4) and in his eagerness to cross the Channel, even in the face of contrary winds and shipwreck (2.6). He encourages the fearful by bringing out holy relics. The *Gesta*'s breathless language here conveys a sense of the man's exuberance as he relishes a meal at sea, with resinous wine, while his ship speeds to England (2.7). After landing at Pevensey (2.8), William joins the small scouting party, returning on foot because of the harsh terrain and even carrying the hauberk of strong William Fitz-Osbern (2.9). Burning with energy, he impersonates his own seneschal so that he can speak directly to Harold's legate and offer the king a contest of single combat (2.11–12). And as he dresses for battle, he starts to put on his hauberk backwards (*sinistra conuersio*), an apparent portent that would terrify anyone else (2.14). The duke only laughs at the meaningless accident, changing bad omen to good by the force of his indomitable will.[66]

But more often the *Gesta Guillelmi* offers standard panegyric, altering its sources to gloss over the duke's errors or to magnify his accomplishments. William of Poitiers may have had before him the *Carmen de Hastingae Proelio* in elegiac couplets. If so, he managed to write a more heroic *Gesta* in prose that contains echoes of Caesar, Cicero, Sallust, and Juvenal, and especially the epic poets Vergil, Lucan, and Statius.[67] His classical references serve to demonstrate the duke's superiority to Caesar or Achilles, Agamemnon or Xerxes, Cicero or Pompey, Titus or Marius, Aeneas or Theseus.[68] He flatters the duke's advisors by comparing them favorably to the Roman senate (2.1), while he elevates the Conquest by likening Harold to Turnus or Hector (2.22), formidable foes of Aeneas and Achilles.

All these epic allusions hammer home a simple message, without the irony of Dudo or the subversion that we will see in William of Apulia. William of Poitiers plays the Roman authors straight. He takes particular delight in comparing his hero's rapid success in England with Caesar's failed British expedition (2.39–40), but the Trojan War and Roman expansion provide irresistible parallels, too (2.26).[69] After all, Agamemnon took only one city, and that by guile after a ten-year siege. Rome obtained her power and wealth by winning one city at a time over many years, while William and his Normans conquered all the English cities in a single battle, one worthy of Statius or

---

66 Like Julius Caesar, Duke William takes no stock in bad omens; cf. Suetonius, *Divus Julius*, 59.

67 Foreville, ed., xxxviii–xliii and notes to the text: 1.10, 13, 18, 19, 22, 30, 33, 44; 2.15, 32, 42. William would not have known all these authors first-hand, but Loud has shown how well he knew Caesar and Sallust ("*Gens Normannorum*," 114). See also Shopkow, *History and Community*, 132–33, 155–56. Orderic Vitalis observes that William of Poitiers imitated Sallust (*EH* 2, p. 258).

68 On this familiar "outdoing topos," see Ernst R. Curtius, *European Literature and the Latin Middle Ages*, trans. Willard Trask (New York, 1953), 162–65). For William of Poitiers' use of this topos and Orderic Vitalis' responses, see Roger D. Ray, "Orderic Vitalis and William of Poitiers: A Monastic Re-interpretation of William the Conqueror," *Revue belge de philologie et d'histoire* 50, no. 4 (1972), 1116–27.

69 Not surprisingly, comparisons of William with Julius Caesar recur in Anglo-Norman poetry. See van Houts, "Latin Poetry," 41–42, 48–49, 56–57.

Vergil, who would have sung the truth and placed William among the gods (2.22). Rome would have rejoiced to serve such a master (2.32).

Comparisons with other Golden Ages only serve to highlight the uniquely pro-Norman view of William of Poitiers. The descriptions of his hero are especially cloying. But perhaps the Norman audience would have found even less to recognize in descriptions of themselves as civilized and civilizing (1.59). Here is a Normandy dearer to the new king than all his recently acquired wealth (2.32, 45), especially precious because of its upright people, faithful to their earthly princes, devoted to Christianity (2.43). This deliberately contradicts the usual view of an unruly populace who need to be kept in close rein by their rulers. The *Gesta Guillelmi* also presents its hero as part of a greater movement of "Norman fighting-men [who] possess Apulia, have conquered Sicily, defend Constantinople, instill fear in Cairo."[70] But this pan-Norman view rings false as well, particularly since this *Gesta* focuses so squarely on the Conqueror, to the exclusion of other Normans, and on England, even to the diminution of Normandy. In the *Gesta Guillelmi* we see the center of gravity moving toward England and away from the duchy.

Maybe the *Gesta Guillelmi* served its author well, ingratiating him further into the favor of his lord. Surely it met an urgent need in King William and his Normans, who sought "legitimisation and justification" for their Conquest and required "abstract moralisations to bury any sense of guilt or shame."[71] But in the long run, this work had little success. For his edition of 1619, André Duchesne found only a single manuscript, whose beginning and end were missing, but even that manuscript is now lost. Surely its classicizing language is no more difficult than Dudo's, whose text survived more robustly.[72] Did the *Gesta*'s toadying, then, ring so false that it had limited appeal beyond the immediate circle of first-generation conquerors? Some signs indicate that later readers did find this text incredible. While Orderic Vitalis used it as a source, for instance, he also showed his disapproval by consistently deflating its panegyric.[73] Today critics acknowledge the *Gesta*

---

[70] 2.32; cf. 1.59. Similarly the *Carmen de Hastingae Proelio* (lines 259–60) has Duke William rouse his troops before Hastings by recalling the exploits of Normans in Apulia, Calabria, and Sicily.

[71] Elisabeth van Houts has identified this need as "the overwhelming reaction of the first generation of Normans" after the Conquest. "The Memory of 1066 in Written and Oral Traditions," in *Anglo-Norman Studies* 19, ed. Christopher Harper-Bill (Woodbridge, 1997), 167–79, at p. 176.

[72] The complete *Carmen de Hastingae Proelio*, whose verse is similarly rhetorical, also survived in just one manuscript, discovered only in the nineteenth century. A second manuscript preserves the *Carmen*'s opening lines. On the transmission of the *Carmen*, see Morton and Muntz, *Carmen*, lix–lxvi. On the reception of the histories by William of Poitiers and William of Jumièges, see Leah Shopkow, *History and Community*, 222–31.

[73] See van Houts, *GND* 1, lxxiv–lxxv, on the way that Orderic's redaction tones down this *Gesta*'s language and enthusiasm.

Guillelmi as an important source for the Conquest of England, but few admire its elegant classicism, monotonous fawning, and nervous self-righteousness.[74]

The Norman conquest of England inspired at least one work of a different sort. The Bayeux Tapestry depicts events from Harold's journey to Normandy, perhaps in 1064, through Harold's death at Hastings and the flight of English combatants before the victorious Normans. Most students of the Tapestry now agree that Bishop Odo of Bayeux, half-brother of William the Conqueror, commissioned or sponsored the work at some point between 1066 and 1082, but that an Anglo-Saxon artist designed it, with Anglo-Saxon embroiderers stitching it in the workshop of Saint Augustine's Canterbury.[75] Odo's presence in this version of the Conquest is so prominent that commentators have imagined the Conqueror's own discomfort if he ever saw the Tapestry.[76]

Many other elements of the Tapestry, in fact, may have disturbed the new king. Not least of these is the elusive meaning of pictures that demand interpretation. While the Latin inscriptions above the scenes often name the actors or describe their activity, they do not report their conversation, attribute motivation, or judge whose cause is right. Viewers must supply all this for themselves. In the opening scene, for instance, Harold and King Edward confer before Harold sails across the Channel (Fig. 1).[77] Norman partisans have

---

74 Ray, "Orderic and William," 1117.

75 Nicholas Brooks argued for a Latin text provided by Odo or his agent: N. P. Brooks and H. E. Walker, "The Authority and Interpretation of the Bayeux Tapestry," *Battle* 1 (1979), 1–34 and 191–99; reprinted in *The Study of the Bayeux Tapestry*, ed. Richard Gameson (Woodbridge, 1997), 63–92. Andrew Bridgeford has most recently challenged that view: "Was Count Eustace II of Boulogne the Patron of the Bayeux Tapestry?" *Journal of Medieval History* 25 (1999), 155–85. Bridgeford suggests that Eustace commissioned the Tapestry as a conciliatory gift for Odo. For the evidence for English design and embroidery of the Tapestry, see Richard Gameson, "The Origin, Art, and Message of the Bayeux Tapestry," in *The Study of the Bayeux Tapestry*, ed. Gameson, 157–211. For the argument that the Tapestry originated in Bayeux, see Wolfgang Grape, *The Bayeux Tapestry: Monument to A Norman Triumph*, trans. David Britt (Munich and New York, 1994), 44–54. The essential edition is still *The Bayeux Tapestry: A Comprehensive Survey*, ed. Sir Frank M. Stenton *et al.* (London, 1965; 2nd ed.). Richard David Wissolik has produced a valuable bibliography of scholarship on the Tapestry: *The Bayeux Tapestry: A Critical, Annotated Bibliography with Cross-References and Summary Outlines of Scholarship 1729–1990*, 2nd ed., Scholars Bibliography Series, vol. 3 (Greensburg, Pa., 1990). To trace the history of this scholarship, see Shirley Ann Brown, *The Bayeux Tapestry: History and Bibliography* (Woodbridge, 1988).

76 H. E. J. Cowdrey, "Towards an Interpretation of the Bayeux Tapestry," *Anglo-Norman Studies* 10 (Woodbridge, 1988), 53; reprinted in *The Study of the Bayeux Tapestry*, ed. Gameson, 93–110, at p. 97.

77 As David J. Bernstein [*The Mystery of the Bayeux Tapestry* (Chicago, 1986), 115] notes, "The scenes of Harold's adventures in Normandy are among the most enigmatic in the Tapestry."

Fig. 1. Edward Rex *with Harold and friend.*

assumed that Edward is charging Harold to promise the English crown to Duke William.[78] But perhaps the king is trying to dissuade the earl from negotiating with the crafty Norman, who holds English hostages whom Harold hopes to retrieve. This is one English view.[79] The Latin announces only, "EDWARD REX" and is otherwise silent about the earl's audience with the king. Whatever his intention, Harold meets disaster when he disembarks on the continent, as Count Guy of Ponthieu takes him into custody, releasing him only to men dispatched by the duke.

Likewise, in the famous scene where Harold, now detained in Normandy by William, swears an oath on two reliquaries, we cannot know precisely what he is swearing. Perhaps he is freely promising the throne to William, as Normans would later claim. On the other hand, he may be acting under duress, swearing allegiance to William in order to win his freedom. If this is so, then the earl finds himself in the uneasy position of conflicting loyalties to Norman duke and English king. The following scenes suggest as much, with Harold approaching Edward in a pose of contrition (Fig. 10). But there is no text to verbalize the author's intention. Some viewers will argue that

---

[78] William of Jumièges [7.13(31)] and William of Poitiers (1.41; 2.12) report this story.

[79] The monk Eadmer presents this scenario in his *History of Recent Events in England*, completed by 1115: *Eadmeri Historia Novorum in Anglia*, ed. M. Rule (RS, 1884), 6–8. The episode does not occur at all in the *Anglo-Saxon Chronicle*. Wace reports both versions, claiming that he has found conflicting reports and cannot judge which is correct (*Rou* 3. 5583–604).

Harold is a conniving perjurer, while others may find him the pawn of William's ambitions or simply the victim of ill winds and bad luck.

So, too, the observer must evaluate William and the Norman cause. The traditional view argues that the Tapestry is a Norman product that proclaims Harold's duplicity and justifies the Norman Conquest.[80] In recent years, however, critics have cited ambiguities in the Tapestry's central narrative that invite alternate interpretation. Some have also looked more carefully at the figures in the top and bottom borders, which the traditional view deemed merely decorative.[81] A few observers have found a pro-English counter-narrative in the alternating pairs of birds and beasts, but especially in the border scenes that allude to animal fables known since antiquity and popularly associated with Aesop.[82] At the very least, these provocative scenes invite viewers to take a stand on the justice of the Norman claims to England.

For expressing dissident views of the oppressed, animal fables have served as a particularly apt vehicle ever since their earliest appearance. The ancients thought that Aesop himself was a slave who invented these fables for social and political commentary that he dared not speak directly. That legend survived into the Middle Ages and continued to articulate the possibilities inherent in this distinctive form of discourse. Widely disseminated in school texts and sermons, fables conveyed moral lessons, and sometimes hazardous opinions, to ordinary people as well as the educated elite. By ancient and medieval convention alike, these tales harbored a deeper meaning beneath the entertaining narrative. To grasp this meaning and its profound impact upon a medieval audience, as Edward Wheatley has argued, "we must be able to

---

80 For support of this view, see Cowdrey, "Interpretation of the Bayeux Tapestry;" Suzanne Lewis, *The Rhetoric of Power in the Bayeux Tapestry* (Cambridge, 1999), especially 30–73. Likewise, J. Bard McNulty [*The Narrative Art of the Bayeux Tapestry Master*, AMS Studies in the Middle Ages, 13 (New York, 1988)] vigorously rejects any notion of a pro-English subtext in the Tapestry, insisting (p. 77) that it presents "an Odonian view of the Conquest," while Daniel Terkla ["Cut on the Norman Bias: Fabulous Borders and Visual Glosses in the Bayeux Tapestry," *Word and Image* 11 (1995), 264–90] finds both a Norman bias and a fluctuating portrayal of Harold, who is not always a villain.

81 McNulty (*Narrative Art*, 22–23) demonstrates the fallacy in this assumption, as he highlights scenes where the border clearly complements the main narrative or where figures point to details in the margins. For the history of this debate, see Bernstein, *Mystery of the Bayeux Tapestry*, especially 128–35.

82 Bernstein, *Mystery of the Bayeux Tapestry*, 124–35, shows how these animals in the borders can subvert any pro-Norman message. Likewise, Bernard S. Bachrach, "Some Observations on the Bayeux Tapestry," *Cithara* 27 (1987), 5–28, at p. 6 argues that the Tapestry's "pictorial narrative . . . may well have had an anti-Norman double meaning." The fabulist Aesop probably lived in the sixth century B.C.E. Fable collections circulated under his name throughout antiquity. Most medieval collections derive from the Latin works of Phaedrus, who wrote under Augustus and Tiberius in the first century C.E. Notes to Phaedrus here refer to this edition: *Babrius and Phaedrus*, ed. and trans. Ben Edwin Perry, Loeb Classical Library (Cambridge, Mass., 1965).

imagine an era during which fable was taken seriously as a vehicle for social, political, and religious communication."[83]

Of the nine Aesopic fables clearly identified in the Tapestry, seven cluster near the beginning, in the section depicting Harold's journey to Normandy as an emissary for his brother-in-law, King Edward the Confessor (Figs. 2–7). The main storyline depicted immediately above them shows Harold embarking from England, sailing toward Normandy, but carried by strong winds to the shore controlled by Guy of Ponthieu, who will have him seized and taken prisoner until Duke William "liberates" him. William parleys with Harold before taking him on a lengthy military operation against Conan, count of Brittany. On their return to Rouen, Harold swears fealty to William, then sets sail for England. As Harold's adventure begins, the border directly below the opening of this storyline presents the seven fables commonly identified as the fox and the crow, the wolf and the lamb, the pregnant bitch, the wolf and the crane, the wolf who reigned, the mouse and the frog, and the wolf and the goat. H. E. J. Cowdrey has summarized the impact of this fable sequence: "The predominant theme is the hidden danger present to the unwary by the crafty and deceitful. There is no question of specific references from the margin to events above in the main story. But the message seems clear: fair appearances like those of Harold are deceptive."[84]

Is Harold the "crafty and deceitful" figure, who will trick the Normans, falsely swearing fealty to William and promising him the throne upon Edward's death, only to snatch it himself? This is the official Norman position, which Odo would have commissioned the embroiderers to represent. But the symbolism of these fables may have suggested an altogether different message to the conquered peoples, both those who designed and embroidered them and those who viewed the finished Tapestry.[85] When we interpret the wolf as a code for Norman, we see a pattern of images proclaiming the lawlessness of Norman aggression.

First consider the scene immediately preceding this sequence. As Harold feasts, taking his last meal on land before sailing toward Normandy, in the

---

[83] *Mastering Aesop: Medieval Education, Chaucer, and his Followers* (Gainesville, Fla., 2000), 3. This book begins with an incident in thirteenth-century Padua when the recitation of an Aesopic fable, interpreted and re-interpreted by successive hearers, led to the imprisonment and decapitation of fable-tellers by a suspicious tyrant.

[84] Cowdrey, "Interpretation of the Bayeux Tapestry," 56. Lewis (*Rhetoric of Power*, 60) repeats this general message: "All the stories deal with trickery, deceit, betrayal, and greed, without exception exemplified by the wrongful appropriation of territory or food." But the viewer must identify the guilty party, English or Norman.

[85] Unlettered viewers would have recognized these ancient fables that passed orally from generation to generation. For the literate, there seems to have been at least one English manuscript which Marie de France translated in the late twelfth century. H. Chefneux, "Les fables dans la tapisserie de Bayeux," *Romania* 60 (1934), 1–35, 153–94.

Fig. 2. Harold prays and feasts . . .

Fig. 4. Harold crosses the Channel . . .

Fig. 3. . . . then embarks with hound and hawk.

Fig. 5. . . . and reaches the French coast.

Fig. 6. Guy apprehends Harold . . .

border below him, two wolves lick their paws (Fig. 2).[86] They may represent the Normans, anticipating their own feast on Harold and the English. Exactly following these wolves in the lower border is a scene commonly assumed to represent the Aesopic fable of the fox and the crow (Fig. 3). In the fable, the fox has tricked the bird into speaking, so that the cheese in her beak will fall into the waiting mouth of the fox. Indeed, the embroiderers have left the cheese suspended in mid-air, midway between beak and fox's jaw. But is it here, as in the usual versions of the fable, a fox that waits to devour the cheese? At least one observer, looking closely at the birds and beasts of the Tapestry, noted that this animal has a wolf's tail.[87] If we take the lupine fox to represent a wily Norman, we find the Norman awaiting a tasty morsel that he has tricked away from its rightful owner.

The Tapestry illustrators thought this fable so meaningful that they inserted it two more times within the narrative of Harold's journey to Normandy.[88] At its second appearance, as Harold rides in William's train against one of the duke's vassals, the fox has already caught the cheese (Fig. 8). Here Harold, and England, seem as good as lost to Norman power. But when this fable recurs for the final time, now in the upper border, the bird has

---

[86] Yapp identifies these as wolves, since they are shaggier than dogs: W. Brunsdon Yapp, "Animals in Medieval Art: The Bayeux Tapestry as an Example," *Journal of Medieval History* 13 (1987), 15–75, at p. 48.

[87] Yapp, "Animals in Medieval Art," 36.

[88] Bernstein has written a fine analysis of this fable's meaning within the Tapestry narrative, showing how it frames Harold's journey to Normandy. *Mystery of the Bayeux Tapestry*, 133–34.

Fig. 7. as animals in the lower border stalk and kill their prey.

the cheese (Fig. 10). At this precise point in the central narrative, Harold has returned safely to England and rides off to meet King Edward. For the moment, Harold is free again, and the English still possess England.

Next in the fable sequence comes a meeting of wolf and lamb at a stream (Fig. 3). In Phaedrus's version of the fable, the first in his collection and so immediately following his disclaimer that these are "just made-up stories," the wolf berates the lamb for muddying his water supply. In fact, the wolf himself stands upstream from the lamb, so if anyone is fouling another's water, it is he. The innocent lamb in the Tapestry drinks peacefully, while the larger wolf stares out at him, panting. Between them, the waves appear to flow toward the lamb and away from the wolf, testimony to the falseness of the wolf's pretext for anger.[89] In Phaedrus, the lamb at first stymies the wolf by pointing out this evidence. The wolf, motivated by hunger rather than truth, makes one more false claim, likewise easily refuted by the lamb, before simply pouncing on its victim and tearing it to pieces. The embroiderers of the Tapestry are warning that Duke William will bring charges, patently false, against the peaceable English, and finding no just cause for his aggression, will attack and devour them in any case.

The next scene in the lower border portrays the fable of the pregnant bitch (Fig. 4). One dog has secured another's permission to deliver her puppies in the other's kennel, but when the owner returns to reclaim her home, she

---

[89] Yapp, "Animals in Medieval Art," 36, observes this movement and supposes that it contradicts the implied message. It does, however, support the story as Phaedrus tells it.

Fig. 8. The fox has the cheese.

meets a snarling brood who refuse to leave. The artisans have managed to make the displaced dog appear cowed by the four beasts who lunge out at her from their comfortable lair. Surely these yapping interlopers are the Normans, who will return Harold's graciousness with their own hostile possession of his territories. As if to clarify its meaning beyond any doubt, the Tapestry repeats this same scene (Fig. 11, in the lower border), as Duke William exhorts his troops before the Battle. The commentary here would suggest to English eyes that William is promising the Normans that they will soon hold lands that rightfully belong to another. And once the Normans with their families and retainers sit securely within English keeps, the owners can never reclaim their properties. Elisabeth van Houts has reminded us that the Conquest traumatized the conquered.[90] This fable of the dispossessed offers an image for their voiceless horror at the ongoing injustice. Against Norman might, the English were helpless, however just their cause.[91]

Following the earlier appearance of these usurping beasts, fourth in the seven-fable sequence, comes the story of the crane who extracted a bone from the wolf's throat (Fig. 4). When the bird tries to claim the promised reward, the wolf shouts, "Ingrate!" and professes incredulity that the crane expects a second reward. The real reward was the bird's survival after sticking his head in the wolf's mouth. This fable usually illustrates the folly

90 "The Trauma of 1066," *History Today* 46, no. 10 (October, 1996), 9–15.
91 Bernstein (*Mystery of the Bayeux Tapestry*, 130–31) and Terkla ("Cut on the Norman Bias," 271) interpret this fable as anti-Harold.

Fig. 9. Harold returns to England . . .

Fig. 10. . . . and approaches Edward.

Fig. 11. William addresses his army.

of dealing with treacherous people, and the sight of the docile crane placing its head in the wolf's jaws must have had a chilling effect on English observers as they watched Harold sail to the wolf's den. The order of the figures reinforces this interpretation, since the observer's eye, moving from left to right, sees the crane stepping forward to meet the waiting wolf.[92] When this fable recurs (Fig. 9), this time in the upper border just at the point when Harold touches English soil again, the figures are reversed: the wolf is standing on the left, apparently surrendering the bird's beak. Harold is home, safe, for the time being, from the wolf.[93] The border narrative punctuates this moment with the third appearance of the fox and the crow, immediately to the right of this wolf and the crane (Fig. 10). And here, too, the embroiderers have reversed the previous order of the figures, now with the wolf on the left, its mouth agape, and the crow in the right, the cheese still in its mouth.

The fifth border scene in the long introductory sequence illustrates the story about the wolf who reigned (Figs. 4 and 5). In the fable, the lion king

[92] Terkla ("Cut on the Norman Bias," 272) sees the crane as representing "William, who has done Harold the services of arming him and investing him with his English lands; the wolf, then, is Harold, who breaks these oaths and betrays William's trust in him."

[93] This repetition in particular argues against the view that the wolf represents Harold. Cowdrey ("Interpretation of the Bayeux Tapestry," 56) has suggested that the fables of the wolf and the crane, along with the crow and the fox "are well chosen to point up Harold's situation: the wolf mocks the crane for a benefit lately conferred (we recall William's recent generosity to Harold in giving him arms); proud of what he has just stolen (we recall that Harold is about to seize the crown), the black-feathered crow sits aloft eager for flattery (we shall soon see Harold in false regality) but the fox cuts him down to size."

decides to pass his power to another, and his animal subjects choose the wolf as his successor. The Tapestry shows the lion standing before a naked human figure and an assembly of eight beasts, with the wolf leading the other animals. Proposed identifications of the naked man have ranged from Adam to an ape.[94] But the general progression is clear: a wolf will receive the throne surrendered by the lion who has no progeny. A Norman viewer could assume that Harold is the new king, whose treachery brings death to his subjects, as in the fable.[95] Indeed, the fable suits this interpretation in its many details, since Harold, like the wolf, succeeds by election of his fellows, who soon meet their deaths for this choice. But an Anglo-Saxon partisan might simply read wolf as Norman, ignoring contravening details in the same way that modern viewers of the Tapestry sometimes overlook particulars that challenge their own prejudices.

The following scene is difficult to interpret, in part perhaps because it has been so extensively repaired (Fig. 5). It is supposed to be the fable of the mouse and the frog, friends who bind themselves together and go out walking. In some versions of the tale, they come upon a body of water and the frog jumps in, drowning his companion. But in later versions, the frog intentionally tricks the mouse into jumping into a river. In any case, the frog loses his life, too, in both variants, since a bird of prey dives down to kill them both once they are flailing in the water. The bird may be William, the ultimate victor against the quarreling English, who should have united to oppose Norman aggression.[96]

We are on surer ground again with the final fable in this series: a wolf and a goat confront one another (Fig. 6). In one fable, a wolf corners a goat, who pleads for the chance to sing a final prayer before the wolf devours him. But the goat uses this opportunity to call for help, and so he escapes. Just at this spot, in the scene above, Harold's ship reaches land, falling into the clutches first of Guy of Ponthieu (Fig. 6) and then of Duke William himself before he can extricate himself and hasten back to England. For the moment the goat has outwitted the wolf.[97]

---

94 Yapp, "Animals in Medieval Art," 38.

95 For this argument, see Lewis, *Rhetoric of Power*, 69; McNulty, *Narrative Art*, 27–29; and Terkla, "Cut on the Norman Bias," 273.

96 Terkla ("Cut on the Norman Bias," 273 n. 48) offers variant readings for this scene, but always makes Harold the frog, "just as I have associated him with every other negatively valenced animal in the previous fables. He can be no other: the Tapestry is decidedly biased in Edward's and William's favor."

97 McNulty (*Narrative Art*, 30) hurries past this scene without comment, perhaps unable to squeeze it into his pattern of pro-Norman commentary. Terkla ("Cut on the Norman Bias," 274), on the other hand, makes the wolf stand for both William and Guy, with the goat as Harold, whose "song" of imprisonment induces William to free him. When the wolf and goat recur in the Tapestry border [Fig. 18], Terkla reverses the roles, finding Harold the wolf as he reveals his true nature.

Fig. 12. Guy brings Harold . . .

Fig. 14. Harold and William arrive at the palace . . .

Fig. 13. . . . to meet Duke William.

Fig. 15. . . . where they parley.

Fig. 16. Horses land at Pevensey . . .

Fig. 17. . . . and the Normans gallop to Hastings.

Fig. 18. Norman knights and archers attack.

The lower border illustration here proceeds with a lively depiction of a topsy-turvy hunt, which ends with one of the hunting beasts devouring the quarry (Fig. 7). This hunting metaphor resumes in the border beneath the scene of William dispatching his messengers to Guy, to arrange for Harold's transfer to his own custody. Here the hairstyles of the hunters identify them as "unmistakably" Norman.[98] In the next scene of the main story rides Harold, with his right hand holding the reins of his prancing steed and with his left hand holding a falcon (Figs. 12 and 13). He is the very picture of the nobleman, proud and free. But directly beneath him in the border, where it immediately follows a Norman hunter with his long club, is the notorious pairing of the naked man and woman. These two face one another, she trying to shield herself, while he advances with arms outstretched and penis erect. This coded message may suggest that Harold is really only changing the appearance of his condition, while in fact he moves from one form of danger and submission to another particularly humiliating and threatening one. Soon Harold and William are meeting face to face (Figs. 14 and 15). Below them in the border a naked man lays down his axe, while above them in the upper border, on the roof of the ducal palace, a lamb extends its left foreleg to touch the outstretched paw of a sharp-clawed beast that looks suspiciously like a wolf. When the lamb parleys with the wolf, the prospects do not seem favorable to the lamb.

Here, as with the Aesopic fables, the border illustrations may harbor a dissident voice. The borders, by appearing merely decorative, become in fact

98 Bernstein, *Mystery of the Bayeux Tapestry*, 125.

a freedom zone for expressing hostility that oppressors may not notice and cannot interpret with certainty, if they do.[99] So for instance, as Norman ships sail toward England and Conquest, a hound chases a hare across the lower panel and increasingly agitated birds shriek a warning. At the moment when these ships land, as the Normans unload their war-horses, two wolves in the upper border chase a deer (Figs. 16 and 17).[100] The animals run from left to right, the direction of the Normans' relentless charge against the English.

When the Norman knights and archers themselves rush against the English foot-soldiers at Hastings, we find the wolf and the goat once more, in the border above the fray (Fig. 18). In their previous encounter in the Tapestry border (Fig. 6), the goat had escaped. But this second meeting recalls another fable in which a wolf tries to persuade a goat to descend from his cliff and enjoy the grassy pasture. In this Aesopic tale, the goat understands that the wolf is only trying to lure him down so he can gobble him up. And so he stays safely on the cliff. Yet here the wolf and goat stand on the same plane. Later Anglo-Norman historians will relate how Harold's family and friends tried to persuade him not to rush into battle with the Normans.[101] To his peril, however, Harold spurns their wise counsel. The wolf has called down the goat. Beneath this scene, in the lower panel, a wolf-like creature holds in its jaws the head and neck of a large bird, whose wings extend in struggle. This wolf, it seems, is devouring the crane at last.

When we read wolf as Norman in these border scenes, we may be seeing the Tapestry as the conquered people saw it. Allusive and ambivalent, the Aesopic fables in the Bayeux Tapestry offer one meaning to a Norman lord but another altogether to a dispossessed Anglo-Saxon. In this respect, among

---

99 Bernstein calls the borders "a realm of freedom" and explains the Aesopic tradition of dissent. *Mystery of the Bayeux Tapestry*, 135. For comparative examples of beast fables used by "underdogs" to express dissent subversively but safely, see Ziolkowski, *Talking Animals*, 6–9.

100 Yapp ("Animals in Medieval Art," 48) writes that these racing beasts might be wolves, though he is not certain of their identification. He concludes: "they are following a deer, as is the habit of wolves." Note the shrieking birds that precede them.

101 See Chapter Five, 187–88. The border scenes here repeatedly present predators stalking their prey. So a fox approaches a donkey in the upper panel, while in the lower panel a bird swoops after a hare. Next, a leopard-like beast creeps toward another donkey, who grazes unawares. In the upper border, two formidable birds frame a single lamb who seems to be fleeing for his life, shortly before Harold falls dead in the central panel, victim of a Norman arrow. While donkeys scarcely glorify the English, neither do they depict them as anything worse than hapless victims. At best, these scenes hint at the inevitability of the Norman victory rather than imply any justice in the Norman cause. Indeed, the terrified lamb – whether specifically Harold or just a generic Anglo-Saxon – suggests innocence, as in the wolf and lamb metaphors in Norman histories. For a discussion of this sequence of border scenes, see Terkla, "Cut on the Norman Bias," 271.

contemporary Norman accounts of the Conquest, the Tapestry best represents the Norman pattern of celebratory text and subversive subtext, featuring the wolf metaphor to insinuate Norman trickery and deceit.

This counter-message within the Tapestry expressly contradicts the Conqueror's official version of Norman justice and right as presented in the *Gesta Guillelmi*, a work that the Tapestry designer seems to have known.[102] As powerful and artistically compelling as these vehicles might be for their competing views, however, it is the humble *Gesta Normannorum Ducum* of William of Jumièges that exercises the greatest influence as the centerpiece of the Norman historiographical tradition. Both in his own redaction of this *Gesta* and in his master work, the *Ecclesiastical History*, Orderic Vitalis will heavily interpret this chronicle of William of Jumièges, imposing views akin to the wolfish commentary of the Tapestry embroiderers.

---

[102] Frank Barlow has summed up the *Tapestry*'s literary connections, including its affinity with the *Carmen* and the designer or artist's acquaintance with the accounts of William of Poitiers and perhaps William of Jumièges, along with an anonymous *Vita Ædwardi Regis* (*Carmen*, lviii–lix et passim).

3

Normans in the South

BY 1066 Norman mercenaries had been fighting in southern Italy for at least a half century.[1] From as early as the reign of Richard II, the riches of Apulia and Campania attracted Normans who were fleeing increased ducal control over an emerging aristocracy in eleventh-century Normandy.[2] Dissidents and losers in feuds, younger sons without inheritance, pilgrims and adventurers saddled up and headed south in search of freedom and fortune.

On this frontier, Norman warriors found themselves in high demand. Local princes, heirs to the great Lombard kingdom crushed by Charlemagne,

---

[1] This chapter draws on my article, "Bohemond and the Rooster," on my unpublished article, "Sicily and the Norman Frontiers," and on my Ph.D. dissertation, "William of Apulia's *Gesta Roberti Wiscardi* and Anna Comnena's *Alexiad*: A Literary Comparison" (University of California, Berkeley, 1975). The classic account of pre-Norman Italy is Jules Gay, *L'Italie méridionale et l'empire Byzantin, 867–1071*, Bibliothèque des écoles françaises d'Athènes et de Rome, 90 (Paris, 1904). See also Barbara M. Kreutz, *Before the Normans: Southern Italy in the Ninth and Tenth Centuries*, Middle Ages Series (Philadelphia, 1991). Jean Décarreaux, *Normands, papes et moines: cinquante ans de conquêtes et de politique religieuse en Italie méridionale et en Sicile (milieu du XIe siècle – début du XIIe)* (Paris, 1974), discusses the Norman conquest; see the review by Armand O. Citarella in *Speculum* 52 (July 1977), 645–48. David C. Douglas, *Norman Achievement*, 34–43, and Kenneth Baxter Wolf, *Making History: The Normans and their Historians in Eleventh-Century Italy* (Philadelphia, 1995), 9–45, provide good summaries. For a detailed account of the Norman period, consult Ferdinand Chalandon, *Histoire de la domination normande en Italie et en Sicile* (1907; reprint, New York, 1960), 2 vols., and the lively volume by John Julius Norwich: *The Other Conquest* (New York and Evanston, 1967), published in England as *The Normans in the South, 1016–1130*. Historians have traditionally placed the first contact in 1016, with the meeting of Norman pilgrims and the Lombard Melus (see below). But H. Hoffman ["Die Anfänge der Normannen in Süditalien," *Quellen und Forschungen aus Italienischen Archiven und Bibliotheken* 49 (1969), 95–144, at p. 101] traced Norman mercenary involvement to even earlier Norman pilgrims who repelled a Muslim assault against Salerno, perhaps in 999.

[2] For the circumstances that propelled Norman emigration to Italy, see G. A. Loud, "How 'Norman' was the Norman Conquest?" 16–20.

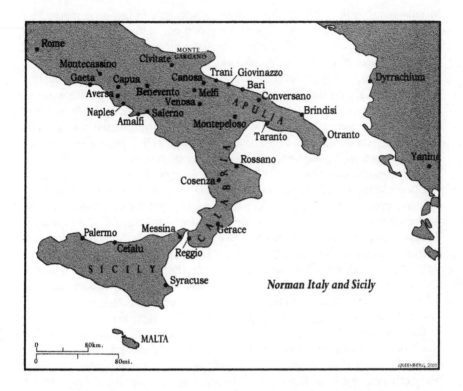

Norman Italy and Sicily

clashed with one another over the boundaries and privileges of their independent principalities and duchies. Some challenged native Italian groups under local control or with ties to Byzantium. External threats heightened the danger, not only from the Byzantines but also from the papacy and German emperors, each of whom claimed territories in southern Italy, fostering disruption. And just off the coast lay Arab Sicily, which could also menace any tenuous peace on the mainland.

Despite the turmoil and violence, southern Italy still boasted prosperous trading cities like Bari, Taranto, Amalfi, and Salerno, which attracted merchants sailing from Alexandria and Antioch – "Arabs, Libyans, Sicilians . . . and Africans," in the words of the Norman historian William of Apulia (3.483). Diverse peoples and cultures uneasily shared the land: Lombard and Byzantine, Jewish and Armenian. Indeed, the Byzantine presence had recently grown, as the empire poured both soldiers and settlers into its last western territories, in a concerted effort to keep southern Italy within its realm.[3] In Calabria, Eastern Orthodox monasteries fostered Greek spirituality and learning, while Campanian cultural centers, especially Salerno and

3 Kreutz, *Before the Normans*, 151.

Montecassino, still cherished the vestiges of ancient civilization preserved by the Carolingian renaissance. This rich mixture of intellectual sophistication and material wealth looked particularly attractive to Norman soldiers of fortune because it seemed ripe for the plucking.

Normans won their first Italian holdings by playing Lombards against Byzantines, fighting for both sides and nearly always becoming the winners themselves. From these early skirmishes, the sons of Tancred of Hauteville emerged as the greatest Norman chiefs. In Normandy, Tancred was a small landholder, whose modest estate could not support his twelve remarkable sons. In about 1035, William, Drogo, and Humphrey, the three oldest boys, headed toward Aversa, where William was to earn the epithet "Iron-Arm" and become the first Norman-Italian count. But a younger half-brother soon eclipsed even William: Robert Guiscard won papal blessing and the title "duke of Apulia and Calabria" at the Synod of Melfi in 1059. In his turn Robert helped the youngest brother, Roger, wrest Sicily from the Saracens, taking Messina in 1061 and Palermo in 1072 and founding a magnificent state that would fuse Norman energy with Byzantine and Arab culture. Robert, meanwhile, consolidated his own power in Italy and then crossed the Adriatic in a bold attack on Byzantium. He died on this campaign in 1085, a venerable warrior pursuing his ultimate dream, the imperial crown.

Such ventures would not go unsung. Historians attached themselves to the new Norman princes and recorded the heroic age of conquest. In the eleventh century, Amatus of Montecassino, William of Apulia, and Geoffrey Malaterra wrote the earliest of these Norman histories in the south. At first sight their works seem to lie outside the Norman historical tradition. Instead of citing Dudo or William of Jumièges for links to the Norman past, for instance, they situated themselves clearly in their Norman-Italian present, using spare local chronicles and oral sources for data. Yet they entered the mainstream of the Norman tradition when Orderic Vitalis wove their stories into his *Ecclesiastical History*. For this reason alone they belong in any reckoning of Norman histories. But there are other reasons as well for including them here. Although Amatus, William of Apulia, and Geoffrey Malaterra wrote during the heady years of Norman adventure, when Norman histories everywhere exhibit the greatest exuberance, in their works, too, lurk angst and censure of the Norman people and princes. The stories these writers tell, and the ways they tell them, fit the pattern of surreptitious commentary on the dark side of Normanness.

Amatus is the earliest of these three and the central figure from whom many Italo-Norman historians drew their information.[4] Writing in the late 1070s, this monk of Montecassino may have witnessed many of the events he

4 *Storia de' Normanni di Amato di Montecassino*, ed. Vincenzo de Bartholomaeis, Fonti per la storia d'Italia, pubblicate dall'Istituto storico italiano per il Medio Evo. Scrittori. Secolo 11, no. 76 (Rome, 1935). See Wolf, *Making History*, especially pp. 87–122.

recorded as he followed Normans in Italy from 1016 to the death of Richard, the Norman count of Aversa and prince of Capua, on March 3, 1078. This *Historia Normannorum* ("History of the Normans") opens with the first people to leave Normandy, whose fields and orchards cannot sustain a growing population (1.1).[5] In Italy the immigrants discover a land of milk and honey (1.19), prosper, and use their new territories as a base for conquests against the infidel in Sicily (1.16). Amatus seems to have seen his book as the joyful record of God's will, announced by Biblical prophecy and realized on earth by pious heroes like Richard of Capua and Robert Guiscard, whom he assiduously refashioned as Christian champions.[6] Since both Richard and Robert were generous benefactors of his monastery, Amatus had ample motivation for praising them, though he himself was a Lombard.[7]

But we no longer have the words that Amatus wrote. The original Latin text of his *Historia Normannorum* has disappeared, replaced by a fourteenth-century Old French version. This *Ystoire de li Normant* is more an adaptation than a precise translation, as we can see by comparing the French text with selections from the Latin, preserved in the second and later redactions of the *Chronicle of Montecassino* written by Leo Marsicanus.[8] At places where the *Chronicle* parallels the *Ystoire* most closely, there are significant textual differences. As Byzantines embark on a Sicilian campaign, for instance, they ask for aid from the Lombard prince Gaimar, who sends three hundred Normans under William, son of Tancred, newly arrived from Normandy. At this point the *Ystoire* includes the following (2.8):

> And to tell the truth, the daring and valor of these few Normans is worth more than the large number of Greeks.

> (Et, à dire la verité, plus valut la hardiece et la prouesce de ces petit de Normans que la moltitude de li Grex.)

The *Chronicle* lacks this sentence. Did Amatus write a Latin version of this, which the *Chronicle* failed to repeat, or did the Old French translator insert it into his text? We cannot resolve these questions or reconstruct Amatus's text precisely. Even less can we determine when the *Ystoire* preserves the mood and tone of Amatus's *Historia* and when it distorts the original spirit. It is

---

5   Marjorie Chibnall gives the date 1080–86 (*EH* 2, p. xxiii, n. 1); R. H. C. Davis followed earlier scholars who suggested 1073–80 (*The Normans and their Myth*, 88).

6   Wolf nicely describes Amatus's rehabilitation of these and other Norman princes (*Making History*, especially 89–92).

7   A. Lentini, "Richerche biografiche su Amato di Montecassino," *Benedictina* 9 (1955), 183–96.

8   Leo Marsicanus and Peter the Deacon, *Chronica Monasterii Casinensis*, ed. H. Hoffman, *MGH SS* 34 (Hanover, 1980).

problematic, therefore, to use the *Ystoire* as if it were an eleventh-century Norman text.[9]

Historians used to think that Amatus served as a source for William of Apulia.[10] Now it is generally agreed that both wrote independently of one another, using a common written tradition.[11] Like Amatus, William traced the paths of various Norman heroes. Indeed, the *Gesta Roberti Wiscardi* is considerably more than Robert Guiscard's *Geste*. The history does feature Robert and conclude with his funeral, but William begins this tale with the arrival of the first Norman mercenaries in southern Italy (c. 1012–17), whose fortunes he followed until Robert's appearance some forty years later, in the second of five books.

We know little about the author. Even his birth as Norman or Italian and status as layman or cleric remain undetermined, although many scholars have searched for clues.[12] References that seem to identify William with the Normans occur in a single dramatic passage (3.199–224) describing the siege of Palermo. Here William repeatedly calls Roger's Norman army *nostri* ("our men"). But this seems to mean "we Christians" rather than "we Normans," as suggested by the following excerpt:[13]

> For he always fought against the Sicilian enemies
> of the divine name, desiring to exalt the holy faith
> by which we all live.   (3.199–201)

Perhaps William was a Lombard at the court of Roger Borsa, the younger son of Robert Guiscard.[14] But the *Gesta*'s brief prologue and epilogue offer only spare biographical details: William claims to write at the request of Roger and Pope Urban II. Other internal evidence dates the poem to c. 1095–99, the years of the First Crusade. Aside from these hints, William's identity remains elusive. At the very least, he is a Norman historian in the same sense as Dudo, writing Norman history at a Norman court for a Norman prince.

---

9 Wolf's assessment is more optimistic; see *Making History*, 89. Cf. Bartholomaeis, *Amato di Montecassino*, lxxxv–cviii. It is difficult to avoid Amatus when discussing Italo-Norman histories, but I use the fourteenth-century text with caution.

10 Aimé, *Ystoire de li Normant*, ed. O. Delarc (Rouen, 1892), lvi–lxiv. For the text of William's history see Mathieu, *La geste de Robert Guiscard*.

11 On the *Gesta*'s sources, which may include lost annals of Bari, see Mathieu, *La geste de Robert Guiscard*, 26–38.

12 Following Chalandon and Manitius, many have espoused the theory of his Italian origin, suggesting Giovinazzo as William's birthplace because of the disproportionate amount of attention this little town receives in his history. See M. Manitius, *Bildung, Wissenschaft und Literatur im Abendlande von 800 bis 1100* (Crimmitschau, 1925), 662; Norwich, *The Other Conquest*, 339–40; and Wolf, *Making History*, 124. Cf. *Gesta* 3.540–605; 627–36.

13 The anonymous author of the *Gesta Francorum* similarly uses *nostri* to mean "we Christians." (See Chapter Four, below.)

14 Wolf, *Making History*, 126–27. Roger got his nickname Borsa, "the Purse," from his childhood fondness for counting the coins in his money bag.

The third historian of eleventh-century Norman adventurers in the south, Geoffrey Malaterra, reveals slightly more about himself. He almost certainly came from the lesser aristocracy in Normandy, where his family's meager patrimony may well have inspired the surname, "Badland."[15] Geoffrey sought the contemplative life of a Benedictine monk before traveling "from across the mountains" to Apulia, then to Catania in Sicily, where he joined the monastery of St. Agata, endowed by Count Roger in 1091. There Geoffrey wrote his history *De rebus gestis Rogerii Calabriae et Siciliae comitis et Roberti Guiscardi ducis fratris eius* ("On the deeds of Roger, count of Calabria and Sicily, and his brother, Duke Robert"), left unfinished in 1098 or shortly after. Geoffrey's history does describe Robert's exploits including even his Byzantine campaign, but it shows a special interest in Roger of Sicily. Malaterra claims to write at Roger's request and to use oral sources. These have given him summary information for Apulia and more detail for Calabria and Sicily. Often he is our only source, particularly for Roger's Sicilian campaigns and for Italo-Norman history following the death of Robert Guiscard. Like William of Poitiers, Malaterra protests that he is eschewing the "new and elegant poetry" in praise of his hero and is honoring the traditional sobriety, lest he risk the charge of adulation. With its florid prose and occasional verse, however, his history often seems to flatter "the very chic (*elegantissimus*) young Count Robert of Calabria" (2.38).

This intense interest in Norman heroes links the three histories and defines the Normanness of these works.[16] All three historians have ample motivation to revel in Norman successes in the south, even more so when they feature the holy war in Sicily. Yet they shade their tales with ominous undertones. William of Apulia shows this most dramatically, and I feature him here, using Geoffrey and Amatus for comparison, though we must always view the latter with suspicion. Let us see now how the Italo-Norman story unfolds.

> When it pleased the King who has the power to change
> eras and kingdoms that the Greeks should no longer inhabit
> Apulia, which they had held so long,
> the Norman people, noted for their fierceness on horseback,
> enter,
> and reign over Latium after driving out the Greeks.

So begins Book One of the *Gesta Roberti Wiscardi*, with God's decision to oust the Greeks from Italy. We readers have no time to ponder the inscrutable design of the Almighty, for at once the *gens Normannorum* ride onto the

---

[15] Huguette Taviani-Carozzi, *La terreur du monde: Robert Guiscard et la conquête normande en Italie. Mythe et histoire* (Paris, 1996), 18.

[16] Davis, *The Normans and their Myth*, 88–89.

scene and fulfill God's will. Here the *Gesta* interjects a breathless account of the Normans' trajectory, along with the etymology of their name: Since the wind they called *nort* carried them to the northern realms, from which they eventually made their way to Italy, these people are called "Northmen, that is, *homines boreales*" (1.6–10). In this account, the Normans are a mysterious folk, driven by winds from some unnamed homeland. Antenor, the Trojans, the Scythians – all are missing from this Italo-Norman narrative. For the *Gesta*, Normandy itself is only a way station in the divinely ordained rush to Italy.

Amatus offers a variant, but equally brief, explanation. His Normans take their name from an island called "Nora," their original homeland, which they left because its fields and trees could not support the vast population (1.1). So they scattered throughout the world, entering the service of others, but ever "wishing to have all people in their own power and control" (*en lor subjettion et en lor seignorie*). "And they took up arms and broke the bonds of peace and drew up great armies of foot-soldiers and knights" (1.2). Of the three early Italo-Norman historians, only Malaterra recalls Rollo (*Rodlo, dux fortissimus . . . ex Norveja*) and his pirate crew, pillaging his way along the western shores until he came to the mouth of the Seine (1.1):

> Along this river, penetrating the deep interior of France with his huge fleet, he observed the charm of these places compared with all the other lands that he had passed through, and he decided to choose this one for himself and embrace it with his love.

Other readers of this passage have noted its aggressive eroticism.[17] Rollo desires the land for the fertility of its streams and fields, and he leaps ashore, at once beginning to subjugate its people to his command (*incolas illius regionis suo imperio subjugare coeperunt*), until some French king ("I think it was Louis II," writes Malaterra vaguely) proposes the pact that cedes the land to Rollo by right (1.2). And from this land and this people come the Normans, whose name Malaterra derives, as does William of Apulia, from the Germanic word for the north wind.

All three historians waste no time in getting the Normans to Italy. In their brief background accounts, Amatus and Malaterra have managed to introduce the Normans' lust for hegemony, but William begins more circumspectly, proceeding quickly to the Normans' peaceable appearance in Italy as pilgrims visiting Monte Gargano to fulfill a vow to the Archangel Michael.[18] But at the holy site they meet Melus, a Lombard nobleman from Bari, whose exotic Greek dress and miter pique their curiosity. His plea further arouses

---

17 Wolf, *Making History*, 149.
18 On the competing versions of this foundation story, see Einar Joranson, "The Inception of the Career of the Normans in Italy – Legend and History," *Speculum* 23 (July 1948), 353–96.

their interest: How happily he would return to his home, from which the Greeks had exiled him, if only some Normans would help him evict the easily routed Greeks. The Norman pilgrims have traveled unarmed. But they ride quickly north, gather companions and weapons, and return to support Melus's insurrection. The Norman onslaught has begun.

When Norman warriors reached Italy, they entered an arena notorious for the savagery of its villains.[19] For Amatus, a partisan of Normans, the true wolves are Lombards like Prince Gisulf II of Salerno (*loup rapace Gisolfe, maistre de tout malice*; "ravening wolf Gisulf, master of every vice"; 4.43; cf. 4.34), whose "insatiable madness . . . seemed to exceed the cruelty of Nero and Maximian" (8.2). Malaterra indicts the entire Lombard people, "a very hateful folk, who always hold a virtuous person suspect" (1.6; cf. 1.13 and 1.28, on the Apulians and Calabrians, respectively). Amatus especially vents his spleen against the Lombard prince, Pandulf III of Capua, who often harried Montecassino, proclaiming him "full of all sin and evil" (2.5; cf. 1.41). Writing in the late 1070s Desiderius, the abbot of Montecassino, recalled God's miracles that punished Pandulf for his predations against the monastery: the emperor Conrad rode against the prince and, with God's aid, wrested from him the lands that he had stolen; and after Pandulf's death, demons tormented him, dragging him by the neck and drowning him over and over in the dark waters of a lake.[20]

Our sources agree: such rogues meet their match in the Normans. For Amatus, this *gent molt robuste et forte, ceste fortissime gent* ("very hardy and strong people, this extremely strong people"; 1.1 and 1.3) rarely makes any pretense of being other than ruthlessly ambitious. Geoffrey Malaterra, too, habitually characterizes the Normans as driven by *aviditas dominationis,* "a desire for absolute power." Echoing Sallust's description of Catiline, the traitor against the Roman republic, Malaterra taints his Norman conquerors with the qualities of a notorious predator.[21]

For his part, William of Apulia marks the Normans' bravery (5.65), but also details their other distinctive traits: Normans are "savage on horseback" (1.4), war-loving (1.145), "a fierce people, barbarous and cruel" (*gens effera, barbara, dira*; 2.427), and especially motivated by greed (1.38).[22] Normally not a poet who repeats constructions simply to fill out the metrical pattern, in

---

[19] Cf. Kreutz, *Before the Normans,* 150–51: ". . . it is particularly important to note the appalling violence of this eleventh-century struggle – and its total disruption of the 'Beneventan' region. . . . It was all reminiscent of the ninth century with its Arab mercenaries; but this was far more brutal and much more widely destructive."

[20] Desiderius of Montecassino, *Dialogi de miraculis sancti Benedicti,* ed. Gerhard Schwartz and Adolf Hofmeister, *MGH SS* 30 (pt. 2), 1.9, p. 1123; and 1.13, pp. 1125–27.

[21] Wolf, *Making History,* 162–68.

[22] Our sources frequently note the Normans' insatiable greed. Desiderius, for instance, assumes that avarice characterizes these people. Greedy Normans are the villains in

six consecutive lines William finds three ways to restate the Normans' tendency to sell their loyalties to the highest bidder.[23] Even a Byzantine commander learns their reputation and tries to buy their loyalty:

> For he hears that the Norman people are always prone
> to greed. They love the most the one who offers most. (2.44–45)

On this occasion the Normans demur, but in other circumstances they turn from their own Norman chiefs to serve a Beneventan prince (1.318–27). This happens just after the Normans have won some measure of peace and returned to their refuge in Melfi. There they build homes for their twelve counts. And then they betray those chiefs, transferring their services to Adenolf of Benevento. What could have provoked such disloyalty to their own compatriots? "Maybe he gave them silver or gold," suggests William – a bribe to activate their usual greed. "What are the limits to which ambition leads? It can topple reasonable senses and break the strong bonds of loyalty." But William also hints at a pre-existing tension between the Normans and their own chiefs, which he labels a natural envy of material success.[24] Perhaps the Normans are resisting constraints imposed by their own proto-chieftains in Italy.

The language of the *Gesta* has already hinted that this is so. Early in Book One, William assesses the Normans as "people loving wars more than peace treaties" (. . . *Bella magis populi quam foedera pacis amantes*; 1.145). Normans would rather fight than accept the constraints of compact and federation. Uneasily the war band confronts the hierarchies forming within territories that come under Norman control. Only a few lines later, William describes this incipient society as a motley crew that welcomes all comers. Anyone who would learn the customs and the language could join them to form "one people" (*gens efficiatur ut una*; 1.168). This passage bears a striking resemblance to Rollo's dream of the multicolored birds in Dudo's account (2.6), but with at least one ominous difference. The recruits are not nesting birds from all nations but "any criminals from the neighborhood (*vicinorum [ali]quis perniciosus*) seeking refuge with them" (1.165). Here is a significant modification of the Norman myth of inclusiveness.

Surely Malaterra was right to insist that only a firm hand could restrain this greedy, unruly lot (1.3). In language and spirit that Orderic Vitalis would later imitate, Malaterra places this candid assessment of the Normans near the beginning of his history:

two of his miracle stories (*Dialogi de miraculis sancti Benedicti*, 1.11, p. 1124, and 1.22, pp. 1138–39).

23 . . . *plus tribuenti/ Semper adhaerebant; servire libentius illi/ Omnes gaudebant, a quo plus accipiebant,/ . . ./ . . . plus dantem pluris habebant* (1.142–44; 147).

24 1.318–20; 2.444–50.

It is a very crafty people, avenger of injuries, scorning ancestral fields in the hope of gaining more elsewhere, eager for profit and power, simulator and dissimulator of anything whatsoever, occupying some mean between largesse and avarice . . . indeed, unless these people are restrained by the yoke of justice, they run completely amuck.

(Est quippe gens astutissima, injuriarum ultrix, spe alias plus lucrandi patrios agros vilipendens, quaestus et dominationis avida, cuiuslibet rei simulatrix ac dissimulatrix, inter largitatem et avaritiam quoddam medium habens . . . quae quidem, nisi jugo justitiae prematur, effrenatissima est.)

For these predators from the north, southern Italy must have seemed like paradise. The early pages of the *Gesta* reflect the joyful promise of a new life in this lush land. William praises Apulia's fertility, which the feminine Greeks do not deserve to possess and enjoy (1.222–28). The panegyric topos of the *locus amoenus* ("charming place") popular with both classical and medieval writers, provides William the opportunity to indulge in *laudes Italiae*. He delights in the beauty and bounty of all Apulia (1.182–83) and especially in the rich cities of Amalfi (3.476–85), Salerno (3.470–76), and Bari (2.12, 480–85). He extols the fertility of Salerno where lovely women and upright men enjoy their Eden amid exotic fruits, nuts, trees, wine, and pure water (3.470–73). To Amalfi's seaport, Arabs, Lydians, Sicilians, Africans, and merchants from Alexandria and Antioch bring their gold and silver and costly garments (3.476–85). But Aversa, the first Norman town in Italy, wins the happiest praise (1.171–73):

> Rich in resources, this profitable spot is also charming;
> it does not lack crops or fruits, fields or orchards.
> No place in the world is more delightful.

In all Norman breasts such wealth inspires "one longing – to take it for themselves" (*Est adquirendi simul omnibus una libido*; 1. 38). Malaterra describes the disastrous effect that three-quarters of a century of Norman rapine would exert upon this prosperous land. He tells of a year without bread or wine (1.27).

But this eventual disaster does not seem to have troubled William of Apulia as he began his tale of conquest.

> I have in mind to tell under what leadership the Norman people
> came to Italy, what was the reason for their staying,
> and following what leaders they won their triumph over Latium.
> (Prologue iii–v)

> (Dicere fert animus, quo gens normannica ductu
> Venerit Italiam, fuerit quae causa morandi,
> Quosve secuta duces Latii sit adepta triumphum.)

William's opening definition of his subject ends with *triumphum*, and the surface story does appear to be one of victory. But these lines ominously recall the thesis statement from Lucan's *Pharsalia*:

> I have in mind to set forth the causes of such great matters.
>
> (1.67)
>
> (Fert animus causas tantarum expromere rerum.)[25]

Lucan's text proceeds:

> A huge task is uncovered, to tell what drove a maddened people
> to arms, what knocked peace out of the world.   (1.68–69)

The allusion is unsettling, but readers of the *Gesta* may well shrug off any apprehension at this point, expecting the mood of this story to be a joyful one. After all, William was writing in the late 1090s, a heady time for all Normans who shared the exhilaration that emanated from the call to Crusade and the Crusaders' victories at Nicaea, Antioch, and Jerusalem.[26] The first three of the *Gesta*'s five books generally fulfill this expectation, creating a mood that is predominantly optimistic.

Even at the start, however, the *Gesta* hints at the devastation this conquest will bring. In an early Vergilian echo, "rumor flies" (*fama volat*; 1.43) with reports that the first Norman mercenaries have reached Campania. The language recalls *Aeneid* 4.184, as a grotesquely winged *Fama* "flies by night" (*nocte volat*) with ominous news:

> that Aeneas, sprung from Trojan blood, had come,
>
> (*Aeneid* 4.191)

corrupting Queen Dido, to her eventual ruin and the destruction of her homeland. The allusion insinuates a foreboding of doom into this narrative of the Norman assault.

The *Gesta* telescopes the ensuing advance of Norman power into a breathtakingly sudden strike. Artfully William of Apulia sets the scene, lingering on the momentary calm when no imperial army threatens the tranquillity

---

[25] Here Lucan mimics the beginning of Ovid's *Metamorphoses*, which William of Apulia also knew:

> In nova fert animus mutatas dicere formas
> Corpora . . .
>
> (I have in mind to tell of figures changed into new
> bodies . . .)

For Lucan's and William's characters, as for Ovid's, big changes lie ahead.

[26] The *Gesta* is dated by its reference to his "divinely inspired" (*nutu stimulata superno*) muster of the *gens Gallorum*, "more powerful than any other people in strength of arms" (3.98–105).

between Greeks and Italians, and only the whisper of a planned Sicilian campaign breaks the silence (1.241–44). And then the Normans launch their attack:

> With the Normans entering the Apulian lands, at once
> Melfi was captured.   (1.245–46)

> (Appula Normannis intrantibus arva, repente
> Melfia capta fuit.)

The Norman onslaught continues with a swift succession of battles, including three in the year 1041 alone (1.396–97).

The *Gesta*'s Books Two and Three proceed to emphasize victories and the confidence of the victors. When Robert Guiscard begins his rise to power in Calabria, the optimism grows, as

> Everywhere the Norman people had an illustrious reputation.
> (2.323)

> (Undique gens clarum Normannica nomen habebat.)

If there are ambiguities in the language that challenge this mood – here, for instance, *clarum . . . nomen* can mean "a notorious reputation" as well as a "famous" one – the surface narrative remains bright. A luminance characterizes Robert's marriage to the Lombard princess Sichelgaita (2.430–543), his victory at Civitate (2.284–85), the subjugation of all Calabria (2.413–517), and victories at sea (3.132–33, 255). The *Gesta* delights in Norman attacks on Muslims in Sicily, where Robert comes to the aid of his brother Roger (3.189–347). Even faced with massive rebellion, "the duke . . ./ is shaken by no terror; whether by craft or by arms [*vel arte vel armis*]/ he conquers everyone" (3.567–69). This book concludes with all insurgencies quashed (3.686–87). Although the following book darkens considerably, as we shall see, it begins by affirming Robert Guiscard's conquest of southern Italy, "its cities and fortresses everywhere subdued" (4.6) and ends by announcing two glorious triumphs, over the German king and the Byzantine emperor (4.566–70).

This double victory caps a long career of conquest. Robert had first taken center stage in the *Gesta* at Civitate in the year 1053, when the Normans defeated the papal forces of Italian and German allies (2.122–256). Nowhere does William of Apulia use the epic style with such gusto as he does here in describing the great battle.[27] As the armies stand ready for the fight, William identifies the valiant warriors on both sides: brave Normans, desperate after three days without bread, determined, if they must die, to perish honorably in combat rather than ingloriously from starvation; and opposite them, the papal

---

[27] Cf. Mathieu, *La geste de Robert Guiscard*, 54–58.

forces, Teutons and fierce Swabians, skilled in sword-play, and noble Italians from Rome and Capua, Sabines and Spoletans (2.122–76). Leading the Normans are the Hauteville brothers, including young

> Robert, who surpassed his elder brothers
> in great-minded courage. He was in this battle.
> He was called Guiscard, because even Cicero
> was not as cunning, or Ulysses as crafty.   (2.127–30)

As the battle begins (2.196), the Norman heroes Richard and Humphrey lead the attack. But Robert will not let his older brother Humphrey outshine him in valor. Here is William's epic account of Robert's *aristeia*, his brilliance in battle:

> . . . finally both sides join battle
> with swords. Extraordinary blows are delivered on either side
> with swords. There you would have seen a human body
> sliced from its head, and horses sliced up, too, along with their
> > riders.
> When Robert saw the enemy pressing his brother
> so fiercely and unwilling to yield to him on any account,
> accompanied by the troops of Count Girard
> and with the Calabrian forces following him,
> which he had been assigned to lead,
> full of courage he rushed boldly into the thick of the enemy.
> He pierces some with his spear and others he wounds with his
> > sword,
> and with powerful hands he strikes terrible blows.
> He fights with both hands, and neither lance nor sword
> was ineffectual, wherever he wished to direct his hand.
> Three times thrown from his horse, three times he regained
> > strength
> and returned to arms with more vigor. Rage itself spurs him on.
> Just as a snarling lion rages, when he fiercely attacks
> weaker animals, if he should encounter any resistance,
> and he grows angrier than if he were fighting
> stronger animals. Now he shows no mercy.
> This one he drags, this he devours, and what he cannot devour
> he mangles, wreaking deadly havoc on every beast.
> Just this way Robert does not cease to slaughter resisting
> > Swabians
> with all kinds of slaughter. With some he cuts off their feet,
> with others, their hands; here he strikes the head along with the
> > body;
> there he slashes the belly with the chest; here he pierces
> the ribs after severing the head. Great bodies
> he cuts down to the size of very little bodies.
> He shows that the prize of courage does not only belong

to great bodies, but often lesser men overflow with it.
No one in this battle, as was pronounced after battle,
conqueror or conquered, issued such great blows.   (2.212–43)

This is an expansive scene, unlike the *Gesta*'s generally lean description.[28]
The poet anticipates Robert's entrance (2.221) with a suspenseful account of
the enemy "pressing fiercely" (*acriter instantes*, 2.217) just as Robert, like a
lion, will soon "attack fiercely" (*acriter invadit*, 2.229). In lines 216–20, the
warrior observes his brother's distress, while the narrative notes the troops at
Robert's command. Then comes a sudden release of tension (2.221):

Irruit audacter medios animosus in hostes.

(Full of courage he rushed boldly into the thick of the enemy.)

First a strong verb, then an adverb and adjective all point to Robert's daring,
as the four dactyls in these six feet reinforce the sense of speed. This critical
line further calls attention to itself through rhyme that William normally uses
sparingly, making -os- the first syllable of three successive feet.

Once in combat, Robert delivers hyperbolic blows, seized by the battle
frenzy sometimes called viking rage, which we will find again in the *Gesta
Francorum* with the character called Mad Hugh.[29] Three times Robert's horse
throws him, and three times the hero re-enters the fray with renewed intensity. This is a set-piece of Norman epic histories, applied also to William the
Conqueror at Hastings in the *Gesta Guillelmi* (2.18) and the *Carmen de Hastingae Proelio* (verses 509–15). Oblivious to his bruising falls and to the
dangers all around, Robert knows only the fury that goads him to slice off
feet, hands, and heads in an orgy of brutality. Repeated forms of *caedere* and
caedes, the verb and noun meaning "slaughter," lead to the alliterative half-
line introducing the mutilation. When Robert proceeds literally to cut the
bodies down to size, equalizing tall and short enemies, the description

---

28 It is difficult to show in translation just how flamboyant this passage is, especially in
    comparison with the rest of the *Gesta*. The poet's one characteristic trait (almost his
    obsession), however, throughout the *Gesta* is a delight in wordplay and repetition,
    which he particularly indulges here. The first three-and-a-half lines of this passage
    contain three sets of puns:

    . . . uterque/ . . . utrimque
    ad gladios . . ./ Fit gladiis . . .
    . . . humanum . . . corpus/ . . . equos hominis cum corpore caesos.

    (. . . both sides/ . . . on both sides
    to swords . . ./ (It) is done with swords . . .
    . . . a human body/ . . . horses sliced along with a man's body.)

29 See Chapter Four, 166–67.

becomes ludicrous, and William wisely shifts the focus to another hero. But first he closes this scene with one final hyperbole:

> No one in this battle, as was pronounced after battle,
> conqueror or conquered, issued such great blows.
>
> (Nullus in hoc bello, sicut post bella probatum est,
> Victor vel victus tam magnos edidit ictus.)[30]

In that second line the alliteration and assonance of *victor* and *victus*, the leonine rhyme of *victus* with *ictus*, and the heaviness of a line with five spondees conspire to emphasize the weight of this pronouncement.

William's account of Civitate not only provokes an epic second-person reference but even moves William of Apulia to introduce two long similes.[31] The Italians flee like doves seeking out mountain ridges where they hope in vain for refuge from the pursuing hawk:

> Routed in flight over valleys and hills fleeing
> they scatter. The force of their flight sends many tumbling,
> to be killed by javelin and sword where they lie sprawling.
> Just as when the hawk attacks airy doves flocking together,
> and makes them seek out rocky ridges
> at the mountain's peak in fugitive flight;
> still he catches them when they cannot seek out any further
> refuge: just so for those fleeing Richard.
>
> (Inque fugam versi per plana, per ardua, cursim
> Diffugiunt; multos cogit subcombere stratos
> Impetus ipse fugae; iaculis caeduntur et ense.
> Qualiter aerias, ubi convenere, palumbes,
> Dum petit accipiter, fugitivo summa volatu
> Et scopulosa facit celsi iuga quaerere montis;
> Quas tamen ipse capit, non possunt amplius ullum
> Quaerere confugium: sic dantes terga Ricardus.)   (2.199–206)

Note the important position of *diffugiunt* and the pause after it (2.200). This unusual enjambment draws attention to the panic among the Italian troops.[32] In literature both ancient and medieval, the speed of bird's flight commonly inspires an epic simile, as when an Arab in the *Song of Roland* mounts his

---

[30] This episode bears notable resemblance to the individual acts of valor in *La Chanson de Roland*, as the twelve peers slay their Saracen counterparts (1247 ff.).

[31] "There you would have seen a human body. . . ." This is a common device in medieval epic; cf. *La Chanson de Roland*, 1581: "Poez saveir que mult grant doel en out."

[32] See, too, how often "flight" occurs in various Latin compounds (-*fug*-); the next three lines feature three more such words, at the beginning, middle, and end of the lines: *Diffugiunt Itali . . ./ . . . fuga . . . / . . . fugit*. As the hawk captures (*capit*) the helpless doves, so Richard captures (*capit*) the fleeing Italians (2.207).

horse Barbarmusch, "swifter than sparrow-hawk or swallow."[33] William's dove metaphor particularly recalls a famous ode of Horace (1.37), on the aftermath of another great battle, Octavian's victory over Cleopatra at Actium.

At first glance, the Horatian ode seems to embrace Octavian's propaganda, inviting Romans to drink and dance in celebration of Cleopatra's defeat and suicide. But a dove simile at the center of the poem shifts the tone, as Horace recalls Cleopatra's flight from Octavian at Actium:

> . . . sed minuit furorem
>
> vix una sospes navis ab ignibus,
> mentemque lymphatam Mareotico
>   redegit in veros timores
>   Caesar, ab Italia volantem
>
> remis adurgens, accipiter velut
> molles columbas aut leporem citus
>   venator in campis nivalis
>   Haemoniae, . . .

> (. . . But the escape of scarcely one ship
>
> from the flames calmed her frenzy,
> and Caesar brought her mind, crazed by Mareotic wine, back
>   to authentic terrors,
>   in hot pursuit with his galleys
>
> as she fled from Italy, just as a hawk
> chases gentle doves or the swift hunter pursues
>   the hare on the plains of snow-covered
>   Thessaly, . . .)

The poem ends with an admiring view of the queen, serene and brave, as she deprives Octavian of his triumph by her suicide. Horace has drawn the reader's sympathies away from Octavian to Cleopatra. The final word of this ode, *triumpho*, belongs emotionally not to the warrior prince but to the woman. William probably had not read Horace's ode, but its famous simile (which Horace had himself borrowed from Homer's description of Achilles pursuing Hector around the walls of Troy in *Iliad* 22.139–40) had moved into the common property of medieval poets.[34]

---

[33] Line 1535. A rout in an epic battle likewise often evokes a dramatic simile. Cf. the *Chanson de Roland* 1874–75:

> Si cum li cerfs s'en vait devant les chiens
> Devant Rollant si s'en fuient paiens.

> (Like the stag running before the hounds,
> so the infidel flee before Roland.)

[34] Mathieu (*La geste de Robert Guiscard*, 65) cites a reference to Horace, but this is an error. The passage at hand (1.356) names not Horace, but Hector.

Like Horace's simile, the *Gesta*'s invites a moment's compassion for the victims of Norman aggression.[35] When the Hauteville brothers crush the Pope's defenders, William seems to experience conflicting sympathies, as indeed do the Norman warriors themselves, if we credit the account of their obeisance to the defeated pope after the battle. But perhaps the *Gesta*'s Horatian simile, at the moment of the Normans' greatest glory – Civitate being arguably as important for the Norman conquest in Italy as Actium had been for Octavian – also signals unease with the heroic conquerors and their autocratic ambitions.

While Horace's simile moves from hawk to hunter, William's second extended simile likens the warrior Robert to a lion attacking his lesser quarry and enraged if any try hopeless resistance (2.228–35). This commonplace epic comparison recalls Vergil's description of Turnus's leonine fury (*Aeneid* 10.454–56) or Roland's response to battle: "He became fiercer than lion or leopard" (*Song of Roland*, 1110; cf. 1888). Among Norman historians, William of Jumièges (3.1), Amatus (2.25), and Malaterra (2.33; 3.1, 11) all compare their heroes to lions. The lion of medieval legend and literature is typically a regal beast, often the symbolic antithesis of the wolf.[36] But consider the *Gesta*'s prolonged description of Robert crazed (*insanit*) with rage (*furor*) and wrath (*ira*). Is this mad despoiler of the flock truly heroic, or is the Norman warrior reverting to a bestial state?

If this scene at Civitate presents Robert as a raging beast, the *Gesta* as a whole makes him a complex character who can show generosity (2.312–13) and kindness to the defeated (2.335–59; 3.149–62, 326–30, 345–46). His eloquence matches his ambitions (2.298–307). But Robert's volatility at Civitate hints at the dangers lurking behind these benevolent poses. For Robert may be compassionate one moment and brutal the next. So he weeps to see his mortally ill brother Humphrey, with whom he had often feuded (2.366–67). Yet immediately after the funeral he rushes back to Calabria to besiege Cariatus and frighten the other cities into submission (2.381–83). In these and other exploits, uncommon luck follows Robert. During the siege of Bari, for instance, the duke sits unguarded in the lodging he had thatched himself and winterized with surrounding foliage (2.555–66). As he dines alone, a would-be assassin throws a spear through the bushes. By chance Robert bends down to spit under the table, and the spear finds only empty space where Robert's head had been just a moment earlier. As the assailant

---

35 Mary Margolies DeForest has argued that the Horatian simile also links Cleopatra's fate with Rome's eventual demise by implying that all powerful states must inevitably collapse. ["The Central Similes of Horace's *Cleopatra Ode*," *CW* 82 (1989), 167–73.] The defeat of one's enemies is but a moment in the cycle of rise and fall.

36 Recall the lions of the bestiaries, and those of saints' lives, who often befriended the saints and acted peaceably. See Alison Goddard Elliott, *Roads to Paradise: Reading the Lives of the Early Saints* (Hanover, N.H. and London, 1987).

runs back to Bari, the rumor of Robert's death elicits cries of joy from the townspeople, until the arrival of Robert, shouting for the people to be quiet, silences their merriment.

Robert is a man of many talents, by which he beguiles friend and foe alike. Resting with his troops in Reggio after taking Bari (3.167–83), he hears about a monstrous fish in the nearby Adriatic. Intrigued by these reports, Robert catches the fish through his own clever devices (*Per varias artes ducis hunc prudentia cepit*; 3.172) – and thereby attracts a crowd of Italians who had gathered along the shore to enjoy the spring air and sweet waters. All admire the hero's skill and the enormous size of his catch, whose dorsal fin measures four palms in circumference. The fish provides food for Robert and his men, for the Calabrians, and even for some Apulians.

Fish stories aside, the *Gesta*'s Robert typically applies his considerable *artes* more directly to acts of conquest. "Longing to seize the land," for example, "he shows love/ to all [the Calabrians]; no master [*dominator*] ever tried to be considered/ more affable or more humble than he" (2.320–22). But as soon as he can assemble another fighting force, he resumes his earlier tactics: "He ordered the looting, burning, and everywhere/ despoiling of the lands that he attacked,/ to instill every terror in the inhabitants" (2.327–29). Such strategic versatility, employed with Robert's usual enterprise, in fact, characterizes Robert as a quintessential Norman warlord, who mixes cleverness with cruelty. So wily was Robert that his nickname, *guiscart*, became his usual epithet, almost a surname. William translates the Old French *guiscart* as *ad omnia prudens* – "valiant under all circumstances." The *Gesta* reinforces this attribute by repeating, like a recurring refrain, Robert's ability to "make the difficult task easy through ingenuity" (*Dux, qui difficilem facilem facit arte laborem*, 5.244). In this instance, Guiscard finds a way to divert water into the Glykes River, surprising a Byzantine fleet at the siege of Durazzo.

But his agile mind often leads him to try more overt treachery. For instance, at the siege of Montepoloso in 1068,

> . . . the duke takes by cunning
> a stronghold that he cannot overwhelm by arms.   (2.460–61)
>
> (. . . dux quod non evalet armis
> Arte capit castrum;)

Robert bribes Godfrey, the guardian of Montepoloso, who owes his loyalty to another (2.459–77). Military strategists of Robert's day might have applauded Robert's ingenuity.[37] And indeed William of Apulia concludes this episode by rehearsing the formula of *ars* over *arma*:

---

[37] Vegetius' *De re militari*, which survives in 150 manuscripts from the tenth to the fifteenth centuries, asserts [*Epitoma Rei Militaris* 3.26, ed. C. Lang (1885; reprint,

> Thus the adroit duke's cleverness more often conquered
> by guile what it could not overcome with weapons.   (2.476–77)

> (Sic ducis astuti prudentia, quod superare
> Non armis potuit, superavit saepius arte.)

Still, the *Gesta* also reminds its readers that Godfrey's act of treachery earns him universal opprobrium:

> . . . But who would trust him after that?
> By all the people of Italy he was branded a traitor.   (2.474–75)

> (. . . sed quis post crederet illi?
> Traditor est Latii populo vocitatus ab omni.)

While the Italians deplored Norman-inspired trickery, such acts delighted their chief perpetrator, as the *Gesta* repeatedly makes clear. Many a celebration of the hero, like this one for instance, highlight the Odyssean agility of Guiscard's mind:

> To his brother Robert he [Humphrey] yielded the conquest
> of Calabria. That young man had a great capacity for hard work;
> Robert was valiant and clever and ready
> to set his hand to any business whatsoever,
> always pursuing lofty goals, and loving praise and renown.
> If victory's palm befell him by guile or by arms [*vel arte vel
> armis*],
> he thought it equally fine, because often what force [*violentia*]
> cannot achieve, the mind's adroitness [*versutia mentis*] can.
> (2.297–304)

Robert's ruses come thick and fast in the *Gesta*. But one in particular so belongs to the Norman canon that it deserves reporting in detail. Shortly after the battle of Civitate, Robert schemes to take a secure fortress, his first in Italy:

> He went off looting here and there,
> but could not capture any stronghold or town;
> he contrives to enter one place by a trick [*arte*];
> but its access was difficult because its numerous neighbors,
> a band of monks living there,
> would not let any strangers enter.
> The cunning man [*versutus*] contrives a clever scheme
> and orders his people to testify that one of them
> has died. Like a corpse, this man was laid out

Stuttgart, 1967), 121]: "It is better to vanquish the enemy by famine, surprise or terror than by open combat, where fortune usually has a more potent role than valor. . . . Opportunity in war is usually more efficacious than courage."

on a bier, and a cloth smeared with wax was ordered
to cover him, concealing his face,
in the Norman custom of veiling cadavers,
swords are concealed in the bier under the corpse's back.
To the monastery's entrance the body is carried
for burial, and a dead man's trick deceives [*defuncti fictio fallit*]
men ignorant of fraud, whom the living could not trick.
And while the funeral seemed to be proceeding in an ordinary
      way,
suddenly the man believed interred rises up.
With swords drawn, his companions attacked
the inhabitants of the place, deceived by guile [*deceptos arte*].
What could the dolts [*stolidi*] do? They cannot defend
      themselves;
they have nowhere to flee. They are all captured. And there
you put your first fortress garrison, Robert.[38]   (2.332–54)

The language and spirit here so purely echo a famous passage in Dudo's history, Hasting's capture of Luna, that William's exuberant re-telling of that tale is as shocking as it is entertaining. It is shocking because the perpetrator here is not an unredeemably pagan viking, but a Christian Norman, who has recently sworn fealty to the pope. How far has this Robert come, in more than a century-and-a-half, from the heathenism of Rollo? William assures his readers that Robert did not destroy the monastery or cast out the monks, though the violence of William's language here may raise suspicions rather than assuage them.[39]

It was the young Guiscard who deceived the monks. But he did not reform as he matured, or give up his roguish ways. In the *Gesta* he remained a trickster to the end, as we shall see, and his persistent affinity for the artful ruse ever marks Guiscard as an archetypal Norman. But William of Apulia also draped his hero in epic trappings from ancient Rome. Of all the *Gesta*'s epic elements, the most conspicuous is its choice of verse over prose and of the archaic dactylic hexameters over the popular rhymed, accentual verse that Malaterra, for example, occasionally introduced into his prose narrative. Like many other Norman historians, William wrote in verse because it could set the proper tone for an epic saga. The classical meter links the *Gesta* to the great works of the old poets, tapping into a venerable classical tradition.[40] But

---

[38] The passage concludes:
    Quid facerent stolidi? Nec se defendere possunt,
    Quo fugiant nec habent; omnes capiuntur; et illic
    Praesidium castri primum, Roberte, locasti.

[39] *Non monasterii tamen est eversio facta,/ Non extirpatus grex est monasticus inde.* (2.355–56)

[40] Umberto Ronca [*Cultura medioevale e poesia latina d'Italia nei secoli XI e XII* (Rome, 1892), 403–409] listed dozens of lines and episodes which he believed were modeled

William also knew how to exploit this tradition to suggest an ambivalence toward conquest and conquerors. Like Dudo before him, William of Apulia used classical models to subvert his ostensible aim of celebrating Norman heroes in high Latin style.

When he prefaced his *Gesta* with allusions to ancient poets singing of their own heroes (Prologue, i–ii), William seemed to have Vergil preeminently in mind. Indeed, he began his prologue by implicitly comparing Norman successes and settlement in Italy with the experience of Aeneas and his Trojans:

> Gesta ducum veterum veteres cecinere poetae;
> Aggrediar vates novus edere gesta novorum.[41]

> (Ancient poets celebrated the deeds of ancient leaders;
> a new poet, I shall try to proclaim the deeds of the new leaders.)

Frequent references to the *Aeneid* pepper the early books of the *Gesta* and buttress its euphoric tone as Normans conquer southern Italy and move into Sicily.[42] Many Vergilian allusions come in battle scenes, but others advance the riches of Italy, as for instance in a catalogue of towns that fall to Guiscard, including "Cosenza, strong in arms,/ and then affluent Gerace."[43]

But the tone shifts in the *Gesta*'s later books, as Guiscard's ambitions provoke rebellions. While the tone darkens, so the predominance of allusions moves from Vergilian echoes to recollections of the *Pharsalia*, Lucan's angry indictment of the civil war that toppled the Roman Republic. William's

---

directly on passages from Horace, Ovid, Statius, Lucan, and especially Vergil. To Ronca, the Normans' initial meeting with Melus (1.24–40) seems reminiscent of Vergil's Sinon episode (*Aeneid* 2.57–198). Robert Guiscard's stratagem of feigning death to gain entry to a fortified place (2.332–54) recalls the Trojan horse; heroic battles of the *Gesta* copy those of the *Aeneid*; Alexios's nocturnal assault on the rebels Bryennios and Basilakios (4.94–121) imitates a similar scene in the *Aeneid* (9.315 ff.). A. Pagano [*Il poema* Gesta Roberti Wiscardi *di Guglielmo Pugliese* (Naples, 1909), 108–18] argued convincingly that these epic episodes were not direct borrowings from Vergil but rather reflect generalized medieval traditions and language. Mathieu (*La geste de Robert Guiscard*, 61–62) concurred: "Guillaume de Pouille montre une certaine familiarité avec Ovide, Virgile, Stace et Lucain, mais les imitations directes ou textuelles sont rares; elles s'apparentent aux expressions qui figurent dans les 'lexiques prosodiques' du temps."

41 Note the artistry of these opening lines of the prologue, with the play of *veterum veteres* and *novus . . . novorum*; *gesta ducum veterum* and *gesta (ducum) novorum*; *veteres . . . poetae* and *vates novus*.

42 Mathieu, *La geste de Robert Guiscard*, 61–62, lists direct quotations and verbal allusions.

43 *. . . Cossentia fortis in armis,/ Tunc quoque dives opum Geratia . . .* , 2.413–14; cf. *Aeneid* 1.14, describing Carthage as "affluent and very harsh in its zeal for war" (*dives opum studiisque asperrima belli*).

Pharsalian allusions signal his disaffection with Guiscard's ruthlessness in pursuit of imperial designs.

Lucan was only twenty-five when his clash with Nero compelled him to commit suicide in 65 C.E.[44] But he left behind both a legacy as a tyrant-hater and an ambitious poem often acclaimed second to the *Aeneid* alone among Roman epics. As he wrote, Lucan kept Vergil in mind. Suetonius described Lucan's first recitation from the *Pharsalia*, which the precocious poet introduced to his audience with this gibe at Vergil's early trifles: "How far do I have to reach to match the 'Culix' ['The Flea']?"

Indeed, many have read the *Pharsalia* as Lucan's ironic response to the *Aeneid*.[45] While Vergil wrote just after the succession of civil wars had ceased at last, when Octavian's victories ended generations of bloodshed and promised peace and enlightened rule, Lucan labored in the full knowledge of Julio-Claudian despotism. This knowledge informs Lucan's portraits of his three Roman "heroes": Julius Caesar, invincible warrior and assured politician, fortune's darling, amoral and utterly self-absorbed; Caesar's opponent, Pompey, vacillating and insecure, an aging warrior who inspires affection and devotion; and the Stoic Cato, relentless in his dedication to liberty, to virtue, and to Rome.[46] Caesar must be the victor when these men clash, but Lucan invests that victory with ironic commentary, having seen the despotism of Caesar and his adoptive son, Octavian, reflected and reaching its logical culmination in Nero, their heir. In a paean to the Stoic holy man, Lucan risks

---

[44] Born into a prominent aristocratic family, Lucan (39–65 C.E.) seemed destined for a life of privilege and comfort. His uncle, Seneca, was tutor to the emperor Nero, only two years older than Lucan, and the young contemporaries may have known each other from boyhood. When Lucan was completing his education in literature, rhetoric, and philosophy in Athens, Nero recalled him to Rome and welcomed him among the group of his intimates. The emperor fancied himself an *artiste*, and for a while he may have thought Lucan a kind of junior colleague in the arts and a kindred soul. The young Lucan was already writing an ambitious epic on the war between Caesar and Pompey, a long poem called the *Civil War*, or the *Pharsalia*, after the decisive battle at Pharsalus. And so Lucan embarked on a promising career in politics, law, and letters, counted among Nero's friends.

But their friendship went badly awry. In his brief *Life of Lucan*, the second-century historian Suetonius writes that Nero ruined one of Lucan's public readings, interrupting the poet to summon the senate forthwith "for no reason except to throw cold water on the performance" (*nulla nisi refrigerandi sui causa*). Lucan retaliated with insults of his own, including an outrageous recitation of Nero's verse at a public latrine. He also joined with Calpurnius Piso and other Romans in a conspiracy to kill the emperor, speaking openly of "the glory of tyrannicide" and threatening "to toss Caesar's head to his pals." Such bluster was bound to attract attention. Permitted to choose how he should die, Lucan committed suicide, but not before sending his father some emendations to his verses.

[45] F. M. Ahl, *Lucan: An Introduction* (Ithaca, N.Y., 1976), 67.

[46] These portraits draw heavily on Ahl's interpretation (*Lucan: An Introduction*), especially pp. 155–57.

Nero's wrath by proclaiming that Cato (rather than the deified Julio-Claudians) has earned the worship of devout Romans:

> See the true father of his country, who most deserves your altars,
> Rome; you will never be ashamed to swear by him,
> and if you ever stand with neck unbound,
> then at that moment you will make him a god.   (9.601–604)

Such characters held strong appeal for medieval writers, who admired Lucan's righteous tone and polemical stance as much as the high drama of his subject, and who generally did not disdain his penchant for the violent and the grotesque. Many thought him Vergil's equal.[47] Norman historians were not, of course, the only ones to love and use Lucan. Suger's prose biographies of French kings, for instance, imitated Lucan rather than Suetonius, who may seem to us a more likely model.[48] But Lucan's passions played particularly well to Normans, with their finely tuned aversions to a feudal system that placed a lord over free men and upset the egalitarian ideal of Norman myth. As Norman historians grasped Lucan's satiric indictment of a fall from republican freedoms to the constraints of tyranny, who could appropriate Lucan's language more aptly than William of Apulia, whose characters fought for control over Italy, as had Caesar, Pompey, and Cato?

But William reserved the strongest Lucan parallels for his final books when Guiscard, like Caesar at the Rubicon, reveals his imperial ambitions by transgressing into forbidden territories. So as Guiscard prepares his ill-starred campaign into the Byzantine heartland, the hero attracts ominous recollections of Lucan's Caesar, openly a tyrant with no further pretensions to benevolent lordship. Against Jordan of Capua, for instance, Guiscard exacts a cruel retribution reminiscent of Caesar's rage vented against innocent Italians. For when Robert's enemy, Henry IV of Germany, swept into Italy, Jordan signed a peace treaty with him, "fearing," writes William, "that he might lose the lordship inherited from his father/ if the king entered Apulia" (5.116–17).

> And because Jordan had yielded to the king's sovereignty,
> the duke despoils his lands with fire and sword.   (5.118–19)

---

47 On the popularity of Lucan, and the accessibility of manuscripts, see Joan Gluckauf Haahr, "William of Malmesbury's Roman Models: Suetonius and Lucan," in *The Classics in the Middle Ages : Papers of the Twentieth Annual Conference of the Center for Medieval and Early Renaissance Studies*, ed. Aldo S. Bernardo and Saul Levin (Binghamton, N.Y., 1990), 170–72; David Knowles, *The Monastic Order in England* (Cambridge, 1963), 526. For Lucan's impact on thirteenth-century French histories, see Gabrielle M. Spiegel, *Romancing the Past: The Rise of Vernacular Prose Historiography in Thirteenth-Century France* (Berkeley, 1993), esp. pp. 152–213.

48 Charles Homer Haskins, *The Renaissance of the Twelfth Century* (1927; reprint, Cambridge, 1972), 224.

(Et quia Iordanis ditioni cesserat eius,
Dux huius terras ferro populatur et igni.)

This last phrase recalls *Pharsalia* 2.445:

Arva premi, quam si ferro populetur et igni.

Lucan's line stands in the midst of a passage on Caesar's rage for war, a rage expended to the detriment of innocent Italian lands and peoples:

Caesar, mad for war, rejoices to find no paths open
except through bloodshed, rejoices that the lands of Italy
which he tramples are not empty of a foe, and the fields he
                    assails, not deserted,
rejoices that he is not even wasting his time on the march, that he
                    wages
battle after battle. Rather than enter open city-gates, he prefers
the ones he has smashed his way through; rather than oppressing
the fields without the farmer's resistance
he prefers to ravage them with fire and sword:
He disdains advancing by an open road and appearing like a
                    proper citizen.
                                        (*Pharsalia* 2.439–46)

The people, who had wavered in their loyalties, lean now toward Pompey (2.453), having experienced the senseless wrath of Caesar.

As we shall soon see, William of Apulia begins to signal distress toward Guiscard's imperial ambitions by showing the reluctance of conscripted Normans to fight this war and by describing the suffering of civilians. But he also introduces another hero to challenge Guiscard's eastern campaign. Early in Book Four, Alexios Komnenos ascends to the throne of Byzantium, first by vanquishing rival claimants, Basilakios and Bryennios (4.81–121), then by overthrowing the aged emperor, Nikephoros Botaneiates, and subduing Constantinople (4.142–62). The *Gesta* showers him with heroic epithets in these passages. Nobly born and raised as a warrior, Alexios is *prudens* (4.96), "vigorous in cunning calculation and bold in combat" (4.82). So he shares Guiscard's essential traits.[49] To emphasize this twinning, the *Gesta* repeats these dual qualities of commander and trickster:

Defeated in battle, Bryennios surrenders and is captured.
Defeated by an Alexine ruse, Basilakios surrendered.   (4.92–93)

---

[49] Anna Komnene, historian and daughter of Alexios, also recognized the qualities that Normans and Byzantines held in common. See Albu, "Bohemond and the Rooster," 157–68.

(Bellando victus cedit capiturque Brienus.
Victus Alexina cessit Basilachius arte.)

William describes this ruse with gusto, detailing Alexios's feigned flight and
surprise attack by night (4.94–119), concluding the episode with this reprise:

> Indefatigable and wary, thus the victor Alexios conquered
> many enemies of the empire by arms and by guile.   (4.120–21)

> (Impiger et cautus sic victor Alexius hostes
> Imperii multos armis superavit et arte.)

Soon this canny warrior will turn his formidable wits against Guiscard.

Any epic hero, of course, needs a worthy opponent to test his mettle. But
the *Gesta*'s sympathies with Alexios surpass this necessity, even making
Guiscard look foolish by comparison. When Alexios captures Constantinople
in 1081, for example, he takes into custody Guiscard's daughter, who was
betrothed to a prince of the imperial family. Hoping to placate Guiscard and
avert his impending attack, Alexios treats the girl with honor (4.155–58). But
Guiscard blunders ahead, meeting the new emperor's conciliatory gestures
with fresh provocation (4.159–70). For he immediately welcomes into his
entourage a "lying impostor" (*mentitus . . . seductor*; 4.162–63) who
pretends to be the ex-emperor Michael VII Doukas, overthrown by Alexios's
predecessor in 1078. "The better to justify his expedition" (4.169–70), Guiscard threatens to restore this "Michael" to the throne that Alexios now holds.

At this point in the *Gesta*, sentiment swings toward Guiscard's adversary,
Alexios Komnenos, who assumes the amiable character of Lucan's Pompey.
But especially does William's portrait of Pope Gregory VII owe something to
Lucan's Cato, the moral voice of the Roman republic. When Gregory dies in
1085, only seven weeks before the death of Robert Guiscard, William eulo-
gizes the pope in terms recalling Lucan's paean to *sanctus* Cato.[50] Both are
holy men swayed by no passions but love of justice. Both are rigorous moral-
ists, yet also moderate and emotionally stable. And both serve the people,
without regard for personal gain or comfort.

It may seem natural to honor Pope Gregory with allusions to a Stoic saint
and martyr. But William is pushing dangerous limits when he risks the wrath
of Guiscard's sons, including his own patron Roger, by criticizing Guiscard
and evoking compassion for his mortal enemy, Alexios. Although the papacy
in William's day was urging rapprochement with Byzantium and opposing
the Normans' Byzantine war, William did not dare support the papal view
openly, even if William's sympathies lay with the Pope's policy and against
Norman aggression. But there was a way for a learned writer to make his

---

[50] Compare William's tribute to Gregory, 5.255–67, with Lucan, *Pharsalia* 2.372–91,
especially 2.376–78, 389.

feelings clear to some in his audience, safely and without fear of reprisal. Near the end of Normandy's first century, Dudo had found Vergil an appropriate vehicle for both honoring and satirizing the newly important Norman counts. A hundred years later, William of Apulia could look back over decades of despotism by ambitious princes, finding Lucan's lens particularly apt. This is a sophisticated alignment, but a learned audience of William's contemporaries, schooled in Vergil and Lucan, could decipher the code and grasp William's argument against the injustice of Guiscard's Byzantine campaign and the ambition of Norman princes.[51]

In his epilogue, William pointedly reclaims the Vergilian comparison, pronouncing Roger Borsa "a duke worthier than the Roman duke Octavian," who should reward his own poet "as he rewarded Vergil." So Vergil literally gets the final word, in a client's plea for a patron's beneficence. Perhaps this petition sufficiently flattered Roger. By this point, however, the narrative has implicitly linked the poet with the dissident Lucan, and Roger's father Robert Guiscard with Lucan's Julius Caesar. For erudite readers, the alignment of Caesar/Guiscard, Cato/Gregory, and Pompey/Alexios does not compliment Guiscard. This shift of poetic model from Vergil to Lucan, furthermore, parallels the *Gesta*'s transition from celebration to threnody.

As we have seen, the predominant mood of the first three books is joyous, culminating in the account of the war for Sicily, William's focus in Book Three. His anti-Muslim fervor nurtured by the First Crusade, William endows the Sicilian enterprise with the attributes of a holy war: in a nod to the Crusaders' victories (3.100–105), the *Gesta* announces that the Holy Land would still be under Muslim domination if the powerful *gens Gallorum*, "incited by divine will," had not opened up the long-barred Holy Sepulcher, "through God's inspiration." Just so, in William's eyes, the Normans struggled in Sicily as *Cultores Christi* (3.218), Christians fortified with the body of Christ (3.236) and earning victory "by divine will" (*nutu divino*; 3.247). In his speech before the attack on Palermo, Robert affirms Christ's imminent aid:

> ... When you see that the time is at hand,
> Rush in! By Christ's mercy the hard-to-capture will open up.
> He makes any difficult task easy.   (3.291–93)

---

[51] William of Apulia was not alone in modeling a Norman prince on Lucan's Caesar. William of Malmesbury did likewise when interpreting the character of William Rufus. See George Meredith Logan, "Lucan in England: The Influence of the *Pharsalia* on English Letters from the Beginnings through the Sixteenth Century" (Ph.D. diss., Harvard University, 1967), 54–55. On the similarities between Lucan's Caesar and Milton's Satan, see William Blissett, "Caesar and Satan," *Journal of the History of Ideas* 18 (1957), 221–32.

(. . . Dum tempus adesse videtis,
Currite! dura capi, Christo miserante, patebit.
Difficilem quemvis facilem facit ipse laborem.)

The Normans celebrate this God-given victory by converting the mosques into churches (3.332–36).

William's enthusiasm for the Norman conquest of Sicily highlights, by contrast, his apparent disapproval of the attack against the Byzantine Empire. A sense of foreboding lingers over the last two books. Through these changes in mood, William implies that divine will, which authorized the wars in Sicily and southern Italy, opposed and doomed Guiscard's assault on the peoples across the Adriatic. This view complemented the interests of William's avowed patrons, Urban II (Pope from 1088 to 1099) and Guiscard's younger son, Roger (duke of Apulia from 1085 to 1111).[52] Urban's policies, pursuing Union of the Churches and *rapprochement* with Alexios Komnenos, followed the precedent of Pope Gregory VII, who not only sought to unite eastern and western Christendom but also often found himself at odds with rebellious Normans and the thrice-excommunicated Robert Guiscard.[53] From Roger's perspective, his father's Byzantine offensive must have seemed a foolish diversion from consolidating Norman holdings in southern Italy, the lands which were Roger's inheritance. Roger may have had another reason, too, for wishing that his aging father had not exerted himself in this endeavor, since it claimed Robert's life before the boy was capable of vigorous rule on his own.

William of Apulia and his patrons must have been of one mind concerning Guiscard's ill-fated campaign against the Byzantine heartland. So immediately after his repeated reckoning of the daring and cunning that won brilliant victories for Alexios Komnenos (4.81–121), William turns to Robert Guiscard cajoling and threatening his mutinous troops (4.122–33). Mustering an army at Otranto, Robert finds that the men long to stay in Italy with their wives and dear children (*uxures et pignora cara*), enjoying the hard-won peace (4.128): "That journey seems to many cruel and unusual."

The language of "cruel and unusual" punishment, which a just leader would not inflict, imparts a melancholy tone to this passage, which recounts the deeply rooted resistance of Normans against a leader eager to expand his powers at the expense of the people's peace. The historian appears to lose heart in solidarity with the reluctant soldiers. Although this final expedition dominates the last two-fifths of his work, William considers it outside his main story of the conquest of Italy, as announced in the prologue (iii–v), and beyond the divine mandate (1.1–3).

---

[52] The *Gesta*'s prologue (vi–xiii) claims that William writes at the behest of both princes.

[53] On the wavering, often hostile, relations between Gregory and Robert, see H. E. J. Cowdrey, *The Age of Abbot Desiderius: Montecassino, the Papacy, and the Normans in the Eleventh and Early Twelfth Centuries* (Oxford, 1983), 122–76.

For Robert Guiscard, however, Italian conquests have only whetted his appetite for the greater riches to which Italy is but a gateway. The mercantile wealth and harbors of Sicily beckon, but Guiscard finds the prestige and opulence of Byzantium especially alluring. This is a land whose affairs William of Apulia knows well. Although the historian of Robert Guiscard and the Normans of the south barely acknowledges Normandy itself – and William never so much as alludes to the Norman conquest of England – yet he repeatedly dwells on details of Byzantine imperial politics, wars, and intrigues.

Not surprisingly, William knows the succession of catapans and generals who directed the campaigns against the Normans in southern Italy: Tornikios (1.57–58) and his legate in the first battle, Leo Pakianos (1.67–70); General Michael Dokeianos, who humiliated the Lombard mercenary Harduin (1.199–215); Michael Dokeianos' replacement, Basil Bojannes' son (1.344–443); the great George Maniakes (1.441–43); emperor Michael V's ineffectual appointee Sinodianos, soon recalled by imperial order (1.405–13); and Stephen Paternos, sent to Bari to assassinate Guiscard (2.542–73). William also relates other incidents of Norman–Byzantine contact: unsuccessful in his rebellion against Guiscard, Jocelyn, lord of Molfetta, flees to Constantinople (2.458) to return in 1071 with a Byzantine fleet (2.540–41). In that same year William has Jocelyn unwittingly play a role in the blinding of the emperor Romanos Diogenes (3.82–90). Another Norman rebel, Robert's recalcitrant nephew Abelard, seeks refuge with the benevolent emperor Alexios Komnenos (3.659–67).

What is unexpected is William's intimate acquaintance with Byzantium's internal politics and her clashes on the eastern frontier. The *Gesta* frequently comments on the succession of Byzantine emperors. Constantine VIII and Basil II are reigning when the Normans first join with Melus of Bari to raid Apulia (1.60–61). It is Michael IV the Epileptic who orders the Sicilian expedition (1.196–98) and later leaves the crown to his nephew Michael when at last he succumbs to his wasting disease (1.402–405). William knows about the blinding of this imprudent Michael V, following his refusal to share power with the Empress Zoë (1.461–67), and Zoë's subsequent marriage to Constantine Monomachos, the enemy of George Maniakes, who then rebelled against the throne (1.468–77). The death of Constantine X in 1067 introduces a long description of the disastrous reign of Romanos Diogenes, with his defeat at Manzikert in 1071, his subsequent capture and a legendary confrontation with the Sultan Alp Arslan. William has the chivalrous sultan put Romanos on a throne beside his own and ask the defeated emperor what he would do if the present roles were reversed. The rough soldier answers (3.61–62):

> If you had subdued me and my men like this, I'd order
> your head cut off or I'd have you hanged on the gallows.

But the sultan offers terms of peace, both generous and humane. Honorably treated by the Turkish prince, Romanos ironically meets his doom at the hands of his step-son, Michael VII.

It is here that William alludes to the First Crusade, claiming that Michael's folly would have left the East to the Turks even to the present time if God had not inspired the Normans to open up the roads to the Holy Sepulcher (3.100–105). As Book Three began with this account of Michael VII's cruel path to power, so Book Four opens with the announcement of Michael's deposition in 1078 and the coronation of the aging Nicephoros Botaneiates (4.71–80). When William introduces the new emperor as "inexperienced in war, but shrewd, with a nimble mind" (4.78–79), he reveals the Norman respect for cleverness. So he also shows interest here in Botaneiates' young lieutenant, Alexios Komnenos (4.73–121), who defeats the pretenders, Bryennios and Basilakios.

By the mid-1070s Guiscard himself had formal ties with imperial politics. When Michael VII offered his own son and heir, Constantine Doukas, as bridegroom for one of Guiscard's daughters, Guiscard dispatched the girl to Constantinople, where the Byzantines re-baptized her in the Greek rite and named her Helena. But the hapless girl never married her prince. Michael's deposition by Botaneiates offered Guiscard a pretext for entering Byzantine territories, to rescue his daughter and restore the dethroned emperor.

William's language, here as elsewhere, acknowledges Byzantine imperial rights over all others in the secular realm. Byzantium is the Holy Empire (*Imperium Sanctum*), controlled by a Ruler of Empire (*Imperii Rector*).[54] By implication this monarch also surpasses lesser princes, including kings (*reges*). The *Gesta* styles Henry as *rex Henricus* (4.32, 172, 176, 549; 5.117), who wears the "crown of the Roman kingdom" (*Romani regni . . . coronam*; 4.31; cf. 4.173). When William extols Guiscard's double victory over both realms, the distinction becomes explicit (4.566–68):

> . . . So at one time were conquered
> Two lords of the earth, that infamous [*iste*] German king
> and the mighty ruler of the Roman Empire.

> (. . . Sic uno tempore victi
> Sunt terrae domini duo, rex Alemannicus iste,
> Imperii rector Romani maximus ille.

This is the Byzantine point of view, but not the opinion of the German "king" and his subjects. Nor is it the universal judgment of Norman historians. For Malaterra, Henry is unquestionably *imperator* (cf. 3.333, 37).

---

54 *Imperium Sanctum* (Holy Empire) 3.662; 4.87, 88, 147; *Imperii Rector* (Ruler of Empire) 3.1–2; 5.35, sometimes also called *Imperium* (4.246, 279, 291, 317) because the meter does not admit *Imperator* (Emperor).

The Old French translator of Amatus bestows the title of *impeor, empeor,* or *impereour* upon German and Byzantine alike (1.24, 25; 3.1); *li impereour de li Grex . . . de l'autre empereor* (1.25). Discovering that his source calls Henry IV "king" at one point, Amatus hastens to explain the discrepancy: the young Henry must not yet have been crowned (6.9). But William of Apulia has absorbed the Byzantine spirit of late eleventh-century Apulia, where the empire had lately been investing considerable attention. This spirit harmonizes with the will of the *Gesta*'s papal patron, who advocated *rapprochement* with eastern Christendom. So William envisions a carefully constructed realm which the Byzantine emperor dominates by divine right. The *Gesta* makes Byzantium the only true empire and the spiritual and political mistress of the western world.[55]

William's Byzantine sympathies contrast with the indictment of Malaterra, who calls the Greeks "always a very treacherous people" [*semper genus perfidissimum* (2.29)], and with the scorn of Amatus, who writes that the Norman mercenaries gauged the Greeks' mettle as soon as they opposed them in Apulia (1.21): "And they commenced fighting against the Greeks, and they saw that they were like women" (*Et commencerent à combatre contre li Grez, et virent qu'il estoient comme fames*). William knows these indictments of the Byzantines.[56] Indeed, he has a Lombard named Harduin make similar insinuations when wooing Norman mercenaries to his cause: "Why," argues Harduin, "should we let wealthy Apulia be held by the effeminate Greeks [*femineis Graecis*], a cowardly people, dissolute, hung over from drinking?" (1.224–27).

But this is not the prevailing view of the *Gesta Roberti Wiscardi,* whose interest in Byzantium colors the portrayal of Guiscard's final attack on the empire. The *Gesta* deflates Guiscard's pretext for invasion, first by narrating how the valiant Alexios (*bellator Alexius*; 4.143) has already exacted vengeance against Michael's usurper, Nikephoros Botaneiates (4.142–46) and has treated Guiscard's daughter Helena with suitable honor (4.154–58), then by ridiculing the "Michael" in Robert's entourage as an impostor (4.162–70). The *Gesta* discloses how absurdly this trickery misfires when Guiscard

---

55 The ties between William of Apulia and Byzantium are complex. The Byzantine historian Anna Komnene, writing in the 1130s and 1140s, somehow knew a source of William's or perhaps the *Gesta* itself. Anna's *Alexiad* translates three brief passages of the *Gesta* nearly verbatim. Anna knew no Latin, so she perhaps relied on a bilingual informant who reported these episodes, all surrounding Guiscard's siege of Durazzo. Though the similarities are limited and brief, their very existence shows how closely William moved toward the Byzantine sphere.

56 This accusation is a cliché among western writers. Décarreaux, *Normands, papes, et moines,* 22. Note that William's indictments of Byzantine foibles and vices appear in Book One: 20, 78–79, 210–12, 223–28, 281–85. And the most virulent critique comes not from the *Gesta*'s narrator directly but from a disgruntled Lombard (1.210–12, 223–28). The *Gesta*'s view of Byzantium softens as the narrative progresses.

exhibits his pseudo-Michael at the siege of Durazzo, hoping that the "imperial" presence will win the people's sympathy and provoke their surrender. Crowned with the diadem and announced with horns and lyres, "Michael" appears before the city. But the pageantry fails to impress the crowd, some of whom had seen the real Michael Doukas. From Durazzo's high walls, laughter and derision greet the spectacle, and the people taunt the charlatan with language that alludes to Lucan's bacchante simile (*Pharsalia* 1.675):

> . . . "That fellow used to
> set tables with goblets full of wine;
> he was only a waiter, and a lowly one at that."   (4.269–71)

It is a humiliating moment and a rare failure for Guiscard, foreshadowing the ultimate disaster of this campaign.

The Normans and their tricks meet their own match in the sophisticated Byzantines. This may be William's point in telling such a memorable and unflattering tale, and narrating it with zest. It is one of three episodes from the *Gesta* that somehow made their way into Anna Komnene's *Alexiad* some four decades later, showing again William's proximity to the Byzantine world, though we cannot see precisely where he got his detailed information on Byzantine internal affairs, just as we cannot pinpoint how Anna received William's stories, if the overlapping tales are not merely a coincidental result of historians working on the same characters and episodes.[57]

The spectacle before Durazzo best illustrates how far the *Gesta*'s sympathies have shaded away from Guiscard as he launches his Byzantine offensive. Warfare still dominates the history but no longer seems glorious. William's persistent interest in military action distinguishes this history from the works of Amatus and Malaterra, who devote more attention to other matters, particularly religion and diplomacy. Perhaps William himself had training or experience that drew him to military history. But the dominance of force may also reflect William's bleak view of his world, where sieges often bring atrocities against civilians. Consider the attention given to the assaults on Bari (2.480–573; 3.111–66), Trani (3.271–390), Salerno (3.424–44), Giovinazzo (3.539–66), Durazzo (4.213–505), and Cephalonia (5.228–34). After the capture of Bari in 1071, naval warfare becomes increasingly important for the Normans, and William's interest in it grows, culminating in his relatively detailed account of a battle against a combined Byzantine–Venetian fleet in 1084 (5.154–98).

In both land and sea battles William shows some concern for military tactics. He describes with relish, for instance, the martial arts and weapons of the Swabians (2.148–63). In two successive Norman victories over the

---

[57] On these three episodes in the *Gesta Roberti Wiscardi* and the *Alexiad*, see Mathieu, *La geste de Robert Guiscard*, 38–46.

Byzantine Michael Dokeianos (1.254–302), William gives numbers of combatants, the condition of arms, and the disposition of battle lines. He also explains the Greek custom of continually sending fresh troops into battle. As Alexios Komnenos presents Robert a unique challenge, so too Alexios's strategic skills fascinate the Norman historian, who reports the competing tricks when Robert and Alexios face one another before Durazzo (4.366–424) and Janina (5.11–18). At the battle for Janina, the emperor arranges wagons along the plain and bars access with threshing sledges that would pierce horses' hooves. But the Normans under Bohemond, protected by dense fog, nonetheless surprise the Byzantines, putting them to flight.

Another form of violence also punctuates William's narrative, especially in the darker final books. Like minor variations on a major theme, rebellions recur throughout the *Gesta*. They begin early. Soon after Melus enlists Normans in his struggle against his Byzantine foes, the Normans are fighting among themselves over the spoils (1.148–52) and forsaking their chosen leaders for the Lombard prince Adenolf (1.318–27). They repeatedly abandon one master to follow another promising greater rewards (1.414–16). A Lombard mercenary may accuse the Byzantines of *avaritia* because they refuse to share their booty with him (1.210–12), but the burden of evidence points to the Normans, as ambitious as they are impecunious, as the most susceptible to charges of greed.

Tensions increase as the Hauteville brothers turn against one another. The *Gesta* reports that Humphrey cedes to Robert the conquest of Calabria (2.297–98). But Robert takes his knights pillaging "wherever he could, especially conducting multiple plundering in those territories which his brother held" (2.310–11). Robert shares the spoils equally with his men, who hold him dear as he does them (2.312–13). But he seems not to have shared his loot or his love with brother Humphrey, who retaliates by seizing Robert while they dine together. Only the swift intervention of another Norman, Jocelyn, prevents Robert from lunging at Humphrey with his sword. In the wake of this episode, Humphrey keeps Robert in custody a short while before releasing him to pursue further Calabrian conquests.

It comes as no surprise when more widespread animosities follow. Guiscard's marriage to Sichelgaita rouses jealousy in the counts, who plot his death (2.444–50). Eventually their scheming leads to rebellion (2.451–79).[58] The conspirators include Geoffrey, lord of Conversano; Jocelyn, the Norman who had prevented Humphrey and Robert from killing one another over dinner; and Robert's own nephew and ward, Abelard. This boy was the son of Humphrey, who had died in 1057, leaving the child to the uncertain care of

---

[58] On the Norman rebellions of the 1070s, see pp. 434–36 in William B. McQueen, "Relations between the Normans and Byzantium, 1071–1112," *Byzantion* 56 (1986), 427–76. McQueen's article stresses "the instability of Norman society" in southern Italy and the weakness of Guiscard's position within this mercenary society.

Guiscard, who had shown a suspicious interest in the boy's inheritance. Robert soon crushed this rebellion by a ruse, bribing Godfrey, the guardian of Montepoloso, the stronghold where Geoffrey had taken refuge.

Upon Guiscard's victorious return from Sicily, another rebellion breaks out, this one engineered by Peter of Trani, who refuses to give up the land conquered by his own father but claimed by Guiscard (3.352–411). As elsewhere, here too William makes no attempt to whitewash Robert and paint the conspirators as culpable. On the contrary, he accords legitimacy to their motives, as he did when Guiscard usurped Abelard's inheritance (2.451–53) and as he will when Guiscard extorts his daughter's dowry from the counts, who complain about the imposition of this novel debt (3.498–508). Such actions finally provoke the Norman lords to a massive rebellion, whose description closes Book Three (*Gesta* 509–687):

> The Norman counts often complained among themselves
> that the duke treated them so badly and so oppressively;
> they hid for a long time the rage of their treacherous hearts.

But gradually they draw into their scheming a widening circle of conspirators, Lombard lords and Norman, all wounded by Guiscard's aggressions.

> This discord not only shatters Apulian lands
> but even prevails on the Calabrians and Lucanian shores
> and as far as Campania.   (3.528–35)

Three of the duke's nephews join the plot, including the aggrieved Abelard.

> . . . Wrath inflamed his nephews
> against him, as he wanted to have dominion over them all.
>   (3.525–26)

This is a classic formulation of the Norman nobles' defiance of another who would be their lord. Close kinship does not tie uncle to nephews with bonds of loyalty or affection. On the contrary, it makes them rivals for property and power.

The resulting chaos brings this Norman world to the brink of madness:

> . . . Fear of attack is everywhere;
> the frenzy of brigands rages in all directions,
> and all over Italy the number of plunderers has grown.
>   (3.530–32)

> (. . . Metus est hostilis ubique;
> Latronum rabies passim bachatur, et omnes
> Per partes Italas raptorum copia crevit.)

Metus ("fear," "dread") is a word Lucan uses often, as he captures the desperation roused by the Roman civil wars. So, too, he frequently associates *rabies* ("rage," "frenzy") with Julius Caesar, the single-minded victor. William's allusions to those wars among kin usurps Lucan's tone and implied criticism of ambitions realized at great cost. William's later assurance that the duke remains calm, and the usual disclaimer *vel arte vel armis/ Omnes exsuperat* (3.568–69), cannot assuage the reader's feelings of uneasiness.

This rebellion spreads to embrace a large number of dissidents (3.528–29). Still, many people remain loyal to Robert, including the inhabitants of Giovinazzo. Although invested by an army of insurgents, the townspeople refuse to capitulate, holding out until Guiscard rescues them by a ruse. He dispatches a messenger with this false report:

> "Here comes Roger, Robert's son," says
> the messenger, "and the duke has given him great bands
> of cavalry and foot soldiers to lead."   (3.562–64)

At this news, the besiegers scatter, leaving the duke victorious as usual (3.567–71). Yet throughout southern Italy the rebels fight on for a second year, and William devotes another hundred lines to the vagaries of this warfare, in a narrative packed with sieges, battles, and vengeance. Inspired by Italian and Byzantine practices, the duke even punishes one hapless rebel, Gradilon, with blinding and castration (3.613–14). And still the revolt continues, until Guiscard forces the counts to capitulate, one faction at a time. When Abelard can no longer resist, he flees to a gracious welcome at the Byzantine court (3.659–63). The last rebels surrender, swearing fealty to their duke (3.685).

> The duke, clever and bold, knows how to bow
> unbending necks and impose an end to wars.   (3.686–87)

So ends Book Three, with Robert compelling the Normans to accept his lordship. It is not a comforting resolution for those who know the Norman antipathy to submission. Surely the subdued will only lie low, awaiting another opportunity.

This struggle for and against domination often leads William of Apulia to probe existential questions, as he laments the passions that condemn men to *ambitio* and *avaritia*, resulting in factions and bloodshed. This dark counter-theme undermines the *Gesta*'s ostensible celebration of conquest and achievement. Indeed, early in Book One, the greed of the first Norman freebooters in the south moves William to a tirade on the folly of ambition, a lament that anticipates the despair of Orderic Vitalis and Wace:

> But since the aspirations of the human mind are prone
> to greed, and money prevails everywhere,
> [Normans] abandoned now this lord, now that,
> always attaching themselves to one who paid more.
> . . .

139

> A great lust for domination thrust those princes
> into wars. Each wishes to be the most powerful
> and strives to encroach on the rights of another.
> From this dry tinder come feuds, battles, deaths;
> and so among mortals woes increase.
> Ah poor men, whatever they venture in this world is vain:
> for empty praise they endure countless toils,
> and more will they suffer when they leave worldly cares.
>
> (1.140–43; 148–55)

> (Sed quia mundanae mentis meditamina prona
> Sunt ad avaritiam, vincitque pecunia passim,
> Nunc hoc nunc illo contempto, plus tribuenti
> Semper adhaerebant;
> . . .
>   Illis principibus dominandi magna libido
> Bella ministrabat. Vult quisque potentior esse,
> Alter et alterius molitur iura subire.
> Procedunt lites hoc fomite, proelia, mortes;
> Inter mortales ideo mala plurima crescunt.
> Heu miseri, mundo quicquid conantur inane est:
> Innumeros vana passi pro laude labores,
> Plus cruciabuntur postquam mundana relinquent.)

The language of this passage emphasizes the folly of this greed and strife. See, for instance, the seductive alliteration and word placement of line 153:

> Innumeros vana passi pro laude labores . . .
>
> (for empty praise they endure countless toils,)

Although *vana* properly modifies *laude*, its position between *innumeros* and *passi* stresses the vanity of the suffering and the countless labors, as well as the emptiness of the praise men seek. These toils lead only to the eternal torments of the damned.

This early lament introduces a dreary note that culminates in a long threnody at the *Gesta*'s close (5.301–22). This tone echoes throughout the *Gesta* as the mighty tumble from the heights. So the Byzantine emperor, Romanos Diogenes, suddenly loses his imperial title and becomes a blinded monk (3.91–92). Often death surprises nobles in the flower of their youth, as Argyrus passes away in disgrace among the Byzantines (2.278–83) and the hot-blooded rebel, Jocelyn, languishes and dies in Guiscard's custody (3.139–41). The most pitiful fall is Abelard's. Displaced by his uncle, Duke Robert, the young man escapes to Alexios Komnenos only to perish as he plans a triumphant return to Italy (3.659–67). William interposes *potentem/ . . . cum fascibus atque triumphis* ("powerful/ . . . with fasces and triumphs" – ancient Italian symbols of victory and honor) with *exul . . . mortuus . . .*

humatus ("an exile . . . dead . . . buried") to make the reader feel the irony of this victory of *mors* over *iuveniles . . . artus* ("death/youthful limbs").

The *Gesta* persists in recalling this theme, the wretchedness of the human condition and the inevitable cruelty of death. This insistence upon *lacrimae rerum* extends beyond the fates of the lords to the struggles of ordinary people for survival, as they suffer for their masters' ambitions. The battle-grounds in these Norman campaigns, after all, rarely pit warriors against one another in open combat, but more often feature sieges of civilian populations in their homes and the despoiling of peasants' lands. The citizens of Trani, for instance, victims of the dissension between Peter II and Robert Guiscard, despair of surviving a blockade (3.379–86), while the dispute between Guiscard and Prince Gisulf reduces the Salernitans to eating dogs, horses, mice, and asses (3.428–30). Evidently moved by their plight, William repeats the story of a man in the camp outside Salerno who smuggled daily rations to his father in the city with the help of his loyal and clever dog.[59] Other families, caught in the feud between Guiscard and the rebel Ami weep inconsolably so long as Ami holds their children hostage. Even as the narrative notes the duke's grace and the parents' joy at their children's return, the *Gesta* lingers over the mothers' and fathers' crying (3.647–49). Such sentiments prepare the reader for the *Gesta*'s sympathies toward the men forced to join Guiscard's war effort against the Byzantine Empire (4.128–33).

When William does not explicitly blame the ambitions of duke or warriors for human sorrows, he often invokes fickle fortune as the culprit. In fact, despite the apparent clash with Christian doctrine, medieval writers often follow their classical models in invoking fortune as the cause of certain events.[60] The prominence of this convention in the *Gesta Roberti Wiscardi* reveals William's debt to ancient literature, especially Lucan's epic. It also reinforces William's bleak outlook, contributing to the sinister counter-tone which prevails in the last two books, since this primitive happenstance can wreak havoc at any moment.

Even in the early books, when William reports the advance of the Normans in Italy and the rise of the house of Hauteville, a foreboding of fortune's vagaries haunts the narrative. From time to time, William reminds his readers that fortune often wavers between two courses and keeps the

---

[59] 3.432–40. Amatus tells another version of this story, with Gisulf as the villain who has a dog killed for delivering bread to a priest inside the city (8.20).

[60] Cf. Otto of Freising, *Gesta Friderici*, ed. Franz-Josef Schmale (Darmstadt, 1965), 310. 2,15: *Porro, ut in rebus caducis ex arridentis fortune blandimento fieri solet, rebus secundis elata in tantam elationis extumuit audaciam. . . .* Amatus 2.31; 5.1, 27. Fortune is important to Malaterra, though he often ignores its dark side; but see 1.16; 2.24, 25, 26; 3.9. On the influence of classical authors, especially Sallust, on Malaterra's references to Fortune, see Loud, "Gens Normannorum," 114; Wolf, *Making History*, 151–52. On the influence of Boethius' *Consolation of Philosophy*, see Beryl Smalley, *Historians in the Middle Ages* (London, 1974), 46–47.

outcome long in doubt, as in the first battle of the Normans and Greeks (1.73) and in Romanos Diogenes' war against the Turks (3.23). Once she has assigned victory, fortune oppresses the losers and favors the victors, as the Normans in Italy learn early, in the wake of their crushing defeat under Melus of Bari (1.114). When fortune does smile, her darlings are still subject to the whims of chance. So the newly chosen leaders of the Normans accept their territories, *nisi fors inimica repugnet* ("unless hostile chance should oppose it"; 1.237). And when the Normans are most confident of fortune's blessings, she strikes them down with cruel irony. So they expect success under Melus's remarkable son Argyrus (1.436):

> . . . if you are our leader, fortune will favor us.

Then Argyrus betrays their trust. Even the best of luck must run out eventually, as illustrated by fortune's chariot (2.35), which overwhelms the wealthy Norman Peter I of Trani and exalts the sons of Tancred for their moments of glory.

Surely immense good luck blessed Robert Guiscard. In his military campaigns and in the many conspiracies against him, he prospered. At the siege of Palermo, for instance,

> Favorable to Robert and wretched for the city was
> Fortune's work . . .   (3.316–17)

Yet the tide turns against him as he embarks on the Byzantine campaign, and ultimately he, too, faces ruin. William classes among *infortunia* the plague that strikes the hero down (5.221).

The attachment of *fortuna* to Guiscard for most of his career is another bond that links the *Gesta*'s Guiscard to the *Pharsalia*'s Julius Caesar. In his epic, Lucan invokes Fortune 146 times, as ill fortune dogs Pompey and good fortune favors Julius Caesar.[61] Likewise, William of Apulia lets fortune, and not heaven, move the pawns in his epic tale, even during the Holy War against the infidel in Sicily (3.316–17). The *Gesta*'s first mention of heaven's intervention is in fact ironic (2.146–47). It comes as William is describing the (false) confidence of the German army while the soldiers await battle at Civitate, where they will fight with the papal forces. Although the Germans anticipate victory with heaven's aid, they are about to lose utterly against the Normans. The second instance occurs as Guiscard consults the leaders of his troops while they expect the imminent arrival of Alexios Komnenos (4.354). The war council urges Robert to steal out of camp and surprise the advancing Byzantine army. But he rejects this advice, venturing the surprising contention that it is vain to seek victory through ruse (*arte*) since success comes

---

[61] On Fortune's influence over the action in the *Pharsalia*, see F. M. Ahl, *Lucan: An Introduction* (Ithaca, N.Y., 1976), especially pp. 293–97.

only at heaven's granting. Surely someone is using irony here, too. Is it Guiscard, the master trickster, teasing his men? Or is it the narrator, mocking Guiscard's implausible excuse? In any case, Robert's mock reverence allows him to neglect their counsel and do as he pleases.

In the invocation of fortune over heaven, the *Gesta*'s classicism and pessimism marry well. The sense of melancholy builds to a climax, until the threnody at Guiscard's death confirms the validity of the counter-themes that converge to dominate the final book. Twice the *Gesta* reveals that Robert sails from Italy never to return, as he bids farewell to his wife and people standing on the Adriatic shore (5.140–42) and leaves unfulfilled his plan to settle in Salerno, resting-place of the apostle Matthew and Pope Gregory VII (5.282–83). Robert's death while on campaign – still a warrior as he approached his seventieth birthday – might have inspired a eulogy like that given his brother Humphrey (2.373–80), where the *Gesta* confines the weeping to two half lines.[62] But the lamentation of Guiscard's wife, Sichelgaita, persists through twenty-two hexameter lines (5.301–22) as her husband lies dying. She lacerates her cheeks and tears out her hair, like any grieving widow (5.300), but her dirge is far from formulaic, as it foretells her own doom and that of her son and his people without Robert's protection. She concludes by admitting the futility of pleading with pitiless death:

> Ah! wretched me! In vain I pray to death always ungracious
> to the suppliant and sparing no one ever.   (5.321–22)

Then her son Roger Borsa takes up the wailing and groaning (5.323–27) until his cries reach the heavens. A child of thirteen, he is losing his father before he is strong enough to acquire new lands or even secure the lands his father had won (5.325–26).

> Who could have kept a dry eye, seeing the tears
> of the people there? Who could have been so long-suffering, so
> > unfeeling
> that he would not suffer along with so many sufferers?
> > > (5.328–30)

The subjective style sustains the dreary mood to the end, as death robs Guiscard of his beloved life (*moriens vita spoliatur amica*; 5.332) and his widow accompanies the body to Italy, his own realm which Guiscard was not allowed to see again while he lived (5.342).

His elder son Bohemond, stricken by a pestilence that was ravaging the Norman army in the winter of 1085, had already withdrawn to Italy for

---

62 C. M. Bowra showed how suitable such a passage might be in heroic poetry: "Both panegyric and lament celebrate an individual's fame at some special crisis, and in so doing endorse a heroic outlook." *Heroic Poetry* (London, 1952), 9.

medical treatment (5.210–27). This leaves young Roger to take counsel with his father's men, who implore him to withdraw from the siege (5.350–52). He knows that he must return to Italy, to secure his inheritance there (5.345–47). This urgency allows him little bargaining room with the troops, who promise their continuing obedience "only if a suitable agreement is offered to them" (5.363). Roger signals his retreat and the Norman army, bereft of Guiscard, succumbs to panic:

> If all the Greeks, Turks, and Arabs
> had attacked them, and from all the world's climes
> armed men were streaming down and assailing them unarmed,
> that would be no greater terror than this terror. (5.368–71)

Guiscard's men abandon their goods, even their clothes and horses, as they swim frantically out to the ships that might take them home. But most cannot reach the fleet, and in desperation they enter the service of the Byzantines, "with the fierceness of their fierce spirit knocked out of them" (5.390). The Norman fleet, meanwhile, has sailed into a storm on the Apulian coast. In the ensuing shipwrecks, when most of the sailors and many soldiers drown, Guiscard's body slips into the sea, to be rescued only with difficulty. Fearing the rotting stench of the putrefying corpse (*foetor . . . nocivus*; 5.397), Sichelgaita hurries the burial.

The remaining ten lines of the *Gesta*, extolling the Hauteville brothers as "without peer from the time of Caesar or Charlemagne" (5.405–406) and praising the beauty of the church that held their bones (5.407–408), cannot erase the gloom of this final book. The emotional center of Book Five, Sichelgaita's lament to Guiscard as he lies dying, has sealed this mood with her ominous prediction:

> "Your son – oh! is left to the wolves, to be torn apart, and so is
> your wife
> and your people, never to be held safe without you." (5.312–13)

> ("Filius ecce lupis sinitur rapiendus et uxor
> Et populus, nunquam sine te securus habendus.")

Sichelgaita does not specify who these wolves may be. Guiscard had many enemies for Roger to inherit. But the customary use of *lupus* as code word for Northman/Norman points us toward the usual suspects. The prevalence of rebellion in the *Gesta* and the ominous mood of the Norman troops on this campaign further suggest that Sichelgaita has reason to fear the treacherous proclivities of Norman lords and warriors, soon to be released from the restraints of Robert Guiscard.

4

The First Crusade and
the Norman Principality of Antioch

From that time on, the infidel Persian people began
to overrun Romania with slaughter and rapine.
At this very moment that land is returning to imperial
authority, but only because the people of the Gauls, who
        overpower every other people
in strength of arms, prompted by divine will,
are restoring it to freedom by conquering the enemy.
God inspired them, arousing them to open up the sacred paths
to the Sepulcher, closed for a long time now.

       (William of Apulia, *Gesta Roberti Wiscardi* 3.98–105)

A S William of Apulia is about to launch his account of the Normans'
campaign against Muslims in Sicily, he pauses to reflect on another holy
war, in progress even as he writes.[1] This is the passage that dates William's
Gesta to the era of the First Crusade, a venture that drew many Normans from
southern Italy, where uncertain prospects following Guiscard's death left
fighting men yearning for adventure and profit elsewhere. These Normans
hurried to answer the Pope's call to rescue the Holy Land.

At this point in his *Gesta Roberti Wiscardi*, while following Byzantine
fortunes, William has just recited the momentous events that led to the
crusade: the emperor Romanos Diogenes' defeat by the Seljuq Turks under
Sultan Alp Arslan at Manzikert in 1071, the treaty negotiated by the emperor
and sultan, and Romanos's blinding, at the command of his step-son Michael

---

[1] The literature on the crusades is particularly rich. See, for instance, Marshall W.
Baldwin, ed., *The First Hundred Years*, vol. 1 of *A History of the Crusades*, ed.
Kenneth M. Setton (Madison, 1969); Jonathan Riley-Smith, *The Crusades: A Short
History* (New Haven, 1987), *The First Crusade and the Idea of Crusading* (Philadelphia, 1986), and *The First Crusaders, 1095–1131* (Cambridge, 1997). This chapter
draws on my article, "Norman Views of Eastern Christendom: From the First Crusade
to the Principality of Antioch," in *The Meeting of Two Worlds: Cultural Exchange
between East and West during the Period of the Crusades*, Studies in Medieval Culture,
21, ed. Vladimir P. Goss and Christine Verzar Bornstein (Kalamazoo, 1986), 115–21.

VII, as he was returning to Constantinople (3.18–92). The torture and deposition of their new ally released the Turks from the compact with the empire. And so these "Persians" (in William's archaizing reference above) swept through "Romania," the Byzantine heartland of Asia Minor. The Seljuqs had already (in 1055) established their own sultanate in Baghdad. From there they invaded Arab-controlled Palestine, taking Jerusalem in 1071, overrunning Syria and capturing the wealthy and commanding city of Antioch (1085). The Christian west felt resulting shock waves, with the disruption of routes for trade and pilgrimage. The Turks even threatened Constantinople as they harried sites along the Bosphorus.

By the mid-1090s a confluence of forces conspired to provoke a response from the west. Alexios Komnenos called for mercenaries to help him push back the Seljuqs from Byzantine lands. Merchants and pilgrims demanded relief from the fresh dangers that plagued their journeys. Pious Christians lamented the subjugation of holy sites. And the pope saw in all this an opportunity to put the unruly energies of the warrior class to some useful purpose. Knights and lords who habitually threatened the peace of western Christendom might better apply their aggressions and martial skills against the infidel. When Urban II preached the Crusade at Clermont in 1095, were Normans high on his wish list of volunteers?[2]

If so, he must have delighted in the roster of nobles who signed on. As David C. Douglas noted, "Among the nine principal leaders in that crusade were a son and son-in-law of William the Conqueror [Duke Robert of Normandy and Adela's husband, Count Steven of Blois], two sons of one of his tenants-in-chief in England [Godfrey and Baldwin, sons of Count Eustace of Boulogne], and a son and grandson of Robert Guiscard [Bohemond and Tancred]."[3] Lesser Norman princes joined them, including two more scions of the house of Hauteville: Tancred's brother, William son of the marquis, and Bohemond's cousin, Richard of the Principate. And in the armies of these Norman chieftains, knights and foot soldiers swelled the numbers of men related by blood or marriage or feudal ties to Normans.

This Norman dominance was possible because the Investiture Conflict continued to alienate Henry IV from the papacy and kept Germans out of this endeavor. The French, too, entered in lesser numbers while their king, Philip I (1060–1108), remained excommunicate for repudiating his wife, Bertha. The English likewise largely stayed at home through the anti-clerical influence of

---

2　On the motivations of churchmen and lay crusaders, see Jonathan Riley-Smith, "The Crusading Movement and Historians," and Marcus Bull, "Origins," in *The Oxford Illustrated History of the Crusades*, ed. Jonathan Riley-Smith (Oxford, 1995), 1–12, 13–33. Riley-Smith and Bull emphasize both the nature of medieval piety and the pope's desire for the liberation of Jerusalem and the peoples of the Levant.

3　*Norman Achievement*, 162. On Norman leaders of the First Crusade, see especially pp. 162–64.

their Norman king, William Rufus, fully engaged with business in his own land. But Robert, duke of Normandy, took the cross, and many Normans followed him. Large contingents of Flemings and Provençals, of course, also joined the First Crusade. But Normans were the most visible and most determined to profit. This is especially true for Normans of the south, so that Evelyn Jamison concluded, "From this point of view the Crusade falls into line as one more enterprise of the house of Hauteville."[4] It is a legacy of Robert Guiscard, who died harboring dreams of eastern domination, that his kin headed east with purpose fully formed. And at Antioch, Bohemond succeeded by founding his own principality (1098–1111), later ruled by Tancred (1111–12), and then by Roger of Salerno, son of Bohemond's cousin, Richard of the Principate (1112–19). Normans expected to gain from the woes of kings, which kept other peoples behind. A few achieved their goals.

A knight in Bohemond's army has left a record of this crusade, the *Gesta Francorum*. This *Gesta* tells us how Bohemond heard about the commotion: An army of pilgrims surprised him as he besieged Amalfi with his uncle, Count Roger of Sicily. Bohemond initiated careful inquiries (*coepit diligenter inquirere*) on the condition of their weaponry, what insignia they wore, and what cry they shouted in battle. By this line of questioning, we presume, he could learn whether these men were prepared for the task and therefore worth joining. More importantly, perhaps, he could ascertain if they already owed some allegiance that would conflict with Bohemond's interests or limit his own prospects. His informant explains:

> They bear arms fit for war. On the right arm or between the shoulder blades they wear the cross of Christ, and with one voice they shout the battle-cry, *"Deus vult! Deus vult!* [God wills it!]"

This answer satisfies Bohemond. Their weapons attest their seriousness of purpose, and furthermore, they fight under no signified chain of command, but only at God's will. This presents an opportunity for Bohemond to slip in and take charge. Already on full military alert, he is ready to move.

> Immediately, inspired by the Holy Spirit, Bohemond ordered the most precious cloak he had to be cut up and made into crosses. Then most of the soldiers who were at that siege rushed to join him with great eagerness, so

---

4 "Some Notes on the *Anonymi Gesta Francorum*, with Special Reference to the Norman Contingent from South Italy and Sicily in the First Crusade," in *Studies in French Language and Mediaeval Literature Presented to Professor Mildred K. Pope*, Publications of the University of Manchester, 268 (Manchester, 1939), 208. See also Douglas, *The Norman Fate*, 156 and 169.

that Count Roger remained almost alone, and he returned to Sicily grieving and mourning because he had lost his army.[5]

Bohemond provisions the troops and pays the expenses in transporting Norman chiefs and vassals from Italy across the Adriatic.

The *Gesta Francorum* lists some of these lords on the march (1.4): Tancred, son of the marquis; Richard of the Principate and Rainulf his brother; Robert of Anse; Herman of Cannes; Robert of Sourdeval; Robert Fitz-Toustan; Humphrey Fitz-Ralph; Richard, son of Count Rainulf; the count of Russignolo with his brothers; Boel of Chartres; Aubré of Cagnano; and Humphrey of Monte Scabioso. These lords with their men follow the ancient Roman road to Constantinople, where Bohemond must deal with his archenemy, the emperor Alexios Komnenos. Having sealed a tenuous truce, Bohemond joins the seven-month siege of Nicaea, which the crusaders capture and return to Alexios, as they have promised to do (1097). After a harrowing march across Asia Minor, the army suffers the long siege of Antioch, chief city of Syria, taking it at last only through treachery master-minded by Bohemond (June 3, 1098). Three days after entering Antioch, the Christians find themselves caught between Turks who still hold the citadel and a formidable army commanded by Kerbogha, emir of Mosul and agent of the sultan. Without food or water, the crusaders despair until revived by the miraculous discovery of a weapon proclaimed as the Holy Lance that pierced Christ's side as he was hanging on the cross. With this assurance of God's favor, they attack fiercely, winning a brilliant victory in the Great Battle for Antioch on June 28, 1098.

Even before the Great Battle, the crusading leaders bicker over their latest conquest. Bohemond ultimately refuses to surrender the prize. Renouncing his vow to persevere until the Holy Sepulcher is again in Christian hands, he settles in and forges a Norman principality at Antioch which his heirs will rule until 1287. The main army, meanwhile, sets out for Jerusalem in the spring, winning the city from Egyptians who had retaken it from the Turks the previous year, and defending it gloriously at Ascalon (August 12, 1099). The *Gesta Francorum* ends here, with rejoicing after the battle.

Besides the *Gesta*'s author, two other participants left histories of this expedition. Raymond of Aguilers, priest and canon of Le Puy, traveled with Raymond of St. Gilles, count of Toulouse, and his Provençals. Fulcher of Chartres, also a priest, served as chaplain to Baldwin of Boulogne, who would become the first Latin king of Jerusalem. Both Raymond and Fulcher

---

5 *Gesta Francorum* 1.3. The text used here is the 1962 edition of Rosalind Hill, who prints the early twelfth-century Vatican ms. and lists few variants. Cf. the editions of Heinrich Hagenmeyer, *Anonymi Gesta Francorum* (Heidelberg, 1890) and Louis Bréhier, *Histoire anonyme de la première croisade*, Les classiques de l'histoire de France au moyen âge, 4 (Paris, 1924).

consulted the anonymous *Gesta Francorum*, which was already available in Jerusalem by the winter of 1101/2 and soon circulated in the west.[6] The *Gesta Francorum* thus became the seminal work in the outpouring of works inspired by the crusade. Directly or indirectly, it influenced nearly every western crusading history.[7]

Medieval historians, like modern ones, were eager to cull the authentic experiences of an eye-witness, but most also felt compelled to alter his rustic language into more elegant Latin. The anonymous crusader, after all, represented a phenomenon still uncommon in the late eleventh century, a knight who could read and write Latin. Perhaps he had entered minor orders of the Church before the death of an older brother recalled him to a secular career. His simple Latin reflects the language of the Bible and the Christian liturgy, at the same time following the cadences of the vernacular which he speaks and hears all around him.[8] Most contemporary readers expected to find history packaged in a more elegant style, and even modern historians sometimes complain about the poverty of his vocabulary or his deviations from classical vocabulary and syntax. Only in recent times have readers in large numbers come to appreciate the virtue of this voice, its authenticity unobscured by layers of literary conceits. In some respects, this crusader's thoughts and feelings lie closer to the surface than those of other historians in the Norman tradition.

The anonymous crusader seems not to know ancient literature at all, unless one phrase preserves a memory of a famous line from Julius Caesar's *Gallic Wars*. As the crusaders set out from France,

Fecerunt denique Galli tres partes.

(After that the people of Gaul made three divisions.)

This mimics, perhaps unconsciously, Caesar's "All Gaul is divided into three parts" (*Omnis Gallia in tres partes divisa est*), and so it is an anomaly in a work that contains no other classical allusions. Nor does the *Gesta* display any knowledge of Norman histories. The textual citations are all Christian. Although direct Biblical parallels generally cluster in the introductory material and speech of Urban II (1.1) or in isolated sections like the strange prophecies of the mother of the emir of Mosul (9.22), religious references pervade the work. Fasting, prayer, communion, martyrdom, relics, and ceremonies of thanksgiving to God set the *Gesta*'s pious tone. This mirrors the intense involvement in a Holy War, and the crusader's spirituality reveals

---

[6] Hagenmeyer first demonstrated that both these writers used the *Gesta*. See his *Anonymi Gesta Francorum*, 39–92.

[7] For a summary of histories that draw on the *Gesta*, see Hill, ed., *Gesta Francorum*, ix–xi.

[8] On his language and style, see Bréhier, xix–xxi.

itself in a confidence in God's miraculous intervention and in a commitment to worship at the holy sites rather than pursue material gain at Antioch.

The benedictions that conclude each of the *Gesta*'s ten books underscore the devotion of a man who nonetheless sees no incongruity between his piety and the call to murder on crusade. Indeed, a single sentence can join both emotions without comment. As the crusaders stand before Jerusalem, for instance, the *Gesta* has them contemplate violence and holy services simultaneously (10.38): "Then our leaders contrived how they could assail the city with siege engines so that they might enter to worship at our Savior's Sepulcher." When these tactics succeed and the crusaders penetrate the sacred city, they pursue the civilians who seek refuge in Solomon's temple and slaughter them until the temple flows with blood. The final sentences in this chapter continue the easy alternation between savagery and reverence as the men sack Jerusalem, then come to pray at the Holy Sepulcher, "rejoicing and weeping for great joy"; the very next morning, these same crusaders are stealing up to the Temple roof to decapitate women and men who cower there. The only Christian to show disapproval is Tancred, and he rages (*iratus est nimis*) presumably because some of the Saracens escape execution by committing suicide, jumping off the Temple's roof. The writer himself expresses no disapproval for any of this behavior, in which he took part. In other words, he shares the full range of emotions and values of his fellow crusaders.

Who then is this man? We know only what we can deduce from the *Gesta*, which does not even reveal his name. He comes from southern Italy in Bohemond's army, and Apulia may well be his home. In a reference that may reveal the crusader's own origins, he makes the emir of Mosul boast that he would pursue his conquests all the way from Antioch to Apulia (9.21). A poor knight, he knows the lesser lords and common people better than he knows the more powerful men on crusade. He identifies with these ordinary Christians rather than with Norman lords. He never tells us what ethnicity he claims, Norman or Italian. The Normanness of the *Gesta Francorum*, then, comes in part from its author's vantage point as he travels and fights among Normans. The writer's eventual disaffection with Bohemond will reveal just how much he has in common with other Norman historians even though he seems not to know the Norman historical tradition that will absorb his work.[9] It is all the more remarkable that a rank-and-file fighting man would come to the same conclusions about his Norman lord as the clerical elites were drawing about Bohemond and other Normans in their apparently more sophisticated histories written in high style. Here in the *Gesta Francorum*,

---

9 See below, Chapter Five, for Orderic's use of the *Gesta*'s material, which he knew through an intermediary text, Baudry of Bourgueil's *Historia Ierosolimitana*.

then, we find independent confirmation of the assessment prevailing throughout the court histories of the Norman tradition.

The *Gesta* even lets us see how its author forms his opinions. This crusader writes on the road, or at least in stages along the way, when he can.[10] His method of composition is a valuable asset because he writes when the memories are fresh. For the reader it also exposes a maturing literary style and evolving sensibilities. So the writer fine-tunes his opinions of the crusading chiefs in general and Bohemond in particular the longer he sees them in action. He becomes more skillful in character development, telling his story more fully and supplying more dialogue. And he writes with a surer voice, revealing a deepening understanding that he is addressing a broad audience with an intense interest in the details of this history. As he is about the relate the capture of Antioch, a defining moment for the crusade, he pauses to explain (8.19):

> I cannot relate [*nequeo enarrare*] everything that we did before the city was captured, since there is no one in these parts, whether cleric or layman, who could write or tell it altogether, just as it happened. But I will tell you a little bit.

The bit that he tells and the way that he tells it, as we shall see, involve choices and selections on his part. Perhaps he has also come to realize that he himself is experiencing the crusade differently, both living and observing it increasingly in terms of his own narrative.

Here is a representative passage from the early stages of the march toward Constantinople, which shows the *Gesta*'s spare style and its author's views as he begins both the crusade and its history (1.4):

> Then we left there [a Bulgarian valley] and came through very rich country, from village to village, from city to city, from castle to castle [*de uilla in uillam, de ciuitate in ciuitatem, de castello in castellum*] until we came to Castoria, where we solemnly celebrated Christmas. And we were there for some days seeking supplies, but those people would not cooperate with us because they feared us a great deal, thinking that we were not pilgrims but that we intended to despoil the land and kill them. So we seized oxen, horses and asses, and everything we could find.

Without a hint of irony, the writer views this pillaging as the logical and natural result of the Castorians' fears. He is equally without recriminations when he observes that the crusaders burned heretics alive in their castle, as the narrative continues:

> Leaving Castoria, we entered Pelagonia, where there was a castle of heretics [*quoddam hereticorum castrum*], which we attacked from all sides, and

---

[10] Bréhier, viii–ix; Hill, 54, n. 7.

soon it fell under our control. So we set it on fire and burned the castle along with its inhabitants. After this we reached the river Vardar, and then lord Bohemond crossed it with his men, but not all, for the count of Russignolo stayed behind with his brothers. The emperor's army came and attacked the count with his brothers and all who were with them. When Tancred heard of this he turned back and, diving into the river, he swam across to the others, and two thousand men plunged into the river to follow Tancred. Finally they came upon the Turcopuli and Patzinaks fighting with our men, and they bravely made a sudden attack and skillfully defeated them. And they captured many of them and led them, with hands bound, into lord Bohemond's presence. He said to them, "Why are you wretches killing Christ's people and mine? I have no quarrel with your emperor." They answered, "We cannot do otherwise. We have been placed at the emperor's command, and we must do whatever he orders." Bohemond let them go away free. This battle occurred on the fourth day of the week, which was Ash Wednesday. Blessed be God in all things. Amen.

With its repetitive vocabulary and syntax and its conversational tone, this is different from anything we have seen, homelier even than William of Jumièges' *Gesta*. The style displays many elements typical of vulgar Latin, and we hear the spoken voice rather than follow the patterns of classicizing high style.[11] The writer uses superfluous prepositions, for instance, as in *per plures dies* (for many days). Once reserved for emphasis, personal pronouns now appear routinely as they did in ordinary speech, and the language has acquired an indefinite article in *quoddam*. Surely this is the language of a man who thinks in the vernacular and translates vernacular conversations into roughly equivalent Latin speech. He also mirrors the values and temperament of his day. The plain language exposes a stark cruelty and primitive violence. From time to time the writer will ponder the crusaders' responsibilities and find their leaders' breaches of faith disquieting, but his usual acceptance establishes him as a man who does not often transcend the prevailing morality. This becomes significant when we consider his eventual disillusionment, on moral grounds, with his Norman prince.

At this point early in the enterprise, disillusionment is still many months away. Here the writer gives Bohemond the honorific *dominus* (lord) and takes pains to contrast the emperor's alleged treachery with Bohemond's magnanimity. He also introduces Tancred's essential qualities in a positive light. A crisis stirs the young man to immediate action, proving him decisive and intrepid (not to say reckless), accomplished in battle, a born leader of warriors. The report of these events exudes sincerity that the commonplace

---

11 John Joseph Gavigan, "The Syntax of the *Gesta Francorum*," *Supplement to Language: Journal of the Linguistic Society of America* 19, no. 3, suppl. (1943), 3–102.

style can only make more compelling. We seem to be hearing the story as it happens or even as if the narrative is telling itself, though in fact the author has selected episodes that reveal a particular point of view. He also takes care to date the heroic moment and to close this book, like the others, with a benediction as a reminder of the crusaders' mission and the author's faith.

Like his contemporary William of Apulia, the crusader does not allow a Norman prince to dominate the narrative. And like William, this historian virtually ignores Normandy and Norman England. Each of these writers is interested primarily in the new venture, and perhaps secondarily in the new identity of the prince as Italian duke or crusading leader. Each looks to the east, without much concern for the old homeland.

We have noted the crusader's one reference to Apulia as the ultimate goal of an arrogant emir (8.19). Three times he distinguishes from the rest of the army Bohemond's *Longobardi*, by which he means southern Italians, including Normans, especially those in Bohemond's retinue (1.2; 8.20). But his usual terms for all crusaders – the word "crusiatus," with all its variants, being a later twelfth-century coinage – are *Franci* and *Christiani*, the *Hierosolimitani* of his full title, *Gesta Francorum et aliorum Hierosolimitanorum* ("Story of the Franks and others who journeyed to Jerusalem"). *Hierosolimitani* ("Jerusalemites") seems to be the term preferred by the participants and those who chronicled their progress, as individual ethnic identities merge, ideally and sometimes in reality, into a single essence identified by the goal of their journey, the recovery of Jerusalem. The symbolic power of this word must haunt the *Gesta*'s final assessment of Bohemond, whose ambitions for land and power divert him from the cause and prevent him from attaining the status of a true Jerusalemite.

Most often the *Gesta*'s author uses the term *Franci* to define the host who march and straggle to the east. Occasionally he restricts the word to the subjects of Philip I Capet, as in 1.2 when the few German-speaking *Alamanni* break off from the *Franci* to travel separately, early in the journey, "because the Franks were being pompous and arrogant" (*quia Franci tumebant superbia*). But such overt ethnic quarreling is rare in the *Gesta*, far rarer than other evidence suggests it actually was. The *Gesta* adopts a more expansive view than other crusading histories, its author being acutely conscious of the common cause. So normally he uses the term *Franci* as a kind of shorthand for the bulk of the crusading army, those who came from French-speaking peoples. This includes the Normans of Normandy and the south as well as other northern French and Provençals. The *Gesta* tells their story, though there are also Italian-speaking *Lombardi* and some *Alamanni* – the "others" of the full title. But the Normans do not constitute a specially designated group of crusaders in the *Gesta*, and no pan-Norman chauvinism dominates the history.

In fact, the only crusader whom the *Gesta* regularly identifies as a Norman is Robert II Curthose, the duke of Normandy and a son of William the Conqueror. Unable to control his Normans at home, Robert had pawned the duchy to his brother, William Rufus, and joined the large numbers of Normans on crusade. The *Gesta's* restriction of *Normannus* to Robert suggests a consciousness, already in the late eleventh century, that Normans live in Normandy and that their diaspora kin are something else – *Longobardi*, in the case of Bohemond and his people from southern Italy and Sicily.

Perhaps it is not surprising, given his ineffectual reign back in the duchy, that Robert the Norman plays a relatively small role in the *Gesta Francorum*, in which other leaders dominate the action. In the list of armies setting out for the Holy Land, the duke appears fourth in Bohemond's band, named after Bohemond himself, Richard of the Principate, and Robert count of Flanders (1.3). We do not hear of him again until he arrives late at the siege of Nicaea, with his brother-in-law, Count Stephen of Blois and Chartres (2.8). From Nicaea he sets out with Bohemond and Tancred, but note the language here: "In one band were the manly Bohemond and Robert the Norman and valiant Tancred and many others" (*vir Boamundus, et Rotbertus Normannus, et prudens Tancredus, et alii plures*). The duke collects no heroic epithets, and indeed virtually disappears from the *Gesta* for some time. On the terrible march from Nicaea to Antioch, Robert is conspicuously missing from the list of leaders who rush to help Bohemond when the Turks attack, fearsome and howling (3.9). He does show up in the battle line that soon forms, but without any of the epithets that here distinguish Bohemond (*vir sapiens*), Tancred (*prudens*), Raymond (*fortissimus miles*), and the count of Flanders (*acerrimus miles*).

Robert's next appearance does not occur until 9.24, when the crusaders find themselves trapped inside Antioch, and he takes the oath (after Bohemond and the count of St. Gilles) promising not to turn tail and flee (9.24). Shortly before this, the duke was missing from the list of crusading leaders (Duke Godfrey, the count of Flanders, the count of St. Gilles, and the Bishop of Le Puy) to whom Bohemond confided his plan for capturing Antioch (8.20). His name appears in the reckoning of combatants at the Great Battle for Antioch (9.29) in the list of leaders (though fourth after Duke Godfrey, Raymond of St. Gilles, and Bohemond) who send Hugh Magnus to summon the emperor from Constantinople (10.30) and again among the leaders adjudicating the dispute between Raymond and Bohemond at Antioch (10.31) and summoned by Raymond when the negotiations fall apart (10.34).

But Robert is about to assume a larger presence, perhaps because Bohemond's withdrawal leaves room for others on center stage. Robert joins the leaders who proceed to Jerusalem (10.34), where he gains prominence among the besiegers (10.37). Though slow to join the armies at Ascalon – like the count of St. Gilles, he refuses to leave Jerusalem until he can get assurances that a battle will occur – Robert enjoys his sole moment of *aristeia* in this fight. It lasts for a single sentence:

But the count of Normandy, seeing that the emir's standard had a golden apple on the end of the staff, which was covered with silver, rushed furiously at him [the standard-bearer] and wounded him mortally.

In his very last appearance, Robert is redeeming this standard from the crusaders who captured it, paying them twenty silver marks, so he can give it to the newly chosen patriarch of Jerusalem "in honor of God and the Holy Sepulcher" (10.39).

This late flurry of heroism notwithstanding, Robert plays a slim role in the *Gesta*, which habitually calls him "count" rather than his proper and more elevated title "duke." This seems a striking slight, especially when we consider what pains other Norman historians took to award the ducal title to Robert's comital ancestors, from Rollo to William Longsword and Richard I. The *Gesta Francorum* never mentions that Robert comes from this line, that he is in fact a son of William the Conqueror. One might argue that the anonymous crusader, as a lesser knight, could not distinguish the rankings of various lords and therefore indiscriminately called them "counts." Yet he seems rather meticulous in his identifications. In the *Gesta*'s pages, for instance, Godfrey of Bouillon is always *Dux Godefridus*.[12] Copyists of the *Gesta* altered the text to improve Robert's position, until one manuscript universally replaces *comes* ("count") with *dux* ("duke") and moves Robert to the top of any list of crusading leaders.[13] But the *Gesta*'s original author, watching the crusaders in action, sees Robert as a lesser player than others. He does not highlight Robert for his position as Norman duke. Indeed, the *Gesta*'s early focus on other Norman leaders comes primarily because its author travels and fights in their company.

It is a dwindling band. When we ask why the Normans disappeared, we must not discount the perils of their way of life. Fully a third of the southern Italian crusaders named in the *Gesta* are dead before 1099, with another quarter unaccounted for.[14] Those young men killed in battle include Tancred's brother, William, cut down along with Godfrey (or Humphrey) of Monte Scaglioso in the battle on the march from Nicaea to Antioch (3.9). This six-hour encounter, writes the *Gesta*'s author, also took the lives of "other knights and foot-soldiers whose names I do not know." If Pope Urban II hoped that the crusade would divert rampaging Normans from western lands, he got his wish: of the *Gesta*'s named southern Italians, only three show up in the later records living out their lives in Italy.[15]

The survivors include Bohemond and Tancred, and the *Gesta*'s treatment

---

[12] Sometimes the juxtaposition is quite striking, as in 9.29, when the crusaders form an additional battle line at Jerusalem "from the ranks of Duke Godfrey and the count of Normandy" (*ex acie ducis Godefridi et comitis Normanniae*).

[13] Roger A. B. Mynors, in Hill, ed., *Gesta Francorum*, xxxix–xl.

[14] Jamison, "Notes on the *Gesta Francorum*," 208.

[15] Jamison, "Notes on the *Gesta Francorum*," 208.

of these two is particularly telling. At first the *Gesta* honors Bohemond by routinely calling him *dominus* ("milord") and often attaching one of these epithets: *bellipotens* ("mighty in war," 1.4), *vir prudens* ("valiant warrior," 2.5; 6.14; 6.17), *sapiens* ("judicious," "counselor," 2.6), *doctissimus* ("very clever," 6.17), *honestissimus vir* ("most honored warrior," 2.6), or *fortissimus Christi athleta* ("most courageous champion of Christ," 5.12). On the way to Constantinople, Bohemond distinguishes himself by urging his people not to plunder from fellow Christians (1.4). Modern editors of the *Gesta* are quick to suspect Bohemond's motives here; Hill footnotes this good deed with the following caveat: "Bohemond had already fought against the Emperor Alexius 1084–5. He seems now to have been anxious to create a good impression, since he hoped to gain a principality in the imperial lands."[16] But the *Gesta*'s author does not yet voice any such suspicions. He portrays his lord as incapable of preventing the looting in this instance, but soon gaining more control over the army, as Bohemond blocks the capture of a well-provisioned fortress and even forces his men to return stolen animals (1.5). In short, he shows himself a responsible commander.

But at Constantinople Bohemond reveals a more troubling side, and the *Gesta* begins to struggle with the evidence of his devious nature. The city elders, "fearing that they would be stripped of their country, took counsel with one another and came up with clever plots (*ingeniosis scematibus*) to make the dukes, counts, and all the leaders of our forces swear an oath of fealty to the emperor" (2.6). The leaders refuse this demand, calling it unjust. At this point the *Gesta*'s author interrupts the narrative with his first overt complaint against the crusading lords:

> Maybe all along we were going be tricked often [*sepe delusi erimus*] by our leaders. In the end what did they do? They may say that they were compelled by necessity to prostrate themselves, whether they wanted to or not, to the will of that wicked emperor.

The episode resumes with Bohemond sealing a secret treaty with that emperor, Alexios Komnenos, who offers him a large stretch of land just beyond Antioch in exchange for his oath of loyalty, freely given. Again the author stops to exclaim:

> Knights so brave and so tough! Why did they do this? Surely they must have been driven by a compelling need.

The writer struggles to find a motive that might exonerate his lord. But through his anguish here he seems to be conceding that the crusading leaders as a group, and Bohemond in particular, sold out their holy cause in these private agreements.

---

[16] *GF*, p. 8.

The *Gesta* implies that as early as 1097, in Constantinople, Bohemond revealed his designs on eastern lands, and perhaps on Antioch itself. Why else would he have negotiated for that particular piece of land, which would be impossible to maintain without control of the city that guarded it? Perhaps these ambitions reanimate Bohemond, for it is at Antioch itself that he has his finest heroic moments, riding ahead of the main army to secure the city gate (5.12), avenging the deaths of his men by attacking Turks "like a very brave champion of Christ" (5.12), volunteering for a dangerous mission with the count of Flanders (5.13), excoriating slackers (6.14), planning strategy and rousing men in battle with a stirring speech (6.17).

So dominant is Bohemond here that all the others insist that he direct the battle, and they press him with a string of admiring attributes:

> "You are wise and valiant, you are grand and splendid, you are brave and ever victorious, you are a director of wars and commander of battles. You take care of this. Let all this rest on you."

> ("Tu sapiens et prudens, tu magnus et magnificus, tu fortis et uictor, tu bellorum arbiter et certaminum iudex, hoc totum fac; hoc totum super te sit.")

The ensuing combat inspires heroic epithets and even the lion similes that epics find *de rigueur*, as Bohemond rallies the flagging troops and charges "like a lion that has been starving for three or four days, and so comes out of its cave roaring and thirsting for the blood of cattle and recklessly falls upon the flocks, tearing the sheep apart as they flee in all directions" (6.17).

This is Bohemond's grandest moment in the *Gesta*. Yet he continues to take the initiative throughout the siege of Antioch, volunteering to escort builders from the harbor so that the crusaders can erect a stronghold (7.18) and carrying on secret negotiations with the defender Firuz (8.20). When the crusaders take the city and almost at once find themselves besieged within it, it is Bohemond who flushes out shirkers by setting fire to their shelters and prodding them out to the walls to fight (9.26). It is no wonder that the emir Kerbogha, chief of the besieging army, asks his mother, "Are not Bohemond and [his nephew] Tancred the gods of the Franks, and do they not deliver them from their enemies?" (9.22).

But Antioch is the turning point in the *Gesta*'s view of Bohemond. We can see this shifting attitude in the very language describing the scheming that will assure Antioch's fall (8.20). For here Bohemond contrives an alliance (*amicitia*) with Firuz, the commander of three towers, with whom he exchanges messengers most amicably (*amicissime*).[17] An *amicus* is a political ally to whom one owes intense loyalty. As *amici*, therefore, Bohemond and

---

17 Firuz may have been a "renegade Armenian," who had personal reasons for betraying Antioch. See Sir Steven Runciman, "The First Crusade: Antioch to Ascalon," in

Firuz freely and gladly (*liberius*; *libenter*) pledge to honor their compact, which offers to Firuz baptism, riches, and distinction in exchange for entry into the city. Confident that his *amicus* will betray Antioch to him, Bohemond approaches the other crusading leaders, self-delight written all over his face (*gauisus serenaque mente, placido vultu*). Here are his pleasant words (*iocunda uerba*), contrived to trick his peers into compliance:

> "Sirs, most gallant knights, see how all of us, great and small, are in such poverty and distress; and we have no idea where we can turn for something better. So then, if it seems good and proper to you, let one of us elect himself above the rest [*eligat se ante alios unus ex nobis*], and if by some way or some contrivance [*ingenio*] he can acquire the city or engineer [*ingeniare*] its capture, either by himself or through others, with one harmonious voice let us cede the city to him as his due [*concordi uoce ei urbem dono concedamus*]."

This carefully crafted statement combines two principles cherished by Norman princes: the elevation of a chieftain from a group of equals and the authorization of artifice or trickery as a legitimate means of winning the contest.

Bohemond's legalese by no means soothes the leaders into compliance. They are adamant in their refusal (*qui omnino prohibuerunt, et denegauerunt*):

> "To no one will this city be handed over, but we will all share it equally; just as we have had equal effort, so from that effort let us have equal privilege."

This response wipes the smile off Bohemond's face and propels him out of the meeting (*paulo minus subridens protinus recessit*). Bohemond's contrasting expressions, as he enters the room and as he leaves it, emphasize his humiliation.

This is not the final verdict, of course. The knowledge that Kerbogha's army is bearing down on them compels the leaders to accept the Norman's deal in the end. So Bohemond resumes discussions with his *amicus* Firuz, pleading with wheedling words (*humillima, maxima, et dulcia*), until he can assure the Christian leaders, "God willing, this night Antioch shall be betrayed [*tradetur*] to us."

The description of the betrayal itself does not present Bohemond in a favorable light. He is absent when his men begin to scale the walls, and Firuz cries in despair, "*Micro Francos echome.*" This is the only time the *Gesta Francorum* allows someone to speak Greek, and the pathos of this lament –

Marshall W. Baldwin, ed., *The First Hundred Years*, vol. 1 of *A History of the Crusades*, ed. Kenneth M. Setton (Madison, 1969; 2nd ed.), 317.

"We have few Franks" – calls attention to this passage and to the sarcasm in Firuz' voice as he invokes Bohemond's heroic epithets: "Where is that really fierce Bohemond? Where is that unconquered warrior?" (*Vbi est acerrimus Boamundus? Vbi est ille inuictus?*) One of the soldiers from southern Italy has to climb back down the ladder and run after his lord, shouting, "Why are you standing here, valiant hero [*uir prudens*]? Why did you come here anyway? Look! we already have three towers!" The soldier's exhortation betrays his exasperation and a hint of irony, too, in the epithet that normally implies respect for both valor and good sense. But the urgent cry of Firuz especially grabs the reader's attention. If it is an authentic quotation, as it seems to be, this is the only language in the *Gesta Francorum* that presents the untranslated words of the speaker. How did this demotic Greek find its way into the *Gesta*?[18] The *Gesta*'s author, who was in the group that broke through a gate after the ladder broke apart, could easily have heard the story from eye witnesses. Perhaps this memorable line, with its taunt to the laggard Norman, also circulated among the crusaders as a challenge to Bohemond's claim to the city. It does spotlight, in a dramatic way, an unheroic Bohemond, conspicuously away from the action at a critical moment in the city's capture.

After Antioch yields to the crusaders, and the Great Battle with Kerbogha seals his victory, the *Gesta*'s author finds that he can no longer serve a master who abandons his holy vow to recover Jerusalem. When Bohemond snatches Antioch for himself and settles in there, his actions shock the pious knight into leaving Bohemond's Italo-Norman army and joining the Provençal knight, Raymond Pilet, and his master, the count of Toulouse, *vir venerabilis Raimundus*. This transfer of loyalties seems to energize the *Gesta*'s author, who vigorously recounts an adventure of Pilet's band, worthy of epic (10.37): in a skirmish outside Antioch, seven hundred enemy knights surround thirty crusaders when a messenger breaks through to Raymond Pilet. "Why are you standing here with these knights?" he cries. "Look! All our men are in terrible straits, trapped by Arabs and Turks and Saracens, and maybe at this very moment they are all dead. Hurry to their aid, hurry!" Raymond's forces attack with such fury that each knight unhorses his opponent, and the survivors retreat in terror.

The crusader's new alignment is particularly striking because the Normans and the Provençals had frequently quarreled. Indeed, those peoples were so culturally and temperamentally alien from one another that a slightly later historian of the crusade would call them, metaphorically, different species. "Like a hen to a duck" seemed the Provençals to the other crusaders, who found them "a little bit effeminate," and the opposite of themselves in "customs, disposition, culture, and cuisine."[19]

---

[18] I am grateful to Patrick Geary for his insight into this passage.

[19] Ralph of Caen, *Gesta Tancredi*, 61: *His, quantum anati gallina, Provinciales moribus,*

Not surprisingly, Bohemond and the Provençal leader, Count Raymond of Toulouse, were at that moment embroiled in a duel over the lordship of Antioch. These two princes had squared off against one another at least as early as Constantinople, when Bohemond bullied Raymond into swearing an oath of loyalty to Alexios (2.6). Now that oath comes back to haunt Bohemond, since Raymond invokes it to explain why he cannot surrender Antioch to the Norman (10.33).

> Noluit comes ad hoc assentire, pro fiducia quam fecerat imperatori.

> (The count was unwilling to agree to this, on account of the oath which he had made to the emperor.)

This reprises the count's arguments, which he had repeatedly made to his colleagues at Antioch (10.31):

> Every day Bohemond kept asking for confirmation of the deal that all the leaders at one point had made to hand over the city to him. But the count of St. Gilles was unwilling to accede to any deal or to give in to Bohemond because he was afraid of perjuring himself before the emperor. There were frequent meetings in the church of St. Peter to find the right thing to do. Bohemond recited his agreement and displayed his list of expenses. Likewise the count of St. Gilles set forth his own words, including the oath that he had sworn to the emperor on Bohemond's advice.

There is delicious irony at play here, as Raymond holds Bohemond to the promises that the Norman had forced on others at Constantinople.

The contrast is stark between the honorable Raymond and Bohemond the opportunist. The crusading leaders, fearful of offending either prince, call it a stalemate and refuse to decide, leaving each claimant to fortify his own strategic sites within the divided city. But the *Gesta*'s author has made his choice. Never again in the *Gesta*'s pages does he call Bohemond *dominus*. Nor does he record Bohemond's subjugation of the new principality. Instead, he takes his narrative on a linear path to Jerusalem. For a brief time Bohemond agrees to go along, too, until the *Gesta* dismisses him by recalling one final act of oath-breaking and treachery at Ma'arrat al-Nu'man. There the squabbling leaders had gathered the armies, with the lordship of Antioch, to the north, still under dispute (10.33). Bohemond makes a solemn promise to spare Turkish leaders of Ma'arrat al-Nu'man, but murders or enslaves all who trust in his protection. Soon after this deceit, he removes himself altogether from the crusading enterprise and returns to hold Antioch as his own domain.

Bohemond's desertion shocked the sensibilities of many. In a letter of

animis, cultu, victu adversabantur. Recueil des historiens des croisades, Historiens occidentaux, ed. Ludovico Antonio Muratori (1866; reprint, Farnborough, England, 1967), 3.599–716.

December 1099 urging recruitment of reinforcements for the crusading effort, Urban's successor Pope Paschal II expressly proclaimed the crusaders who remained in Antioch excommunicate until they fulfilled their pledge to go on to Jerusalem.[20] The *Gesta Francorum* anticipates this stance through its nagging concern about leaders who betray the crusading cause by slipping away at critical moments. Apparently wanting to record the cowardly as well as the valorous for posterity, the *Gesta*'s author expressly names deserters like William of Grandmesnil, his brother Aubré, Guy Trousseau, and Lambert the Poor, who climb down from Antioch's walls and scurry to the port, where they terrify the sailors into departing. Indeed, the *Gesta* ironically positions Bohemond as a harsh judge against such runaways. When Tancred catches William the Carpenter sneaking away from the siege of Antioch, he returns him to Bohemond's custody, where William huddles all night in Bohemond's tent "like a lousy castoff" (*uti mala res*), suffering the Norman's chastisement (6.15):

> Oh, you miserable disgrace to all France, you criminal embarrassment to all the people of Gaul! Oh, you most worthless of all the people whom the earth has to endure, why did you behave so disgustingly and run away? Maybe you wanted to betray [*tradere*] these knights and Christ's host just as you betrayed [*tradidisti*] those others in Spain.

Bohemond releases William to his own custody only on the condition "that he swear with all his heart and mind that he will never turn away from the journey to Jerusalem whether for good or for ill." The *Gesta*'s author will not forget how emphatically Bohemond pressed this oath on others before he betrayed it himself.

Paralleling Bohemond's descent to ignominy, and ultimately to oblivion, in the *Gesta*'s pages is Alexios's ascent. It has been a commonplace assumption that the *Gesta*'s author despised the Byzantines and their ruler from first to last, and it is true that the early books often reflect that hostility.[21] But even here the attitude is more complex. The *Gesta* introduces the emperor as a concerned Christian who warns Peter the Hermit, leader of a ragtag band of poor pilgrims, not to cross the Bosphorus to Asia Minor until reinforcements arrive (1.2). The author acknowledges that only the severe misconduct of the

---

[20] Heinrich Hagenmeyer, *Epistulae et Chartae ad historiam primi belli sacri spectantes: Die Kreuzzugsbriefe aus den Jahren 1088–1100* (Innsbruck, 1901), 176.

[21] Bréhier, iv–v; Hill, xii. Historians continue to repeat Bréhier's assessment here. Kenneth Baxter Wolf considers the *Gesta Francorum* consistent in its portrayal of Bohemond "as a *miles Christi* par excellence, dedicated to the success of the pilgrimage," and likewise consistent in its presentation of Alexios as an "*iniquus* and *infelix* emperor," tenacious in his efforts "to subvert a holy enterprise." "Crusade and Narrative: Bohemond and the *Gesta Francorum*," *Journal of Medieval History* 17 (1991), 211, 213.

Latins provokes the emperor to send them across to certain death and to rejoice in their defeat: in Constantinople they sack and burn palaces, and even steal lead from church roofs to sell for their own profit; in Asia Minor they continue to misbehave, looting and torching both homes and churches until the Turks end their rampage.

As hostilities mount between crusaders and Byzantines, the *Gesta* does launch some vituperative attacks against Alexios. When Godfrey of Bouillon arrives next and his troops plunder imperial territory, the "wicked emperor" (*iniquus imperator*) has his Turkish mercenaries assault and kill the marauders (1.3), but he also promises alms to the poor among them. With the crusading leaders in Constantinople for negotiations, "the emperor, distraught and seething with rage, was plotting how he might snare these soldiers of Christ with deceit and cunning," but God's grace protects them (2.6). Alexios, "full of false and wicked designs," does at least manage to profit from the westerners' valor by receiving Nicaea after their long siege and letting the inhabitants go free without penalty (2.8), though once again the emperor aids the poor in thanksgiving (3.9). From Nicaea the army moves on to Antioch, with Bohemond determined to surrender no more hard-won cities to Alexios.

While describing the suffering crusaders encamped outside Antioch, the *Gesta* unleashes one final onslaught against Byzantine authority, this time in the person of Tatikios, the imperial representative with the western army (6.6). That enemy (*inimicus*), "fashioning all sorts of lies," declares that he will travel to Byzantium, leaving behind his tents and household as surety, and return with many ships laden with grain, wine, barley, fresh meat, flour, cheeses, and all necessities, including horses for battle. As Tatikios abandons the crusaders, the *Gesta* makes a damning pronouncement: "he remains in perjury, and he will always remain so."[22]

Meanwhile, Alexios is personally leading a Byzantine army to aid the crusaders at Antioch. When these desperately needed reinforcements turn back to Constantinople, the *Gesta* does not even hurl a pejorative epithet at the emperor, but places the blame squarely on *imprudens* ("cowardly") Count Stephen of Blois, son-in-law of William the Conqueror, and other deserters among the crusading army. Feigning illness at Antioch, Stephen had withdrawn to a nearby mountain where he could spy on the "countless

---

22 Alexios's daughter, the distinguished historian Anna Komnene, reports Tatikios's version of the tale in *Alexiad* 11.6.1–2. She says that Bohemond tricked Tatikios into believing that his life was in danger and that he should escape while he could. With Tatikios gone, Bohemond could claim that the Byzantines forfeited any rights to Antioch by abandoning the crusaders in their direst need. McQueen ("Relations between the Normans and Byzantium," 454) assesses the evidence, both western and Byzantine, surrounding Tatikios' departure and finds for the Byzantine view: Bohemond almost certainly met with Tatikios and persuaded him to leave, hoping by this to secure Antioch for himself.

tents" of the Turkish army below. Then Stephen lingers only long enough to strip his camp of valuables before fleeing in terror to the west. Encountering Alexios and his army, Stephen persuades the emperor that the Christians, recently trapped inside the city, must surely be dead (9.27). In a meeting with his advisors, Alexios reports this news to Bohemond's half-brother Guy, qualifying the report with the disdainful aside, "just as that miserable count, so shamefully fleeing, relates" (*sicut iste infelix comes turpiter fugiens narrat*). Guy reacts by raging against an unjust God, bemoaning Bohemond's supposed death, and then assailing Stephen's character.[23]

It is significant that the *Gesta* passes by an opportunity for invective against the emperor here, at the nadir of the crusade, and instead, features the emperor's disgust with the cowardly Stephen, which Guy emphatically seconds. Perhaps the *Gesta*'s author does not so much intend to elevate Alexios as he means to excoriate the deserters. But he does seem to sympathize with Alexios's noble intentions, thwarted at great cost to the crusaders who remained at Antioch. The narrative reinforces the shared sense of doom, as Christians howl in grief and die by the roadside, in the retreat of the emperor's army.

After the Great Battle for Antioch, the crusaders send Hugh Magnus to Constantinople, asking Alexios to receive the city and fulfill his obligations there. "He went," notes the *Gesta* tersely, "but he never came back" (10.30). The writer comments no further, leaving open the possibility that the fault does not lie with the emperor. This silence, too, is noteworthy, given Bohemond's insistence that Alexios had forfeited his rights to Antioch by failing to show up there. Disappointed by Bohemond's rapacity and the desertion of other crusading princes, the author of the *Gesta* has modified his feelings about Bohemond's archenemy, perhaps coming to appreciate the moral and political complexities that Alexios faced, or even to sympathize with the emperor's viewpoint as did his new lord Raymond of Toulouse, who honored his solemn oaths (10.31; 10.34). Just as the *Gesta Roberti Wiscardi* shifts its sympathies away from Robert Guiscard, so its contemporary *Gesta Francorum* reaches a hostile opinion of Guiscard's son.

And what of Tancred, the other Norman prince highlighted in the *Gesta Francorum*? Tancred does pursue the journey all the way to victory at Jerusalem, though at least one historian has presumed that he did so essentially as an agent for Bohemond.[24] The *Gesta* presents a Tancred endowed with prodigious energy and ambition, a perversely petulant opportunist. The *Gesta*'s author does not doubt his bravado and charisma, proved early on the crusade

---

23 Bréhier (ed. *GF,* vii) and Steven Runciman ("Antioch to Ascalon," 320, n. 11) thought this a later interpolation. But Rosalind Hill (ed., *GF,* 63) correctly defends its authenticity. By this point in the narrative, the crusader has cultivated a talent for these psychologically revealing vignettes.

24 Runciman, "Antioch to Ascalon," 327.

when he dives into the Vardar and swims across to rescue the rearguard (1.4). But on other occasions his rashness and self-absorption provoke Bohemond to anger, as when Tancred longs to capture a Christian fortress and steal its provisions (2.5).

Only with difficulty can Bohemond control his intemperate nephew, and as soon as Bohemond goes ahead to Constantinople leaving the young man in charge, Tancred shows his preference for pillage over lawful trade by leading the army to a lush valley and ravaging it to his heart's content (2.5). Once he reaches Constantinople, Tancred sneaks across the Bosphorus with his Norman kinsman, Richard of the Principate, to avoid swearing an oath of loyalty to the emperor (2.7). Soon he is taking his men on another plundering expedition away from the main army (4.10), this time losing any claim to Tarsus because he refuses to share it with Count Baldwin, who offers him half. But it is not in Tancred's nature to share, so he stalks off to win Adana and Missis (classical Mopsuestia) "and very many castles" for himself. Always looking out for his own interests and habitually strapped for cash, he demands a sizable reward for defending a fortress outside Antioch (8.19): "If I knew what profit I'd gain, I'd zealously guard the castle with just my own men."

Though he is among the poorest and youngest of the crusading leaders, Tancred manages to call attention to himself with predictable regularity, often through brash or unconventional behavior. When the other leaders swear a simple oath to stay and fight at Antioch, for instance, he modifies his oath, promising also that he will march to Jerusalem if only he has forty knights in his service (9.24). The *Gesta Francorum* offers one final view of the young hothead, irate (*iratus est nimis*) when he sees Saracens jumping to their deaths from Solomon's Temple and so avoiding decapitation (10.38).

If the Tancred of these vignettes seems to be the quintessential Norman prince, a slightly later Norman history confirms this view. The *Gesta Tancredi* ("The Story of Tancred") by Ralph of Caen extols Tancred's exploits of the heroic years, from 1096 to 1104. Born in Caen about 1080, Ralph journeyed to Norman Antioch in 1107 or 1108. After serving Tancred there, he completed his *Gesta* between 1112 and 1118, using the history of Fulcher of Chartres and oral sources, including, so he claims, the testimony of Bohemond and Tancred themselves. In a scene recalling Dudo's alleged encounter with the aged Duke Richard I, Ralph imagines the Norman princes calling to him from the grave (Preface): "*Tibi loquimur; in te confidimus*" ("To you we speak; in you we have complete confidence"). He wrote independently of the *Gesta Francorum*, which was circulating in the west and in Jerusalem. Was it not available in Norman Antioch, or did Ralph know it but choose not to use it? Either possibility suggests that the Norman powers in Antioch found the *Gesta Francorum* insufficiently zealous in support of the Norman cause.

Ralph's panegyric more than makes up for that deficiency. Yet he also

164

vaguely confirms the view of Bohemond presented in the *Gesta Francorum*, while conveying more explicitly Tancred's jealousy and suspicions. Tancred is guarding the highways when Antioch falls and so misses the glory of its capture and the first booty. "Oh Bohemond, Bohemond, my blood relative," he cries at the news, "you let others know, but kept it a secret from me!" (70). Tancred is sure that envy compels Bohemond to mistreat him so. And Ralph takes Tancred's side, by implication condemning Bohemond for abandoning the march to Jerusalem. Tancred, by contrast, "a second Julius Caesar," continues the march, believing nothing accomplished until Jerusalem falls (96). Occasionally Ralph of Caen shows Tancred's petulant side, but more often he invests his master with all the magnificence that his classicizing style can muster.

> O ubi, et quando, et quis in filiis hominum
> par tibi, Tancredi!   (7)

> (Oh where and when and who among the sons of men is
> your equal, Tancred?)

Ralph's Tancred is "a man who is not a man, but a lion," superior to Ajax, Hector, Achilles (128). But these antique heroic comparisons cannot do him justice. Outside Jerusalem a hermit accosts him with more fitting praise: "Guiscard, conqueror of Alexios, lives still in you, Tancred!" (113).

Tancred may indeed bear an uncanny resemblance to his grandfather. But the *Gesta Francorum* makes no such claim, disillusioned as its author ultimately is with the house of Hauteville. A recent immigrant directly from Normandy to Antioch, on the other hand, Ralph of Caen comes late to the crusading enterprise. Lacking the cachet of a participant in the conquest, Ralph must find his own way to establish an identity and a sense of belonging in the new land, whose masters he serves. He does this by claiming a Norman chauvinism for the warrior ruling class of Antioch and attaching himself, as a genuine Norman from the Norman homeland, to Tancred and the Hauteville line. So his opening paragraph of chapter one rehearses Norman exploits:

Tancred, the most illustrious shoot from illustrious stock, had exceptional parents, the marquis and Emma. So to be sure, he was scarcely ignoble as a son from such a father. But as a nephew, from his mother's brothers, he was far more elevated still [*longo sublimior*]. The family on his father's side, you see, considered it sufficient to win praise in their local neighborhood. But his mother's brothers transported the glory of their martial exploits above and beyond their fatherland, Normandy. Indeed, who would not commend the commendable achievement of Guiscard, whose triumphant standards, so they say, caused both the Greek and the German emperor to tremble on the same day? For he personally liberated Rome from the German, but he subjugated the territory of the Greeks by defeating their king through the agency of his warlike son, Bohemond. The rest of [Emma's] brothers, eleven in number, were intent on waging war on

Campania, Apulia, and Calabria. Roger must be singled out for special mention here since, in subduing the heathens of Sicily, he won glory second only to Guiscard's among the brothers. But the narrative which launched me into this digression lets me dwell on this no longer. So now I return to Tancred.

But Ralph injects many reminders of Tancred's Norman lineage into his *Gesta Tancredi*, just as he frequently asserts his own Normanness.[25] Ralph lived to adulthood in Normandy, and his story of Tancred and Antioch sometimes draws his memory back to the homeland. When he describes the crusaders' siege of Antioch in 1098, for instance, he recalls "a terrifying red glow" visible then in the night sky over Normandy, a sign that inspired viewers to shout, "*Oriens pugnat*" ("The East is fighting"; 57). Ralph adds this testimony:

> I myself saw that sign when I was still a young man living in my paternal home in Caen, when I had not yet seen Antioch, or even heard about it, except in name only. . . .

The author of the *Gesta Francorum*, however, neither emphasizes Normanness nor invokes Normandy. A devout Christian and a fighter with no hint of the bureaucrat or the sycophant, he can develop a view at once more critical and more universal.

This view honors the non-Norman princes who show particular valor, like Baldwin during a Muslim attack (5.13), or piety, like Raymond when, in a humble gesture designed to break the deadlock after Antioch, he walks barefoot from Ma'arrat al-Nu'man to Kafartab (10.34). The *Gesta Francorum* especially features memorable deeds performed by lesser Norman knights whom the author knows more intimately than he knows the princes. One of Bohemond's followers, for instance, a man called "Bad-Crown" or "Ill-Tonsured" (*Mala Corona*), musters the forces that will launch the crusaders' final assault on Antioch (8.20). Soon nearly sixty brave fighters are scaling the wall to a tower held by Firuz (8.20). Once inside the city, these Normans defend it valiantly. Trapped in a tower after his two comrades have left to tend their wounds, a single soldier from the army of Godfrey of Monte Scaglioso fights off a Turkish attack (9.26). Three spears break in his hands, but he defends the tower in daylong combat. The *Gesta*'s most recent editor

---

25 On Tancred as heir to Hauteville glory, see how he earns the epithet *Wiscardida*, "Guiscard's scion" [e.g. *Gesta Tancredi* 36, where lengthy panegyric leads Ralph to apply the Vergilian tag, *parcere subjectis et debellare superbos* (*Aeneid* 6.853). Like the idealized Romans of *Aeneid* 6, the heroic Tancred must "spare the conquered and war down the arrogant"]. Although Ralph favors Tancred's maternal lineage, he cannot resist using the honorific "Marchisides" ("son of the marquis") with great frequency.

suggests that this Norman, Mad Hugh or Hugh the Berserk (*Hugo Insanus*), had reverted to the ancient Scandinavian tradition of blind fury in battle.[26]

But the admiration of the *Gesta*'s author reaches beyond the Christian army to embrace even the valiant enemy. Here is a famous passage honoring them after the battle for Nicaea, all the more significant since it immediately follows a reckoning of the Normans who died in this contest (3.9):

> Who will ever be knowledgeable and learned enough to dare describe the prowess, fighting skill, and bravery of the Turks, who thought they could terrorize the Franks by threatening them with their arrows, as they terrorized the Arabs, Saracens, Armenians, Syrians, and Greeks? But, if it please God, they will never be as good as our men. Still, they claim that they come from the same stock as the Franks [*de Francorum generatione*], and that no one is a natural born knight aside from the Franks and themselves. Here's the truth, which no one dares deny: surely if they had ever been confirmed in the faith of Christ and holy Christendom, and had been willing to confess the One God in Three Persons, and had believed faithfully and righteously that the Son of God was born of a virgin mother, suffered and rose from the dead and ascended into heaven in the sight of his disciples and sent them the consolation of the Holy Spirit in all its perfection, and that he is reigning in heaven and on earth, then no one could find stronger or braver or more resourceful fighters. And yet by God's grace they were conquered by our men.

This passage, of course, highlights the victors' success against such warriors even as it privileges Christian doctrine. Indeed, the excursus on Christianity serves almost as an apology for the writer's praise of the infidel. But the praise itself still stands as a display of respect for the enemy.

Later, at Antioch, the oddly tragic figure of Kerbogha, emir of Mosul, confirms this sense of the Turks' prowess, while adding dimensions of humanity and honor. We see these qualities especially in Kerbogha's exchange with an emir to whom he entrusts the citadel of Antioch (9.21):

> And so when he received the citadel, Kerbogha summoned one of his emirs, whom he knew to be a truthful, gentle and peaceable man, and said to him, "I want you to enter and hold this citadel as my liege man [*in fidelitatem meam*], since I have known for a very long time that you are a man of the best character [*fidelissimum*], and so I beg you to protect the stronghold by every possible device."

The emir is forthright in setting limits to his loyalty: if the Franks defeat Kerbogha, he will surrender the citadel at once. Kerbogha accepts these conditions: "I know you to be so honorable and brave that I will agree to whatever you think is right." This exchange corroborates the body of

---

[26] Hill, 61, n. 1.

evidence suggesting the *Gesta*'s developing view that, just as a Norman prince can be an oath-breaker, traitorous to the cause of his people, so a Turkish prince can be honest and loyal.

The *Gesta*'s author shows considerable interest in Muslims, who howl like savages in battle (3.9; 7.18) and speak with eccentric diction when he gives them voice (4.10). The *Gesta*'s quirkiest anecdote features a long conversation between Turks, as Kerbogha's mother tries to dissuade her son from battle with the crusaders (9.22). She has searched the Christian scriptures, the Koran, and the stars for prophecies concerning her son. All of these predict his defeat at Antioch. The author delights in Kerbogha's supposed misconceptions about the crusading heroes and their religion, imagined errors that the writer ironically matches with his own ignorance of the Islamic world. Confusing Arabs and Turks, the crusader also has them swearing "by Mohammed and by the names of all [their] gods" (9.21) and worshipping idols. As he cannot distinguish Arabs from Turks, so he assumes that the Muslims see a monolithic Christian people and identify the western crusaders as the same stock who defeated their armies in Syria and Asia Minor during the Byzantine wars of the previous century (9.21). Perhaps here he is trying to show the Muslims' ignorance, but maybe he too can envision a united Christendom, minimizing the differences between Orthodoxy and Catholicism in this ecumenical view.

Even as the *Gesta* displays a fascination, sometimes even empathy, with various peoples, its heroes most often are common folks in the Christian host, not only soldiers but also the women who aid them, as here before Nicaea (3.9):

> The women among us, too, gave us great relief that day, since they kept fetching water for us combatants to drink and steadfastly kept encouraging those who were fighting and defending them.

This attention to ordinary women and men signals a change even from the *Gesta Roberti Wiscardi*, which shows William of Apulia's sensitivity to the distress of soldiers and their families when Guiscard launches his Byzantine venture (4.128–32) and to parents whose children are taken hostage (3.647–49). Medieval histories often ignore the lower classes, but crusading chronicles cannot neglect the suffering and terror that dog the army. Even Ralph of Caen with his eagerness to please an elite audience, repeatedly notes the hunger, thirst, cold, and inadequate supply of weapons and horses (e.g. 54, 57, 60, 64, 73, 97, 123). All this the anonymous crusader experienced first-hand. He has witnessed the people's piety and courage in daily struggles for existence. As their leaders wrangle and as Bohemond connives, the knight and his comrades confront Muslim armies, hunger, and thirst.

Almost every page of the *Gesta* testifies to the travails of the journey over nearly impassable mountains and through waterless wastelands (4.11) where provisioning the army is a constant preoccupation (e.g. 4.11; 5.13; 6.14;

6.15). The sieges offer nightmarish horrors, which the *Gesta* describes with precision. During the march from Nicaea to Antioch, for instance, a band under the Italian Rainald meets a Turkish ambush, and the survivors flee to a nearby stronghold (1.2):

> The Turks besieged it at once and cut off their water-supply. Our men suffered so greatly from thirst that they bled their horses and asses and drank their blood. Some let down belts and small garments into a sewer and squeezed out the liquid into their mouths. Some urinated into one another's cupped hands and drank. Others dug the moist earth and lay down on their backs because they were so parched with thirst. But the bishops and priests comforted our men and urged them not to despair.

It is a scene that will repeat itself, with terrible variations, throughout the crusade, but most memorably inside Antioch (9.26; cf. 9.23; 10.33; 10.37):

> Those profane enemies of God held us shut up in the city of Antioch so that many died of hunger, since a small loaf of bread sold for one bezant. I will not even speak of wine. They sold and ate the meat of horses and asses. And they sold a hen for fifteen *solidi*, an egg for two, and a nut for a *denarius*; everything was very expensive. So intense was their hunger that they cooked and ate leaves from figs and vines, and thistles and all trees. Some cooked and ate the skins of horses and camels and asses and oxen or buffaloes. These afflictions and many other agonies which I cannot name we suffered for the name of Christ and to free the way to the Holy Sepulcher.

These recitals of deprivation repeatedly recall the Pope's call to crusade (1.1):

> "Brothers, you must suffer many things for the name of Christ – misery, poverty, nakedness, persecution, want, weakness, hunger, thirst, and other such woes, just as the Lord said to his disciples, 'You must suffer many things for my name.'"

The enduring heroism of the crusade lies in the people's suffering like the disciples, and these very travails which test their faith ultimately bear witness to their worth as champions of Christ.

The heroism of the crusaders' hunger and thirst and fatigue often dominates the narrative, but of course the *Gesta Francorum* also features the horror of battle, the carnage and taking of prisoners, public executions and enslavement. In this war, all is fair, including psychological torture of civilians caught in the great sieges. Before Antioch's gate the crusaders behead Turkish captives, hoping to distress their allies in the city (5.12). Turks wail in grief as the Christians dig up their dead, decapitate the corpses, and load four horses with their heads, a gift for the emir of Cairo (7.18). When they take cities, the crusaders show no mercy to men or women, the great and the small. So at al-Bara, Count Raymond of St. Gilles kills *omnes Saracenos et*

Saracenas, maiores et minores (10.30), at Antioch the Christians fill the streets with their bodies until no one can endure the stench (8. 20), and in Jerusalem they burn mountains of corpses, so many that only God can number them, including bodies of people slaughtered in the Holy Sepulcher itself (10.38–39).

The *Gesta* conveys the sense that these often brutal crusaders are moving through dangerous spaces. Enemies lurk everywhere: in the court of Constantinople, at water holes, behind the next ridge. Not even a fortified encampment can promise sure protection. Outside Antioch the Saracens pepper Bohemond's camp with arrows and claim at least one casualty, a woman (5.12). In any given instance the local Armenians and Syrians may or may not prove friendly. Sometimes they are war profiteers, spies, and suppliers for the enemy (5.12; 6.14; 8.19), or heretics eager to join the Saracens in battle against the crusaders (3.9; 8.20; 9.21; 10.34); but sometimes they are supportive fellow Christians who succor crusaders in distress (2.5), or at least silently applaud Christian successes when they cannot express open support (7.18).

And then, of course, there is the Muslim enemy, whose howling can magnify the terror of an attack (3.9):

> Continuo Turci coeperunt stridere et garrire ac clamare, excelsa voce dicentes diabolicum sonum nescio quomodo in sua lingua. Sapiens vir Boamundus videns innumerabiles Turcos procul, stridentes et clamantes demonica voce protinus iussit omnes milites descendere, et tentoria celeriter extendere.

> (At once the Turks began to screech and yip and yell, in a loud voice making some devilish sound in their own language. The wise hero Bohemond, seeing countless Turks in the distance screeching and yelling in a demonic voice, straightway ordered all the knights to dismount and pitch their tents quickly.)

Here the Turks expressly sound like devils and demons (*diabolicum sonum*; *demonica voce*); and the *Gesta*'s language here recalls the Christians' linking of Islam with the devil, for instance by calling mosques "homes of the devil" (7.18; 10.31) or by assuming that Turks join "the devil and his angels" at death (7.18). But their cries also invoke folk memories of witches, whose shrieks by night foretell some doom.[27] Again outside Antioch (7.18), when Turks ambush a band of Christians, the Muslims "began to screech and jabber and yell with a mighty yelling" (*coeperunt stridere et garrire ac clamare uehementissimo clamore*), until a counter-attack left the survivors

---

[27] Cf. Petronius, *Satyricon* 63, where their screeching signals the presence of invisible witches, in a story that immediately follows the tale of a howling werewolf (62).

"no longer daring to whoop and jabber [*clamitare uel garrire*] day and night as they used to."

In this uncertain and often terrifying world the poor and weak must have defenders. They cannot count on their lay princes, whose weaknesses lie exposed in self-serving deals with Alexios, the power struggle at Antioch, and Count Stephen's pusillanimous whining. Already in its second chapter (1.2), the *Gesta* notes the first traitor of the crusade, a German commander who deserts his troops holing up against a Turkish attack in a fortress near Nicaea. Their leader's betrayal abandons many men to death, with the survivors being used for target practice by their captors or sold off into slavery and led away to Khorosan, Antioch, and Aleppo. Even this early in the *Gesta*, the text dwells on their lord's treachery:

Denique dominus Alamannorum concordatus est cum Turcis, ut traderet socios illis, et fingens se exire ad bellum, fugit ad illos et multi cum eo.

(Then the lord of these Germans came to an agreement with the Turks to betray his companions to them, and pretending to go out to battle he fled to them, and many went with him.)

As the crusaders face every danger, with no assurance of their leaders' loyalty or protection, their plight lends poignancy to the death of the people's champion, the Bishop of Le Puy (10.30):

There was great trial and tribulation and terrible grief in the whole army of Christ since he was a supporter of the poor and a counselor of the rich, and he used to keep the clergy within proper bounds and preach to the knights and admonish them, saying, "None of you can be saved unless he honors the poor and succors them. You cannot be saved without them, and they cannot live without you. They ought to offer daily prayers for the forgiveness of your sins to God whom you offend in many ways every day. And so I beg you, for the love of God, that you love them and aid them as much as you can."

This message of Christian charity harmonizes with the *Gesta*'s simple and direct style, with its reminiscences of the Vulgate, and with its conviction that the ordinary crusaders are the heroes of this venture. In the *Gesta*'s version, this bishop works to harmonize the conflicting interests of the weak and the powerful, honoring the poor over the sinful rich. The bishop's sympathies, as expressed here, represent those acquired by the *Gesta*'s author himself.

At its conclusion the *Gesta Francorum* remembers these poor as the core of the crusading army, when the defeated emir of Egypt cries out in despair (10.39):

I have been conquered by a tribe of beggars, unarmed and impoverished, who have nothing but a sack and satchel. . . . I led two hundred thousand soldiers here to battle, and I see them fleeing with slack reins along the road to Cairo, and they do not dare turn back against the Franks. I swear by Mohammed and by all the majesty of the gods that I will never levy another army, because I have been driven out by a foreign people.

At Antioch Kerbogha had written his sultan an exulting letter, mocking the miserable weapons captured from poor Franks (9.21). Through the emir's lament, the *Gesta* answers this Muslim vainglory, delighting in the image of poor knights overcoming formidable odds by God's grace. The concluding threnody also returns the *Gesta* to its beginnings and the Pope's call for a crusade, with the poverty and suffering that it must entail (1.1). This is a neat reinforcement of the writer's acquired point of view, that ordinary women and men have brought the journey to a successful conclusion in Jerusalem.

But if Jerusalem is the resolution toward which the *Gesta* moves, Antioch is the point of crisis, the watershed for the history and historian alike. The sieges and battles for Antioch fill half of the *Gesta*'s pages, consuming chapters 12–32 out of thirty-nine and almost exactly the middle half of the chronicle's pages.[28] Antioch is literally at the center of the *Gesta*. At Antioch the crusade nearly falters and dies until Bohemond, in the nick of time, persuades a defender to betray his city. At once blockaded within, sandwiched between a besieging army and the men in the citadel, the crusaders lose heart until a miracle revives them. In all of the *Gesta Francorum* its sober author records only three miracles, each one known by reliable testimony and occurring in the charged atmosphere of Antioch. These miracles, with the accompanying dreams and visions, offer windows into the crusaders' minds.

The first such episode concerns a priest named Stephen, who approaches the leaders while they agonize, trapped in Antioch and despairing. He tells them how, as he lay cowering in the Church of St. Mary, Jesus appeared to him, with his mother Mary and St. Peter, and Jesus said (9.24):

> "I have aided you well, and I will aid you yet again. It was I who allowed you to hold the city of Nicaea and to win all your battles, and I led you all the way here, and I have suffered along with you all the troubles that you have endured in the siege of Antioch. See how I gave you help just when you needed it and put you safe and sound into the city, and now see how freely you are taking your wicked pleasures with Christian women and wicked pagan women, so that a vast stench goes up to heaven."

Only the fervent intercession of Mary and Peter persuades Jesus to offer absolution and relief from their pressing woes. Here, reports the priest, are Jesus' instructions and promise (9.24):

---

[28] Wolf believes that the *Gesta Francorum* devotes so much attention to Antioch because its author wants to highlight the heroic Bohemond and avoid condemning Bohemond for failing to complete his pilgrimage to Jerusalem. "Crusade and Narrative," 215.

"Go then and tell my people that they should return to me, and I will return to them, and within five days I will send them great help [*magnum adiutorium*]. And every day let them sing the response, '[The kings of the earth] have gathered together,' [Psalm 47:5] all of it, along with the refrain."

The priest swears to the princes that he tells the truth, offering to verify his story through trial by ordeal. He is willing to hurl himself off a tower; and, if an injury proves his guilt, he proposes this punishment: "behead me or throw me into a fire." On the Gospels and a crucifix he swears again before the Bishop of Le Puy. His earnest piety convinces many of his sincerity (9.24).

All our leaders met together to deliberate that very hour, deciding that they all should swear an oath that none of them should flee, not to save his life nor to escape death, so long as they lived.

Bohemond characteristically swears first, while Robert the Norman appears only third on the *Gesta*'s list. Tancred, equally true to his character, modifies his oath in a flourish of bravado. But the substance of these oaths does not seem to embody the promise that Jesus wanted to extract when he confronted the priest about lustful acts with bad women. Can it be that this vision and the response actually reveal the sins, committed or contemplated, by priest and lay princes, respectively? Can we penetrate here the consciences of guilt-ridden men? This seems a likely explanation, though the bishop, seizing the moment, may have contrived this oath to forestall a rash of devastating desertions from the nobility.[29] Stephen of Blois had fled only a day before Antioch fell to the crusaders, and Bohemond's brother-in-law, William of Grandmesnil joined him a week later, having slipped through Kerbogha's blockade. Surely many others were thinking of escape, and their mass departure from Antioch would have doomed the crusade altogether.

But a second vision energizes the dispirited army, rescuing the crusaders at their direst moment and therefore salvaging the entire expedition (9.25).[30] Even before the Christians took the city, St. Andrew the Apostle visited the priest Peter Bartholomew, urging him to go into the Church of St. Andrew as soon as he can enter the city, there to find the lance that pierced Christ's side when he was dying on the cross. The saint even transported the priest miraculously into the city to see the very spot in advance. Once the crusaders hold Antioch, Andrew comes to Peter Bartholomew again, hounding him until he, like Stephen, discloses his message to the crusading leaders and shows them the very place in the church.

---

29 Runciman, "Antioch to Ascalon," 321.
30 Runciman ("Antioch to Ascalon," 322, n. 12) briefly surveys contemporary accounts of the episode.

And thirteen men dug there from morning until evening, and so that man found the lance just as he had predicted. And they received it [*acceperunt*] with great joy and awe, and tremendous rejoicing arose in the whole city. From that hour we received [*accepimus*] among ourselves a plan of war.

(9.28)

With the same verb the writer describes the acceptance of the lance and the simultaneous acceptance of a new and aggressive strategy. This miracle restores the crusaders' faith and their nerve at the same time.

The *Gesta Francorum* conveys the energizing effects of this discovery, which rescued the crusade from its lowest depths. Just in the previous chapter (9.27) the *Gesta* spotlighted invective by both Alexios and Guy against the traitorous Stephen of Blois, one of the most powerful lords affiliated with the Norman camp. With the discovery of the lance (9.28) the *Gesta* signals confidence in a miracle featuring Provençals allegedly favored with heavenly guidance. If this narrative lacks the fervor of the account by the Provençal chronicler Raymond of Aguiliers, still the *Gesta*'s confidence in this miracle is significant. Because the Provençals were touting this discovery as their own, and because the lance might therefore signal divine authorization for Provençal claims on Antioch, the authenticity of the lance became an intensely partisan issue. Tancred and Bohemond were already feuding with Count Raymond of Toulouse, and the lance becomes the focal point of their dispute. Though usually quite willing to embrace the miraculous (e.g. 106, 120), on this point Ralph of Caen presents the hostile view of the Norman princes (100–102), who wonder why St. Andrew would favor a man of such low estate with this revelation. "Who hid the lance," asks Bohemond in the *Gesta Tancredi*, "and why? *O rusticitas credula!*" When Peter Bartholomew dies after an ordeal by fire, Ralph and his Normans exult in their supposed vindication (108–10). The author of the *Gesta Francorum* fails to mention Peter's trial. His report of the episode suggests that he is transferring his emotional allegiance to Raymond from Bohemond, whose bald self-interest is jeopardizing the fragile morale of the crusading army.

The confidence inspired by this discovery propels the crusaders to launch an attack against their besiegers. And so the starving and depressed men who had been sulking inside houses and unwilling even to defend the walls hurl contemptuous orders to Kerbogha, that he should remove his army from Christian lands. The astonished Turk responds with equal defiance:

"We neither welcome nor want your God or your Christianity, and we spit on you and them altogether."

With insults successfully exchanged, the crusaders fortify themselves through fasting, processions, confession, communion, almsgiving, and masses, then rush out to fight the Great Battle for Antioch (9.29). Into the fray the Bishop of Le Puy carries the holy lance, whose presence invigorates the crusaders. Surprised by the Christians' self-confidence, Kerbogha takes precautions for a possible retreat, then withdraws a bit while his army divides into two wings, hoping to trap the crusaders between them. The Christians at once adjust their own lines to counter the Saracens' strategy. A fierce battle ensues until the *Gesta* records its third and final miracle, unexpected aid from an army of warrior saints:

> And there came down out of the mountains infantry, countless men riding white horses and carrying banners all white. So when our men saw this host, they had no idea what was happening or who these men were, until they realized that this was the help from Christ [*adiutorium Christi*; that is, the aid promised Stephen in the first miraculous vision], led by the [soldier] saints, George, Mercurius, and Demetrius. This account is absolutely true, for many of our men saw it.

Now the Turkish lines can no longer hold. Setting the grass afire to signal defeat to their companions back at the camp, they flee in panic, abandoning abundant food, livestock, and pavilions laden with silver and gold.

This is the emotional high point of the *Gesta Francorum*, which lingers for a parting look at Antioch, "very lovely and distinguished," with its citadel and double walls of stone, its public buildings, churches, and 360 churches, nestled between high mountains and the Orontes River, here called Farfar (10.33). "This is a city," the description concludes, "of enormous prestige."

> For seventy-five kings first established it, chief of whom was King Antiochus, from whose name it is called Antioch. The Franks besieged that city for eight months and a day, and after that, they were blockaded inside for three weeks by the Turks and other pagans in larger numbers of people than had ever gathered together before, whether Christian or pagan. With the help of God [*adiutorio Dei*] and the Holy Sepulcher, nevertheless, they were defeated by the Christian people of God [*a Christianis Dei*], and we rested, with joy and great delight, in Antioch for five months and eight days.

The language of this passage again recalls the miracles that saved the crusaders at Antioch. And just as the help of God rescued the crusading enterprise, so the recipients of that aid are classified finally as "the Christian people of God," stripped of ethnic identities that alienate one from the other. And so too, the *Gesta*'s author will never identify Antioch as a Norman principality.

The long bickering of the crusading princes, provoked by Bohemond's intransigent ambitions, disturbs the interlude at Antioch and complicates the narrative of victory. When the army finally proceeds to Jerusalem, the *Gesta*'s author is riding with the forces of Raymond of St. Gilles. The capture of Jerusalem itself occupies a relatively brief space in this history, which seems to find even this event anticlimactic after Antioch. But the *Gesta Fran-*

corum does allot one fine anecdote to its conclusion. On August 12, 1099 (a Friday, the *Gesta* informs us) the crusaders fight at Ascalon to defend their conquest of Jerusalem. God stuns their foes and grants the Christians an easy victory (10.39):

> The enemies of God stood blinded and struck senseless, and seeing the soldiers of Christ, they saw nothing though their eyes were wide open. And they dared not rise up against the Christians, so shaken were they by God's power.

In their panic the enemies climb trees or jump into the sea or simply fall to the ground, while the defeated emir of Egypt cries out in despair. Here again the language stresses the victory of Christians aided directly by their God.

Much of the *Gesta*'s considerable appeal lies in the sobriety with which it presents this story, a sobriety that complements its ultimate conviction that the true victors are the ordinary crusaders and their God. We can readily imagine what Dudo or William of Poitiers or Malaterra might have done with the same material. But we need not simply imagine. Many writers yielded to the impulse to put the *Gesta* into "literary form," including Guibert of Nogent, Baudri of Bourgueil, and Robert the Monk.[31] The Norman chauvinist, Ralph of Caen, packaged the same story in ornate prosimetrical form, calling on all the trappings from the rhetorical style: wordplay, repetition, and quotations from Horace and Vergil and Lucan, punctuated by the supine exclamation *mirabile dictu!* ("remarkable to relate"; cf. 140). This pompous syntax encourages excesses, like the list of verbs concluding the verses that honor Hugh Magnus for his exploits at Dorylaeum (27–32):

> Aggreditur, lacerat, fugat, insequitur, premit, arctat,
> Fulminat, exsultat, fremit, exclamat, furit, ardet.
>
> (He attacks, tears to shreds, routs, pursues, harries, presses,
> thunders, runs riot, roars, shouts, rages, blazes.)

As Tancred's brother William dies in battle and the surviving crusaders flee, the *Gesta Tancredi* mourns (22):

> O bellum miserabile! O fuga lugubris! O damnum in damno! O in vulnere vulnus!
>
> (Ah, wretched war! Ah, grievous flight! Ah, loss amid loss! Ah, wound amid wound!)

With more felicity Ralph's crusaders burst into a joyous hymn as the army proceeds to Jerusalem (111), but the damage is done. The second-rate

---

[31] Frederic Duncalf, "The Councils of Piacenza and Clermont," in *A History of the Crusades*, ed. Baldwin, 1. 239.

bombast – including the insistence that Tancred is *alter Julius* ("a second Caesar") – seems foolish after the simplicity of the *Gesta Francorum*.

But we do need the *Gesta Tancredi* if we want to follow the Norman heroes, Bohemond and Tancred, in their pursuits, as they create their Norman principality at Antioch. Yet even this work does not follow their tale to the end. After the death of Bohemond back in Apulia in 1111 and the death of Tancred in 1112, Ralph stopped writing, having gotten only as far as 1104 in the narrative. Bohemond left a young son, the future Bohemond II, for whom Tancred served briefly as regent. With Tancred's death, the regency devolved on a Hauteville cousin, Roger of Salerno, son of Richard of the Principate.

Thanks especially to the war-loving energy of Tancred, Norman Antioch was a formidable power, surpassing the other crusader states, even Jerusalem. Heavily fortified and nearly impossible to take by siege – as the crusaders themselves had discovered – Antioch still controlled large territories and oversaw considerable commerce. But with prince Roger's death in 1119, at the battle that Christians would remember as the *Ager Sanguinis* ("Field of Blood"), the Norman presence at Antioch weakened irreparably, not least because this debacle wiped out Roger's predominantly Norman army. Baldwin II took over the regency, and the French played an increasing role at the principality, even as disputes over the succession sapped Antioch's strength. The brief rule of Bohemond II (1126–30) could not significantly restore the balance of power to the Normans. Bohemond II also died in battle, leaving a daughter, Constance, whose marriage to Raymond of Poitiers (1136–49), son of Duke William IX of Aquitaine, opened the door to southern French influences, which finally ousted the remaining Norman elements at Antioch. Through Constance, the heirs of Bohemond I ruled Antioch until 1287, but by then they had long since ceased to consider themselves Norman.[32]

In any event, the crusading account by a participant in the Norman forces never truly acknowledged Antioch as a Norman possession. The *Gesta*'s implicit renunciation of Bohemond's ambitions, in fact, adds a note of irony to assertions that Bohemond used the *Gesta Francorum* to support his claims to the principality. Twentieth-century readers suggested that Bohemond ordered new passages inserted into the *Gesta Francorum*, and then carried the interpolated text with him through Italy and France in 1105 and 1106, essentially using the *Gesta* as a tool for recruitment and fund-raising to support new campaigns for Antioch.[33] Louis Bréhier argued, for instance,

---

[32] Davis, *The Normans and their Myth*, 9.

[33] Cf. Louis Bréhier, ed. *GF,* v–viii; August C. Krey, "A Neglected Passage in the *Gesta* and its Bearing on the Literature of the First Crusade," in *The Crusades and Other Historical Essays presented to Dana C. Munro*, ed. Louis J. Paetow (New York, 1928), 57–78. See also Harold S. Fink, "The Foundation of the Latin States, 1099–1118," in *The First Hundred Years*, ed. Marshall W. Baldwin, 391.

that the cluster of Biblical citations in chapter one and the Christian erudition of Kerbogha's mother indicate such additions. But the author may simply have known – perhaps intuitively, rather than by explicit example – the historical convention that introductions should be more elaborate than the main text. His style generally changes in direct address, and he always makes Saracens talk in an odd way.[34] Other differences stem from the varying conditions under which he wrote, or from the increasing skill and expansiveness of his prose as he gained experience.

For readers who believe that Bohemond inspired an interpolated text, the most important supposed addition is the passage concerning Bohemond's secret deal with Alexios at Constantinople (2.6). But no manuscript evidence supports this theory, and both the language and the sentiments of this episode sound authentic. Indeed, it seems plausible that Bohemond and Alexios should come to terms, with the emperor here promising Bohemond remote lands in exchange for good behavior and oaths of fealty. In the *Gesta*'s version, Alexios offers Bohemond the territory beyond Antioch, but not the city itself – a distinction that the Norman prince would have avoided if he were inventing the terms a decade after the supposed meeting. Finally, if Bohemond had a scribe add this passage, he would also have eliminated references to his own binding oaths, with their suggestions of any debt to Alexios as his overlord, and he might have taken care as well that the scribe remove the critical remarks that circumscribe the *Gesta*'s account of this secret treaty.

There is no secure evidence that Bohemond ever adduced the *Gesta Francorum* as testimony for his heroism and for his ownership of Antioch. If he knew the work well, he could not have been altogether satisfied with the way the *Gesta* portrayed him. Bohemond's recruiting tour aimed to attract more partisan enthusiasts to Antioch, men who had not witnessed his ready sacrifice of the common goal to his own ambitions. On this triumphal journey, Bohemond promulgated the heroic view of his exploits, and he basked in the adulation of adoring crowds. One of the Normans inspired to immigrate to Antioch, Ralph of Caen, wrote a history that presented this view for the most part, though Ralph focused on Tancred as the truest descendant of the house of Hauteville in his own generation.[35] But Ralph's sycophantic pose does not make the *Gesta Tancredi* a characteristically Norman history. On the contrary, the *Gesta Francorum* fits the Norman pattern more closely by

---

[34] Hill, xvi.

[35] The *Gesta Tancredi*, for instance, presents Tancred's view of the crusaders' passage through Constantinople on their way to Jerusalem (11). Here Tancred laments Alexios's alleged seduction of Bohemond: "Venit ad regnum, invenit jugum" ("[Bohemond] came for a kingdom; he got a slave's yoke"). Tancred's jingle ends with a nice pun in *jugum*, which means both "yoke" and "acre."

opposing the ambitions of a prince when these violate the people's needs or the dictates of the historian's conscience.

Its very rejection of Normanness makes the *Gesta Francorum* a Norman tale. Its author did not write, as some have assumed, for a Norman patron and a Norman audience.[36] Nor is the *Gesta*, as some routinely assert, "a pro-Norman chronicle."[37] Nor is it a work that "thoroughly idealizes Bohemond," as others have claimed.[38] Yet its very disenchantment with an ambitious Norman lord aligns the *Gesta* squarely with the viewpoints expressed in the central works of the Norman historical tradition. The *Gesta*'s author was not consciously working within that tradition. Nonetheless, the *Gesta Francorum* entered its mainstream in the twelfth century through the writings of the pan-Norman historian, Orderic Vitalis.

---

[36] Cf. David C. Douglas, *The Norman Achievement*, 103.

[37] Harold S. Fink, "The Foundation of the Latin States," 391.

[38] Hans Eberhard Mayer, *The Crusades*, trans. John Gillingham (1972; reprint, Oxford, 1978), 46.

5

Orderic Vitalis

> . . . mortalium robur labile est subitoque ceu flos foeni marcet. . . .
> (. . . mortal vigor is fleeting and withers suddenly like the flower of
> the field. . . .)
>
> (*Ecclesiastical History* 2.80)

THE crusade left a deep and lingering mark on twelfth-century Europe. A generation after the anonymous *Gesta Francorum*, Orderic Vitalis devoted one of the thirteen books in his *Ecclesiastical History* to the crusader's tale. While covering the millennium from the Incarnation to his own day, Orderic found good reason to emphasize the five years from Clermont to the immediate aftermath of Ascalon. To his mind, that spiritual and material adventure directly illustrated God's providential plan at work on earth, the glory of championing God's cause, and the vanity of worldly ambitions. Orderic's writing presents a monastic point of view, to be sure. But his experiences as a resident in what was essentially a Norman war zone on the duchy's southern frontier, and as an acute student of the Normans, from their origins to the women and men of his own era, left him especially world-weary.[1]

The dean of Norman historians was born in England, in the border region near Shrewsbury.[2] Orderic never mentions his mother, whom we presume to be English. His Norman father, Odelarius of Orleans, had come to England two years after the Conquest, immigrating with Roger of Montgomery, future earl of Shrewsbury (1074–94). A learned clerk and one of Roger's chaplains, Odelarius had lofty ambitions for his oldest son. So when Orderic was five years old, in 1080, Odelarius sent him to study with an English priest in Shrewsbury. For the first ten years of his life, the boy lived among the conquered English, his mother's people. In 1085 he obeyed his father's

---

[1] Kathleen Thompson, "Orderic Vitalis and Robert of Bellême," *Journal of Medieval History* 20 (1994), 134.

[2] *EH* 6, p. 52. On Orderic's life and times, see Chibnall, *World of Orderic Vitalis*.

wishes and traveled to Normandy, to enter the monastery of Saint-Évroul, far from family ties and home.

There Orderic lived until his death, probably in 1142. Throughout a long lifetime he worked in the scriptorium copying texts and writing his own, occasionally visiting other monasteries and once even returning briefly to England.[3] His travels gave him first-hand information on sites, events, and people. But he spent most of those years at Saint-Évroul, dwelling "in a barren countryside amid the worst possible neighbors" (*EH* 3, p. 118; cf. 2, p. 148). There he never lost his sympathy for the English or forgot that he had come as a foreigner to Norman soil (cf. *EH* 3, p. 6). He called himself *Vitalis Angligena* "Vitalis of English birth" or "*Ordricus Angligena.*"[4] Yet Saint-Évroul enjoyed far-flung contacts with all the Norman world, dispatching its monks to be abbots elsewhere or watching its benefactors' sons seek their fortunes in the east or the south. Orderic gathered oral reports, too, from frequent visitors to his monastery. From all these connections Orderic could learn about Lombards, Syrians, crusaders, Byzantines, Arabs, and Turks.

Orderic also relied on his access to a rich collection of manuscripts, including annals, chronicles, saints' lives, monastic charters, and letters. Bede's *Historia Ecclesiastica gentis Anglorum* ("Ecclesiastical History of the English People") was a constant inspiration for Orderic, showing him the path toward broader historical sensibilities. The *Historia Langobardorum* ("History of the Lombards") of Paul the Deacon also taught Orderic how to write the history of a people who rose from barbarism to become civilized players on the world stage. But for the material of his own Norman history, Orderic needed Norman sources, and he found those that took him to the core of the Norman historical tradition. His care in citing these sources makes it easy to see what he knew by reputation or by the perusal of texts discovered in other monastic libraries. Orderic recognized the eloquence of Dudo's "panegyric rich in changing styles and meters," though he preferred the abridgment and continuation by William of Jumièges, whose work he knew intimately.[5] For the life of William the Conqueror he copied William of Poitiers so faithfully that from Book Four of the *Ecclesiastical History* we may be able to retrieve the lost conclusion of the *Gesta Guillelmi*.[6] Through Saint-Évroul's ties with southern Italy, he heard reports of Malaterra's recent *Historia Sicula* (*EH* 2, p. 100) and probably gained access to some of Amatus's sources. Orderic's account of the crusade follows the *Gesta Fran-*

---

3 On his travels, see Chibnall, *EH* 1, pp. 25–27.

4 Chibnall (*World of Orderic Vitalis*, 3) discusses his persistent use of *Ordricus* (and not *Ordericus*) *Angligena*. On his position as an Anglo-Norman historian, see Antonia Gransden, *Historical Writing in England c. 550 to c. 1307* (Ithaca, N.Y., 1974), 151.

5 *EH* 2, pp. 2, 4; cf. 3, pp. 304, 6. For Orderic's sources, consult Marjorie Chibnall's introductions to the individual volumes of her edition, especially 1.48–97.

6 Chibnall, ed., *EH* 2, p. xviii.

corum, which he knew through an intermediary source, Baudri of Bourgueil's literary adaptation, the *Historia Ierosolimitana*.[7]

The *Ecclesiastical History* is the masterpiece of this historical tradition, but all the evidence indicates that it reached only a small audience.[8] Its length made it too cumbersome for ready copying or wide circulation. For three-fourths of the text, the only surviving medieval manuscript is the autograph, whose few marginal notes imply infrequent use. Wace knew this work, as did Robert of Torigny, who culled many of Orderic's data for his own more popular history, and in this way Orderic's material entered the mainstream of later medieval historical writing.[9] It is odd, however, that Robert did not quote directly from the master whom he may have known. Though Robert's monastery was close to Saint-Évroul and though the prior of Bec was a fervent book-collector, he never bothered to transcribe the *Ecclesiastical History*.

While Orderic's masterwork almost passed into oblivion, his insertions into William of Jumièges' *Gesta Normannorum Ducum* won him a large readership. Before 1109 the young monk was copying the *Gesta* in Saint-Évroul's scriptorium and breaking into the text to add tiny notes or entire chapters whenever he saw fit.[10] As it happened, these became practice exercises for the great task that he would soon begin. The interpolations deserve our attention, not only because they anticipate so many characteristics of that larger work, but especially because they reveal the workings of Orderic's mind as he restores Norman treachery and violence to the *Gesta*'s more wholesome picture.

Orderic made a few additions to the early books of William's *Gesta*, for example recovering some of Dudo's material about Rollo and re-emphasizing Rollo's Danish connection, which William of Jumièges had obscured. But the majority of Orderic's notes interrupt William's final chapter on the Conqueror. There Orderic sometimes adds simple details like names and dates. More often he balances the ducal view with information critical of the duke. He offers the infamous story, for instance, of the young duke's siege of Alençon in 1051, when the defenders taunted the Bastard from the safety of their

7   Chibnall, ed., *EH* 5, pp. xiii–xv.
8   For documention of this evidence, see Roger D. Ray, "Orderic Vitalis and his Readers," *Studia Monastica* 14 (1972), 17–33.
9   Chibnall, ed., *EH* I, pp. xvii and 114. Wace used parts of Books Seven and Eight. For the relationship between Orderic and Robert, see Marjorie Chibnall, "Orderic Vital and Robert of Torigni," *Millénaire monastique de Mont-Saint-Michel* 2 (Paris, 1966), 133–39.
10 Elisabeth van Houts has questioned whether Orderic in fact wrote these interpolations: "Quelques remarques sur les interpolations attribuées à Orderic Vital dans les *Gesta Normanorum Ducum* de Guillaume de Jumièges," *Revue d'histoire des textes* 8 (1978), 213–22. Following Delisle and Marx, Marjorie Chibnall believed that these additions were "the unaided work of Orderic" (Chibnall, ed., *EH* I, p. 30).

walls, mocking his mother's lowly birth from a family of tanners [7.(18)]. So vexed was the young duke by these insults that he mutilated thirty-two of the offenders when he took their fortress, ordering his men to cut off their hands and feet.

As we have seen, the dukes found themselves particularly threatened by charges of illegitimacy, and historians repeated them at their own risk. But Orderic exposes Duke William's vulnerability on this charge time and again, as at 7.(3), when he has William's distant cousin, Roger of Tosny, refuse to acknowledge the boy as duke. Roger boasts descent from Rollo's uncle, Malahulc, so he thinks his own claim, though remote, beats a bastard's, as Orderic explicitly states: "When he learned that young William had succeeded his father in the duchy, he became vehemently indignant and arrogantly scorned to serve him, saying that a bastard [*nothus*] should not rule over him and the other Normans." Here Orderic proceeds to name William's mother, becoming the first historian to do so: "For William was the son of Duke Robert's concubine, Herleva, the daughter of Fulbert, the duke's chamberlain, and he was despised by the native nobility and especially by the descendants of the dukes Richard, inasmuch as he was a bastard [*utpote nothus*]."

Orderic reminds us that this humiliation dogged Duke William even as he was about to sail against England. For here [7.(33)] Orderic interjects a note alleging William's fright at the threats of Conan, count of the Bretons, who dispatches an envoy to terrify William with this message:

I hear that you intend now to cross the sea and get the kingdom of the English for yourself. I am very glad to hear it, but I entreat you to return Normandy to me. For Robert, duke of the Normans, whom you pretend is your father, commended all his inheritance to my father Alan, his cousin, as he was about to go to Jerusalem. Then you along with your accomplices [*complicibus tuis*] killed my father Alan with poison at Vimoutiers in Normandy, and you invaded his land, which I could not defend because I was just a boy, and you have held it until now against all right [*contra fas*], because you are a bastard [*nothus*]. So now either hand over Normandy, which you owe me, or I shall bring war upon you with all my troops.

Orderic allows Conan his own defiant voice and never contradicts the charges that link William's bastardy to unlawful lordship, wrongful seizure, thuggery, and poisoning.

Orderic does avow that "God deigned to snatch [the duke] from his enemy's threats," but at once he undermines any sense of divine justice by identifying the agent of William's rescue: it is a Breton magnate, Conan's own chamberlain and the very man sent to Normandy with Conan's warning. Ensuing events strongly suggest that the duke has corrupted this Breton envoy during their parley. For when Conan's emissary returns to Brittany, he smears poison on his lord's gloves, reins, and horn.

183

Conan's demise from this poisoning deepens the suspicion that William had in fact poisoned Conan's father.[11] This fresh murder, moreover, leads directly to Orderic's encomium of the duke's enemy [7.(33)]:

> He was very wise and virtuous and a lover of justice. If he had lived longer, so people say, he would have done many good deeds and he would have governed his territories in a manner beyond reproach. But the traitor [*proditor*], aware of his guilt, soon fled from Conan's siege-army and reported his death to Duke William.

Is it any surprise when Orderic, in the sentence immediately following this account, strips the honorific *princeps* ("prince") that William of Jumièges gave his duke and omits the legitimizing phrase awarded to Duke William as he resumes his preparations against England? Where William of Jumièges has "the prince who by right (*iure*) ought to have been crowned with the royal diadem," Orderic is silent.

Occasionally Orderic alters William's sense by commandeering one of his sentences in a way that challenges its original meaning. In one example [7.11(27)], William of Jumièges describes Duke William's capture of Mayenne, a fortress in Maine: "Having besieged it for some time with all his resources, he finally took it by throwing fire inside it [*igneque iniecto*] and burning it to the ground." William of Poitiers supports this account with a detailed portrait of the castle, high on a cliff above the river Mayenne, unapproachable from any direction by knights or foot-soldiers or by siege-engines of any sort (*GG* 1.40). Indeed, he uses the same words (*iniecti ignes*) to explain how the duke captured Mayenne, apparently by throwing firebrands or shooting burning arrows over the walls.[12] But Orderic corrects the record as he copies William of Jumièges [7.11(27)]. In place of William's vague injection of fire, Orderic inserts an incident that he may have received through oral tradition: "Having besieged it for some time with all his resources, [the duke] finally took it after it was set on fire [*igneque iniecto*] by two boys who had entered it covertly as if to play with the children of the town, and so he burned it to the ground."

Orderic's emendation places this exploit squarely within the viking/Norman tradition of taking a fortified place through an artful ruse. Employing children as the perpetrators may be so inglorious that a chronicler and panegyrist of Duke William's own day used discretion in omitting that detail. But Orderic's insertion seems plausible as a venerable Norman trick updated for conditions of the mid-eleventh century, when Normans burned fortified towns instead of monasteries.

---

[11] Only Orderic claims poisoning as the cause of Conan's death: van Houts, ed., *GND* 2, p. 164, note 2.

[12] On the use of fire in siege warfare, see Davis and Chibnall, ed., *GG*, p. 66, note 1.

When Orderic is not incriminating the duke or removing rhetoric of praise, he frequently directs attention away from ducal authority and toward the resistance of Norman or Breton nobles. While William of Jumièges emphasized the duke's control over the forces of anarchy, Orderic stresses the opposite, adding much information about the chaos during the minority of William the Bastard as nobles harry the countryside. Even in the lifetime of the boy's father, Duke Robert I, William of Bellême and his sons stir up trouble. To the *Gesta*'s account of their perfidy, Orderic adds details that expose gratuitous violence. When "a good and kindly soldier" greets Warin, one of the sons, with a friendly smile, Warin responds by chopping off his head (6.4). Choked by a demon, Warin gets his due, as does his brother, Robert, when foes axe him to death in prison, retaliating against the brutalities of his men (6.7). Vengeance and counter-vengeance continue with vigilantism and murder when men least expect harm, "just as they all deserved," in Orderic's pronouncement [7.(2)].[13]

Time and again Orderic infuses the *Gesta* with reminders of traitorous Normans. William of Jumièges dared not risk "inexorable hatred" by naming the magnates who ran roughshod over Normandy when William the Bastard was a young child, since these same men had become the duke's liegemen, "on whom the duke has heaped great honors" [(*Gesta* 7.1(1–4)]. But in his account Orderic inserts three chapters [7.(2)–(4)], names names and damns the perpetrators along with the crimes. Here is the first of these chapters:

Now Hugh of Montfort, son of Thurstan, fought with Walkelin of Ferrières, and in that battle both were killed. Furthermore, the madness [*rabies*] of certain people breaks out and reigns supreme, at great damage to the country. So one morning while riding, Gilbert, count of Eu, son of Count Godfrey, the clever and brave guardian of William (still a boy, though his lord), while talking with his fellow countryman Walkelin of Pont-Échanfroi and suspecting no evil, was killed along with Fulk, son of Giroie. Next Turold, tutor of the young duke, was slain by renegades faithless to the country [*perimitur a perfidis patrie desertoribus*]. Osbern, too, steward of the ducal household, son of Herfast brother of Countess Gunnor, one night while he and the duke were sound asleep in the duke's bedchamber at Vaudreuil, in a sudden attack by William, son of Roger of Montgomery, had his throat cut as he lay in bed. At that time Roger was in exile in Paris because of his treason [*pro perfidia sua*], and his five sons Hugh, Robert, Roger, William and Gilbert were in Normandy, deeply implicated in committing awful crimes. But not much later William met his just reward, God's retribution for the aforementioned wickedness that he had performed. For Barnon of Glos, Osbern's provost, wishing to avenge the

---

13 On Orderic's disdain for Robert of Bellême, see Kathleen Thompson, "Robert of Bellême Reconsidered," *Anglo-Norman Studies* 13, ed. Marjorie Chibnall (Woodbridge, 1991), 261–84, and "Orderic Vitalis and Robert of Bellême," 133–41.

unjust murder of his lord, one night gathered some ready fighters and entered the house where William and his accomplices were sleeping, and butchered them all on the spot, just as they all deserved [*omnes simul sicut meruerant statim trucidauit*].

In Orderic's version, as the young duke matures he tries to control "the sons of discord, who rejoice in dissension and strive to afflict people who want to live in peace" [7.(4)]. When the unruly magnates "see that they cannot harm the ordinary people as much as they would like," they "scheme to overthrow the country" by colluding with the French King Henry. In such circumstances, righteous men must continue to take the law into their own hands. So when the gang headed by William Sor's sons commandeers the church of St. Gervais at Séez as their hideout, the local bishop, the aged Azso, forces them out by tearing down the walls [7.(13)]. The country people join in exacting retribution. A peasant axes to death Richard, the eldest Sor boy, who had tortured him, while other peasants chase down his brother Robert and kill him as he plunders their land [7.(14)]. "Robbers and wreckers of churches" should beware, writes Orderic, for they will suffer a like fate. Or maybe not, in this lawless world. But if they should prosper, he continues, resorting here to his favorite Biblical admonition, let them know that "worldly pleasure passes away in an instant like smoke and brings everlasting grief."

Orderic's villains often seem frighteningly real. Leblond has argued that these immoderate rogues are the truest representatives of the Norman character.[14] Consider, for instance, Orderic's portrait of Mabel of Bellême, the enemy of Saint-Évroul, who inherited a wicked temperament from her father and passed it along to her sons [7.(16)]:

After William Talvas was driven from his own land by his son, as I related above, he roamed about, staying in one household after another, wretched and despised by all. Finally he sought out Roger of Montgomery and willingly offered him his own daughter, Mabel [*filiam suam, nomine Mabiliam*], and granted him every privilege which he himself had lost through laziness and vice. Now Roger, who was brave and upright and mature in his deliberation, decided that this would be in his own best interests and acquiesced in everything. So he received the wanderer in his own household and married his daughter in lawful wedlock. The aforementioned woman was petite and very talkative [*loquax*], quite ready to do evil, shrewd [*sagax*] and witty, and exceedingly cruel and bold [*audax*]. In succeeding years she bore five sons and four daughters, whose names are as follows: Robert, Hugh, Roger the Poitevin, Philip, and Arnulf, Emma, Matilda, Mabel, and Sibylla. In their character, the girls surpassed their

---

14 Bernard Leblond, *L'accession des Normands de Neustrie à la culture occidentale (Xème–XIème siècles)* (Paris, 1966), 144–50.

brothers, for they were honorable maidens, kind to the poor and monks and other servants of God. But the boys became savage [*ferales*] and rapacious, greedy oppressors of the weak. How cunning or warlike or treacherous they were, how arrogantly they swaggered over their neighbors and peers, and then perished under them for their villainies, it is not our business to relate in this place where we have resolved to publish the deeds of the great Duke William. Let us therefore leave those affairs and direct our pen back to the narrative.

But Orderic cannot keep his pen on the duke's business for long. He incorporates jingles and rhymes into his prose to mock Mabel as truly her father's daughter and to underline her less appealing traits. Orderic finds Normans like Mabel too compelling to ignore. And he is drawn to the dark atmosphere surrounding these Norman nobles, whose children often inherit their parents' evil nature, just as violence begets more violence.[15]

It is one mark of Orderic's genius that he gives these Normans their own voices, and voices that ring true. Historians ancient and medieval felt free to invent plausible dialogue, and Orderic follows this custom with skill, transporting us into the minds of his characters and giving us entry into their intimate conversations, as Orderic imagined them. When Bishop Ivo rousted out brigands by burning the church where they were hiding, for instance, Pope Leo reproaches him [7.(15)]: "What have you done, knave? By what law should you be condemned for having dared to burn your mother?" ["Quid fecisti, perfidi? Qua lege damnari debes, qui matrem tuam cremare ausus es?"] The direct accusation brings us to the heart of Ivo's dilemma. Plain language also marks the conversation between Count William Werlenc and a knight in his household, Robert Bigot, who wants to leave Normandy [7.(19)]:

> "I am oppressed by poverty, my lord, and here in our homeland I cannot earn a living. So now I will go to Apulia, to live more honorably there." William replied, "Who persuaded you to do this?" He answered, "The poverty that I suffer." The count then said, "If you are willing to trust me, you will stay here with us. For within eighty days you will have such circumstances in Normandy that you will be able to steal with impunity any resources that you see."

Perhaps this dialogue was invented to justify Duke William's confiscations and the exile of alleged plotters, but it implicates the men convincingly, even as it shows the lure of Apulia, which beguiled impoverished Normans.

Orderic often gives a voice to dissident Normans. But he also lets an Anglo-Saxon speak, offering one English voice that condemns Harold Godwinson for his impetuosity before Hastings [7.(35)]. With the support of

---

15 Cf. 6.4; 7.7; 7.(10).

his mother and friends, Harold's brother Gyrth tries to persuade the reckless king to withdraw from the battle:

> Dearest brother and lord, you ought to temper your honor with a moderating discretion. Just now you have come back exhausted from battle with the Norwegians, and now again you are hastening to fight against the Normans. Please rest! [*Quiesce, queso*] You should want to conduct yourself cautiously. That is what you promised Normandy's ruler with sworn oaths. Beware not to incur [*incurras*] perjury. Don't rush into [*corruas*] disaster for such a crime along with the flower of our people and forever after be an abiding disgrace for our descendants. I am free of any sworn oath to Count William and owe him nothing. Boldly, therefore, I am ready to vie with him on behalf of my only brother. But you, my brother, rest in peace however you see fit and wait for the war's outcome. Don't let the fair liberty of the English perish through your disastrous defeat [*pernicie*].

It is wise counsel, offered with compassion and a sense of impending tragedy. Earl Gyrth's speech must represent one opinion commonly held by the conquered English of Orderic's day. In this view, at the very least Harold had sworn to engage in no hostilities against William. His oath-breaking, combined with his folly in meeting the Norman forces so soon after fighting the Norwegian invaders, seals England's doom. Here is a Harold so hell-bent on self-destruction that Gyrth's admonition only provokes him to hurl abuse on his brother and kick away his mother (*pede procaciter percussit*), who was fondly clinging to him. The harsh sounds and alliteration of Orderic's prose highlight Harold's brutality and petulance.

Orderic's rendering of this scene draws the readers' sympathies to the people doomed to lose their fair liberty (*clara libertas*) for such a king. This portrayal reflects Orderic's conviction that the sins of Harold's father, Godwin, haunted Godwin's son and destined England for ruin. He rails against Godwin's influence and guile, contrasting him with Edward the Confessor, pious and sworn to perpetual virginity [7.(9)]. Though Harold's truculence propels the English toward Hastings, the ultimate cause of England's ruin is Godwin's murder of Alfred Ætheling, for which the Normans act as God's avengers (7.36).

Orderic's personal history leads him to England and to these sympathies with the English people, damned by the sins of arrogant lords. But the ties of his monastery and its patrons often take him to Apulia, where Bishop Ivo canvasses friends and relatives for funds to rebuild the church that he had destroyed [7.(15)] and where banished nobles find a profitable exile [7.(19), (29)]. Two chapters summarize Arab attacks on the Italian coast and the recruitment of Norman mercenaries by Lombards who need their military aid against these Saracens and Byzantine armies as well [7.(29)–(30)]. Here Orderic recounts the growing Norman hegemony in the south. He especially cites Robert Guiscard's conquest of Apulia, Calabria, and Sicily and his invasion of the Byzantine Empire, where Orderic claims he routed Alexios Komnenos in retaliation for his rebellion against the Emperor Michael Doukas. In fact, Alexios had rebelled against the man who dethroned Michael Doukas. Despite this error in detail, the breadth of Orderic's geographic range, which extends from Spain [7.(3)] to Constantinople [7.(15)], remains impressive. A single Norman family can divert his narrative to any part of that world and beyond, as the descendants of Giroie terrorize barbarians "in England or Apulia or Thrace or Syria" [7.(11)]. R. H. C. Davis argued that the unusually close ties of Orderic's monastery to these far-flung Norman freebooters have given us a deceptive view of the Normans in their widely scattered possessions as a single and distinct people.[16] But Orderic's experience left him certain that this was so. By their distinctive behavior as much as by their family ties, these adventurers reveal themselves as Normans.

Orderic's curiosity about Normans and their exploits knows no limits, and only with difficulty can he pull himself back to Normandy and the course of events there. Within the duchy he takes a particular interest in monastic history. The interlude of tranquillity produced by Duke William's iron fist especially pleases the monk because it diverts the nobility from their bellicose pursuits to the construction of churches and the endowment of monasteries [7.(22)]. Orderic's investigations into monastic history, like his later treatment of the crusade, provide admirable outlets for his interests, a mixture of spiritual and secular that would later confound critics of the *Ecclesiastical History*, but seems so natural to the writer himself.[17]

Frequent Biblical references comment on the ways that Norman history confirms the scriptures. So when all the Sor brothers meet violent ends, Orderic exclaims:

> See! In them we truly saw fulfilled what we have heard in the epistles of Saint Paul the apostle [I Cor. 3:17]: "If any man defile the temple of God, him shall God destroy." [7.(14)]

Later Orderic excuses the murder of Englishmen during the Conquest by quoting the psalmist's warning against lawbreakers, an admonition that they had ignored to their peril [7.(36)]. Maxims from everyday parlance further reinforce the moral tone:

> But the treachery of evil men does not cease from disturbing the peace of good men. [7.(13)]

---

[16] *The Normans and their Myth*, especially pp. 63–64.

[17] For analysis of the criticism and Orderic's response, see Ray, "Orderic and William."

But as the common proverb states, "A fool is chastened not by words, nor by examples, but by blows, and then just barely, and he does not really fear until he feels the hard strokes." [7.(19)]

Perhaps nothing confirms the monk's religious passions so much as his enthusiastic reaffirmation of miracles: a demon strangles the wicked Gunther of Bellême as his comrades watch [6.(4)]; God points out the site of a future monastery through an angel [7.(23)]; holy relics work cures on Cyprus [7.(26)]. Yet for Orderic the spiritual, mysterious, and moral messages complement rather than invalidate his human interest and compassion. Sometimes he inserts into the *Gesta* local tales that take the narrative suddenly into the villages or countryside. He describes, for instance, the theft of a holy woman's pig by Arnulf, son of William Talvas, and the robber's murder that very night [7.(12)]. Sometimes he follows the genealogies of Saint-Évroul's benefactors, a practice he would further develop in the *Ecclesiastical History* for the edification of monks who must pray for their souls. Orderic may have had the same motivation here. But he seems particularly driven to fill in the gaps in the *Gesta*'s narrative, to identify the interrelationships among the powerful Normans who contest the duke's sovereignty, and to bring the various threads of the story up to his own time. All his concerns strain against the pat and tidy ducal view. His interpolations into the *Gesta Normannorum Ducum* show the young Orderic redirecting the Norman historical tradition toward a new, more universal history, and one profoundly critical of both duke and Norman lords.

Orderic's designs for his *Ecclesiastical History* evolved over time.[18] At the request of his abbot and brother-monks, he began a history of Saint-Évroul. He soon found that he could not discuss the monastery's affairs without treating the Norman families that had so influenced Saint-Évroul, as benefactors or oppressors. The deeds of these magnates made sense only within the larger context of Norman activity everywhere, especially in the duchy and the Anglo-Norman *regnum*. Sometimes he returned to the internal business of his monastery, enumerating donations and miracles alike. With the book that became the seventh, at the center of his thirteen-volume history, Orderic moved more decisively to the secular realm, summarizing Norman, French, and English affairs to the death of the Conqueror in 1087. The remaining books continue this history, in more detail, until 1141. As he worked on these later sections, Orderic also wrote Books One and Two, chronicling the lives of Jesus and the apostles, and listing the succession of both popes and lay rulers in Western Christendom. Within this structure, the progression is often thematic rather than strictly chronological, with numerous digressions to illustrate an important point or simply report news that intrigued Orderic,

---

[18] On the emerging development of his plans for this work, consult Chibnall's introduction to her edition (1.31–39) and Gransden, *Historical Writing in England*, 152–53.

and with repetitions as Orderic revisits significant persons and events from different perspectives. The final result is an *Ecclesiastical History* that duplicates the chaos of the Norman realm as Orderic knew it. And if it is styled a "church history," fully "five-sixths of it deals with the emergence of the duchy of Normandy and the great Norman expansion into England, southern Italy, Spain and Antioch."[19]

At first he wrote slowly, perhaps somehow constrained by deference to his master in the scriptorium, John of Rheims, who died in 1125.[20] But once Orderic's friend Warin of Les Essarts assumed the abbacy of Saint-Évroul, Orderic's pace quickened. As Marjorie Chibnall has shown, Orderic composed the bulk of his masterwork between 1123 and 1137, precisely the years when Warin was abbot.

In all his historical writings, before and after 1123, Orderic enjoyed considerable license to express his own views, untrammeled by any lord's demands for adulation or the sanitizing of unsavory deeds. For the *History*, however, he did encounter an unusual problem with sources. He had material for the early years: Dudo and his successors had told their story of the duchy, from its origins to the Conquest of England; William of Apulia and other Italo-Normans traced Norman advances in the south, while crusaders left records of their adventures in the east. But for the history of the Anglo-Norman realm, including the duchy itself, after the Conquest, Orderic found few written sources. No doubt this lapse occurred in part because the Conqueror's immediate successors did not patronize historians. But it also happened because the final years of William the Conqueror were so bleak, the succession so troubled. Who could discern the meaning behind the distress that followed, the rebellions, chaos, and disloyalty of the king's sons?[21]

For answers, Orderic searched the memories of friends and acquaintances, near and far. He does not turn away from the uncomfortable, often nasty, truths he learns, but examines these post-Hastings years in some detail. He depicts the Conqueror as a man tormented in his last days, grieving over the Norman passion for insurrection that extends even to his own children (4.82). The dying king holds little hope for Normandy or England under his fractious sons, Robert Curthose, William Rufus, and Henry. The oldest of these, Robert, is the least promising of the three, and King William predicts ruin for Normandy with him as duke – "a haughty and foolish cipher [*superbus . . . et insipiens nebulo*], who surely will be stricken with grim, protracted misfor-

---

19 Marjorie Chibnall, "Feudal Society in Orderic Vitalis," in *Battle* 1, ed. R. Allen Brown (1979), 35.
20 Marjorie Chibnall, *EH* 1, p. 32.
21 For an account of these years, see Hollister, "Normandy, France and the Anglo-Norman *Regnum*," and J. H. Le Patourel, "The Norman Succession, 996–1135," *English Historical Review* 86 (1971), 225–50.

tune" (4.92). In Orderic's version, William leaves England to no heir, because he feels that the unjustly subdued land is not his to bequeath, but he prays that William Rufus will secure God's favor and keep the kingdom (4.92–94). The youngest, Henry, is chagrined to receive no land, but only a fortune of five-thousand pounds in silver (4.94).

The struggles among the brothers soon begin, while Orderic aligns with the younger two against Robert, whom he often attacks for his weakness and misrule.[22] Eager to escape the feuding that his languor has encouraged and to atone for his sins, Robert welcomes the call to the First Crusade and mortgages the devastated duchy to William Rufus to finance his expedition (5.26). Orderic's portrait of Robert jibes with his fitful presence in the *Gesta Francorum*, where he rarely cuts a heroic figure. Before Robert can return from Jerusalem, King William Rufus dies during a hunt in the New Forest, killed instantly by an errant shot, and Henry takes the crown. At this point, in the year 1100, Orderic delights in a competent lord (5.294–98) and applauds his action in usurping Robert's claim to England [6.14–16). "Afterwards," writes Orderic, "Duke Robert returned in Normandy, to become even more despised than before by his men. In that enterprise, indeed, he gained nothing for himself except fear and toil and disgrace" (6.16).

Shortly after Robert reclaims his duchy, he finds his nobles in rebellion (5.308–20). He controls Normandy "in name only." For his "indolence and lasciviousness" make him "an object of contempt to the restless and lawless Normans [*inquietis et exlegibus incolis*]. Theft and rapine occurred incessantly, and disasters multiplied everywhere to the ruin of the whole country." In 1101 Norman magnates send one messenger after another to Robert's brother, King Henry of England, offering him Normandy. Although Orderic has painted Robert as a wastrel, he decries the results of these disloyal pleas: "So both peoples were corrupted by the threatened treachery, and both plotted how to harm their lords. Some rebels took up open war against loyal neighbors and stained the bosom of their nurturing land with plundering, fires, and bloody slaughter." At last Robert sails to England, eager for battle and guided to shore by sailors who have deserted his brother. "Robert's fleet," writes Orderic, "was quite unlike his father William's fleet, for it reached Portsmouth harbor not through the courage of the army but through the contrivance of traitors." This insurrection ends with an unexpected truce between the brothers, but in 1106 Henry brings his army to Normandy to defeat Robert at Tinchebrai. Robert will spend the rest of his life in prison, dying there in 1134, while Henry governs England and Normandy until his own death in the following year.

At first Henry I enjoys the acclaim and stability that his just governance brings (6.98, 100). But he too must endure plots and personal tragedy. With

---

[22] E.g. 4, pp. 146–54; 4, p. 162; 4, p. 178; 4, p. 286; 5, p. 26; 5, pp. 300–302; 6, p. 46.

the wreck of the White Ship during a channel crossing in 1120, he loses his sons William and Richard. Suddenly bereft of a male heir, Henry looks to his daughter Matilda, whom he marries to Count Geoffrey of Anjou in 1128. This union does produce a son, but the future Henry II is only three years old when his grandfather dies in 1135, and the crown passes to Stephen of Blois, son of the elder Henry's sister Adela and the Count Stephen censured by the *Gesta Francorum* for his desertion at Antioch. This succession initiates a long civil war between King Stephen and the count and countess of Anjou. The *Ecclesiastical History* breaks off soon after Geoffrey and Matilda seize control of Normandy in 1140.

Conflicts among Normans, treachery and insurrections, these are primary patterns throughout Orderic's history. When the death of Henry I sets off a new round of civil wars (*intestinis . . . guerris*), for instance, Orderic appraises the Norman character:

> But though Normandy was not disquieted by external forces, nevertheless she by no means enjoyed peace and security, since she was perniciously harassed by her own children, and she suffered ceaseless pangs in her womb, like a woman in labor. If the Norman people were to live according to God's law and be united under a good prince, they would be as invincible as the Chaldaeans were under Nebuchadnezzar and the Persians and Medes under Cyrus and Darius and the Macedonians under Alexander, as their victories in England and Apulia and Syria repeatedly testify. But since strife cuts them off from one another and arms them in lethal fashion against their own flesh and blood [*in sua uiscera*], they defeat themselves even though they are victors over external forces, and while their hostile neighbors look on with derision, they cut one another's throats mercilessly, so that the eyes of their mother Normandy continually weep.

Whenever the reins of power slacken, the Normans rise up in rebellion, as upon the death of Henry's brother, William Rufus:[23]

> In the month of August, as soon as the unfortunate king's death was known in Normandy, the madness of the turbulent Normans [*turgentium furor Normannorum*] was roused against their own flesh and blood.

This passage introduces another period of vengeance and counter-vengeance, as Normans "rose up against one another with all their energies now that no one was reining them in, and by their mutual slaughter and pillaging they stripped the wretched land that had no governor."

This mayhem provokes Orderic's most famous assessment of the Normans as unruly:[24]

---

[23] 5, p. 300. Cf. the anarchy under King Stephen (6, pp. 492–94).

[24] 5, p. 24. This echoes the Conqueror's warning to his rebellious son, Robert Curthose (3.98): *Normanni semper inquieti sunt, et perturbationes ardenter sitiunt.* ("The

The Normans are an untamed people [*indomita gens Normannorum est*], and if they are not kept in line by a firm ruler they are very quick to commit wrong. In all communities, wherever they may be, they seek to rule and many times collude against truth and loyalty through the restless zeal of their ambition. This the French and Bretons and Flemings and their other neighbors have frequently experienced. This the Italians and Lombards and Anglo-Saxons have endured to the point of extermination.

Orderic fears that this unrestrained passion is the dark legacy from the Normans' "Scythian" past (5.24). Immediately following Orderic's statement about the bellicose nature of Normans, he traces their lineage, roughly as Dudo had reported it, from Scythian to Trojan to Dane to Norman. It is no wonder, Orderic concludes, punning with *auster* ("the south wind") and *aquilo* ("the stormy north wind"), that "their bold harshness [*austeritas*] has proved as threatening to their delicate neighbors as the chilling north wind [*aquilo*] to tender flowers."

Upon the death of Henry I, the last surviving son of William the Conqueror, this scene of chaos repeats itself, here described in rhymed couplets (6.452):

> Occidit Henricus rex prima luce Decembris,
> Lugubris incumbit patriae contritio membris.
> Tollere quisque cupit iam passim res alienas,
> Rebus in iniustis en quisque relaxat habenas.
> Ecce gehennales furiae mortalibus instant,
> Arma parant, ad bella uocant, et spicula donant.
> Normanni furtis insistunt atque rapinis,
> Mutuo iam sese perimunt capiuntque ligantque,
> Incendunt aedes et in illis quicquid habetur,
> Non parcunt monachis, mulieres non reuerentur.

> (King Henry died on the first of December;
> mournful sorrow weighs down all parts of the land.
> Everywhere now each man longs to plunder others' possessions.
> In lawless affairs, look! each rides roughshod.
> See how the hellish furies press on mortals;
> they take up arms, call to war, give out arrows.
> The Normans take to theft and rapine;
> they slaughter and capture and bind one another;
> they burn buildings and whatever is contained inside;
> they do not spare monks nor respect women.)

Normans are always restless, and they thirst after disturbances with a blazing passion.") Orderic has King William profess the same judgment as he lies dying (*EH* 4, p. 82).

With no sympathies for Norman propensities toward aggression, Orderic remains receptive to the viewpoints of peoples they set out to conquer. Against fresh Norman claims, for instance, he acknowledges the "ancient right and venerable liberty" of Greeks in Apulia (2.100); and despite the vigorous propaganda of Antioch's Norman rulers, he repeatedly suggests that the Syrian principality belongs to the Byzantine emperor.[25] The welcome that the Byzantines extended to English exiles, driven from their homeland after 1066 by Norman conquerors, played some role in favorably disposing Orderic to the eastern Christians (2.202–204). As Alexios Komnenos receives these expatriates into his palace, making them guardians of his person and the imperial treasures, Orderic's narrative repeats the Byzantine view of Normans as treacherous people (*malefidi*) and the Empire's "public enemies." He points out that they offered haven to Alexios's rival, while he praises Alexios as a man "whom God defends and cherishes" (4.14–16).

But it was the behavior of Normans in England that assured that Orderic would become the Norman historian most critical of his people and most sympathetic to victims of Norman assaults. From his childhood in his mother's homeland, he must have recalled stories of Norman atrocities, of the arrogance of men he indicts as "fools and sinners."[26] This assessment comes in a passage (2.260–70) that mentions the Domesday Inquest, evidence that Orderic here is including conditions during his own last days in the land of his birth. He draws a damning picture of Normans running wild and terrorizing the English.

This section begins with King William's distribution of English lands and titles among his Norman vassals, men like Hugh of Avranches, who received the county of Chester and "wrought much bloodshed among the Welsh" (2.260–62):

> He was not so much generous as prodigal, and he always dragged around with him an army rather than a household. In his giving and taking he kept no reckoning. Every day he devastated his own lands, since he approved of fowlers and hunters much more than farmers or monks. He was a slave to his belly's gluttony, so that he could scarcely move, so weighed down was he by a huge mass of flab. He completely abandoned himself to carnal lusts, and by his concubines he had many children, boys and girls who nearly all perished wretchedly, swallowed up by various disasters.

---

[25] 5, pp. 354, 6; 6, pp. 102, 4; 6, pp. 502–508.

[26] 2, p. 268. Cf., for instance, 4, p. 278, when he describes Norman lords plotting "a heinous conspiracy" against King William Rufus: "Many of the Normans who had grown rich in England, having acquired wealth from the labor of others, became extremely haughty, spurred on by the troublesome restlessness of their burning greed and pride."

Some Norman lords Orderic recalls fondly, like Roger of Montgomery, in whose employ Orderic's own father, Odelerius, served. But more, like Hugh, are tyrants, including the supposed patron of the Bayeux Tapestry (2.264–66):

> What shall I say about Odo, bishop of Bayeux, who was an earl palatine and brought fear to all the tenants of England everywhere and laid down the law at this place and that, like a second king? He held pre-eminence over all the other earls and magnates of the realm. . . . In this man, if I am not mistaken, were vices mixed with virtues, but he abandoned himself more to worldly affairs than to spiritual contemplation. Monasteries of holy men complained intensely that Odo was doing them great damage and was violently and unjustly plundering their endowments of great antiquity, given to them by pious Englishmen.

The litany of complaints against Norman oppressors leads Orderic to a deeply felt diatribe (2.268):

> So when the Normans had accumulated too much of the wealth that others had gathered in, they went on an arrogant rampage and were unscrupulously smiting the native peoples, stricken by the rod of God for their sins. They remind us of the Vergilian couplet:
>
> > Ah, the human mind, ignorant of fate and what will be,
> > and how to hold restraint when elated with good fortune.[27]

This is Vergil's comment on the folly of Turnus, enemy of Aeneas and his Trojans. Just at this point in the *Aeneid*, Turnus has slain Pallas, a prince dear to Italians and Trojans alike. Exulting in this victory, Turnus strips Pallas of his belt, taking it as a trophy, the gold hilt dripping with the young prince's blood. At precisely this moment, Vergil interrupts the narrative with the lament that Orderic repeats. Turnus does not know that this mark of his conquest will seal his own doom at the end of the *Aeneid* (12.940–52). Orderic seems to understand the context for this couplet, though he most likely drew his Vergilian references from *florilegia* or *exempla*, that is, from collections of lines appropriate for expressing certain sentiments, and not directly from the Vergilian corpus.[28] Still, he uses this allusion with apt precision. Their despoiling of the treasures of the innocents will inevitably lead to a just retribution for the Normans, as this passage recalls over and over again.

Orderic's text continues (2.268):

> Noble maidens endured shame from lowly soldiers and wept for their disgrace at the hands of foul good-for-nothings. Matrons, refined and born

---

[27] Vergil, *Aeneid* 10.501–502, though Orderic writes *mens hominis* ("the mind of man") for Vergil's *mens hominum* ("the mind of men").

[28] Chibnall, *EH* 1, p. 63.

to nobility, mourned their loss, bereft of their husbands and almost all their friends, and preferred death to life. Toadies fawned on the ignorant, who turned foolish with pride that they were drenched in such power, and they came to think that they could do whatever they wanted. Fools and sinners! Why did they not ponder in their hearts, with all contrition, that they had conquered their enemy not by their own strength but at the will of God, who directs everything, and that they had subdued a people greater than themselves and more wealthy and more ancient, and among whom many saints and wise men and powerful kings had led brilliant lives, and won all sorts of acclaim at home and on the battlefield?

This encomium to the English concludes with another warning to the Normans (2.268):

Ceaselessly they should dread this statement of truth and plant it in the depths of their heart: "By the same measure by which you have measured, so it will be meted out to you again."[29]

Now Orderic turns on the churchmen "who appeared wise and pious" but served at the royal court, slaves to their own greed and ambition. "Hirelings" (*stipendiarii*), "not monks but tyrants" replaced the legitimate abbots, whom they chased from their offices "unjustly and without a hearing at any synod." These new shepherds behave like wolves among defenseless sheep (*qualis inter lupos et bidentes sine defensore solet fieri*; 2.270), as demonstrated by the example of Thurstan of Caen, tyrannical abbot of Glastonbury Abbey. When his monks refused to abandon their ancient English chant, first learned from disciples of Gregory the Great, and adopt the unfamiliar Norman chant, Thurstan directed his retainers to surprise the monks at choir and shoot arrows at them.

Orderic writes that he could tell many such stories, but he will turn his pen to a more edifying tale. And so he reports the resistance of Guitmund, "a venerable monk of the abbey which is called the Cross of Helton." Pressed by King William to take high office, Guitmund refuses in a speech that remains one of Orderic's finest creations.[30] Orderic has Guitmund tell William that the king cannot simply appoint whomever he wishes. Only a proper canonical election can decide such matters. But Guitmund's indictment goes further:

"After lying awake and mulling everything over in my mind, I do not see what right I have to preside over a body of men whose foreign customs and barbarous language I do not know, and whose fathers and dear relatives and friends you have killed by the sword or disinherited by driving them into exile or imprisoned or put them into an intolerable servitude that they do not deserve."

---

[29] The quote from Luke (6:38) is another of Orderic's favorites. Cf. *EH* 4, p. 14.
[30] On this speech and its sources, see Chibnall, *EH* 2, pp. 270–79.

Scripture forbids anyone's advancement under these circumstances, but it especially condemns the circumstances themselves, that is, the plundering of England by the Normans. "I adjudge all England to be the spoils of one big looting [*amplissimam praedam*]," intones Orderic's Guitmund, "and I dread any contact with it and its treasures, just as I avoid a blazing fire." The holy man reminds King William that kingdoms inevitably collapse, and he launches into a discourse that repeats Orderic's recurring theme of the vanity of worldly ambitions. The Babylonians, Medes, Persians, Macedonians, and Romans – all have fallen in their time. Here Orderic remembers Antenor and the line from Troy to Dacia/Denmark: "One group of Trojans under Aeneas won the kingdom of Italy. Another group with Antenor made the long and difficult journey to Dacia, where they settled and have lived up to the present day."

Guitmund's long speech begins to attract millennial implications, as he reckons the years in each cycle of rule: Persians conquer Babylonians and reign for two-hundred-and-thirty years before Alexander the Great fractures their empire; one thousand-and-eighty-nine years after its foundation, the temple of Jerusalem falls, destroyed by the Romans; Anglo-Saxons have been controlling the Britons for about six-hundred years. "All these peoples, swollen with pride in their conquests, in just a little while succumbed to wretched death. And now tormented by the same agonies that afflict their victims, they groan without hope of respite in the sewers of Hell."

The very next word (after *gemunt in cloacis Erebi*) is *Normanni*. The damned despots of ages past, writhing now in Hell, lead Orderic to the period of Norman hegemony: "The Normans under their duke Rollo wrested Neustria from Charles the Simple, and now have held it for a hundred and ninety years while the Gauls contested their claims and often challenged them in an outbreak of war." The fulfillment of all these cycles leads to one conclusion: "These signs, therefore, portend the end of the world," with attendant earthquakes, famines, plagues and signs from heaven.

Throughout Guitmund's address to King William, we hear the voice of despond that recurs throughout the *Ecclesiastical History*. Given the character of the Normans and the sins of their princes, Orderic sees much to despair in the domain he surveys. As a sexagenarian, he laments this vision in a long rhymed hexameter poem that introduces Book Eleven.[31]

> ... While I hope for renowned deeds and would like to write of wonders,
> in Christ's name filling my parchment with miracles;
> while I love to praise the one who rules the whole world,

---

31 *EH* 6, pp. 8–12.

who can free us easily from all woes,
I am forced to speak of dark deeds I see and suffer.
I relate the capricious acts of fickle men;
for love of the world drags mankind to perdition,
and the file of justice does not smooth away the rust from them.
. . .
Holy king, good Jesus, Chief Priest, save us.
Do not let the old serpent poison us with the damned;
but draw us up, purged of sins, from the sea of the world,
and mercifully unite us with the saints in the court of heaven.
Amen.

Much that he has witnessed and studied has provided evidence for Orderic's primary moral theme: the vanity of hope in worldly affairs. A commonplace for Christians, this is nonetheless a sentiment that the historian feels deeply.

He deplores not only the treachery and the mayhem. Orderic the moralist also inveighs, repeatedly and at length, against the new manners and effeminate fashion that betray an unseemly attachment to the most transitory sensual delights:[32]

So after the death of Pope Gregory and William the Bastard and other pious princes, the honorable customs of our fathers were almost completely eradicated in the lands of the west. Our ancestors used to wear decent clothes, nicely fitted to the shape of their bodies and suitable for riding and running and performing every task that they should reasonably perform. But in these wicked days the practices of olden times have almost completely given way to novel fads.

"Effeminates began to take charge all over the world," dictating trends that swept courts and castles. Soon townspeople and peasants were imitating these fashions as well. So men grew unkempt beards rather than risk a stubble that chafed the ladies' delicate skin. Young men did shave their heads from the forehead back to the crown ("like thieves," writes Orderic), but kept their hair long and free in back ("like whores"), in defiance of their fathers' customs and the teachings of St. Paul. They curled these fancy locks with hot irons and affected foppish dress, tight shirts with wide sleeves that draped over their hands, and flowing gowns and mantles that swept along the ground, collecting dust and dirt. To complete the look, men wore shoes originally designed by the count of Anjou, Fulk le Rechin, to conceal his bunions. The toes of these shoes bent up and around, "like scorpions" or "serpents' tails." "Freighted with these frivolities, they can scarcely walk quickly or do anything at all useful," complains Orderic, though they apparently find these

---

[32] 4, pp. 186–88; cf. 4, p. 268; 6, pp. 64–66; 6, pp. 190–92.

outfits suitable for their new occupations: sleeping all day, and drinking and gambling all night. What has become of the Normans?

Watching from his heavenly throne, God afflicts the transgressors with disease and wars and with authorities who are hypocrites (4.190). Good men grieve and complain, but they are helpless before the reprobates. If the ancient commentators could materialize in Normandy – "Persius and Plautus and other biting satirists" – "they would find ample matter for criticism and public ridicule" (4.190). But in Orderic's own day, poets like Blitherus the Fleming "brilliantly pointed out the downfall of the world" (4.190), and one Giroie Grossivus included this poem in a letter he wrote to the bishop of Lisieux:

> The lamp of virtue, which shone in the previous age,
> shot all its radiance straight up to the stars.
> In our times the world is wrapped in darkness.
> And the light, now extinguished, cannot restore itself.
> No righteous man exists today, or anyone who cares about
> righteousness,
> No value or honor or love of righteousness.

A gray mood dominates the *Ecclesiastical History*, where a recurring metaphor, borrowed from the scriptures, runs like a refrain:

> . . . All flesh is grass, and all the goodness thereof is as the flower of the field: The grass withereth, the flower fadeth: because the spirit of the Lord bloweth upon it: Surely the people are grass. The grass withereth, the flower fadeth, but the word of our God shall stand forever.
>
> (Isaiah 40:6–8; cf. I Peter 1:24–25)

Under Orderic's pen, this image evokes melancholy, since he directs it toward the transience of life and happiness more than toward the eternity of God's word. The untimely deaths of promising young men are the most poignant reminders of this flower of the field. Robert, son of Giroie, is a brave warrior (*heros*) who weathered many conflicts, but a playful moment at home leads to his demise, "for mortal vigor is fleeting and withers suddenly like the flower of the field" (2.80). A woman survives ordeal by red-hot iron to prove her claim that her two sons are illegitimate children of Duke Robert Curthose. But their rise in fortune puts them both in peril. "Those two brothers were brave and likable, but they soon withered, in an instant, like the flower of the field," as one perished in a hunting accident, and the other on crusade (5.282). Bohemond II, son of the great Bohemond, assumed his father's position as prince of Antioch, "and flourished [*floruit*], but soon withered away like the loveliest flower" (6.108). Baldwin VII became count of Flanders when he was still a teenager, and his future looked bright, "but he withered in a moment, like the loveliest flower, grazed by the slightest wound" (6.162). Indeed, on campaign against King Henry, Baldwin brings on a fatal illness by eating fresh meat, drinking mead, and sleeping with a woman – all of this in one night, too soon after suffering injury in battle.[33]

This metaphor can lead Orderic to a common rhetorical device, but one that he feels deeply: *Ubi est . . .* ? Where is a once-great figure now?

> Verily the glory of the world falls and shrivels like the flower of the field; and just like smoke it dissipates and passes away. Where is William Fitz-Osbern, earl of Hereford, regent of the king, steward of Normandy, and master of the soldiers, eager for battle? He was, of course, the first and greatest oppressor of the English, and supported a vast following through his foolhardiness, by which he brought ruin and wretched death to many thousands. But the just judge sees all things and to each person will render just as he deserves. Oh, too bad! See how William has fallen. The bold athlete got what he earned.[34]

Orderic can invest this image with irony that occasionally, as here, crosses over to sarcasm. He finds a rough justice in the death of William the Conqueror, whose last breath prompts his wealthier attendants to ride off to protect their property, leaving the servants to pillage the bed-chamber of its linens and bedding and even the kings' clothes (4.100–102), and provoking Orderic's exclamation: "O worldly pomp, how despicable you are, how completely vain and fleeting! How rightly you are compared to bubbles of rain-water, one moment raised up and inflated, and suddenly reduced to nothing." Humiliating events twice interrupt the solemnity of the state funeral, upstaging the eloquent eulogy of Bishop Gilbert of Évreux. First, Ascelin son of Arthur steps forward to forbid burial on a site that William had stolen from his father. The assembled company must pay him recompense on the spot before the interment can proceed (4.106). And then, when attendants are forcing the corpulent body into a coffin "fashioned, through the masons' carelessness, too short and too narrow," the bowels burst, assailing the congregation with a stench so foul that the frankincense from the censers cannot overpower it (4.106). Orderic rehearses these ignominies one more time before repeating the message here for all who scheme for earthly glory or wealth (4.108):

> All flesh is grass, and all the glory thereof is as the flower of the field. The grass withers, and its flower falls. But the word of God remains forever.

Orderic returns again and again to stories that feature the irony of expectations dashed. Sometimes, as with the Conqueror's death, Norman preda-

---

[33] 6, p. 190. The metaphoric commentary on Baldwin's death (6, p. 162) has a Catullan twist: *sed quasi flos gratissimus levi lesura tactus in momento emarcuit*; cf. Catullus 11, lines 22–24: . . . *qui illius culpa cecidit velut prati/ ultimi flos, praetereunte postquam/ tactus aratro est.*

[34] 4, pp. 318–20.

tion meets with a rough justice, and Orderic gives an approving nod to the twist that fortune has applied. So, for instance, Orderic recalls how William displaced English peasants along with their parish churches, to create the New Forest where he might indulge his passion for hunting. But that forest, Orderic notes, would claim two of William's sons, Richard and William Rufus, and his grandson Richard – all killed hunting there (5.282–84). Rufus ignores the warnings of churchmen, who have had visions and preached sermons foretelling his demise because he allows "the leprosy of villainy" to stain England with "unbridled lust" and "insatiable greed" (5.286). From the pulpit the abbot of Shrewsbury thunders: "Behold, a sudden revolution will be upon us. Not much longer will effeminates rule. . . . Lo, the bow of divine anger is bent against the reprobates, and the arrow swift to wound is taken from the quiver." And the very next morning Rufus sets off to hunt, laughing off the warnings of Abbot Serlo: "Does he think that I follow the practice of the English, who give up their journeys and business because of the snores and dreams of little old women?" These are the king's last recorded words, as he soon steps into the path of an arrow shot by one of his closest friends – an arrow that Rufus himself had just given as a gift.

Occasionally Orderic allows a touch of cruelty in these accounts when the mighty fall. So, for instance, a hermit shows unusual zest in interpreting another vision for Rufus's mother Matilda, wife of William the Conqueror: the dream of trampled flowers in a meadow must foretell the indignities and horrors that a Norman woman will suffer after her husband's demise (3.104–108). But sometimes these tales elicit a purer compassion from Orderic. He writes that *pietas* alone moves him to report the sinking of the White Ship, the tragedy of King Henry's reign (6.294–306) and a story laced with ironies. For "after many labors" Henry had resolved matters in Normandy at last, and so decided to sail to England to reward his loyal knights with lands there. Henry permits a captain named Stephen to carry his sons, William and Richard, in his White Ship. Stephen wins this honor not only because he offers the king a mark of gold, but also because he reminds the king that his father had ferried Henry's father, William, across the Channel to meet Harold at Hastings. But drunken sailors scrape the ship across a rock at sea, and the ship goes down with all aboard except Berold, a butcher of Rouen and the poorest of all the passengers, protected from the chilly waters by his rams' skin coat. At the news, King Henry falls to the ground wailing like Jacob at the loss of Joseph or David at the murder of Amnon or Absalom. "All universally lament for Prince William . . . so suddenly lost with the flower [*tam subito lapsum cum flore*] of the highest nobility" (6.300).

Though Orderic hopes to make some sense of the human experience, often he must acknowledge life's impenetrable mysteries. When he marvels at the phenomenon of many people drowning in various places near Saint-Évroul during a single hour, he admits his imperfect understanding and explains his motive in recording such events (6.436):

> I cannot determine the divine scheme by which all things happen, and I cannot explain the hidden causes of things. But I am simply carrying out the request of my fellow monks that I produce an annalistic history [*annalem historiam simpliciter actito*]. Who can fathom the inscrutable? For the benefit of succeeding generations I make careful note of events as I have seen or heard of them, and I glorify Omnipotent God in all his works, which are truly just. Let each one examine this according to his own inspiration by divine providence, and if he should determine anything useful to himself, let him cull it for his salvation however he wishes.

This attitude gives Orderic the freedom to indulge his own fascination for anecdotes and his talent for characterization without demanding that a tale be obviously edifying. But often his stories comment on the futility of human struggles. While Duke Robert II besieges Courcy, for instance, men fight desperately around the fortress's oven, placed between the siege machinery and the city gate. In one skirmish, twenty men perish, men "who did not taste any of the loaves bought with their blood" (4.234). For stark horror, nothing can match King Henry's tormenting of the captured rebel Conan, son of Gilbert Pilatus (4.224–26). Possessed with a demonic rage, the king drags his enemy high up into a tower overlooking Rouen, forcing him to survey in all directions the land he had tried to conquer, the forests, the Seine, and the fair city. Ignoring Conan's pleas for mercy, Henry hurls him from the tower window to his death.

But in the pages of Orderic's *Ecclesiastical History*, the Norman penchant for treachery and guile rival their passion for pure violence. Shortly before his death, for instance, Orderic described an incident that had recently occurred at Lincoln Castle.[35] Many of the Anglo-Norman nobles were in rebellion against King Stephen, but this stronghold remained in the control of loyalists, who protect Lincoln in the king's name. Two countesses have come for a friendly visit with the wife of the knight in charge of the castle's defense. The women spend the day in laughter and easy conversation until the Earl of Chester arrives, conspicuously unarmed, to retrieve his wife. Suddenly the three knights with him snatch up weapons and expel the guards as the earl's brother and armed knights burst into the castle to take their place. In a moment Lincoln Castle is in the hands of the rebels, thanks to friendship betrayed.

---

[35] 6.538. The year was 1141. The discussion of this episode comes from my article, "Predatory Friendship: Evidence from Medieval Norman Histories," in *The Changing Face of Friendship*, ed. Leroy S. Rouner (Notre Dame, Ind., 1994), 115–29. In that paper I explored many of the ideas developed here, and I thank the University of Notre Dame Press for permission to incorporate sections of that article into this work.

Treachery involving family and friends looms large in the Orderic's work. See, for instance, how he has William the Conqueror interpret his own life and times. As this king lies dying (4.80–94), he anticipates the chaos under his quarrelsome sons, even as he confesses his own crimes and aggressions. The list is long, as he admits: "For I was brought up in arms from childhood, and completely polluted with much bloodshed. I can by no means calculate the evils that I committed in the sixty-four years that I have lived in this troublous life."[36] But at once William launches into his life-story, recalling the treachery and terror that shaped his boyhood from the moment when his father committed the duchy to him – "I was a tender little boy, only eight years old" – and left on pilgrimage (4.82):

"My own subjects often schemed against me [*insidiati sunt*], and wickedly [*nequiter*] inflicted grave damage and injuries upon me. They treacherously [*fraudulenter*] killed Thurkill my tutor, Osbern son of Herfast, steward of Normandy, and Count Gilbert, father of his country, with many other loyal friends of the duchy. And so by these experiences I came to know the value of my people's fealty. Many times, secretly by night, I was smuggled out of the ducal bedchamber by my uncle Walter, for fear of my kinsmen, and taken to the cottages and hideouts of the poor, so I would not be discovered by the traitors [*a perfidis*] who sought my death."

These are the crimes that Orderic had inserted into the *Gesta Normannorum Ducum* [7.(2)–(4)], but their recital here invokes unusual pathos.

The old king remembers these childhood traumas, inflicted over and over again even by his own kin, as bitter woes that informed his character. They taught him the true nature of his own people, whom he can never trust. So William proceeds directly to this assessment of the Normans, with their penchant for insubordination (4.82):

If the Normans are governed by a good and strict rule, they are very vigorous, and they all excel unvanquished in difficult circumstances, and they fight bravely to conquer every enemy. But when no one controls them, they maul and devour one another [*sese uicissim dilaniant atque consumunt*], for they long for rebellions, hanker after seditions, and are ready for every abomination. So they should be restrained by the strong arm of the law and compelled by the reins of discipline to walk the path of justice. But if they are allowed to go at will like a wild ass, they themselves and their prince will be overwhelmed by disgraceful anarchy and poverty. This I learned long ago from ample experience. My closest friends and relatives, who ought to have protected me by all possible means against all men, frequently conspired and rose up against me, and took from me almost all my inheritance from my father.

36 William was perhaps aged fifty-nine when he died. On the controversy over his date of birth, see Douglas, *William the Conqueror*, 380.

William goes on to enumerate many of these insurrections and insults, including the verbal abuse from his own cousin Guy: "He called me a bastard and cursed me as low-born and unfit to rule." A few years later, two of William's uncles, another William and Mauger, Archbishop of Rouen, level a similar charge – "they belittled me, calling me a bastard" – as prelude to their own rebellion. William's speech, in all this passage, is peppered with words of deceit. But his language also abounds with first-person pronouns in oblique cases, with William presenting himself as the innocent victim, scarred by betrayals from his nearest and dearest, until he can strike back. It is a memorable apologia for a life of bloodshed.

The theme of treachery that pervades William's death-bed speech often attracts the wolf metaphor in Norman histories. Orderic alludes to the Normans' bestial nature here, when he describes their characteristic behavior: "they maul and devour one another." It must be clear by now, from Orderic's outspoken assessment of Norman people and princes, that he felt no need to conceal his criticism in symbolic language, inscrutable to all but select readers. Since Orderic could write whatever he pleased, did he still find the wolf metaphor necessary or useful?

Apparently he did. Nearly forty times, wolves appear in Orderic's *Ecclesiastical History*, almost always as beasts of the imagination. Only once or twice are they flesh-and-blood animals. Even in these instances, they are as much figurative as real. When the monastery of Saint-Évroul sends its first monk to Heudicourt in the Vexin, Roger of Hauterive finds a wasteland where wolves growl at the door of his wattle-and-daub chapel, as if chanting the responses while he sings Matins (2.150–52). There may be wolves in those wilds, but their howling also signals that Roger's establishment is bringing Christianity to a wilderness long abandoned to primitive forces.

In a later book (5.372) Orderic tells the fanciful tale of a Muslim princess, daughter of Yaghi-Siyan, who weeps upon her release from a Christian prison, because she will no longer eat "the excellent pork that Christians enjoy." Her Muslim compatriots, Orderic reports, refuse pork, but do "greedily devour the flesh of dogs and wolves" (*canum et luporum carnes auide deuorent*). Orderic's language here suggests that the infidel assume a bestial quality themselves as they consume animals that neither Christian nor Jew will eat. In this war between Christian Normans and Muslim Turks, therefore, which are the wolves? Orderic has played with this idea a few pages earlier in his *History* (5.362) when he has Melaz, the beautiful daughter of the Turk who holds Bohemond captive, plot to free the Christians before she runs away in feigned terror. "I will flee from you," she promises, "as if I am running from wild wolves."

For Orderic, as for earlier writers, *lupus* is often a code word for non-Christian predators of Christian sheep. So Saul's conversion experience transforms him from ravening wolf (*de rapaci lupo*) to gentle lamb St. Paul (1.173). In the battles for the Holy Land, Muslims (*gentiles*) pursue crusaders, sparing none from slaughter, "more savage than wolves" (5.132). When the second wave of crusaders reach Cappadocia in 1101, they fear just such an attack from the infidel Turks, "who, by their nature, like wolves thirst for the blood of sheep" (5.326). And when Belek of Baghdad lies in ambush for King Baldwin of Jerusalem, who is traveling to Edessa for the Easter feast, the sultan hides in a dense grove of olive trees, lurking there "like a wolf" (6.110). In earlier years, of course, the wolves were Danes, who "ravaged nearly all the island of Britain and destroyed sacred building, mangling and scattering the Lord's sheep, like wolves" (1.154; cf. 2.244, 6). When Gerbert, archbishop of Rouen, transferred Rollo's body to the new cathedral church, he gave his tomb a new epitaph inscribed in golden letters that summarize Rollo's exploits as a viking and end with his conversion (3.90, lines 15–19):

> After much carnage, looting, torching, and bloodshed,
> he made a profitable compact with the eager Franks.
> As a suppliant he gained baptism from Franco,
> and so every sin of his former existence perished.
> Before, he was a wolf to the meek, but then becomes a lamb.
> May peace caress him, so changed, before God.

Most often Orderic uses the wolf/sheep metaphor to indicate bad ruler-ship, or no rulership at all, in a Christian community, especially a monastery. So when the Normans impose tyrannical abbots on the English, the outcome is "just like what usually happens between wolves and defenseless sheep" (2.270). When "a contemptible little fellow" bribes the duke with 140 silver marks to buy the abbacy of Saint-Pierre-sur-Dive, the monks scatter to other monasteries, fleeing this Robert "as from the sight of a ravening wolf" (6.72). A good abbot, on the other hand, like a good shepherd, protects his flock even "in the midst of wolves" just as Évroul does by refusing to flee when a pestilence attacks his monastery (3.292). Holy relics can defend townspeople as surely as an abbot watches over his monks. So the Myreans lament the theft of St. Nicholas's remains (4.64):

> To whose care do you entrust us, your own sheep, o shepherd?
> While you forsake your flock, soon the wolf will arrive.

The number of Orderic's wolf metaphors accelerates in his later books, when Orderic repeatedly deplores the rapacity of William Rufus and Robert Curthose, who pillage church property by delaying episcopal appointments: a church without a bishop, "like a shepherdless flock, lay exposed to the teeth of wolves," that is, "to plunderers rather than guardians."[37] King William Rufus indulges in melodrama when he invokes Robert's practices as a pretext

---

[37] 4.174 and 6.142; cf. 5.322.

for attacking him in Normandy: "See how the holy Church directs its tearful complaint my way from across the channel, wet from weeping every day in sorrow because, without a just defender and patron, it sits amid enemies, like sheep amid wolves" (4.178). But Rufus, too, empties the treasuries of church or monastery whenever a bishop or abbot dies leaving "the Lord's sheep, without their shepherds, prey to wolf-bites" (5.202).

Biblical antecedents for the wolf/sheep metaphor make it a natural symbol for monastic travails. So Cluniac monks, surprised by a wave of oppression, "fled to their monastic folds like sheep from the jaws of wolves" (6.310). Enmity between brother-monks is "wolfish discord," and Saint-Évroul's abbot Osbern pleads with Pope Alexander to intercede, "since you ought to nurture the Lord's sheep and protect them from the snares of wolves" (2.110, 112). But anyone held prisoner by an enemy was said to be "in the wolf's jaws." A wealthy burgess named John spends four months in the custody of his lord's foe because the count of Meulan cannot readily spring him *de ore lupi* (6.46). Secular princes, in Orderic's view, much like abbots or bishops, also must guard their flocks. So Orderic chides King Stephen for allowing his rival, Henry's daughter Matilda, to join fellow rebels in England. He has let the wolf into the sheepfold (6.534). In an earlier passage, King Henry accuses his lethargic brother, Duke Robert, of leaving the Normans "like sheep in wolves' teeth" (6.56), and Count Helias of Maine breaks his vow to go on crusade because he fears leaving Le Mans vulnerable to William Rufus: "God has deigned to commend to me," he tells the king, "the stewardship over Maine, which I ought not to lay aside lightly or foolishly, lest I betray the people of God to predators, like shepherdless sheep to wolves" (5.230).

As they are here, the ravening wolves in Orderic's most explicit metaphors are typically Normans. But not always. On campaign in Byzantine territories, Robert Guiscard hesitates to answer the summons from Pope Gregory, who needs his aid against the German sovereign, Henry, because he fears to abandon his men "very few in number amid many clever and cruel enemies, like sheep among wolves" (4.20). After one unsuccessful foray into Normandy, the French King Louis rallies his troops for another attempt (6.244):

So the men of Burgundy and Berry, Auvergne and Sens, Paris and Orleans, Vermandois and Beauvais, Laon and Étampes, and many others set out like wolves greedy for their prey, and as soon as they left their homes, they began to steal whatever they could, even in their own territories.

Orderic goes on to describe these plunderers in terms often reserved for Normans in Norman histories:

This untamed people insatiably lusted after spoils, and they sacrilegiously pillaged churches along the way and tormented monks and clergy near their borders as if they were enemies.

Attacks by Normandy's neighbors provoke wolfish banditry (6.472). And when a hermit in Germany presents his prophecies to Queen Matilda, he reports a vision of rapacious animals, signifying "the French and Bretons, Flemings and Angevins and other people along the borders, who envy Normandy's success; and they are ready to fall upon its riches like wolves on their prey" (3.106).

Yet nearly always in Orderic's *History* the lupine outlaws are the Normans themselves. At the death of King Henry, Normandy "suffered miserably from her viper brood," who "ran out greedily on that very day like ravening wolves after wicked plundering and pillaging."[38] In the ensuing turbulence "the Normans chewed each other to pieces with their own teeth, as we read in symbolic language about the beast in the Apocalypse." This is the mysterious ten-horned animal described in Revelation 17:16, whose havoc foretells the end of the world much as the Fenris wolf signals the apocalypse in the mythology of pagan Scandinavia. This beast Orderic compares with rampaging Normans.

Twice more the wolf appears with apocalyptic warnings. In one of these passages, the prophecies of Merlin predict a time "when the teeth of wolves shall be blunted" (6.384). Perhaps this foretells the demise of Norman power. But then again, if we identify these wolves as Normans, we ought to define the rest of Merlin's beastly company – the kites and dragons, the lion cubs that metamorphose into fishes and the dogs with mutilated feet. Orderic borrows some of these creatures for his own apocalyptic poem, where the wolf is one of many incarnations assumed by the devil, that venomous serpent and "wicked ten-horned beast" (6.10, 12):

> Alas! the death-bringing serpent infects mortals with a venom
> that makes them mad and makes them annihilate one another.
> . . .
> In the Scriptures handed down from heaven the spiteful foe
> of the human race is called by many names.
> He becomes lion or wolf, dragon, partridge, and basilisk,
> kite, boar, fox, dog, bear, leech, horned serpent
> and savage snake, when he lies in wait for us
> and plots destruction for the foolish by force or by guile.

Orderic writes that this bleak vision comes from his many years of witnessing calamities, the work of the devil (6.8).

In the most distinctive of his wolf metaphors, Orderic probes at the core of woes that torment his memory. These images link wolves explicitly with fugitives and rebels, tricksters and traitors. Rising up against King Henry, the

---

[38] 6.450; cf. 6.458–60, where a famous archer, Robert Bouet, gathers an outlaw gang and tries to steal sheep from monastic lands, "like wolves after their prey."

Britons in Wales burn the castle of Pain Fitz-John and "mercilessly cut down" all the women and men they find inside (6.442). "After this villainy was committed, everyone, both natives and foreigners, headed for the woods like wolves and acted like public enemies, killing and pillaging and burning." In another story, this one joining devil and wolf, Orderic recalls a miracle reported by Abbot Warin of Saint-Évroul (3.348–58). The villain of this piece is one Robert, nicknamed "Malarteis," from the Latin, Orderic explains, meaning *malus artifex*, that is, "evil-doer" or "evil trickster." "For he was rightly called "A Thousand Wiles' Contriver" (*mille artifex*), ostensibly "a minister of King Henry, but really a servant of the devil armed with the teeth of a wolf." Orderic writes that Malarteis was a paid informant, who invented lies when he could find no genuine crimes, until the miraculous appearance of St. Benedict, St. Etheldreda, and her sister St. Sexburga exposed his treachery.

Finally, Orderic attributes to an English earl, Waltheof of Northampton, a speech that offers a definitive defense of loyalty and condemnation of treachery (2.314). Weary of Norman predation, in 1075 many of the earls joined a rebellion fomented by Ralph of Norwich and his brother-in-law, Roger of Hereford. When messengers reach Waltheof, hoping to recruit him to their conspiracy, he disdains their offer of shared power over England, refusing to break his oaths to William. "Every person in every land," declares Waltheof, "must keep absolute fealty to his lord." He continues:

> King William lawfully received the oath of fealty from me, as a lord from his vassal. And so that I would always remain loyal to him, he gave me his niece in marriage. He also granted me a rich earldom and counted me among his closest friends. How could I be unfaithful to such a lord, unless I willed a complete breach of my faith? I am well known in many lands, and it would cause great infamy if – heaven forbid! – I were publicly disgraced as a sacrilegious traitor. No good song is ever sung about a traitor. All peoples curse the apostate and the betrayer as a wolf, and judge him worthy of hanging, and they tie him on the gallows, if they can, and brand him with every sort of abuse and insult. Achitophel and Judas schemed to commit the crime of treachery, and both killed themselves the same way, by hanging, as they were worthy of neither heaven nor earth. The law of England punishes the traitor by cutting off his head, and deprives his whole progeny of their inheritance, their birthright. Heaven forbid that I should stain my honor with heinous treachery, and that such filthy disgrace should be noised abroad about me. The Lord God who by his might delivered David from the hand of Goliath and Saul, Adarezer and Absalom, has by his grace rescued me, too, from many dangers on sea and on land. To him I faithfully commend myself, and in him in all faith I hope that I commit no treachery in my life nor become like the fallen angel Satan through apostasy.

It is no coincidence that Orderic lets an Englishman express these sentiments, dear to his own heart, and curse the traitor as a wolf or devil. Treason and rebellion are characteristically Norman crimes, he suggests, noting – both correctly and precisely – that English law condemns traitors to beheading. Norman law decreed only confiscation and imprisonment for the same offense.[39] The righteous tone of Waltheof's diatribe makes it clear that he, at least, wants no part of such men. And through Waltheof, Orderic articulates his own longing for an orderly society and his own indictment of the treason and riot that unhinge his Norman world.[40]

Though Orderic yearns for tranquillity, at times his history revels in the epic spirit of the immediately preceding age.[41] He tells us himself that in at least one instance he could choose between two sources, a prose *vita* or a jongleur's song, both celebrating Saint William of Gellone, a contemporary of Charlemagne (3.218). The *chanson de geste* is in the air, coloring Orderic's sometimes heroic treatment of the crusade and distorting his portrayal of Robert Guiscard's Byzantine campaign, which Orderic anachronistically invests with the crusaders' zeal.[42] Into the *Gesta Normannorum Ducum*, Orderic had already inserted epic adventures. The most fantastic of these concern Normans of the south, especially Thurstan Scitel, who showed his mettle when he fought Lombards in Apulia [*GND* 7.(30)]. He confounds his enemies by snatching a goat from a lion's mouth and then hurling the lion over the walls of the ducal palace at Salerno. But as the mighty, in Orderic's stories, often fall from glory, just so this exhibition of prowess causes Thurstan's downfall, since jealous Lombards lead him to a dragon's lair. The "flame-vomiting dragon" incinerates Thurstan's shield – "amazing to relate!" (*quod mirum dictu est*).[43] Thurstan slays the beast before he himself succumbs to its poisonous breath (*uenenoso flatu infectus*) two days later.

Of course, epic had influenced the Norman historical tradition from the first, when Dudo saw Vergil's *Aeneid* as one paradigm for the transformation from Northmen to Normans. Dudo's work is part mock-epic, but William of

---

39 Chibnall, *EH* 2, p. 314, n. 1.
40 King William suspected Waltheof of collaborating with the rebels and had him executed. Orderic reports that his severed head finished the Lord's Prayer, which Waltheof had begun to recite as he knelt before the executioner, and that his relics worked miracles (2, pp. 320–22; 346–48). His English compatriots made pilgrimages to his tomb. When a Norman monk named Ouen ridiculed the pilgrims and slandered Waltheof, "saying that he was a good-for-nothing traitor [*nequam traditor*] and deserved to be punished for his crime with decapitation," the Norman became instantly ill and died a few days later.
41 See Chibnall's introductions, especially vol. 4, p. xxiv; 5, p. xxvi; 6, p. xxii; and Robert B. Patterson, "Review of Marjorie Chibnall, ed. and trans., *The Ecclesiastical History* of Orderic Vitalis, V: Books IX and X," *Speculum* 52 (October 1977), 945.
42 Chibnall, ed., *EH* 4, p. xxvi; Mathieu, ed., *Gesta Roberti Wiscardi*, 15.
43 Note Orderic's nod to Vergil's characteristic expression of wonder: *mirabile dictu* ("wonderful to relate"): *Georgics* 2.30; 3.275; *Aeneid* 1.439; 2.174; 4.182; 7.64; 8.252.

Poitiers and Malaterra later found a purer heroic mode the appropriate vehicle for recounting Norman conquests. Even the sober William of Apulia chose the epic meter for his history of Robert Guiscard. But Orderic was writing in a new era, and his *Ecclesiastical History* breaks new ground for Norman histories by introducing elements from the emerging tales of romance: an odd surrealism hovers about the miracles related by Ralph, bishop of Coutances, including the descent of burning candles onto an altar at Séez and their strange markings which learned men try to interpret (4.266); young men sit in the great hall of Conches and tell the lady Isabel their dreams (4.216–18); a Muslim princess rescues Bohemond from his imprisonment and wins a noble Norman husband, though not the one she wanted (5.358–78). Many of Orderic's tales feature women, who belong to romance as surely as they are alien to epic: William, son of Robert Curthose, learns a murder plot from his mistress, who weeps as she washes his hair (6.374); in Tarragona, Spain, a countess dons armor and patrols the walls during her husband's absence, encouraging the guards to watch for lurking Saracens (6.404); Giroie's son Robert teasingly snatches apples from the hand of his wife Adelaide as he sits by the fire, and he eats two before he heeds her warning that they are poisoned (2.80).

Why was Adelaide holding four poisoned apples? And why do poisoning and the suspicion of poisoning recur so often in Orderic's pages, with even Duke Richard III among the possible victims?[44] Orderic is the first known historian, for instance, to repeat the story that both Alan III and his son Conan II, successive counts of the Bretons, died by poison administered with the collusion of Normans. Orderic not only inserts this tale into the *Gesta Normannorum Ducum*, but he also makes the alleged poisoning of Conan one of the charges that inflame English earls against King William in 1075 (2.312), and he repeats three times the accusation that Alan died by poison.[45] Here is one instance (3.88):

> In Normandy in these times many evils were vilely perpetrated. For the Normans poisoned Alan, count of the Bretons and guardian of their own duke [young William the Bastard], and then with their cruel weapons cut down his successor Count Gilbert, son of Godfrey, and slaughtered one another in unbelievably fierce feuds almost daily.

For Orderic, this poisoning is but one sign of Norman criminality. Never mind that this alleged poisoning, like the others, cannot be proved. The detailed account of Conan's death, in particular, strains our credulity.[46] But

[44] *EH* 3, p. 84.

[45] *GND* 7. (38); *EH* 2, p. 304; 3, p. 88; 4, p. 76: "when Alan had been destroyed by a lethal dose of poisoned potion, through the treachery of the Normans . . .".

[46] David C. Douglas, "Appendix F: On Poisoning as a Method of Political Action in Eleventh-Century Normandy," in *William the Conqueror*, 408–15, at 415.

Orderic found the stories plausible. Sometimes he does signal that he is reporting hearsay, as when he writes that Robert of Bellême poisoned Giroie "through the agency of Robert of Poillé, so they say" (*ut dicunt*). But in one sense, it does not matter whether or not Normans of the Conqueror's day, or Orderic's, were busily poisoning each other. The significant fact is their belief that this was occurring. "An apprehension of venom" does "haunt the households of the Norman aristocracy" in these years, while the thought rarely seems to occur, for instance, among pre-Conquest Anglo-Saxons just across the Channel.[47] Distrust and anxiety fomented in these households make poison another apt metaphor for the Norman world that Orderic knew. His Normans might equally dread poisoning from a human foe, or from the Serpent's venom (6.8–12), or from "the poisoned darts of their own sins" (4.174).

An eery sense of foreboding pervades many of Orderic's tales, like the grotesque story of the priest Walchelin, which comes straight from the milieu that would nourish Chrétien de Troyes in the next two or three decades. Returning one night from visiting a sick parishioner, Walchelin witnesses an army of hellishly tormented knights, women, and clerics (4.236–50). A giant forces him to watch the company as it marches by: the dwarves, Ethiopians, and demons he calls "Herlechin's household." The trembling priest interviews some and learns the awful tortures of the damned. The passage perfectly captures the dark and magical mood of romance.

A similar mood haunts the cryptic Prophecies of Merlin, which Orderic is the first Latin historian to excerpt from Geoffrey of Monmouth's *History of the Kings of Britain* (6.380–88). Orderic interprets a small part of it, construing two dragons as the brothers William Rufus and Robert, with Henry as the "lion of justice." He claims that he could decipher more, but much remains obscure and threatening. The prophecies, like Herlechin's clan, illustrate the anxiety of the age and foreshadow new trends in Norman historical writing, which will culminate in the vernacular romance-histories.

Little wonder that Orderic's Norman society of brigands and tricksters inspires this retreat into bleak and inscrutable mysteries, or that people within this society express a sense of alienation. At the end of his long life, as he was completing his *Ecclesiastical History*, Orderic still feels the grief suffered decades before, when his father sent him from England to the monastery in Normandy. Even as an old man, he invests the event with the language of abandonment (6.552–54):

> And so, glorious God, who commanded Abraham to depart from his homeland and kin and father's house, you inspired my father Odelerius to renounce me entirely [*ut me sibi penitus abdicaret*] and to bind me completely to you. So, weeping, he handed me over [*tradidit*], a weeping

child, to the monk Rainald, and bound me over into exile [*in exilium destinauit*] for love of you, and he did not see me ever again. . . . So I left behind my homeland and parents and every relative and intimates and friends [*patriam et parentes omnemque cognationem et notos et amicos reliqui*], and they weeping and wishing me well, commended me with kind prayers to you, almighty God.

Orderic assures himself that his father meant only to offer him eternal salvation, and that both the intentions and the results were sublime. But his vocabulary of betrayal and loss, echoing Dudo's account of vikings exiled by their kin to a life of predation, argues a counter view. Perhaps Orderic has unconsciously extended the mythic identity formation of his people into the realm of his own personal development, making it the template for his own life story.

William the Conqueror's death-bed lament (4.82) also haunts this recollection of Orderic's childhood trauma. Both speakers, frail men in their sixties, are recalling a moment in their youth – Orderic is ten, William eight – when their fathers abandoned them. Both work the first-person pronoun to evoke sympathy for themselves as victims. Of course, their own individual betrayals were as different as they could be, with one child thrust into the political arena and the other, into the monastic fold. But both men, monk and king, have internalized the pain of betrayal, embedding in themselves the Norman anomie.

6

Conclusion:
Wace and Vernacular Romance-History

Toute rien se torne en declin,
tout chiet, tout meurt, tout vet a fin;
hons meurt, fer use, fust porrist,
tour font, mur chiet, rose flaistrist,
cheval trebuche, drap vieillist,
toute ovre faite o mainz porrist.
Bien entent et connoiz et sai
quer tuit morront et clerc et lai,
et moult ara lor renommee
aprés lor mort corte duree,
se par clerc nen est mis en livre;
ne peut par el durer ne vivre.[1]

(Wace, *Roman de Rou*, Appendix, 65–76)

Everything turns to ruin,
everything falls, everything dies, everything comes
    to an end;
a man dies, iron wears out, wood rots,
the tower collapses, the wall founders, the rose
    withers,
the horse stumbles, clothing grows old,
every work made by hand rots away.
I understand and comprehend and know
that all will die, both cleric and laity,
and their renown will last
but a brief moment after their death
if it is not put in a book by a cleric;
it cannot last or survive by any other means.

---

[1] *Le Roman de Rou de Wace*, Société des anciens textes français, ed. A. J. Holden (Paris, 1970), 2.311.

A generation after Orderic put down his pen, Wace was writing a romance-history of the Normans for the court of King Henry II, where vernacular literature was finding an eager audience.[2] Wace had already completed a mythic history of Britain, the *Roman de Brut* ("Romance of Brutus"), in French verse.[3] So he must have seemed a promising choice when Henry, great-great-great-great-great-great-grandson of Rollo, commissioned him to write a vernacular verse history celebrating his Norman ancestry.

Born around 1110 on the island of Jersey, at that time subject to the rule of the Duchy of Normandy, and educated at Caen and Paris, Wace matured into a talented poet.[4] His occasional verses (*serventes*) and saints' lives brought him some renown. In 1155 he completed the *Roman de Brut*, which followed Geoffrey of Monmouth's *Historia Regum Britanniae* ("History of the Kings of Britain") in tracing the Britons back to Brutus, their first king and a descendant of the Trojan Aeneas. This *Brut*, with its fanciful genealogy and imaginative details, Wace presented to the new queen of England, Eleanor of Aquitaine.[5]

The queen could not have found comfort in Wace's view of her adoptive

---

2 Jean Blacker, " '*La geste est grande, longue et grieve a translater*': History for Henry II," *Romance Quarterly* 37 (1990), 387.

3 *Le Roman de Brut de Wace*, Société des anciens textes français, ed. Ivor Arnold (Paris, 1938–40), 2 vols. In this period, *roman* means a text in the vernacular rather than Latin. But the *roman* is not simply *gesta* "romanced." As Gabrielle Spiegal has noted, the writers of verse *romans*

> created a distance between source and translation in which the creative imagination of the writer found legitimate room for play. Both Benoît de Saint-Maure's *Roman de Troie* and Wace's *Roman de Brut* locate their tales within a literary space suspended between history and fable, where, Wace proclaimed, the reader will find 'ne tut mençunge, ne tut veir' (line 9793). Neither wholly a lie nor wholly true, the image of the past offered in the *romans* of Benoît and Wace is a fiction that purports to tell the truth about past facts, and thus is a fiction implying that its fiction is not simply a fiction. By means of this 'fictional factuality' the *roman* formulates its own reality, which exists somewhere in the interstices between fable and history. [*Romancing the Past*, 62].

With this in mind, I translate *roman* as "romance," though I understand that it may be a term best left untranslated or designated (as Holden calls it) "a 'geste' of the Normans" (*Rou* 3.10).

4 For a reconstruction of Wace's life and times, see Judith Weiss, *Wace's Roman de Brut/A History of the British: Text and Translation*, Exeter Medieval Texts and Studies (Exeter, 1999), xi–xiii.

5 Laȝamon, author of another *Brut* in the early thirteenth century, reports this presentation to Eleanor, though extant versions of Wace's *Brut* contain no dedications. Laȝamon, *Le Roman de Brut*, Early English Text Society, 250, 277, ed. G. L. Brook and R. F. Leslie (Oxford, 1963, 1978), 1. lines 20–25. The foundation myth implicating Brutus dates back to a chronicle of the 820s, the *Historia Brittonum*, by a Welshman who came to be identified as Nennius. [Nennius, *British History and the Welsh Annals*, ed. and trans. John Morris (London, 1980).]

people. Like Geoffrey's *Historia*, the *Brut* features cycles of treachery and discord, culminating in the treason of King Arthur's queen, Guinevere, and nephew, Modred. This pattern ultimately derives from Old and New Testament models followed by many medieval historians.[6] But Wace intensified this sequence of betrayals and invested the narrative with a baleful tone, substituting melancholy for the tragedy he encountered in his chief source.[7] As he wrote the *Roman de Rou* ("Romance of Rollo") on the Norman ancestors of Eleanor's husband King Henry II, he sank even further into despond. Wace was transferring into French verse the myths that he found in his Latin predecessors, recalling the fractiousness and treachery that had brought disastrous consequences. These stories propelled Wace, like Orderic before him, to observe the doom that hovers over all human experience: "Everything turns to ruin."

This Judeo-Christian topos recalls the scriptural admonition: "Lay not up for yourselves treasures upon earth, where moth and rust doth corrupt . . ." (Matthew 6:19).[8] But even as Wace recalled the inevitable decay of the material world, he also promised to elevate his patron, King Henry II, beyond it. So Wace made a proposition that would have startled Orderic, for he was not offering solace of heavenly bliss if Henry lived a Christian life, but rather eternal fame if Henry would sponsor his work. After all, argued this historian-for-hire, even Alexander and Caesar would have faced oblivion if writers had not rescued their memory for posterity.[9] Wace's argument made particular sense in an age when the written record was taking precedence over oral tradition, and the personal voice was triumphing over the corporate.

This was one of several attempts by the poet to wrest payment from his patron, despite fitful progress on the *Rou*. Wace interrupted his narrative repeatedly to announce his poverty and to beg for recompense.[10] Though

---

6   See Introduction, p. 4.
7   Judith Weiss (*Wace's Roman de Brut*, xix) shows how Wace has added both nuance and detail to underline "Geoffrey's theme of domestic treachery as the frequent cause of national disaster."
8   The topos appears in such disparate works as the eleventh-century *Vie de saint Alexis* and the late twelfth- or early thirteenth-century verses of the *Hávamál* (*The Sayings of the High One*), a Scandinavian poem that preserves some Eddic material. Stanzas 76 and 77 of the *Hávamál* begin this way:

> Dayr fé, dayia fraendr,
> deyr siálfr it sama.

> (Cattle die, kinsmen die,
> one day you die yourself.)

Both these stanzas end by observing that only one's reputation survives death. [Trans. Patricia Terry, in *Poems of the Vikings: The Elder Edda* (Indianapolis, 1969), 24]. I am grateful to Michael Jones and Paul Hyams, who sent me to these verses.
9   *Rou*, Appendix, 47–64.
10 Cf. *Rou* 1. 8–16, 20–23; 2.4420–25; 3. 143–76; 3. 5115–20; 3. 5315–16. On Wace's begging in the *Roman de Rou*, see Jean Blacker, *The Faces of Time: Portrayal of the*

minnesingers and troubadours habitually decried the death of *noblesce* ("nobility") and its companion, *largesce* ("lavish generosity"), this panhandling seems inappropriate in a history where the convention decrees more subtlety, or at least relegates such pleas to the prologue or epilogue. Wace praised *largesce* too loudly and complained too bitterly to win the sympathy he desired. Finally he quit in mid-course, tossing a testy farewell after relating the victory of Henry I over Robert Curthose at Tinchebrai.[11]

For his part, Wace's sometime patron, Henry II, had already transferred the commission in about 1174 to a certain Benoît, probably Benoît de Sainte-Maure, who had recently completed his *Roman de Troie* ("Romance of Troy"), one of the *romans antiques*, Old French romances set in the ancient world.[12] With the *Chronique des ducs de Normandie* ("Chronicle of the Dukes of Normandy"), though, Benoît lost control of his material, inflating the *Rou*'s 16,000 lines into more than 44,000.[13] Despite its length, Benoît's *Chronique* also breaks off with Henry I, whose grandson and namesake never got the complete Norman history he desired.

Henry II must have especially wanted the missing piece, which would presumably tout his own mother, the Empress Matilda, as the legitimate heir of her father Henry I after the White Ship debacle claimed Henry's sons and another daughter. Young Henry held the county of Anjou from his father, Count Geoffrey V, and the duchy of Aquitaine from his wife, Eleanor, but he was king of England only because he could force the claim of his Norman mother, to whom Henry I had bequeathed his lands. For some time his cousin Stephen had successfully challenged this inheritance, and only King Stephen's death in 1154 ended the civil wars and reunited the Anglo-Norman realm under Henry II. At the age of twenty-one, King Henry II Fitz-Empress ruled with his queen Eleanor over a vast *regnum* that embraced England, Normandy, Anjou, Maine, and Aquitaine. Still, challenges to Henry's authority persisted: Thomas Becket's murder, feuds among the Norman nobility, and the rebellions of his sons left Henry vulnerable. In the long line of Norman princes who craved legitimizing histories, Henry II felt that need as urgently as any and worked harder than most to enlist writers to his cause.

Past in Old French and Latin Historical Narrative of the Anglo-Norman Regnum (Austin, 1994), 180–81. On the mutual disillusionment of poet and king, see Urban Tigner Holmes, Jr., "Norman Literature and Wace." in *Medieval Secular Literature: Four Essays*, ed. William Matthews (Berkeley and Los Angeles, 1965), 64–66.

[11] 3. 11,419–30; 3. 11,439–40.

[12] *Le Roman de Troie*, Société des anciens textes français, ed. L. Constans (Paris, 1904–12), 6 vols. This romance found a large audience and was even translated into Greek in the fourteenth century. [Elizabeth M. Jeffreys, "The Judgement of Paris in Later Greek Literature," *Byzantion* 48 (1978), 113–14.]

[13] *Chronique des Ducs de Normandie, par Benoît*, ed. Carin Fahlin. 3 vols. (Uppsala, 1951, 1967. Vol. 3 published posthumously by Östen Södergård, Uppsala, 1967.)

But neither Wace nor Benoît provided the Norman history that Henry wanted.

And so Norman historical writing virtually ends with two unsatisfying verse histories quitting in mid-course. After the *Rou* and the *Chronique*, only one vernacular history of the Normans survives from the Anglo-Norman realm. In undistinguished prose, this *Histoire des ducs de Normandie et des rois d'Angleterre* ("History of the Dukes of Normandy and the Kings of England") recites ducal history from Rollo to John.[14] In Normandy itself, Stephen of Rouen, a monk of Bec, completed the last Latin history of the duchy in 1169.[15] This verse history, *Draco Normannicus* ("the Norman Dragon") places Henry II and his mother, Matilda, within the context of Norman and French relations from the viking origins of the duchy to their own day. But Stephen holds little hope for the Normans' future once Henry II resolves to divide his holdings among his sons and let them do homage to the French king for Henry's lands within France. Stephen knows that the Normans' realm, like all empires, must fall in its turn. That inevitable Norman decline, he believes, is occurring in his lifetime, and the end is near.

If "the Anglo-Norman empire of the twelfth century was the marvel of its day," as Charles Homer Haskins famously pronounced it, someone should have informed its own Norman historians.[16] To Wace, Benoît, and Stephen, the Norman princes and people failed to offer satisfying narratives.[17] The tenth century had presented heroic tales of vikings Christianized and dukes increasingly civilized and empowered. The eleventh tendered conquests in England and Syria, Italy and Sicily. But who could glorify or even make sense of the feuds and unrest that followed in the twelfth? Pressed to carry Norman history up to his own age, for instance, Wace excavated the distant past for his title, the *Romance of Rollo*, and barely touched his own century.

Wace was not alone in his preferences. Few people in the twelfth century wanted to read Norman history, and fewer sought it out as their own. While Henry II sponsored Wace and Benoît, Henry's sons did not imitate this inclination. King Richard I inspired jongleurs' songs and a metrical chronicle that romanticized his adventures on the Third Crusade but did not set his exploits in a Norman historical context.[18] Nor did his brother John commission histo-

---

14 Anonymous of Béthune, *L'Histoire des ducs de Normandie et des rois d'Angleterre*, Société de l'histoire de France, ed. F. Michel (Paris, 1840). On this end work of the genre, see Jean Blacker, *"La geste est grande,"* 394.

15 Stephen of Rouen, *Draco Normannicus*, in *Chronicles of the Reigns of Stephen, Henry II, and Richard I*, ed. Richard Howlett, RS 82, 4 vols. (London, 1885), 2.589–781.

16 Here Haskins was especially writing about Norman institutions: *The Normans in European History*, 23.

17 Leah Shopkow, *History and Community*, 116–17, outlines the decline of even monastic annals in Normandy during the twelfth century.

18 On *L'Estoire de la Guerre Sainte*, see Antonia Gransden, *Historical Writing in England*, 238–42.

ries to validate his ancestral claim to Normandy, as he might have done when France reclaimed the duchy. Twelfth-century England produced a bountiful literature in French, but little on the history of the Normans.[19]

The Norman ethnic identity, always problematic, was waning in England, not only for its king, who was as much Angevin as Norman, but also among the assimilating nobility and churchmen. The monk William of Malmesbury, for instance, invoked his mixed heritage – "since I carry the blood of both peoples" – as the reason for his alleged objectivity.[20] While this freed him to be critical of Normans, however, it did not propel him to feature their past. In his various Latin histories, he wrote of Glastonbury abbey, the English churchman St. Dunstan (909–88), English pontiffs and English kings.[21] For men and women of the court, too, even while Anglo-Norman French remained their spoken language, their preference for English history and legend over Norman betrays another allegiance.[22]

Judging from both the manuscript evidence and citations from contemporaries, few people were reading either Wace's *Rou* or Benoît's *Chronique*, whereas Wace's *Brut* found a sizable audience. While the *Rou* survives in seven manuscripts, only three of which predate the seventeenth century, the *Brut* survives in at least eighteen, plus a dozen fragments.[23] In its manuscript

---

19 Ian Short, "Patrons and Polyglots: French Literature in Twelfth-Century England," *Anglo-Norman Studies* 14, ed. Marjorie Chibnall (Woodbridge, 1992), 229–49.

20 *Gesta Regum Anglorum*, Book 3, Prologue; vol. 1, p. 424 of the OMT, ed. R. A. B. Mynors, R. M. Thomson, and M. Winterbottom (Oxford, 1998).

21 *The Early History of Glastonbury: An Edition, Translation and Study of William of Malmesbury's "De Antiquitate Glastonie Ecclesie"*, ed. and trans. John Scott (Woodbridge, 1981); *Vita Sancti Dunstani*, in *Memorials of St. Dunstan, Archbishop of Canterbury*, ed. William Stubbs, RS (London, 1874); *The Historia Novella of William of Malmesbury*, ed. and trans. K. R. Potter. Nelson's Medieval Texts (London, 1955); *Willelmi Malmesbiriensis Monachi de Gestis Pontificum Anglorum Libri Quinque*, ed. N. E. S. A. Hamilton, RS (London, 1870); *De Gestis Regum Anglorum*, OMT (1998), 2 vols.

22 The ability to speak French, especially the elegant Continental French rather than the Insular dialect, became the pride of a small elite. Ian Short has reviewed W. Rothwell's arguments on the primacy of English as a living spoken language even among the aristocracy, with Anglo-Norman French becoming "perhaps as early as the end of the 12th century . . . an artificial language of culture." "On Bilingualism in Anglo-Norman England," *Romance Philology* 33 (1980), 467–68. For the gradually evolving identity, linguistic and ethnic, of Anglo-Normans, see Ian Short, "*Tam Angli quam Franci*," 153–75.

23 On the manuscripts of the *Rou*, see Holden, ed., 3.19–24. For the *Brut*: Judith Weiss, *Wace's Roman de Brut*, xxvii–xxix. Of the *Rou* manuscripts, only one transmits the first two books, which describe the viking roots and the transformation from Northmen to Normans – subjects, apparently, of the slightest interest to twelfth-century audiences. Geoffrey of Monmouth's Latin *History of the Kings of Britain*, on the other hand, survives in 215 manuscripts, including fifty from the twelfth century. On its popularity and importance, see Francis Ingledew, "The Book of Troy and the Genea-

transmission, Wace's *Brut* sometimes is found along with Geffrei Gaimar's *L'Estoire des Engles* ("History of the English"), written c. 1135–40 and the earliest of these vernacular histories to come down to us. The *Roman de Brut* presents a legendary history of the Britons from their Trojan origins to the coming of the Angles, while Gaimar's *Estoire* supplies its sequel, treating English history from Hengist to Henry I. This *Estoire* was originally the second half of a two-part series, but Wace's superior literary skills eclipsed Gaimar's, and his *Brut* soon replaced Gaimar's part one, now lost. In turn, Laȝamon and Robert Mannyng of Bourn produced new versions of Wace's *Brut* in Middle English, while French writers of romance, including Chrétien de Troyes, mined the *Brut* for material and imitated its style. A French prose *Brut* circulated widely throughout the fourteenth century.[24]

Both Gaimar, in the lost part one, and Wace, in his *Brut*, were translating into French verse the most celebrated Latin history of their age, Geoffrey of Monmouth's history of the kings of Britain from Trojan ancestors to Angle invasions.[25] Geoffrey's *History* created a sensation when it appeared in the late 1130s, with its array of dragons and incubus demons, shrinking "the dividend of facts . . . to vanishing point."[26] We may agree with Southern that "it was time for history to come under a new management," but Geoffrey's "history" captivated twelfth-century audiences with its fanciful stories of an ancient golden age for Britons, crowned by continental conquests over Romans and French before ending in tragedy with the subjugation of Celtic Britons by the Germanic Angles and Saxons. Beyond this disaster, however, Geoffrey foretold a glittering future with a mysterious rebirth for the Britons. Perhaps his contemporaries read this as a promise that they themselves would eventually subdue their Norman captors and replace their Normanness with a more righteous essence, symbolized by King Arthur. In his interpretation of Geoffrey's Prophecies of Merlin, Orderic Vitalis hints broadly at this Norman demise.[27]

The "matter of Britain" and Arthurian romance appealed to English audiences, even to the Anglo-Normans among them, in part because it willed

---

logical Construction of History: The Case of Geoffrey of Monmouth's *Historia regum Britanniae*," *Speculum* 69 (July 1994), 665–704.

24 Ian Short, "*Tam Angli quam Franci*," 174.

25 *The Historia Regum Britannie of Geoffrey of Monmouth I: Bern, Burgerbibliothek, MS. 568*, ed. Neil Wright (Cambridge, 1984), and *The Historia Regum Britannie of Geoffrey of Monmouth II: The First Variant Version, A Critical Edition*, ed. Neil Wright (Cambridge, 1988). For an English translation, see *The History of the Kings of Britain*, trans. Lewis Thorpe (Harmondsworth, 1966).

26 Southern, "Aspects of the European Tradition, I," 195.

27 Chibnall, ed., *EH* 6.380–88. Orderic chose an extract from the Book of Merlin, which concluded on this point (386): ". . . through [this pestilence] Normandy will lose both islands and be stripped of her former dignity. Then the inhabitants (*cives*) shall return to the island."

away the Normans. Everywhere the Normans had gone, they were dissociating themselves from their Norman past and aligning themselves with the peoples of their new homelands. At Antioch, the *Gesta Tancredi*, completed by 1118, was the last panegyric to a Norman prince of the East. In the South, after the funereal ending of the *Gesta Roberti Wiscardi*, only Geoffrey Malaterra's *History* continues the narrative of the Norman conquest from the Normans' perspective.[28] This *History* ends in 1098, and for decades after that the sources offer only pieces of the story. Alexander of Telese, abbot of the monastery of St. Salvatore, attempted a sycophantic history of King Roger II (1130–54), but his work – the last to celebrate a Norman king of Sicily – breaks off in 1136.[29] Writing after 1154, Falco of Benevento took his *Chronicle* up to 1139, but his was the work of a Lombard partisan, who dismissed the Normans as "little better than a bunch of uncivilized brigands."[30] When Hugo Falcandus produced his *Historia de Regno Siciliae* ("History of the Kingdon of Sicily") in the 1180s, he railed against King William I (1154–66), a tyrant forever designated as "William the Bad," but the anarchy after William's reign he found even worse than the king's cruelty.[31] In about 1195 Peter of Eboli was eulogizing his patron, the German Emperor Henry VI, for his conquest of Sicily that same year.[32]

The Norman principalities were disappearing with their histories. Or perhaps more accurately, Normans everywhere were assimilating into something else, until they transformed themselves out of business and, for all practical purposes, vanished from the face of the earth, leaving Normanness as an intermediary stage on the way to other identities – French or English, Italian or Sicilian or Levantine. By the time that John lost Normandy to King Philip Augustus in 1204, Bohemond's heirs were still holding Antioch but no longer considering themselves Norman.[33] In Sicily a German reigned, helped to power by the insurrections of Norman magnates.

Normans on the southern frontier had seemed an unstoppable power in the eleventh century. But their frontier experience highlights the cultural struggle within Normanness, the battle between the old egalitarian warrior society, celebrated in Norman myth, and the emerging counts, duke, and kings who would rule in despotic splendor. Distrusting the Norman nobles, Roger I of

---

28 On this hiatus in the historical record, see Donald Matthew, *The Norman Kingdom of Sicily*, Cambridge Medieval Textbooks (Cambridge, 1992), 19.

29 Alexander of Telese, *Ystoria Rogerii Regis Siciliae, Calabriae atque Apuliae*, Fonti per la storia d'Italia, 112, ed. L. De Nava (Rome, 1991).

30 Norwich, *Normans in the South*, 340. Falco of Benevento, *Chronicon*, Cronisti e scrittori sincroni napoletani editi e inediti, 1, ed. G. Del Re (Naples, 1845), 161–252.

31 Graham A. Loud and Thomas Wiedemann have translated *The History of the Tyrants of Sicily by "Hugo Falcandus" 1154–69*, Manchester Medieval Sources Series (Manchester and New York, 1998).

32 *Liber ad Honorem Augusti di Pietro da Eboli*, Fonti per la storia d'Italia, 39, ed. G. B. Siragusa (Rome, 1906).

33 R. H. C. Davis, *The Normans and their Myth*, 9.

Hauteville cultivated others at his court, appointing Muslims and Byzantines as his ministers. When Roger died in 1101, his eventual heir, Roger II, was barely five years old, but as he grew to covet Byzantine lands and powers, he also affected the court ritual and the autocratic ways of an emperor, whose subjects had to prostrate themselves in his presence. In 1130 he took the title "King of Sicily" and styled himself lord of Calabria and Apulia, of Capua and Naples and Benevento.

Roger's imperial manners and ambitions brought him onto a collision course with Norman vassals and neighbors, not to mention the pope and the German emperor. A massive rebellion broke out in 1131, supported by Emperor Lothar and Pope Innocent II, with rippling effects that extended throughout Roger's long reign and into that of his son William I (1154–66). Like his father, William had learned to loathe and distrust the nobles, who in turn deeply resented his power and autocratic rule. He withdrew to pleasure palaces and his harem, emerging to crush insurrections and punish rebels with hanging, blinding, or drowning.[34] The survivors remained restive, even through the reign of his son, William II the Good (1166–89). In the turmoil following the death of this William, who left no children, many Norman nobles welcomed the German invaders, whose presence soon exterminated any Norman cultural identity still remaining in the Kingdom of Sicily.[35]

By the early thirteenth century, were there people anywhere, aside from a few nostalgic aristocrats, who wanted to identify themselves as Normans in diaspora? The historians of the old Norman principalities offer few signs that ethnic Normans survived in a meaningful way. Few Normans expressed solidarity with their compatriots elsewhere, for instance, or looked back to Normandy as their motherland.

For the failure of Normans to survive and flourish, the histories offer clues, often in their surface stories, but especially in their deep mythic structures and with a depressed or weary tone. Wace is no exception. Born and raised among Normans, he absorbed the literary tradition of Norman histories. While Wace never names his sources for the *Rou*, it is clear that he used Dudo of Saint-Quentin, William of Jumièges, William of Poitiers, William of Malmesbury, and Robert of Torigny.[36] Perhaps he also knew the *Carmen de Hastingae Proelio*. Although Orderic's *Ecclesiastical History* did not circulate far, Wace found the only copy of Books Seven and Eight that has survived to the present day. At Caen where he was living and writing, St. Stephen's held this manuscript.[37] From Orderic, Wace learned the events surrounding the death of William the Conqueror. His version of King

---

[34] John Julius Norwich, *The Kingdom in the Sun, 1130–1194* (New York and Evanston, 1970), 169.

[35] See R. H. C. Davis, *The Normans and their Myth*, 71–100.

[36] On Wace's Latin sources, see Holden, ed., 3. 101–68.

[37] Chibnall, *EH* 1, pp. xxi–xxii; 114; and *EH* 4, pp. xxi–xxii.

Harold's death at Hastings, on the other hand, suggests that he had also seen the Bayeux Tapestry.[38] Since Wace was a canon of the Bayeux Cathedral, he may well have studied this work. But Wace also shows a lively interest in oral sources that led him directly to individual memories and personal recollections. "Wace was not interested in the Norman nation," writes Elisabeth van Houts on his account of 1066, "or the collective Norman memory; he was a local historian writing the history of the Cotentin soldiers based on interviews and historical archival research."[39]

But this passion for eye-witness accounts reveals more than local interests and an inquiring mind. In Wace, it signifies the withdrawal from the public sphere into the realm of personal experience and private life. In his *Roman de Brut*, Wace had already depoliticized the "matter of Britain" that he found in Geoffrey's *Historia*.[40] While Orderic copied the Prophecies of Merlin, in abbreviated form, soon after Geoffrey wrote them, for example, Wace refuses. Although elsewhere he follows his model closely, now and then almost producing a literal translation, here Wace demurs:[41]

> Ne vuil sun livre translater
> Quant jo nel sai interpreter.   (1.7339–40)

> (I do not wish to translate his book
> because I do not know how to interpret it.)

Indifferent to its impact on his generation, Wace protests that he is simply omitting material that he does not understand. This may be the truth, since the prophecies are undeniably cryptic and defy ready decipherment. But perhaps Wace also had no feeling for the optimism that they proffered. In place of Geoffrey's hopeful ending, Wace substituted his own observation that, despite the wishes and the prophecies, Arthur never did return to save his people.

The Prophecies of Merlin inevitably enter the political sphere, difficult terrain for Wace to navigate, and territory that he avoided if he could. When the subject matter of the *Rou* forced Wace to handle political affairs, he discharged his duties with workmanlike resolve. Often his sources led him to the wars of the dukes and Anglo-Norman kings, where he could escape into

---

38 Matthew Bennett, "Poetry as History? The 'Roman de Rou' of Wace as a Source for the Norman Conquest," in *Anglo-Norman Studies* 5, ed. R. Allen Brown (Woodbridge, 1989), 21–39. In an article in the same issue, David Bernstein agrees ("The Blinding of Harold and the Meaning of the Bayeux Tapestry," 47).

39 "Memory of 1066," 178.

40 Jean Blacker, "The Depoliticization of the Arthurian World in the *Roman de Brut*," in *The Arthurian Tradition: Essays in Convergence*, ed. Mary Flowers Braswell and John Bugge (Birmingham, Al., 1988), 54–74.

41 On the frequent equivalence between the *Historia* and the *Brut*, see Margaret Houck, *Sources of the Roman de Brut of Wace*, University of California Publications in English 5, no. 2 (1941), 161–356.

the heroic realm of battle. But these contests sometimes unmask Wace by revealing his sympathies for the French or for Norman rebels. In particular, Wace champions Robert Curthose over Henry, stressing Robert's courtesy and willingness to compromise in order to preserve peace with his brother, as well as his legitimate right to both England and Normandy since he was the older of the two. The details as much as the broad strokes betray Wace's compassion for Robert, or at least his distaste for those lords who betrayed him.[42] So, for instance, he depicts the garden where the men of Caen seal their conspiracy (3.11,297–308):

> At this time there was a garden
> at Caen near Saint Martin's
> between Saint Martin's and the wall
> which is near Arthur's gate:
> there the men assembled
> and pledged their word
> to betray Duke Robert.
> You may hear a miracle disclosed!
> For ever since this meeting
> – I can assure you this is true –
> the garden never fructified.
> It bore neither apples nor any other fruit.

Henry's cause did attract some of the noblest knights, who gave up their lives on his behalf. Here men lament for Brun, a warrior without equal, killed in a joust with a knight from Bayeux (3.11,041):

> "... Brun, dan Brun, Brun gentil ber! ..."
>
> ("... Brun, lord Brun, noble baron Brun! ...")

The sorrowful lyric that follows does not comment on the justice of the cause for which Brun died, but instead recalls the human cost of Henry's invasion of Normandy. The best men on both sides are lost. In Wace's pages, Henry I wins the war by might, not right.[43] This could not have pleased Henry II, whose kingship derived from Henry I through Matilda. Surely Wace understood all this. But the closer he came to his own age, the more difficulty he encountered in producing the panegyric that Henry was expecting. His tone grows more strident in the critique of Henry I, until Henry II dismisses him at last.

---

[42] U. T. Holmes, Jr., "Norman Literature and Wace," 65–66, suggested that Wace's dangerous sympathies, as much as his slow pace, led to his dismissal. Matthew Bennett raised the issue of betrayal in a footnote to his "Poetry as History?" 37–38.

[43] Wace often notes, for instance, that Henry's ready supply of cash attracts allies away from his brother: cf. 3. 10,854–904; 3. 11,159–62.

For much of his *Rou*, in fact, Wace is ambivalent, even incoherent in his judgments. His motives for writing are clear: he needs the income that patronage should bring.

> Jeo parouc a la riche gent,
> ki unt les rentes e le argent,
> kar pur eus sunt li livre fait
> e bon dit fait e bien retrait.   (*Rou*, 3.163–66)

> (I speak to the rich folk,
> who have revenues and money,
> because it is for them that books are made
> and good tales made and good deeds told.)

Lack of payment agitates him. But if the subject of Norman history drives him, too, this is rarely apparent. When he does display passion, as in his indictment of Henry I, his views send him into a collision course with his king. No wonder then that he has often remained almost defiantly free of opinion, to the point of annoying his readers, even while he repeatedly directs attention to his own state of mind.

From false start to false start, from beginning to end, the narrator's presence dominates the *Rou* more than in any other Norman history, excepting only Malaterra's. Wace habitually uses the first person and introduces his own name into the text.[44] Authorial interjections are a distinctive feature of twelfth-century narratives, consonant with the movement toward private and individual expression.[45] But Wace's subjective style draws particular attention toward his own idiosyncratic and sometimes mean concerns, away from the larger issues that inform other histories.

The political and social atmosphere of the Norman world encouraged such detachment. Wace was distressed to have to record the discord among the Conqueror's sons, which threatened to tear apart a Norman unity that was already strained. In his own day, he found the same scene being played out at the court of his patron in the sedition within the family of Henry II. Wace's temperament, honed in an alienating environment, directs him inward, away from analysis of these societal problems. He claims neither the requisite interest nor even a modest grasp of political affairs.

The *Rou* speaks out for chivalry, *largesce*, and the propriety of feudal law, but not for the Normans, whose very name Wace writes infrequently. Preoccupied with his private discomfort at the perceived demise of chivalric virtues, when confronted with others' political motivation, he repeatedly

---

44 E.g. 1.3; 2.443; 3.11,439.
45 For both commentary and bibliography, see Peter Damian-Grint, "Truth, Trust, and Evidence in the Anglo-Norman *Estoire*," in *Anglo-Norman Studies* 18, ed. Christopher Harper-Bill (Woodbridge, 1996), 63–78.

shrugs. Two counts war against one another. Wace writes only, "I do not know [if it happened] over moveable property or over land" (3.2132). English king and Norman duke come to blows. Wace explains, "I do not know [if they fought] out of anger or out of envy" (3.1058). At first Wace's *ne sai* seems the voice of an honest historian who knows his limits and remains impartial when the evidence is inconclusive or absent.[46] But repeated over and over, this clause becomes a litany of futility.[47] "I do not know" begins to sound like "I do not care" as Wace's professions of ignorance slide into acedia. More than Orderic, who came to understand the inscrutability of God's plan, Wace drowns in its mystery.

Like Orderic, Wace dwells on the inevitability of death even for the loveliest of children (cf. 1.847–52), and like Orderic, he readily harbors a suspicion of foul play in hastening that demise. So, for instance, he reports the death of Duke Robert I on his return from pilgrimage to Jerusalem (3.3211–14):

> He made his return as far as Nicaea;
> there he died by a poison [*par un toxiche*],
> which a knave – God curse him! –
> had given him treacherously [*par felunie*].

Wace also shares Orderic's feeling for the surprising turns of fortune's wheel and the folly of delighting in success. So as King Harold Godwinson exults in his victory over the Danes and rushes headlong toward Hastings, Wace warns (3.6677–82):

> But the man who boasts is a fool;
> a moment of joy is quickly gone,
> bad news soon comes along;
> the man who kills others can soon die himself.
> Often the heart of man rejoices
> when his own misfortune is near.

Such aphorisms suit a man who has internalized the wolfishness of his culture and finds no hope in the stories he must tell.

The composition of the *Rou* shows how Wace labored over his material. After analyzing the four sections of the *Rou*, separated and rearranged in the manuscripts, the *Rou*'s editor, A. J. Holden, proposed the following scenario

---

46 Peter Damian-Grint, "Truth, Trust, and Evidence," 74–75, lists examples of this topos in Wace's *Rou*. The frequency of its appearance, he believes, "underlines both Wace's thorough research and his scrupulous care in following his material."

47 As Jean Blacker notes, "These quasi-formulaic claims of ignorance occur roughly every hundred lines throughout the third part of the poem." ["Wace's Craft and his Audience: Historical Truth, Bias, and patronage in the *Roman de Rou*," *Kentucky Romance Quarterly* 31 (1984), 362.]

for the history's construction.[48] Wace began in eight-syllable verse and wrote 781 lines on the viking invasions before he abandoned this first effort (which Holden prints as an Appendix). Probably Wace saw this as a false start because it put too much weight on the early years and the viking heritage. When he began anew in 1160, he experimented with the fashionable longer lines of Alexandrine *laisses*, stanzas of unequal length, each of which keeps one rhyme throughout. These 4425 lines describe Rollo's foundation of the duchy and the history of the dukes until 965. At this point, Wace interrupted his task to write a new prologue in Alexandrine *laisses*, summarizing the subject matter of his entire poem in inverse order from Henry II to Rollo. In this preface, usually called *La Chronique Ascendante des Ducs de Normandie*, he tried to write panegyric, whitewashing his criticisms of the dukes and affirming his loyalty. Here the French are the villains who "always want to disinherit the Normans," by force, if they can, or by treachery (*par traïsons*).[49] The *Chronique Ascendante* aims to correct the main narrative and assuage Henry II, by affirming his mother's title, for instance, to the lands and powers of her father, Henry I.

After this effort, Wace suspended his writing for several years, perhaps stung by the *Rou*'s cool reception. When he resumed, sometime after 1170, he returned to the octosyllabic rhymed couplets of the more popular *Brut*, in 11,440 lines covering the years from 965 to 1106. He must have added some interpolations to the earlier sections, too. But by 1173, when Henry's imprisonment of Eleanor signaled a breach in Wace's support, he essentially abandoned the project, quitting for good in the following year when Henry replaced him with Benoît.

Wace was never able to forge a unified whole from the parts of his *Rou*. Often he obscures the larger picture by featuring self-contained episodes, which begin with some variation of the formula, *A cel terme ke jeo vus di* ("In the period that I am telling you about. . . .").[50] An occasional reprise signals that a tale has ended or sums up recent developments.[51] This fits a common pattern of medieval narrative, in which episodes come one after another without joining to fashion an interconnected story line.[52] Commentators have observed that this pattern suits oral delivery, when a series of anecdotes would thrill and edify listeners as they dine or lounge in the great hall

---

48 Holden, ed., III. 9–13. See Ray, "Orderic Vitalis and his Readers," on the various parts of the work (pp. 9–13) and on the manuscripts (pp. 19–34). See also A. J. Holden, "L'authenticité des premières parties du *Roman de Rou*," *Romania* 75 (1954), 22–53; and Gaston Paris's review of Andresen's edition: *Romania* 9 (1880), 592–614.

49 1. 54–58.

50 3. 2521; cf. 3. 2427; 3. 4619.

51 E.g. 3.10,295–99; 3.10,329–30.

52 William Ryding, *Structure in Medieval Narrative* (The Hague, 1971), 44; cf. Nancy Partner, *Serious Entertainments: The Writing of History in Twelfth-Century England* (Chicago, 1977), chapter 8, "The Question of Literary Form," especially pp. 201–203.

of a castle. But perhaps the fragmentation also occurs when a writer does not want to think too hard about the larger view of his disturbing tale. So Wace dwells, instead, on details within the individual episodes, on clothing, manners, and fine conversation, blazing the way into the emerging genre of romance.[53]

Wace would like to please his patrons and sing a heroic song. For some brief moments he succeeds. So he has the jongleur Taillefer lead the charge at Hastings, singing about the champions of the Franks' heroic age, "of Charlemagne and Roland,/ of Oliver and the vassals/ who died at Roncevaux" (3.8016–18).[54] Taillefer's *chanson* implicitly links Norman warriors to an imagined era of valor, but for Wace that world, like its heroes, is dead. He can re-enter it only with fleeting encounters in battle.

As a whole, the *Rou* lacks both the surety of epic and its structured plot with characters and events proceeding to a certain end, grand or tragic. Instead, Wace was drawn to the attributes of romance, with its series of incidents or adventures strung loosely together, its idealized portraits of chivalric knights. Some of his predecessors among the Norman historians had homogenized the dukes so that it is difficult to distinguish one from the other. Consider, for instance, the portrayal of the three Richards by William of Jumièges. But no one had yet made Rollo as generous as any idealized knight (2.1190–93) and a peace-loving saint:

> Pais ama et pais quist e pais fist establir . . .
>
> (Peace he loved, and peace he sought, and peace he had established.)

Wace redrew the early dukes with the broad strokes of romance, making them lords whose munificence put to shame the parsimony of his contemporaries, especially King Henry.[55]

But Wace also grew up hearing jongleur's songs about the dukes'

---

53 In his *Epic and Romance* (London, 1926), W. P. Ker assessed Wace's role in the creation of the romance: "Description, conversation, development of love motifs, chivalric treatment, portrayal of character, fine use of the octosyllabic rhymed couplet – all these novelties make him cofounder of the romance type that developed after 1150 with the *Roman de Thèbes*."

54 Taillefer makes his earliest appearance, under the equivalent Latin name *Incisor-ferri*, in the *Carmen de Hastingae Proelio* (389–404) as a *histrio* or *mimus*, who rides out before the Norman army at Hastings, ennobling the faint-hearted by juggling with his sword and then killing the Englishman who raced forth to confront him. For other accounts of this episode by twelfth-century historians Henry of Huntingdon and Gaimar, as well as its connection with the *Chanson de Roland*, see David C. Douglas, "The 'Song of Roland' and the Norman Conquest of England," *French Studies* 14 (1960), 99–116.

55 Cf. 1.8–16; 2.2309–429; 3.167–72; 3.5115–18.

treachery and violence, as he recalls here even concerning William Longs-word, whom Dudo had charged with monastic longings (2.1361–65):

> Minstrels I heard in my childhood, singing
> how William had Osmund blinded long ago
> and gouged out both eyes of Count Riulf
> and had the valiant Anschetil killed by trickery [*par enging*]
> and Balzo of Spain protected with a shield.

Wace reports that he will not repeat these stories since he cannot confirm their truth (2.1366–67). But of course, he has repeated them, if only in passing, and the damage is done in the text, as it must have been also in Wace's consciousness during his impressionable youth.

Wace found Longsword's son, Richard I, more amenable to romantic revi-sions. Expanding upon the material he read in Dudo's fourth book, Wace adapted Richard's story to entertain a courtly audience. An episode from Richard's minority offers an example of Wace at work (2.2772–820). Here King Louis, enraged because Osmund has smuggled Richard out of his custody, has ravaged the Norman countryside and entered Rouen with his army. In Dudo's brief account (4.83) a young French knight observes the rich holdings of Bernard the Dane and asks the king to grant him all of Bernard's property, along with his beautiful wife (*uxorem praepulchrae speciei*). When the other young knights hear of this, they also petition Louis:

> Drive these alien Normans out of here, and annihilate them, we beseech you. Hand over their wives to us and grant us their fiefs.

The mere mention of possibly purloined wives invites Wace to imagine the feelings of Norman ladies and lords who hear rumors of the French knights' desires. So Wace develops Dudo's spare account, fewer than thirteen lines of prose in Lair's edition, into forty-nine lines of iambic hexameter. Now when Bernard's wife hears the rumors, she becomes sad and grieves. In Dudo's passage, Bernard discreetly consults with his peers, but Wace has him brood, vowing to keep his lady and make Louis sorry if he tries to take her. As the news spreads through Normandy, the ladies become terrified, preferring death to disgrace. Bernard's wife will escape across the salt sea or take the veil rather than be given to another so long as her husband lives. For his part, Bernard stands ready to defend "his wife dear beyond compare." If the French dare take her, all Normandy will rise up and fight. But the real action here is personal and internal, just as in romance.

This section in alexandrine *laisses* continues well into the reign of Richard I, until the peace of 965. Using data culled from Dudo, it presents Richard as the consummate diplomat and trickster and fighter, though not the preacher – both Wace and Benoît suppress Richard's long sermon to convert the Danes summoned to fight the French.[56] Wace opened his new section in octosyllabic couplets, now called Part Three, with the death of Emma, presumed to be Richard's first wife, and then reported the marriage to Gunnor and the account of their children. But at this point, in place of the panegyric that occupies most of the remaining chapters in Dudo's history, Wace turned from his written authority to popular legends, to fill Richard's missing years with *aventure*.[57] These revisions have disturbing overtones.

The first of these episodes introduces Richard as a knight-errant, fond of riding alone after dark and visiting isolated churches (3.273–336). In one of these he finds a corpse on a bier, which the duke must walk by to pray at the altar. Even when the body stirs, Richard remains intrepid. Only when the devil stands up, with arms outstretched as if he wants to take the duke with him to hell, does Richard deign to run him through with a sword, before coolly returning to his horse and riding off. But remembering that he has left his gloves on the lectern, he goes back to retrieve them.

The next tale, the legend of the drowned sacristan, also occurs by night (3.337–510). A monk, a sacristan from the abbey of Saint-Ouen, has arranged a tryst with a lady. On his way to this assignation, however, he trips in the darkness, falls off a bridge, and drowns. Both an angel and a devil show up to claim his soul. After much wrangling, they agree to refer the case to the duke. Aroused in his bedchamber, Richard bids them restore the soul to the body and the body to the bridge. If the sacristan keeps his rendezvous, the devil will get his soul, but if he chooses to resume his life of righteousness, his soul belongs to God. When the monk comes to his senses, he flees to the abbey in terror. In the morning he repeats this story before the duke and the assembled monks, and soon all Normandy is chanting this rhyme (3.509–10):

> Sire muine, suëf alez,
> al passer planche vus gardez!
>
> (Sir monk, proceed with care,
> watch out when crossing a bridge!)

The next misadventure has no happy ending (3.511–60). One morning during a hunt, Richard stumbles upon foul play in the forest of Lyons. In a secluded clearing he discovers a knight and a lovely, if disheveled, lady. When the man sees the duke, he decapitates his companion. Richard cries out in rage, then strikes off the knight's head with one blow. Wace reports that no one knew the identities of the victims or dared to record the duke's vengeance

---

[56] Dudo 4.121. On Wace and Benoît, see Holden, ed., 3.131–32.

[57] *Rou* 3.273–654. On this Richard of legend, see Joseph Bédier, "Richard de Normandie dans les chansons de geste," in *Les Légendes Épiques* (Paris, 1926–29), 4 vols., 3rd ed., 4.3–18. Bédier found Richard in virtually all the *chansons de geste*, including the *Chanson de Roland* 3044–51.

before this. That tale reminds Wace of another which does not directly involve the duke but concerns one of his huntsmen in that same forest (3.561–610). The rogue takes his pleasure of a lady he finds all alone, but when he tries to leave her, she hurls him up into a tree – Wace does not know if she kicked him or punched him with her fist – and she disappears. When at last the huntsman's companions come on the scene, they manage to get him down only with difficulty. Even a beautiful woman may not be quite what she seems.

The last tale in the series takes us back to Richard, now in his bedchamber. His clergy and noblemen have persuaded him to marry Gunnor, whom he has long kept as a concubine. On their wedding night, Richard is astonished to find his bride facing him in bed, rather than turned away as she had always done before. Is this a position of power, or even a threatening gesture? Richard is naturally edgy, and perhaps we are, too, after hearing the previous story. Gunnor answers his questions with a smile (3.634–45):

> "Milord, it is not that way at all.
> I used to lie in your bed.
> I used to do your pleasure.
> Now I lie in my own. I will lie
> on whatever side I wish.
> I am a lady, and since I lie in my own bed,
> I will lie as I please.
> Up until now this bed was yours,
> but now it is both mine and yours.
> I was never confident here before
> nor was I ever free from fear with you.
> Now I am somewhat at ease."

And so the duke and his duchess turn to face one another, smiling and talking (3.646–48).

In these episodes Wace has taken Richard to face the devils of the wilderness and the graveyard, to witness incomprehensible evils and demonic temptations. Most of these stories feature the duke as a lonely warrior against dark and mysterious forces that lurk beyond a realm of reason. Some of the tales present Richard's fearlessness and reputation for justice, though they occur against a backdrop of immorality or, at best, amorality.[58] Yet the duke's precipitate act of decapitation unsettles Wace. Before Wace put this incident in his *Rou*, he claims, no one dared record the sin (*le pechié*) that Richard committed in slaying the knight without giving him a hearing. Indeed, no words at all were exchanged in this vignette, presented in pantomime until the duke shouts out his own horror at seeing the lovely woman murdered. We

---

[58] On the "flexibility of morality" in romance, see W. T. H. Jackson, "The Nature of Romance," *Yale French Studies* 51 (1974), especially pp. 15–16.

never learn the identity of the mysterious knight and the lady whose beauty moved the duke even as he viewed the decapitated corpses.

These stories serve to create a mood of anxiety or horror as they present the loneliness of a single human being confronting the inexplicable. The private terrors known to Wace's Richard mirror the chaos in Wace's own society, internalizing the public disarray and taking us deep into the romantic consciousness. Even the conjugal bed gives Richard a small fright before it offers him solace in the most private realm.

If Wace's Richard I is as much romantic hero as warrior, the battles of his descendants let Wace do some of his best writing in the heroic mode.[59] Wace knew how to use the racing octosyllabic lines to capture the frenzy of duels, the fast and noisy action of combat. So Richard II and his Normans rout the forces of Odo of Chartres, repeating their battle cry, "*Deus aie!*" ("God help us!").[60] The victors continue to shout as they hunt down the fleeing enemy (3.1662–65):

> Quant cil que chacent l'unt truvé,
> demandent lui: "U sunt, u sunt?"
> e il lur dit: "La vunt, la vunt!
> Puignez, puignez! jas trovereiz."

> (When those who are hunting found him,
> they demand: "Where are they, where are they?"
> And he says to them, "There they go, there they go!
> Attack, attack! Now you will find them.")

The long account of the hostilities between Duke Robert I and Count Alan of Brittany infuses another confrontation with epic intensity, as the Bretons answer the Normans' "*Deus aie!*" with their own "*Maslou, Maslou!*" (3.2679–82). The narrative comes alive in such scenes, with the flight and the chase, the drama of a life-and-death struggle.[61] Wace's description of Val-ès-Dunes is so vivid and detailed that readers have assumed that he surveyed the battlefield, which was near his home in Caen. His version of Hastings attracts special attention, not only by its length (3.7313–8972), but also by the care lavished on individual acts of valor, styles of combat and weaponry.

Wace devotes over six-thousand lines, nearly half of the *Rou*, to William the Conqueror (3.3241–9340), often following the rhetorical tradition established by William of Poitiers and incorporating from Orderic scenes that compare the mettle of Harold and William. With Orderic, Wace has William trip and fall just after the landing near Hastings (3.6573–82), then as he

---

[59] Matthew Bennett, "Wace and Warfare," in *Anglo-Norman Studies* 11, ed. R. Allen Brown (Woodbridge, 1988), 37–57.

[60] 3.1607, 1624.

[61] Cf. 3.2721–26.

prepares for battle, start to put his armor on backwards (3.7499–530). His attendants interpret both actions as inauspicious. William himself, however, turns potentially damaging omens to beneficent signs by promptly reinterpreting them.

Contrasting anecdotes define Harold as a figure lacking William's cleverness and strength of will. Cursed with an inflexible moral sense, Harold refuses to destroy English lands around the Norman position, though his advisors feel that only such drastic measures will assure their success (3.6925–54). Harold's temper flares up as he wrangles with his brother Gyrth over strategy and threatens the monk Huon Margot whom William sends as envoy (3.7010–54; 3.6801–804). Gyrth must restrain him from striking the monk. Wace comments that "Harold was extremely haughty,/ and it is said that he sometimes became hoarse from screaming" (3.6797–98). Harold sends his own envoy to William, claiming that he was coerced into swearing fealty in Normandy and had not acted of his own free will (3.6815–24). If William will only leave England now, Harold promises, he will pay his expenses.

The duke's response comes quickly:

> "Thanks for the kind offer,
> but I have by no means come
> to this country with so many shields/French coins [*escu*]
> to receive his English pennies [*esterlins*],
> but rather to have the whole land
> just as he swore to me
> and as Edward gave it to me."[62]   (3.6848–54)

Before sending the messenger back to the king, William honors him with a horse and fine clothing. The news chastens Harold, as he recalls his own mistreatment of Huon Margot.

This Harold is no hero. But the dual loyalties of Wace's Anglo-Norman tradition surface with the Conquest. Wace offers both the English and the Norman versions of Harold's journey to Normandy: Harold intended either to rescue hostages from William's grasp or to reaffirm Edward's promise to leave his realm to the Norman duke (*Rou* 3.5583–604). The presentation of both stories as equally credible, indeed with the English version given first, casts a shadow of doubt over the Norman claim to England. As the troops muster for the battle that will determine England's fate, Wace takes us inside the English camp as well as the Norman. So we watch the English carousing while the Normans pray (3.7327–34):

---

[62] Wace's double-entendre, with *escu* as both "shield" and "coin," shows that the word must have acquired its second meaning earlier than linguists have believed. Etymological dictionaries typically date this meaning from the time of St. Louis (thirteenth century).

> All night long they were eating and drinking,
> never once lying in bed that night;
> you would have seen them carrying on,
> prancing and leaping and singing.
> "Bublie," they cry, and "weisseil"
> and "laticome" and "drincheheil,"
> "drinc hindrewart" and "drintome,"
> "drinc helf" and "drinc tome."

Soldiers who prepare for war this way may seem doomed, but Wace describes their day-long resistance in a battle that ranges over sixteen-hundred lines and makes us share the grief that their defeat brings to England.[63]

When Wace located Orderic's Books Seven and Eight, he discovered an interpretation of this Conquest that rang true to him. So he transcribed Orderic's account of the last days of William the Conqueror, including the death-bed speech, with its characterization of the Normans:

> "Orgueillos sunt Normant e fier
> e vanteor e boubancier
> toz tens les devreit l'en plaisier,
> ker mult sunt fort a justisier. . . ."   (3.9127–30)

> ("The Normans are arrogant and proud,
> and boastful and presumptuous,
> They need to be restrained all the time,
> for they are very difficult to control. . . .")

Wace's Conqueror goes even beyond Orderic's, though, in hammering home the illegality and immorality of the Conquest:[64]

> "Engleterre conquis a tort,
> a tort i out maint home mort
> les eirs en ai a tort ocis
> e a tort ai le regne pris;
> e ço que j'ai a tort toleit,
> ou jo nen aveie nul dreit,
> ne dei mie a mon filz doner
> ne a tort nel dei eriter."   (3.9141–48)

> ("England I conquered wrongly,
> Wrongly there many men died;
> Their heirs I have wrongly killed
> And wrongly I took the kingdom.
> And what I have wrongly taken,

---

[63] 3.7331–32; 3.8835–38; 3.8949–72. For the drinking scene Wace may have embellished a passage from William of Malmesbury (*Gesta Regum Anglorum* 3.241).

[64] Wace, *Rou* 3.9141–48. Cf. Orderic, *EH* 4.92–94.

> to which I had no right at all,
> I ought not give any bit of to my sons
> nor should they inherit any of it, wrongly."

Wace writes more directly than he had ever dared before, emboldened here by Orderic's license. The repetition of *a tort* – "wrongly" – pointedly answers the Norman propaganda of the 1060s and 1070s, as presented by William of Poitiers' insistence upon the justice of the Conquest. Wace's patron, Henry II, could not have liked Wace's version of his great-grandfather's confession that England did not belong to him or to his heirs.

So long as Wace continues writing, the prevailing tone is bleak, whether he is narrating the great events of Norman history or revealing personal disappointments, a duke's or his own. So he lingers on the infirmities and tragedies of King William's last days, having passed over most of his twenty-one-and-a-half years of kingship in a few lines. When the French king taunts William, now a sick old man, the Conqueror sets out to burn French lands, but suffers from the enterprise and must return to his bed, from which he dispatches this message to Paris (3.9071–76):

> "When I get up," he said,
> "I will go to mass in his lands.
> I will carry to him a rich offering.
> I will offer him a thousand candles.
> My wicks will be of wood,
> and iron [*fer*] will shine on high instead of fire [*feu*]."

The offering that William promises will be an army, with their iron-tipped lances visible from afar, and not mere arsonists.

Yet despite William's bravado, he meets humiliation at the moment of his death, as the servants ignore the still warm corpse to hurry around the palace, stealing tapestries and whatever else they can (3.9239–46). Wace dwells on the details, especially those garnered from Orderic's moralizing account. So Wace reports how, after a full day of looting, William's retainers finally carry the body to Caen for burial. Even there, commotions twice interrupt the solemnity of his funeral, while the spectators rush away to put out a fire and again while they join the wrangling over the legal possession of William's burial plot (3.9266–340).

> And those who go and those who come
> consider such a thing a great marvel
> that the king who had conquered so much,
> who had taken so many cities and so many castles
> should not have enough land free
> for his body to lie in after death.   (3.9319–24)

Wace brings this scene to life with the full force of its irony and pathos. But he applies the same dramatic skills to his own personal disappointments.

He has heard marvelous tales about fairies in the forest of Brocéliande and the fountain of Berenton there, where hunters collect water in their horns, sprinkling the stones where the water bubbles up and consequently calling down cooling rains. After a futile investigation, Wace berates himself:

> La alai jo merveilles querre,
> vi la forest e vi la terre,
> merveilles quis, mais nes trovai,
> fol m'en revinc, fol i alai;
> fol i alai, fol m'en revinc,
> folie quis, por fol me tinc.   (3.6393–98)

> (I went there seeking marvels,
> I saw the forest and I saw the land,
> I sought marvels, but I found none,
> I came back a fool, I went there a fool;
> I went there a fool, I came back a fool,
> I sought folly, and I hold myself a fool.)

Literary critics sometimes evoke this passage to illustrate Wace's modern sensibilities, his sound judgment, and insistence upon rational evidence.[65] Wace has indeed learned an ironic skepticism. He displays this when he has William at Hastings mock the fortune-teller who did not suspect his own end (3.6561–70), and when he has Gyrth ridicule his brother Harold for rushing into battle ill-prepared yet confident of victory because it was a Saturday, and his mother had always said that Saturday was his lucky day (3.7923–24). In the Brocéliande passage, however, Wace turns the rebuke against himself with a disturbing persistence in the stressed *fol . . . fol . . ./ fol . . . fol . . ./ folie . . . fol . . . .* These expressions of self-contempt reveal more than the disappointment of an historian chagrined by his gullibility. While he thinks himself obviously a fool for believing in fairies and a magic fountain, after all, he does not seem to have questioned the eery adventures of Richard I, dark tales that affirm the powers of evil demons.

A sense of gloom lingers over the *Rou*. This mood, usually attributed simply to Wace's peculiar disposition or his penury, may ultimately derive from the disloyalties and insecurities of his Norman world. In the final year when Wace was writing (1173/4), a Norman prince was once again fighting with his kin, as King Henry II was suppressing a rebellion of his own sons and holding his wife Eleanor in prison for her complicity with their sons' cause. With this insurrection in his mind, Wace ends his narrative in the aftermath of Tinchebrai, railing against the disloyalty that brought Henry I to

---

[65] Charles Foulon, "Wace," in *Arthurian Literature in the Middle Ages: A Collaborative History*, ed. Roger Sherman Loomis (Oxford, 1959), 98.

the battlefield against his elder brother Robert Curthose, leading to so many deaths and the long imprisonment of Robert.

> Grant honte fait, ne poet graignor,
> qui traïst son lige seignor.   (3.11,383–84)
>
> (He earns disgrace – none could be greater –
> who betrays his liege lord.)

This is a dangerous sentiment for Wace to express. His patron Henry II was the grandson of Henry I and so owed his throne, according to Wace's view, to a brother's treachery against brother.[66]

Betrayal has loomed large in Norman histories. In their uncertain world, Norman historians of the twelfth century have found their own voices for lamenting this treachery. These voices more and more replaced echoes of ancient authors with the new language and tone of romance. Only in the *Chronique Ascendant* (14–16) did Wace evoke Vergil, for instance, here recalling the benevolent patronage of the arts in the time of Vergil and Horace, and in the time of Alexander or Caesar or Statius. Nor did he feature the mythic Trojan origins of his Normans. Even in the *Rou*, Trojan ancestry belongs especially to the Britons.[67] The *Rou* proper, discounting the false start that modern editors print as an appendix, begins with Rollo and his Danes.

If the Anglo-Normans seemed uninterested in probing their distant Norman ancestry, their fascination with British origins was another matter altogether. So the Anglo-Normans demonstrated a fascination for the mythology advanced by Geoffrey of Monmouth, who amplified the origin myth found in the *Historia Brittonum* attributed to Nennius. This story produced a Trojan ancestor of the Britons, Brutus, great-grandson of Aeneas. Wace repeated that genealogy in his *Brut*, again intensifying the treachery in the old tale. Before Brutus' birth, soothsayers foretold that this illegitimate child would kill both his parents. Although the murders proved unintended – his mother died in childbirth, and his father, fifteen years later, perished from an ill-aimed arrow during a hunt – still the boy's kin banished him from Italy. So he fled, a patricide and exile, to Greece, where he joined the descendants of Trojans who had escaped their city with Hellenus. By a ruse, Antenor engineered the slaughter of the Greek overlords and freed these Trojans from their bondage.

But the Trojans soon realized that their freedom came at a terrible cost: So treacherous was Brutus' stratagem and so awful the Trojans' vengeance

---

[66] Here Wace rejects the accounts of William of Malmesbury and Orderic Vitalis, who defended the rights of Henry I against his "rebel" brother. See Jean Blacker, "*La geste est grande*," 391.

[67] Appendix 80–83.

against their masters that they could not stay in Greece without fear of just retribution. They must sail away as exiles yet again, first to a deserted island where Brutus prayed for guidance in the remnants of an ancient temple. While Brutus slept, the goddess came to him in a dream, prophesying that he would build a new Troy on an island called Albion, far to the west. Again the Trojan wanderers set sail, past the straits of Gibraltar, surviving an attack by pirates and the sweet enchantment of the Sirens' song, until they landed on the Spanish coast. There they met descendants of Antenor's band and welcomed them and their leader, Corineus, into their ships, which sailed along the coast to the mouth of the Loire, where they provoked a battle with the Poitevins, pillaged the land, and built a fortress at Tours. After more warfare against the French, the Trojans decided to sail off again, and at last they arrived at the island home foretold by the goddess. There on Albion they destroyed a race of giants and claimed the land as their own. Brutus then renamed the island Britain, after himself, called his Trojan companions the Britons, and built New Troy, which would become London.

The wanderings of Brutus thus echo the patterns that Dudo had attached to the Antenor/Rollo myth – patterns of betrayal and exile by kin, of rapine and violence. These foundation myths by Dudo and Wace invert the themes that distinguish Vergil's Aeneas as the creator of a new civilization destined for greatness. In founding New Troy in Britain, Brutus was only establishing a western outpost for this repetitive mayhem. Ever since antiquity, Old Troy had held an ambivalent place in the mythic imagination, home to the heroic Hector, but also home to traitors like King Laomedon and Antenor.[68] Medieval traditions amplified this treacherous connection, until Troy became a hotbed of treason and the city where Criseyde betrayed her beloved Troilus. By the early fourteenth century, anti-English polemicists were using the Britons' putative ancestry to explain their supposed capacity for evil.[69]

Even as Anglo-Norman writers transferred their interest in Norman ancestry to the supposed heritage of their new homeland, they did not shake their sense of despair in a hostile world. So Wace's voice is relentlessly personal, often depressed, critical of leaders, in harmony with the voices of romance. The very movement from the surety of epic to the anxiety of romance, a shift that occurs throughout twelfth-century literature, is a natural progression for a society burdened with profound conflicts in its social structure and with systemic uncertainties in its patterns of friendship and loyalty. If the outward signs of the canker are betrayal and rebellion, the internal signs are anomie and alienation.

Sometimes the rapid assimilation of Normans into other cultures is reck-

68 On Laomedon, see Chapter One, pp. 13–14, n. 27.
69 Beaune, "The Political Uses of the Trojan Myth," 233.

oned as one sign of their success.[70] Yet their willingness to shed one ethnic identity for another may signal not strength but rather a profound dissatisfaction with the strictures of Normanness, both cultural and mythic. The anxiety of Wace's narrative, indeed, seems the natural end for a literary tradition that begins with lupine metaphors for Dudo's Northmen and features the darkening tone of the *Gesta Roberti Wiscardi*, the disillusionment of the *Gesta Francorum*, and the lamentations of Orderic Vitalis. These writers do not inspire confidence that the Normans improved the societies they invaded. Their narratives suggest, on the contrary, that Normans oppressed their new lands with the consequences of a traitorous and violent history. And only by submerging their Norman identity could newly forged societies hope to escape the burden of Normanness.

[70] Haskins, *The Normans in European History*, 247.

Works Cited

Primary Sources

Aimé. *Storia de' Normanni di Amato di Montecassino*, Fonti per la storia d'Italia, pubblicate dall'Istituto storico italiano per il Medio Evo. Scrittori. Secolo 11, no. 76, ed. Vincenzo de Bartholomaeis (Rome, 1935).

―――. *Ystoire de li Normant*, ed. O. Delarc (Rouen, 1892).

Alexander of Telese. *Ystoria Rogerii Regis Siciliae, Calabriae atque Apuliae*, Fonti per la storia d'Italia, 112, ed. L. De Nava, (Rome, 1991).

Anonymous of Béthune. *L'Histoire des ducs de Normandie et des rois d'Angleterre*, Société de l'histoire de France, ed. F. Michel (Paris, 1840).

Bede. *Ecclesiastical History of the English People*, Oxford Medieval Texts, ed. B. Colgrave and R. A. B. Mynors (Oxford, 1969).

Benoît. *Chronique des Ducs de Normandie*, ed. Carin Fahlin. 3 vols. (Uppsala, 1951, 1967; vol. 3 published posthumously by Östen Södergård, Uppsala, 1967).

―――. *Le Roman de Troie*, Société des anciens textes français, ed. L. Constans (Paris, 1904–12), 6 vol.

The Carmen de Hastingae Proelio of Guy Bishop of Amiens, Oxford Medieval Texts, ed. Catherine Morton and Hope Muntz (Oxford, 1972).

Desiderius of Montecassino. *Dialogi de miraculis sancti Benedicti*, ed. Gerhard Schwartz and Adolf Hofmeister, *MGH SS* 30 (pt. 2), 1111–51.

Dudo of Saint-Quentin. *De moribus et actis primorum Normanniae ducum, auctore Dudone Sancti Quintini decano*, ed. Jules Lair (Caen, 1865).

―――. *Dudo of Saint-Quentin, History of the Normans*, trans. Eric Christiansen (Woodbridge, 1998).

Eadmer. *Historia Novorum in Anglia*, ed. M. Rule (RS, 1884), 6–8.

Epistulae et Chartae ad historiam primi belli sacri spectantes: Die Kreuzzugsbriefe aus den Jahren 1088–110 (Innsbruck, 1901).

Falco of Benevento. *Chronicon*, Cronisti e scrittori sincroni napoletani editi e inediti, 1, ed. Giuseppe Del Re (Naples, 1845), 161–252.

Flodoard of Reims. *Les Annales de Flodoard*, ed. Philippe Lauer (Paris, 1905).

Geoffrey Malaterra. *De rebus gestis Rogerii Calabriae et Siciliae Comitis et Roberti Guiscardi ducis fratris eius*, Rerum Italicarum Scriptores, 2nd ed., vol. 5, pt. 1, ed. Ernesto Pontieri (Bologna, 1925–28).

Geoffrey of Monmouth. *The Historia Regum Britannie of Geoffrey of Monmouth I: Bern, Burgerbibliothek, MS. 568*, ed. Neil Wright (Cambridge, 1984).

―――. *The Historia Regum Britannie of Geoffrey of Monmouth II: The First Variant Version, A Critical Edition*, ed. Neil Wright (Cambridge, 1988).

―――. *The History of the Kings of Britain*, trans. Lewis Thorpe (Harmondsworth, 1966).

Gesta Francorum. Heinrich Hagenmeyer, ed., *Anonymi Gesta Francorum* (Heidelberg, 1890).

Gesta Francorum et aliorum Hierosolimitanorum, ed. and trans. Rosalind Hill (London, 1962).

Gesta Francorum. Histoire anonyme de la première croisade, Les classiques de l'histoire de France au moyen âge, 4, ed. Louis Bréhier (Paris, 1924).

Guillaume de Poitiers, *Histoire de Guillaume le Conquérant,* Les classiques de l'histoire de France au moyen âge, ed. Raymonde Foreville (Paris, 1952).

Hávamál. Trans. Patricia Terry, "Sayings of the High One," in *Poems of the Vikings: The Elder Edda* (Indianapolis, 1969), 13–38.

Hugo Falcandus. *The History of the Tyrants of Sicily by "Hugo Falcandus", 1154–69,* trans. Graham A. Loud and Thomas Wiedemann, Manchester Medieval Sources Series (Manchester and New York, 1998).

Inventio et miracula Sancti Vulfranni, ed. J. Laport (Rouen, 1938).

Jordanes, *De origine actibusque Getarum,* ed. Theodore Mommsen, in *MGH AA* 5, pt. 1 (Berlin, 1882), 56–138.

Laʒamon. *Le Roman de Brut,* Early English Text Society, ed. G. L. Brook and R. F. Leslie (Oxford, 1963, 1978), 2 vols.

Leo Marsicanus. *Chronicle of Montecassino.* Leo Marsicanus and Peter the Deacon, *Chronica Monasterii Casinensis,* ed. H. Hoffman, *MGH SS* 34 (Hanover, 1980).

Miracula sancti Benedicti, ed. Eugene de Certain (Paris, 1858), 71–73.

Nennius. *Historia Brittonum,* ed. and trans. John Morris, *British History and the Welsh Annals* (London, 1980).

Orderic Vitalis. *The Ecclesiastical History,* Oxford Medieval Texts, ed. and trans. Marjorie Chibnall (Oxford, 1969–80), 6 vols.

———. *The Ecclesiastical History of England and Normandy,* trans. Thomas Forester (London, 1853–56).

Otto of Freising. *Gesta Friderici,* ed. Franz-Josef Schmale (Darmstadt, 1965).

Peter of Eboli. *Liber ad Honorem Augusti di Pietro da Eboli,* Fonti per la storia d'Italia, 39, ed. G. B. Siragusa, (Rome, 1906).

Phaedrus. *Babrius and Phaedrus,* Loeb Classical Library, ed. and trans. Ben Edwin Perry (Cambridge, Mass., 1965).

Planctus. "Complainte sur la mort de Guillaume Longue-épée," in Philippe Lauer, *Le règne de Louis IV,* Bibliothèque de l'École des hautes études 127 (Paris, 1900), 319–23.

Planctus. "Der planctus auf den Normannenherzog Wilhelm Langschwert (942)," ed. Phillipp August Becker, *Zeitschrift für französische Sprache und Literatur* 63 (1939), 190–97.

Planctus. www.ukans.edu/carrie/Planctus

Ralph of Caen. *Gesta Tancredi,* in *Recueil des historiens des croisades, Historiens occidentaux,* ed. Ludovico Antonio Muratori (1866; reprint, Farnborough, 1967), 3.599–716.

Stephen of Rouen, *Draco Normannicus,* in *Chronicles of the Reigns of Stephen, Henry II, and Richard I,* RS 82, 4 vols., ed. Richard Howlett (London, 1885), 2.589–781.

Vegetius. *Epitoma Rei Militaris,* ed. C. Lang (1885; reprint, Stuttgart, 1967).

Wace. *Le Roman de Brut,* Société des anciens textes français, ed. Ivor Arnold (Paris, 1938–40), 2 vols.

————. *Le Roman de Rou*, Société des anciens textes français, ed. A. J. Holden (Paris, 1970), 3 vols.

————. *Le Roman de Rou et des ducs de Normandie*, ed. Hugo Andresen (Heilbronn, 1877–79), 2 vols.

Warner of Rouen. "Satire de Garnier de Rouen contre le poète Moriuth (X–XIe siècles)," ed. H. Omont, *Annuaire-Bulletin de la Société de l'Histoire de France* 31 (1891), 193–210.

William of Apulia. *Gesta Roberti Wiscardi*, ed. and trans. Marguerite Mathieu, *La geste de Robert Guiscard*, Istituto Siciliano di studi Bizantini et neoellenici, testi e monumenti 4 (Palermo, 1961).

William of Jumièges. *Gesta Normannorum Ducum*, ed. Elisabeth M. C. van Houts, *The* Gesta Normannorum Ducum *of William of Jumièges, Orderic Vitalis, and Robert of Torigni*, Oxford Medieval Texts (Oxford, 1992, 1995), 2 vols.

————. *Gesta Normannorum Ducum*, ed. Jean Marx (Rouen and Paris, 1914).

William of Malmesbury. *The Early History of Glastonbury: An Edition, Translation and Study of William of Malmesbury's "De Antiquitate Glastonie Ecclesie,"* ed. and trans. John Scott (Woodbridge, 1981).

————. *Gesta Regum Anglorum*, Oxford Medieval Texts, ed. R. A. B. Mynors, R. M. Thomson, and M. Winterbottom (Oxford, 1998–99), 2 vols.

————. *De Gestis Pontificum Anglorum Libri Quinque*, RS, ed. N. E. S. A. Hamilton (London, 1870).

————. *The Historia Novella of William of Malmesbury*, Nelson's Medieval Texts, ed. and trans. K. R. Potter (London, 1955).

————. *Vita Sancti Dunstani*, in *Memorials of St. Dunstan, Archbishop of Canterbury*, RS, ed. William Stubbs (London, 1874), 250–324.

William of Poitiers. *Gesta Guillelmi*, Oxford Medieval Texts, ed. R. H. C. Davis and Marjorie Chibnall (Oxford, 1998).

Ysengrimus. *Ysengrimus: Text with Translation, Commentary and Introduction*, ed. and trans. Jill Mann (Leiden, 1987).

Secondary Works

Ahl, F. M. *Lucan: An Introduction* (Ithaca, N.Y., 1976).

Albu, Emily. "Bohemond and the Rooster: Byzantines, Normans, and the Artful Ruse," in *Anna Komnene and her Times*, ed. Thalia Gouma-Peterson (New York and London, 2000), 157–68.

————. "Dudo of Saint-Quentin: The Heroic Past Imagined," *The Haskins Society Journal* 6 (1994), 111–18.

————. "The Normans and their Myths," *The Haskins Society Journal* 10 (forthcoming).

————. "Norman Views of Eastern Christendom: From the First Crusade to the Principality of Antioch," in *The Meeting of Two Worlds: Cultural Exchange between East and West during the Period of the Crusades*, Studies in Medieval Culture, 21, ed. Vladimir P. Goss and Christine Verzar Bornstein (Kalamazoo, 1986), 115–21.

————. "Predatory Friendship: Evidence from Medieval Norman Histories," in *The*

Changing Face of Friendship, ed. Leroy S. Rouner (Notre Dame, Ind., 1994), 115–29.

———. "Scandinavians in Byzantium and Normandy," in *Peace and War in Byzantium: Essays in Honor of George T. Dennis, S. J.*, ed. Timothy S. Miller and John Nesbitt (Washington, D.C., 1995), 114–22.

———. "William of Apulia's *Gesta Roberti Wiscardi* and Anna Comnena's *Alexiad*: A Literary Comparison" (Ph.D. diss., University of California, Berkeley, 1975).

Amory, Frederic. "The Viking Hasting in Franco-Scandinavian Legend," in *Saints, Scholars and Heroes: Studies in Medieval Culture in Honour of Charles W. Jones*, ed. M. H. King and W. M. Stevens (Collegeville, Minn., 1979), 265–86.

Arnoux, Mathieu. "Classe agricole, pouvoir seigneurial et autorité ducale. L'évolution de la Normandie féodale d'après le témoignage des chroniqueurs (Xe–XIIe siècles)," *Le moyen âge*, 5th ser., 6 (1992), 35–60.

Bachrach, Bernard S. "Some Observations on the Bayeux Tapestry," *Cithara* 27 (1987), 5–28.

Baldwin, Marshall W., ed., *The First Hundred Years*, vol. 1 of *A History of the Crusades*, ed. Kenneth M. Setton (Madison, 1969).

Barlow, Frank. "The *Carmen de Hastingae Proelio*," in *Studies in International History Presented to W. Norton Medlicott*, ed. K. Bourne and D. C. Watt (London, 1967), 36–67; reprinted in *The Norman Conquest and Beyond* (London, 1983), 189–222.

Bates, David. *Normandy before 1066* (London and New York, 1982).

Beaune, Colette. "The Political Uses of the Trojan Myth," in *The Birth of an Ideology: Myths and Symbols of Nation in Late-Medieval France*, trans. Susan Ross Huston, ed. Fredric L. Cheyette (Berkeley, 1991), 226–44.

Bédier, Joseph. "Richard de Normandie dans les chansons de geste," in *Les Légendes Épiques* (Paris, 1926–29), 4 vols., 3rd ed., 4. 3–18.

Bennett, Matthew. "Poetry as History? The 'Roman de Rou' of Wace as a Source for the Norman Conquest," *Anglo-Norman Studies* 5, ed. R. Allen Brown (Woodbridge, 1982), 21–39.

———. "Wace and Warfare," in *Anglo-Norman Studies* 11, ed. R. Allen Brown (Woodbridge, 1988), 37–57.

Bernstein, David J. "The Blinding of Harold and the Meaning of the Bayeux Tapestry," *Anglo-Norman Studies* 5, ed. R. Allen Brown (Woodbridge, 1982), 40–64.

———. *The Mystery of the Bayeux Tapestry* (Chicago, 1986).

Bisson, Thomas N. "The 'Feudal Revolution,' " *Past and Present* 142 (1994), 6–42.

Blacker, Jean. "The Depoliticization of the Arthurian World in the *Roman de Brut*," in *The Arthurian Tradition: Essays in Convergence*, ed. Mary Flowers Braswell and John Bugge (Birmingham, Ala., 1988), 54–74.

———. *The Faces of Time: Portrayal of the Past in Old French and Latin Historical Narrative of the Anglo-Norman Regnum* (Austin, 1994).

———. " '*La geste est grande, longue et grieve a translater*': History for Henry II," *Romance Quarterly* 37 (1990), 387–96.

———. "Wace's Craft and his Audience: Historical Truth, Bias, and Patronage in the *Roman de Rou*," *Kentucky Romance Quarterly* 31 (1984), 355–62.

Blissett, William. "Caesar and Satan," *Journal of the History of Ideas* 18 (1957), 221–32.

Bloch, Marc. *Feudal Society*, trans. L. A. Manyon (Chicago, 1961; reprint, London, 1989).

Bouet, Pierre. "Dudon de Saint-Quentin et Virgile: *L'Énéide* au service de la cause normande," *Cahiers des Annales de Normandie* 23 (1990), 215–36.

———. "De l'origine troyenne des Normands," in *Mélanges René Lepelley: Recueil d'études en hommage au Professeur René Lepelley*, ed. Catherine Bougy, Pierre Boissel, and Bernard Garnier (Caen, 1995), 401–13.

Bowra, C. M. *Heroic Poetry* (London, 1952).

Braund, Susan H., trans., *Lucan, Civil War* (Oxford, 1992).

Bridgeford, Andrew. "Was Count Eustace II of Boulogne the Patron of the Bayeux Tapestry?" *Journal of Medieval History* 25 (1999), 155–85.

Brooks, N. P., and H. E. Walker, "The Authority and Interpretation of the Bayeux Tapestry," *Battle* 1 (1979), 1–34 and 191–99; reprinted in *The Study of the Bayeux Tapestry*, ed. Richard Gameson (Woodbridge, 1997), 63–92.

Brown, Shirley Ann. *The Bayeux Tapestry: History and Bibliography* (Woodbridge, 1988).

Busch, Silvia Orvietani. "Luni in the Middle Ages: The Agony and the Disappearance of a City," *Journal of Medieval History* 17 (1991), 283–96.

Chalandon, Ferdinand. *Histoire de la domination normande en Italie et en Sicile* (1907; reprint, New York, 1960), 2 vols.

Chefneux, H. "Les fables dans la tapisserie de Bayeux," *Romania* 60 (1934), 1–35, 153–94.

Chibnall, Marjorie. "Feudal Society in Orderic Vitalis," *Battle* 1, ed. R. Allen Brown (Ipswich, 1979), 35–48.

———. "Orderic Vital and Robert of Torigni," *Millénaire monastique de Mont-Saint-Michel* 2 (Paris, 1966), 133–39.

———. *The World of Orderic Vitalis: Norman Monks and Norman Knights* (1984; reprint, Woodbridge, 1996).

Citarella, Armand Q. Review of *Normands, papes et moines*, by Jean Décarreaux, *Speculum* 52 (July 1977), 645–48.

Coupland, Simon. "The Rod of God's Wrath or the People of God's Wrath? The Carolingian Theology of the Viking Invasions," *Journal of Ecclesiastical History* 42, no. 4 (1991), 535–54.

Cowdrey, H. E. J. *The Age of Abbot Desiderius: Montecassino, the Papacy, and the Normans in the Eleventh and Early Twelfth Centuries* (Oxford, 1983).

———. "The Anglo-Norman *laudes regiae*," *Viator* 12 (1981), 37–78.

———. "Towards an Interpretation of the Bayeux Tapestry," *Anglo-Norman Studies* 10 (Woodbridge, 1988), 49–65; repr. in *The Study of the Bayeux Tapestry*, ed. Gameson, 93–110.

Curtius, Ernst R. *European Literature and the Latin Middle Ages*, trans. Willard Trask (New York, 1953).

Damian-Grint, Peter. "Truth, Trust, and Evidence in the Anglo-Norman *Estoire*," *Anglo-Norman Studies* 18, ed. Christopher Harper-Bill (Woodbridge, 1996), 63–78.

Davis, R. H. C. "The *Carmen de Hastingae Proelio*," *EHR* 93 (1978), 241–61; reprinted in R. H. C. Davis, *From Alfred the Great to Stephen* (London and Rio Grande, Ohio, 1991), 79–100.

———. *The Normans and their Myth* (London, 1976).

Décarreaux, Jean. *Normands, papes et moines: cinquante ans de conquêtes et de politique religieuse en Italie méridionale et en Sicile (milieu du XIe siècle – début du XIIe)* (Paris, 1974).

DeForest, Mary Margolies. "The Central Similes of Horace's *Cleopatra Ode*," *CW* 82 (1989), 167–73.

Deskis, Susan E. "The Wolf doesn't Care: The Proverbial and Traditional Context of Laȝamon's *Brut* Lines 10624–36," *Review of English Studies* n.s. 46 (1995), 41–48.

Douglas, David C. *The Norman Achievement, 1050–1100* (Berkeley and Los Angeles, 1969).

———. *The Norman Fate, 1100–1154* (Berkeley and Los Angeles, 1976).

———. "Rollo of Normandy," *EHR* 57, no. 228 (October 1942), 417–36.

———. "The 'Song of Roland' and the Norman Conquest of England," *French Studies* 14 (1960), 99–116.

———. *Time and the Hour: Some Collected Papers of David C. Douglas* (London, 1977).

———. *William the Conqueror: The Norman Impact upon England* (Berkeley, 1964).

Drell, Joanna. "Cultural Syncretism and Ethnic Identity: The Norman 'Conquest' of Southern Italy and Sicily," *Journal of Medieval History* 25 (1999), 187–202.

Eliade, Mircea. *Zalmoxis, The Vanishing God*, trans. Willard R. Trask, Comparative Studies in the Religions and Folklore of Dacia and Eastern Europe (Chicago and London, 1972).

Elliott, Alison Goddard. *Roads to Paradise: Reading the Lives of the Early Saints* (Hanover, N.H. and London, 1987).

Foulon, Charles. "Wace," in *Arthurian Literature in the Middle Ages: A Collaborative History*, ed. Roger Sherman Loomis (Oxford, 1959), 94–103.

Gameson, Richard. "The Origin, Art, and Message of the Bayeux Tapestry," in *The Study of the Bayeux Tapestry*, ed. Gameson (Woodbridge, 1997), 157–211.

Garnett, G. "Coronation and Propaganda: Some Implications of the Norman Claim to the Throne of England in 1066," *TRHS*, 5th ser., 36 (1986), 91–116.

Gavigan, John Joseph. "The Syntax of the *Gesta Francorum*," *Supplement to Language: Journal of the Linguistic Society of America* 19, no. 3, suppl. (1943), 3–102.

Gay, Jules. *L'Italie méridionale et l'empire Byzantin, 867–1071*, Bibliothèque des écoles françaises d'Athènes et de Rome, 90 (Paris, 1904).

Glosecki, Stephen O. "Wolf," in *The Encyclopedia of Medieval Folklore*, ed. Carl Lindahl and John Lindow (forthcoming).

Goffart, Walter. *The Narrators of Barbarian History (A.D. 550–800): Jordanes, Gregory of Tours, Bede, and Paul the Deacon* (Princeton, 1988).

Gransden, Antonia. *Historical Writing in England c. 550 to c. 1307* (Ithaca, N.Y., 1974).

Grape, Wolfgang. *The Bayeux Tapestry: Monument to a Norman Triumph*, trans. David Britt (Munich and New York, 1994).

Haahr, Joan Gluckauf. "William of Malmesbury's Roman Models: Suetonius and Lucan," in *The Classics in the Middle Ages: Papers of the Twentieth Annual Conference of the Center for Medieval and Early Renaissance Studies*, ed. Aldo S. Bernardo and Saul Levin (Binghamton, N.Y., 1990).

Haskins, Charles Homer. *The Normans in European History* (New York, 1966; reprint, Boston and New York, 1915).

———. *The Renaissance of the Twelfth Century* (1927; reprint, Cambridge, 1972).

Hoffman, H. "Die Anfänge der Normannen in Süditalien," *Quellen und Forschungen aus Italienischen Archiven und Bibliotheken* 49 (1969), 95–144.

Holden, A. J. "L'authenticité des premières parties du *Roman de Rou*," *Romania* 75 (1954), 22–53.

Hollister, C. Warren. "Normandy, France and the Anglo-Norman *Regnum*," *Speculum* 51 (April 1976), 202–42.

Holmes, Urban Tigner, Jr. "Norman Literature and Wace," in *Medieval Secular Literature: Four Essays*, ed. William Matthews (Berkeley and Los Angeles, 1965), 46–67.

Houck, Margaret. *Sources of the Roman de Brut of Wace*, University of California Publications in English 5, no. 2 (1941), 161–356.

Howorth, Henry H. "A Criticism of the Life of Rollo, as Told by Dudo de St. Quentin," *Archaeologia* 45, no. 2 (1880), 235–50.

Huisman, Gerda C. "Notes on the Manuscript Tradition of Dudo of St Quentin's *Gesta Normannorum*," *Anglo-Norman Studies* 6 (1984), 122.

Ingledew, Francis. "The Book of Troy and the Genealogical Construction of History: The Case of Geoffrey of Monmouth's *Historia regum Britanniae*," *Speculum* 69 (July 1994), 665–704.

Jackson, W. T. H. "The Nature of Romance," *Yale French Studies* 51 (1974), 12–25.

Jamison, Evelyn. "Some Notes on the *Anonymi Gesta Francorum*, with Special Reference to the Norman Contingent from South Italy and Sicily in the First Crusade," in *Studies in French Language and Mediaeval Literature Presented to Professor Mildred K. Pope*, Publications of the University of Manchester, 268 (Manchester, 1939), 183–208.

Jeffreys, Elizabeth M. "The Judgement of Paris in Later Greek Literature," *Byzantion* 48 (1978), 112–31.

Joranson, Einar. "The Inception of the Career of the Normans in Italy – Legend and History," *Speculum* 23 (July 1948), 353–96.

Jordan, Victoria B. "The Role of Kingship in Tenth-Century Normandy: Hagiography of Dudo of Saint Quentin," *The Haskins Society Journal* 3 (1991), 53–62.

Ker, W. P. *Epic and Romance* (London, 1926).

Knowles, David. *The Monastic Order in England* (Cambridge, 1963).

Kreutz, Barbara M. *Before the Normans: Southern Italy in the Ninth and Tenth Centuries*, Middle Ages Series (Philadelphia, 1991).

Krey, August C. "A Neglected Passage in the *Gesta* and its Bearing on the Literature of the First Crusade," in *The Crusades and Other Historical Essays presented to Dana C. Munro*, ed. Louis J. Paetow (New York, 1928), 57–78.

Lair, Jules. ed. *Étude sur la vie et la mort de Guillaume Longue-Épée, duc de Normandie* (Paris, 1893).

Leblond, Bernard. *L'accession des Normands de Neustrie à la culture occidentale (Xème – XIème siècles)* (Paris, 1966).

Lentini, A. "Richerche biografiche su Amato di Montecassino," *Benedictina* 9 (1955), 183–96.

Le Patourel, J. H. "The Norman Succession, 996–1135," *EHR* 86 (1971), 225–50.

Lewis, Suzanne. *The Rhetoric of Power in the Bayeux Tapestry* (Cambridge, 1999).

Lifshitz, Felice. "Dudo's Historical Narrative and the Norman Succession of 996," *Journal of Medieval History* 20 (1994), 101–20.

Logan, George Meredith. "Lucan in England: The Influence of the *Pharsalia* on English Letters from the Beginnings through the Sixteenth Century" (Ph.D. diss., Harvard University, 1967).

Loud, G. A. "The '*Gens Normannorum*' – Myth or Reality?" *Anglo-Norman Studies* 4, ed. R. Allen Brown (Woodbridge, 1982), 104–16, 204–209.

———. "How 'Norman' Was the Norman Conquest of Southern Italy?" *Medieval Studies* 25, ed. Antonia Gransden (Nottingham, 1981), 13–34.

Lund, Niels. "Allies of God or Man? The Viking Expansion in a European Perspective," *Viator* 20 (1989), 45–59.

Manitius, M. *Bildung, Wissenschaft und Literatur in Abendlande von 800 bis 1100* (Crimmitschau, 1925).

Matthew, Donald. *The Norman Kingdom of Sicily*, Cambridge Medieval Textbooks (Cambridge, 1992).

Mayer, Hans Eberhard. *The Crusades*, trans. John Gillingham (1972; reprint, Oxford, 1978).

McNulty, J. Bard. *The Narrative Art of the Bayeux Tapestry Master*, AMS Studies in the Middle Ages, 13 (New York, 1988).

McQueen, William B. "Relations between the Normans and Byzantium, 1071–1112," *Byzantion* 56 (1986), 427–76.

Mickel, Emanuel J. *Ganelon, Treason and the* Chanson de Roland (University Park, Pa. and London, 1989).

Monson, Don A. "Andreas Capellanus and the Problem of Irony," *Speculum* 63 (July 1988), 539–72.

Musset, Lucien. "Le satiriste Garnier de Rouen et son milieu (début du XIe siècle)," *Revue du Moyen Age latin* 10 (1954), 237–67.

Niermeyer, J. F. *Mediae Latinitatis Lexicon Minus* (Leiden, 1976).

Norwich, John Julius. *The Kingdom in the Sun 1130–1194* (New York and Evanston, 1970).

———. *The Other Conquest* (New York and Evanston, 1967; published in England as *The Normans of the South*).

Onslow, Richard William Alan. *The Dukes of Normandy and their Origin*, ed. A. L. Haydon (London, 1947).

Pagano. A. *Il poema* Gesta Roberti Wiscardi *di Guglielmo Pugliese* (Naples, 1909).

Paris, Gaston. "Review of Hugo Andresen, ed. *Roman de Rou et des ducs de Normandie*," *Romania* 9 (1880), 592–614.

Partner, Nancy. *Serious Entertainments: The Writing of History in Twelfth-Century England* (Chicago, 1977).

Patterson, Lee. *Chaucer and the Subject of History* (Madison, 1991).

Patterson, Robert B. "Review of Marjorie Chibnall, ed. and trans., *The Ecclesiastical History* of Orderic Vitalis, V: Books IX and X," *Speculum* 52 (October 1977), 945.

Pfister, Christian. *Études sur le règne de Robert le Pieux (996–1031)* (Paris, 1885).

Potts, Cassandra. "*Atque unum ex diversis gentibus populum effecit*: Historical Tradition and the Norman Identity," *Anglo-Norman Studies* 18, ed. Christopher Harper-Bill (Woodbridge, 1996), 139–52.

Prentout, Henri. *Étude critique sur Dudon de Saint-Quentin et son histoire des premiers ducs Normands* (Paris, 1916).

Ray, Roger D. "Orderic Vitalis and his Readers," *Studia Monastica* 14 (1972), 17–33.

————. "Orderic Vitalis and William of Poitiers: A Monastic Re-interpretation of William the Conqueror," *Revue belge de philologie et d'histoire* 50, no. 4 (1972), 1116–27.

Reinhold, Meyer. "The Unhero Aeneas," *Classica et Mediaevalia* 27 (1966), 195–207.

Riley-Smith, Jonathan. *The Crusades: A Short History* (New Haven, 1987).

————. *The First Crusade and the Idea of Crusading* (Philadelphia, 1986).

————. *The First Crusaders, 1095–1131* (Cambridge, 1997).

————, ed. *The Oxford Illustrated History of the Crusades* (Oxford, 1995).

Ronca, Umberto. *Cultura medioevale e poesia latina d'Italia nei secoli XI e XII* (Rome, 1892).

Rowley, Trevor. *The Norman Heritage, 1055–1200* (London, 1983).

Runciman, Sir Steven. "The First Crusade: Antioch to Ascalon," in Marshall W. Baldwin, ed., *The First Hundred Years*, 308–41.

Ryding, William. *Structure in Medieval Narrative* (The Hague, 1971).

Searle, Eleanor. "Fact and Pattern in Heroic History: Dudo of Saint-Quentin," *Viator* 15 (1984), 119–37.

————. *Predatory Kinship and the Creation of Norman Power, 840–1066* (Berkeley, 1988).

Shopkow, Leah. "The Carolingian World of Dudo of Saint-Quentin," *Journal of Medieval History* 15, no. 1 (1989), 19–37.

————. *History and Community: Norman Historical Writing in the Eleventh and Twelfth Centuries* (Washington, D.C., 1997).

————. "Norman Historical Writing in the Eleventh and Twelfth Centuries" (Ph.D. diss., University of Toronto, 1984).

Short, Ian. "On Bilingualism in Anglo-Norman England," *Romance Philology* 33 (1980), 467–79.

————. "Patrons and Polyglots: French Literature in Twelfth-Century England," *Anglo-Norman Studies* 14, ed. Marjorie Chibnall (Woodbridge, 1992), 229–49.

————. "*Tam Angli quam Franci*: Self-Definition in Anglo-Norman England," *Anglo-Norman Studies* 18, ed. Christopher Harper-Bill, (Woodbridge, 1996), 153–75.

Shwartz, Susan M. "The Founding and Self-betrayal of Britain: An Augustinian Approach to Geoffrey of Monmouth's *Historia Regum Britanniae*," *Medievalia et Humanistica* n.s. 10, ed. Paul Maurice Clogan (Totowa, N.J., 1981), 33–53.

Smalley, Beryl. *Historians in the Middle Ages* (London, 1974).

Smith, Anthony D. *The Ethnic Origins of Nations* (Oxford, 1986).

Southern, R. W. "Aspects of the European Tradition of Historical Writing: I. The Classical Tradition from Einhard to Geoffrey of Monmouth," *TRHS*, 5th ser., 20 (1970), 173–96.

Spiegel, Gabrielle M. *Romancing the Past: The Rise of Vernacular Prose Historiography in Thirteenth-Century France* (Berkeley, 1993).

Stenton, Sir Frank M. *et al.*, ed. *The Bayeux Tapestry: A Comprehensive Survey* (London, 1965; 2nd ed.).

Taviani-Carozzi, Huguette. *La terreur du monde: Robert Guiscard et la conquête normande en Italie. Mythe et histoire* (Paris, 1996).

Terkla, Daniel. "Cut on the Norman Bias: Fabulous Borders and Visual Glosses in the Bayeux Tapestry," *Word and Image* 11 (1995), 264–90.

Thomas, Hugh M. Forthcoming work on assimilation and ethnic identity in England after the Norman Conquest.

Thompson, Kathleen. "Orderic Vitalis and Robert of Bellême," *Journal of Medieval History* 20 (1994), 133–41.

———. "Robert of Bellême Reconsidered," *Anglo-Norman Studies* 13, ed. Marjorie Chibnall (Woodbridge, 1991), 263–86.

van Houts, Elisabeth M. C. "The *Gesta Normannorum Ducum*: A History without an End," *Battle* 3 (1981), 106–18.

———. "Historiography and Hagiography at Saint-Wandrille: The '*Inventio et Miracula Sancti Vulfranni*,'" *Anglo-Norman Studies* 12 (1989), 233–51.

———. "Latin Poetry and the Anglo-Norman Court, 1066–1135: The *Carmen de Hastingae Proelio*," *Journal of Medieval History* 15 (March 1989), 39–62.

———. "The Memory of 1066 in Written and Oral Traditions," *Anglo-Norman Studies* 29, ed. Christopher Harper-Bill (Woodbridge, 1997), 167–79.

———. "The Political Relations between Normandy and England before 1066 According to the *Gesta Normannorum Ducum*," *Actes du Colloque international du Centre national de la recherche scientifique, nr. 611: Études Anselmiennes*, ed. Raymonde Foreville (Paris, 1984), 85–97.

———. "Quelques remarques sur les interpolations attribuées à Orderic Vital dans les *Gesta Normanorum Ducum* de Guillaume de Jumièges," *Revue d'histoire des textes* 8 (1978), 213–22.

———. "Scandinavian Influence in Norman Literature of the Eleventh Century," *Anglo-Norman Studies* 6 (1983), 107–21.

———. "The Trauma of 1066," *History Today* 46, no. 10 (October, 1996), 9–15.

Vessey, D. W. T. C. "William of Tyre and the Art of Historiography," *Mediaeval Studies* 35 (1973), 433–55.

Wallace-Hadrill, J. M. "The Vikings in Francia," in *Early Medieval History* (Oxford, 1975), 201–36.

Weiss, Judith. *Wace's Roman de Brut / A History of the British: Text and Translation*, Exeter Medieval Texts and Studies (Exeter, 1999).

Wheatley, Edward. *Mastering Aesop: Medieval Education, Chaucer, and his Followers* (Gainesville, Fla., 2000).

Wissolik, Richard David. *The Bayeux Tapestry: A Critical, Annotated Bibliography with Cross-References and Summary Outlines of Scholarship, 1729–1990*, 2nd ed., Scholars Bibliography Series, vol. 3 (Greensburg, Pa., 1990).

Wolf, Kenneth Baxter. "Crusade and Narrative: Bohemond and the *Gesta Francorum*," *Journal of Medieval History* 17 (1991), 207–16.

———. *Making History: The Normans and their Historians in Eleventh-Century Italy* (Philadelphia, 1995).

Yapp, W. Brunsdon. "Animals in Medieval Art: The Bayeux Tapestry as an Example," *Journal of Medieval History* 13 (1987), 15–75.

Ziolkowski, Jan M. *Talking Animals: Medieval Latin Beast Poetry, 750–1150* (Philadelphia, 1993).

Index

Abelard, nephew of Guiscard, 133, 137–41
Absalom, 202, 209
Achilles, 86, 121
Actium, 121–22
Adalberon, bishop of Laon
    as recipient of Dudo's letter, 8, 10, 36, 40
Adana, 164
Adela, xi, 1 n. 2, 146, 193
Adelaide, 211
Adenolf of Benevento, 114, 137
Aeneas, 25, 38, 44, 86, 198, 215, 237
Aeneid. See Vergil
Aesopic fables, 42, 90–105
Æthelred II, 71–72
Agamemnon, 86
Agata, St., monastery of, 111
Ager Sanguinis, 177
Alan III, count of Brittany, 74, 183–84, 211, 232
Albion, 238
Aldrevald of Fleury, 52, 57
Alençon, siege of, 182–83
Alexander the Great, 193, 198, 216, 237
Alexander, pope, 207
Alexander of Telese, 221
Alexiad. See Anna Komnene
Alexios Komnenus,
    in the *Gesta Francorum*, 148, 152, 154, 156,
        160–63, 174, 178
    in Orderic, 188–89, 195
    in William of Apulia, 129, 132, 134, 140,
        142
Alfred Ætheling, 72 n. 43, 74, 78, 188
Alp Arslan, 133–34, 145–46
Amalfi,
    riches of, 107, 115
    siege of, 147
Amatus of Montecassino, 108–12, 122, 135
    as panegyrist, 3
Amazons, 62
Ami, 141
Anchises, 16, 25
Andrew, St., in visions at Antioch, 173–74
Angles, 220
Anglo-Saxon Chronicle, 89 n. 79
Anna Komnene, 136
Antenor
    in Dante, 14 n. 31
    in Dionysios of Halicarnassus, 15
    in Dudo, 13–15, 37, 38

    in Orderic, 198
    in Wace, 237–38
    in William of Jumièges, 14 n. 31, 62–63
Antioch
    description of, in the *Gesta Francorum*, 175
    taken by Turks, 146
    besieged by crusaders, 148, 154, 157,
        162–63, 169–70, 172–75
    miracles at, 172–74
    Great Battle for, 174–75
    Norman claims to, 156–57
    Norman principality of, 1, 147–48, 165,
        177–78, 221
Apulia, 87
    Normans drawn to, 106, 187
    in the *Gesta Francorum*, 150, 153
    praised by William of Apulia, 115
Arabs,
    in Sicily, 117
    in southern Italy, 115, 188
    See also Sicily
Argyrus, son of Melus, 142
Armenians, 170
    in southern Italy, 107
Arnulf I, count of Flanders
    in Dudo, 21, 23, 24, 27, 29–32, 39
    in William of Jumièges, 65–66, 68
Arnulf, son of William Talvas, 190
Arthur, king, 220, 223
Ascalon, battle at, 148, 176
Ascelin, son of Arthur, 201
Athelstane, 60
Aubré of Cagnano, 148
Aubré of Grandmesnil, 161
Augustine, 4–5, 52
Aversa, 108
    riches of, 115
Baghdad, 146
Baldwin (of Boulogne) I, 146, 148, 164, 166
Baldwin (of Le Bourg) II, count of Edessa, king
        of Jerusalem,
    regent of Antioch, 177
    captured by Turks, 206
Baldwin II, count of Flanders, 74
Baldwin III, count of Flanders, 67, 74
Baldwin VII, count of Flanders, 200–201
Bari, 107
    Norman siege of, 122–23, 136
    riches of, 115

251